MW01617766

E. S. Paxson

To
My Mother and Father

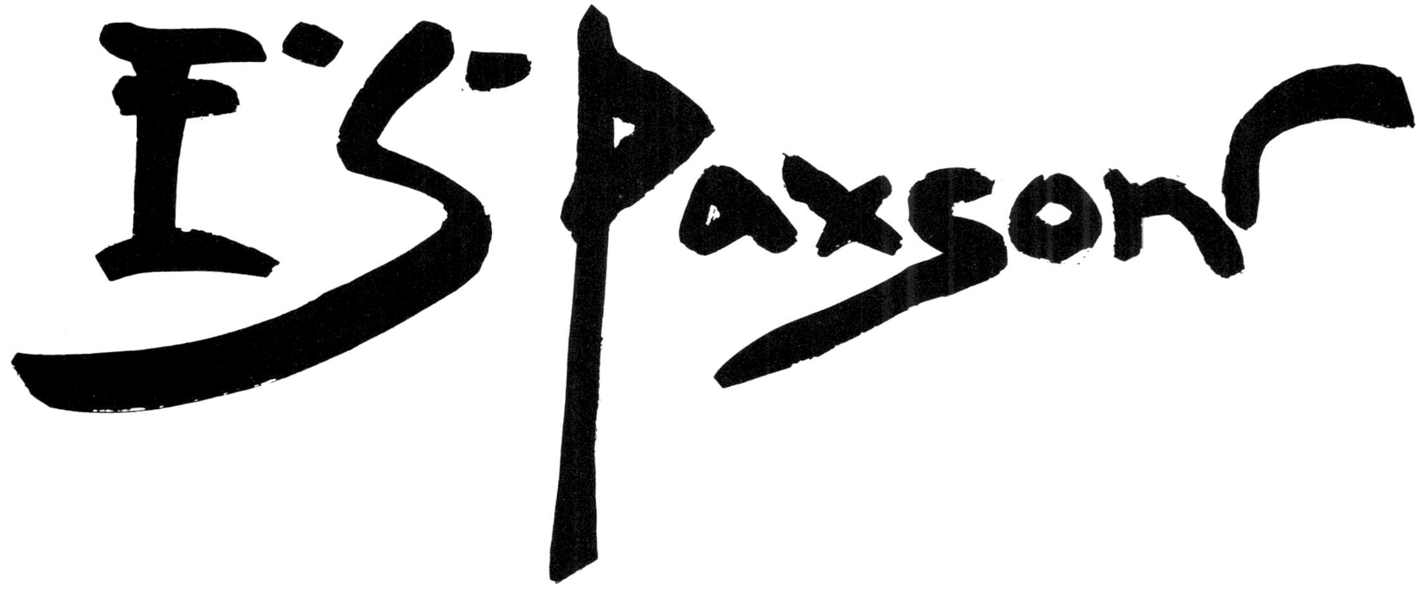

E.S. PAXSON: FRONTIER ARTIST

WILLIAM EDGAR PAXSON, JR.

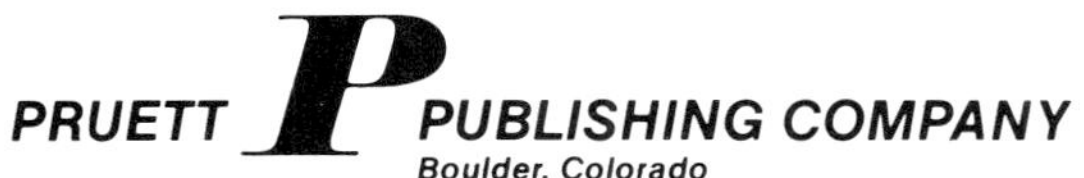
PRUETT PUBLISHING COMPANY
Boulder, Colorado

First Edition
1 2 3 4 5 6 7 8 9

Printed in the United States of America

Library of Congress Cataloging in Publication Data

Paxson, William Edgar, 1948-
E.S. Paxson, frontier artist.

Bibliography: p.
Includes index.

1. Paxson, E. S., 1852-1919 . 2. Painters—United States—Biography. 3. West (U.S.) in art. I. Title.
ND237.P257P39 1984 759.13 [B] 84-4771
ISBN 0-87108-663-8

Acknowledgements

For their contributions of pictorial material, I would like to thank the Missoula Museum of the Arts, the Montana Historical Society, the Buffalo Bill Historical Center, the Thomas Gilcrease Institute of American History and Art, the Rockwell Museum, Stremmel Galleries, Petersen Galleries, the University of Montana, the Missoula City-County Library, the Missoula Women's Club, the Dillon School District, Maxwell Galleries, the Pacific Northwest Indian Center, David Bird Burnham, Mr. and Mrs. S. H. Rosenthal, Laurence Rockefeller, James Fowler, Jimmie and Sydney M. Shoenberg, Jr., Bob and Billie Anne Baird, Robin MacNab, Dr. Van Kirke Nelson, C. W. Edwards, John and Debbie Capps, SLM, Inc., Martin and Penny Kodner, Robert and Felice Rubin, Alfred E. and Judy Goldman, Ray and Maxine Howser, Robert and Juanita Ellithorpe, Susan Sorelle, Michael McCullough and Jim Browne.

For their cooperation in my research efforts, I would like to thank Lory Morrow, Patti Dean and the library staff at the Montana Historical Society, the Missoula Museum of the Arts' staff, Bonnie Weber at the Whittier Public Library, Albert Partoll, George Stratford, William J. B. Burger, Bob Ward and the Hale family. Further, I would like to express appreciation to Harold Davidson, Graham Pomeroy, Jon Schulman and Cork Millner for their expert advice; David Hunt and Dr. Patricia Trenton for their critical reading of the manuscript and Lenora Koelbel for her encouragement and helpfulness.

I am very grateful to the many owners of Paxson paintings in Montana, Washington, Oregon and California who graciously welcomed me into their homes, showed so much interest in my project and allowed me to photograph their paintings. For giving me a home away from home I am indebted to Margaret Paxson, Lyn Dartnell and Gary Preston. I owe special thanks to Kate O'Neill for providing me with an ideal writer's hideaway and for much encouragement.

Laura Dartnell deserves recognition for her charcoal portrait of the artist, her great-grandfather, from whom she has quite possibly inherited her considerable artistic ability.

My greatest thanks go to my mother Dorothy and my father William Edgar, Sr. and my cousin Elizabeth Paxson Dartnell. This book would have been many times more difficult to complete and far less comprehensive were it not for their dedication over the past twenty-five years in collecting and preserving source material about the life and art of E. S. Paxson.

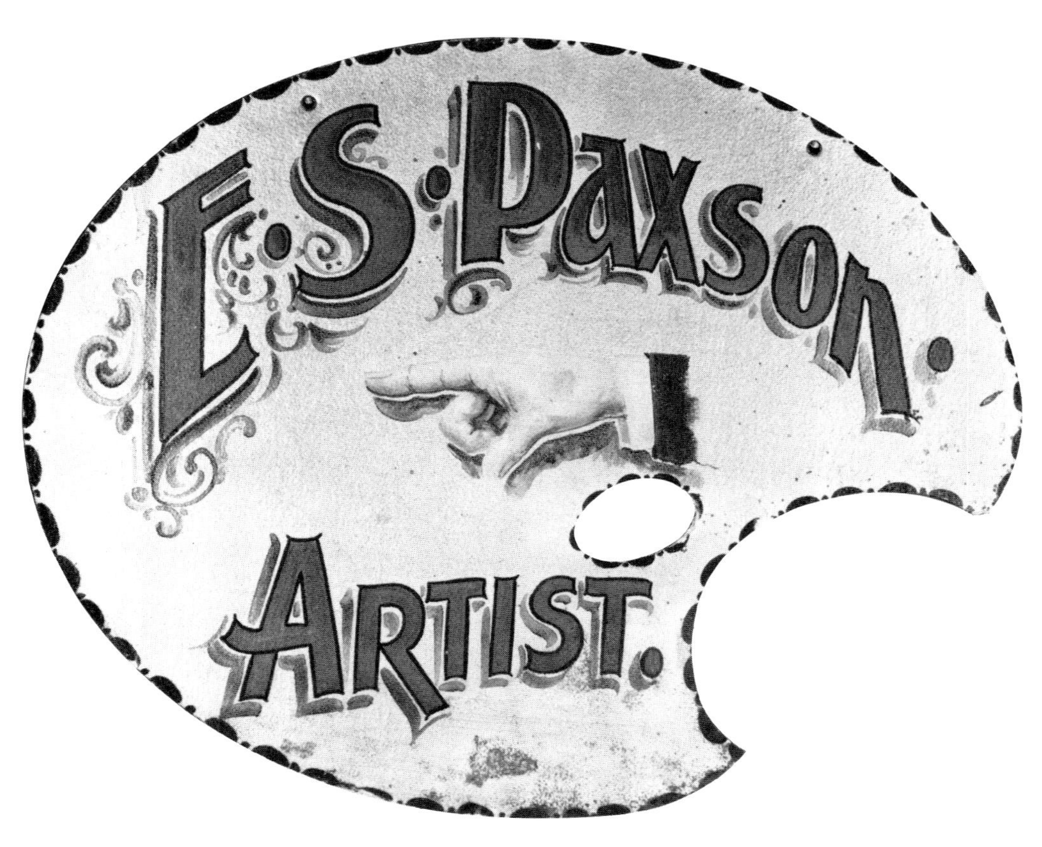
E.S. Paxson.
ARTIST.

Contents

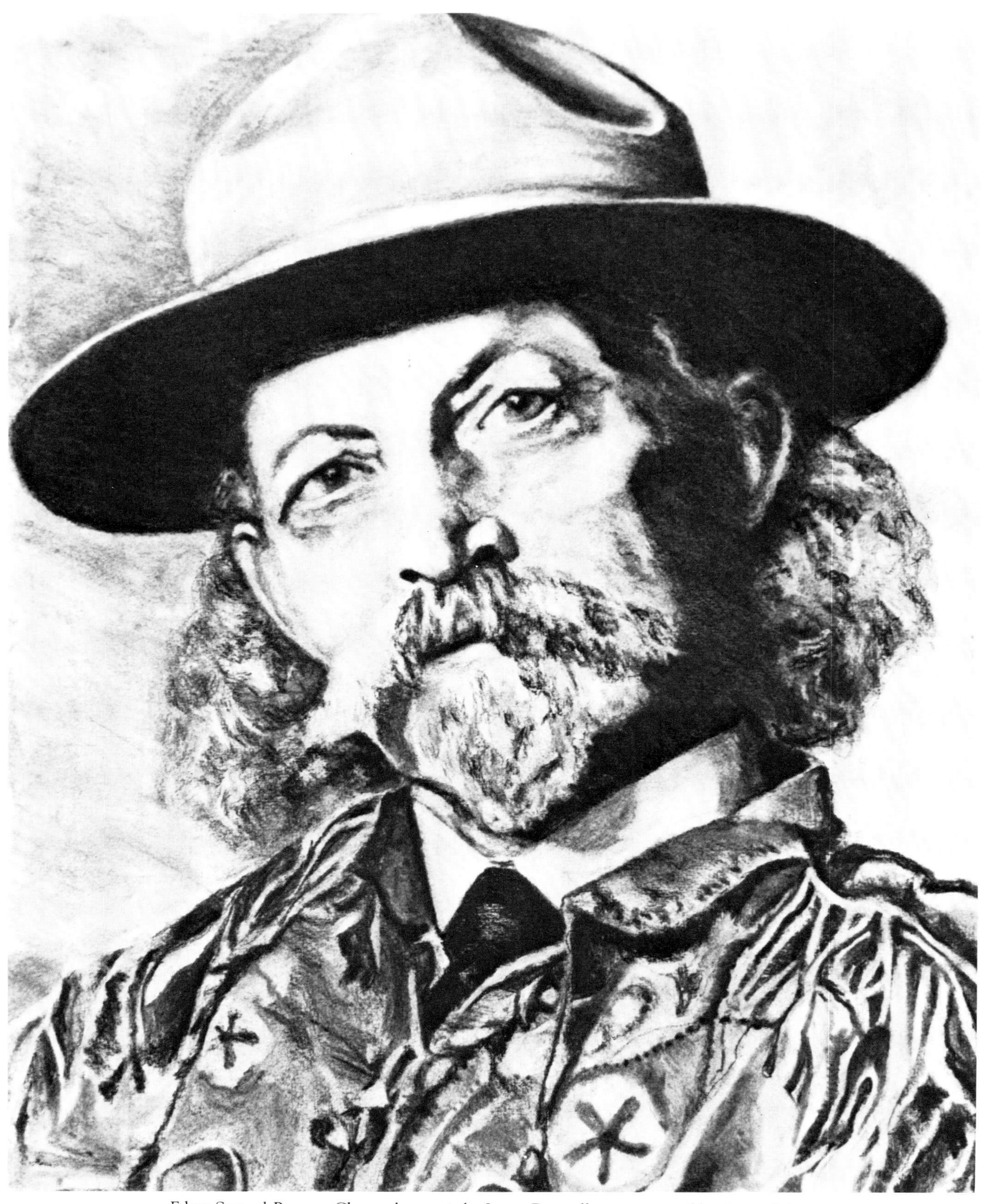

Edgar Samuel Paxson. Charcoal portrait by Laura Dartnell, a great granddaughter of the artist.

Introduction

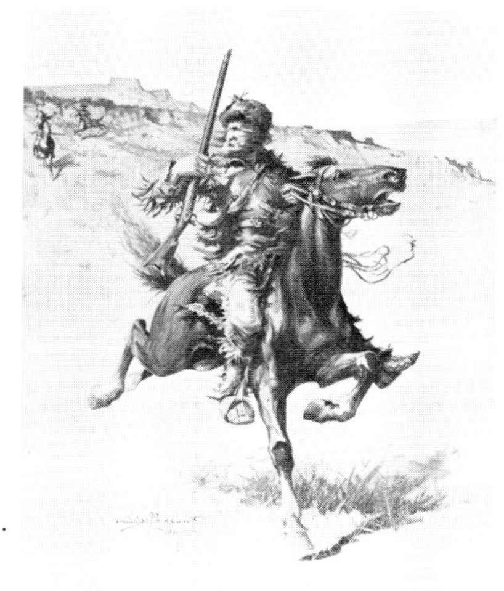

"Beaver Dick." Watercolor, 1901.
Outdoor Life.

In August 1877 the fledgling settlements of Montana Territory were in an uproar: Indians were on the warpath. Chief Joseph and his Nez Percé were on the march toward Canada, having passed through much of the territory, battling and skirmishing with federal troops along the way. In the southwestern part of the territory and neighboring Idaho, angry Bannock and Shoshone were worrying white settlers and cattlemen. Late in the month, about two weeks after the fight on the Big Hole River between the Nez Percé and General Gibbon's troops, three white men, scouts hired by local cattlemen to look out for Indians, set up camp. They had sighted Indians the day before and were on the alert. One of the scouts later recalled:

> Towards evening some shots were heard away up the range. Perhaps half a mile away a man on a horse appeared in full jump, his arms swinging and hair flying. Close in his rear, coming like the wind was (*sic*) seen two bucks, stripped to breechcloth and mocassins. Now and then smoke in little puffs would roll from the arms of the pursuers, while the significant pop! pop! pop! vibrated sharply through the hills.

The three scouts ran toward the chase, up a sagebrush-covered slope, firing a few shots at long range as they went. The Indians whirled and made for the timber above, while their intended prey fled straight down the hill to safety.

Finishing his recollection, the scout described the fleeing horse and rider, "I can see him now, an old pinto horse stumbling down the rough hill through dusty sage, in an old rusty saddle, on his back an old man in tattered buckskins, long grey hair flying from beneath an old beaver-skin cap, in his hand an old Hudson Bay gun, powder horn, bullet pouch etc., and long fringes flopping in the air."[1]

The old man was Beaver Dick, a trapper, a mountain man "of the old school." The young scout who told the story was Ed Paxson, then twenty-six years old. In 1901, Edgar Samuel Paxson, artist, recorded the story in watercolor, investing it with all the drama he felt that day in 1877. And importantly for us today, he painted the incident and so many others with a commitment to historical authenticity.

Historians were rare in Montana Territory in those frontier days. Pioneers were naturally expending all their energy dealing with the problem of survival. Recording history was left mostly to those on the other end of a telegraph line many miles to the east. Rarer still on the frontier was a man like Edgar Paxson, an historian with an artistic genius.

Today interest in western art is burgeoning. Now there are many gifted and well-trained artists painting the West as it was. But in those days when the frontier was fading, it took artistic pioneers with vision—men such as Paxson, his famous contemporaries Charles Russell and Frederic Remington and a few others—to blaze a trail that the many that follow have built into a broad thoroughfare. Were it not for the frontier artists who recorded history as they lived it, much of what was the real West would be lost to us now.

Until the western art boom of recent years, the name E. S. Paxson had fallen into relative obscurity while some of his contemporaries, especially Russell and Remington, were well known. Why this is so has puzzled many who know Paxson art and feel that his best work is no less masterly than the best work of the others. Indeed, several shrewd western art collectors quietly searched out and purchased Paxson paintings in past years and are now benefiting greatly from the western art boom because of their foresight.

Paxson's lack of renown is at least partly attributable to his unassuming nature. He often said he disliked interviews and "blowing his own horn," as he put it. Russell, too, was modest but had a hard-driving business manager in his wife Nancy. Remington was a New Yorker with many means of widespread publicity. Both Remington and Russell spent considerable time in the East. Paxson made only two brief trips east to promote his work, in 1893 and 1903. Although the second boosted his career considerably, he never went farther east than Chicago and while he was away, he sorely missed his "mountain home," as he lovingly called it. After 1903, he never left it again for business purposes.

Fortunately for us, Paxson's sense of history was stronger than his modesty. Otherwise this biography would have suffered from a lack of source material. He must have known the value of his work for future generations because he regularly kept a detailed journal from the time of his service in the Spanish-American War in 1898 until his death in 1919. In addition he kept scrapbooks with newspaper clippings back as far as the 1880s about himself, his friends and Montana history in general. In his journals he frequently related incidents of his youth and his early days in Montana. And he habitually made marginal notations in historical books and novels as he read them, showing up inconsistencies and elaborating on the history and any personal relationship he had with places and events.

Undoubtedly some important source material has been lost over the last sixty years since Paxson's death. And those who knew him have nearly all passed away. This writer's father (Edgar's grandson) is one of the few still living to have known the artist. As a boy, he lived with his grandfather from 1912 to 1916 in Missoula, Montana. Some of his memories of "Grandpa" at his easel, or in town with his cronies exchanging yarns, are still vivid. With these memories as a beginning, he has dedicated the last twenty-five years to gathering material for this story of Edgar S. Paxson, scout, hunter, soldier, artist and pictorial historian.

In addition to accumulating biographical material, William Paxson, Sr. has traced hundreds of Paxson paintings. Many of these were originally purchased from the artist for a few dollars and handed down within Montana families, never having been seen publicly or even photographed. Many are reproduced for the first time in this volume.

Other Paxson paintings have disappeared from sight over the years due to the artist's obscurity. A number of these are major works, the only records of which are old photographs or lithographs. These are reproduced as necessary in this volume in an effort to give the most complete representation possible of Edgar S. Paxson's art.

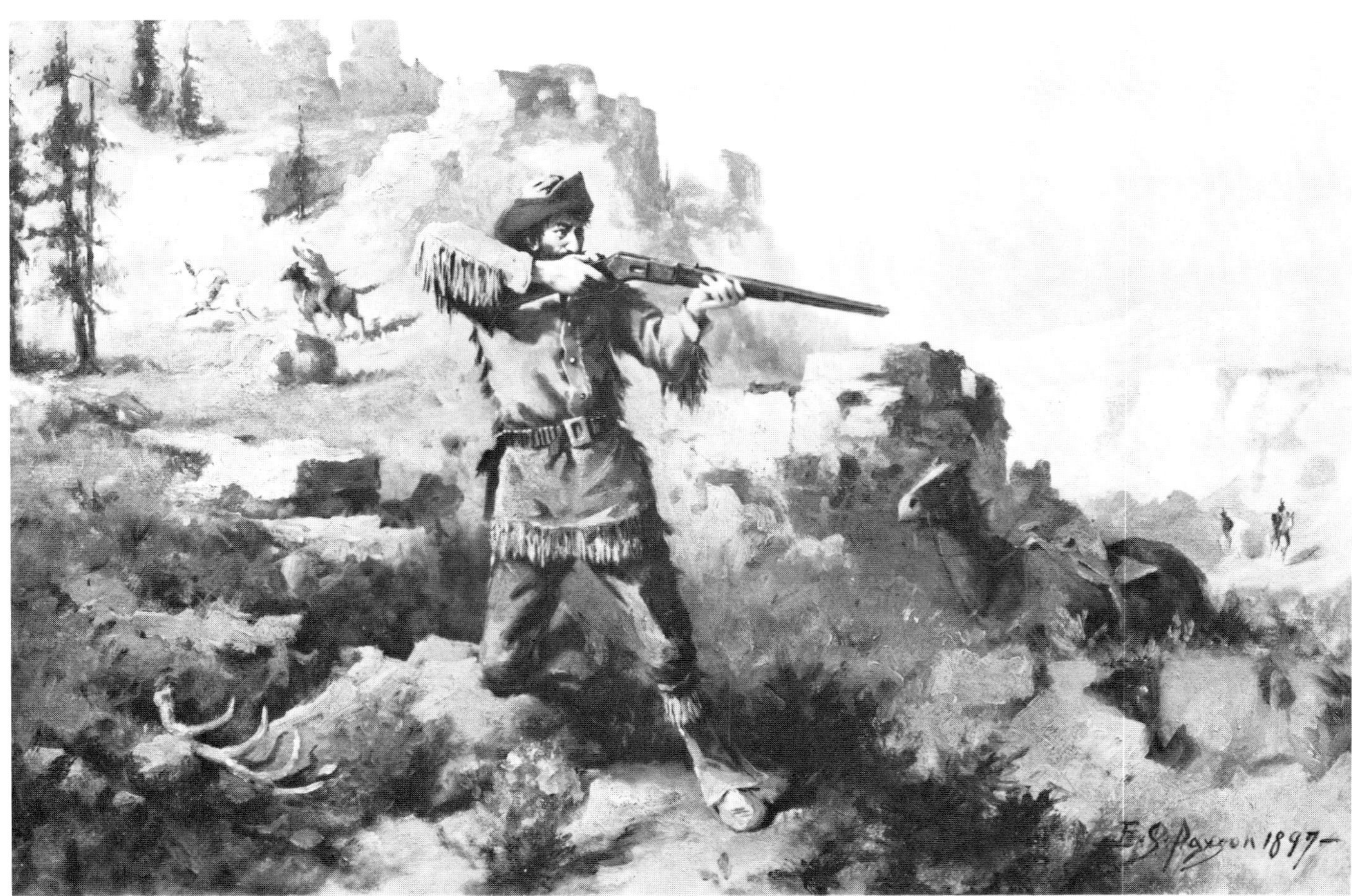

"The Trapper," oil on canvas, 1897, 12 x 18. *Wunderlich & Company, Inc.*

1

Childhood

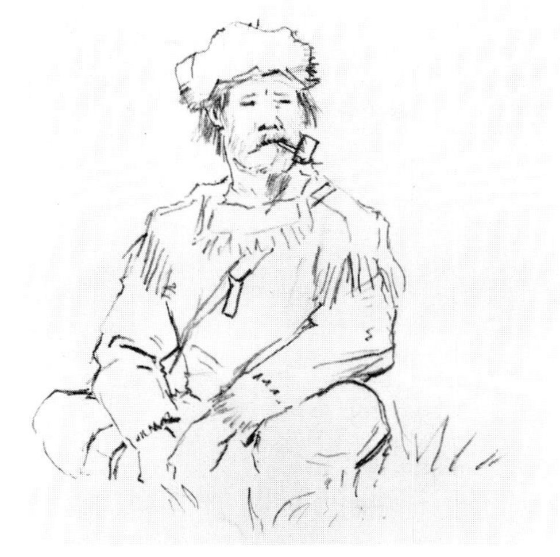

"At Campfire," Pencil, 1902. *Private Collection.*

Edgar Samuel Paxson's ancestors were Quakers. The first to come to America from England settled in Bucks County, Pennsylvania, in 1682. They were nearly all hard-working and successful farmers. Through the generations, continuing into Edgar's childhood, families were large and close-knit. Children were brought up in the simple habits, moderate tastes and honest purposes of Quaker rural society.

Most of Edgar's ancestors inclined to be liberal and progressive in their Quakerism. In 1827, when the Society of Friends split into two groups, the conservative orthodox faction and the progressive Hicksites, his family followed the Hicksites. During Edgar's childhood, Quakerism was losing its hold on many of the clan. They lost interest in the religious dogma and spent their moral enthusiasm in advancing popular reforms. Several were active in the anti-slavery movement, providing their homes as stations on the Underground Railroad. Several, including Edgar's father, although bred in Quaker pacifism, went to war to emancipate the slaves. Only a generation earlier, Edgar's grandfather Samuel Hambleton had gone to jail for refusing military duty owing to his Quaker principles. And Samuel's Uncle Moses and Moses' son Aaron refused conscription into British forces near Toronto where they lived during the War of 1812. Aaron died in a Canadian jail and Moses fled to the United States, losing his farm for his beliefs.[1]

Although as a child Edgar spent much of his time with his Quaker aunts and uncles and lived with his grandfather Samuel for a time, he went the way of most of his generation by giving up Quakerism. Very soon he ceased using "thee" and "thou" in his speech, but throughout his life he retained the forthright honesty and morality learned in his childhood. He never joined another church, although he professed a belief in God and in his later years attended a Presbyterian and a Congregational church occasionally. He was never very fond of sitting through a church meeting unless the sermon held some interest for him, perhaps historical. It is quite possible he shied away from going to church out of memory of those interminable Sunday Quaker meetings of silent prayer which, as he once recalled, he endured as a young boy anxious to be out in the woods.

It is no surprise that Edgar headed for the Montana frontier as a young man. His ancestors had traditionally sought out the frontiers of civilization. Since coming to America, they had been subduing the wilderness, offspring continually striking out westward as the frontier receded across the continent. Besides being farmers, several were trailblazers and skilled hunters in Pennsylvania and western New York. Some had considerable local reputations. Edgar's great-grandfather Jonas Hambleton was often compared in family legend to his contemporary, Daniel Boone. Jonas brought his family through the wilderness of western New York to the shores of Lake Erie where they settled in 1809. Soon other families of the Hambleton and Paxson clans from Bucks County joined them in what came to be called Erie County. By April 25, 1852, the day Edgar was born, the little villages of Webster's Corners, East Hamburg, and East Aurora, all not far from the budding town of Buffalo, were full of Paxsons and Hambletons. Edgar's parents William Hambleton Paxson and Christiana Hambleton Paxson had a home in East Hamburg, now called Orchard Park, where Edgar, brothers Everett and Robert and sister Florence grew up.

From his birth Edgar was bred for the frontier life. A neighbor, "Aunt" Triphene, who was with Christiana when he was born, was the first white person born on the nearby Seneca Indian Reservation. She used to thrill the little boy with stories of the time she was a girl on the New York frontier when the Senecas, one of the powerful Five Nations of Iroquois, ranged the woodlands led by the famous chief Red Jacket.[2]

When a little older, Edgar eagerly listened to stories

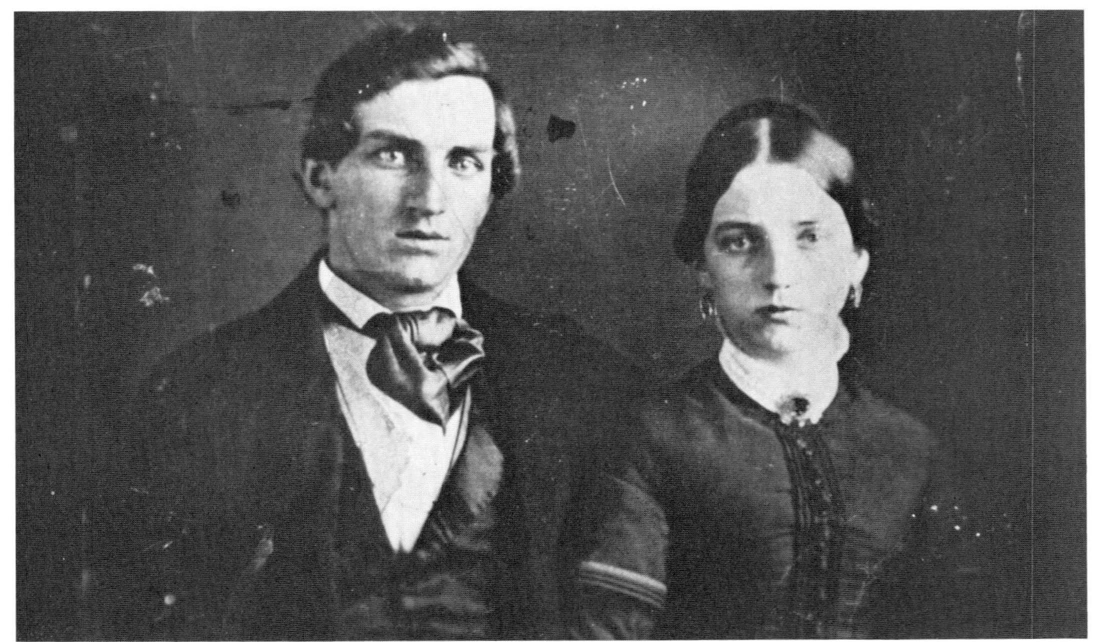

The artist's parents, William Hambleton Paxson and Christiana Hambleton Paxson. From an 1850 tintype.

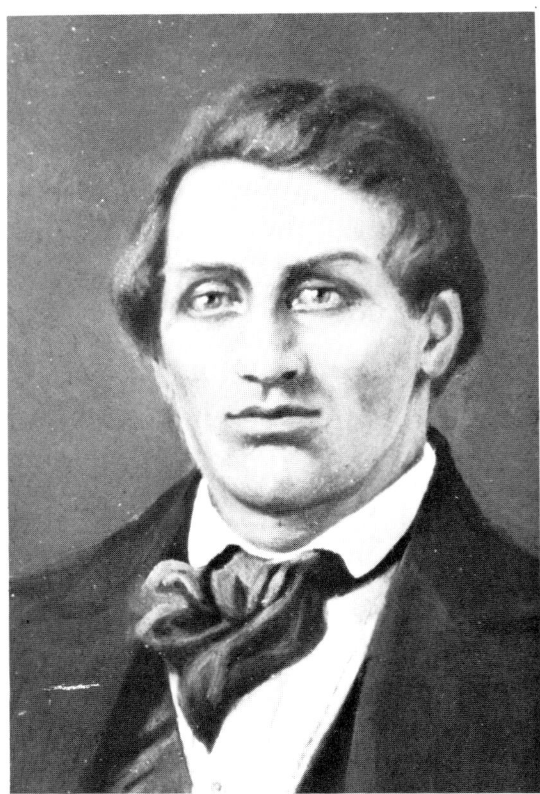

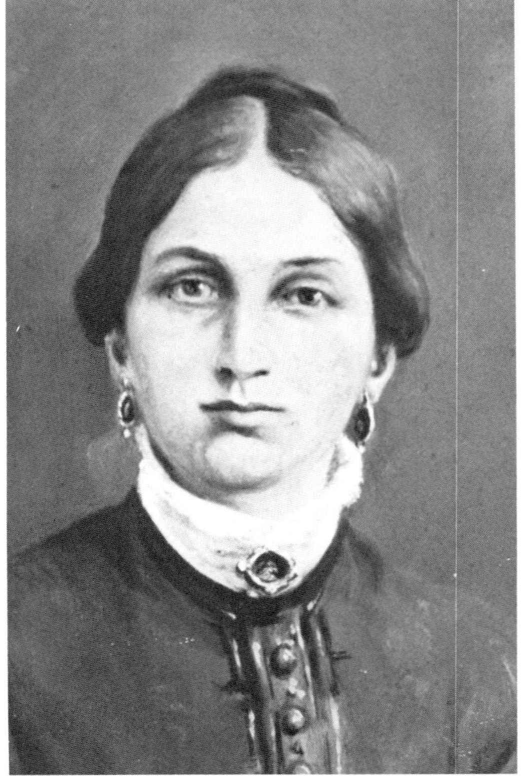

Oil portraits of his parents done by the artist in 1916 from the 1850 tintype shown above.

and lessons about woodlore and hunting told him by his grandfather and thirteen uncles, all of whom were skilled woodsmen. When the time was right, young Edgar was given an old flintlock rifle, as long as he was tall, and taught to use it. From then on he spent as much time as he could hunting rabbits, squirrels and partridges, proud to contribute to the family larder. At night he made bullets, a task required of every hunter in those days, by melting down the empty leaden canisters which had held the gunpowder he used. This done he would often sit before the fireplace on a buffalo robe, reading books about hunting adventures or the ways of the woodsman. Some of the books that young Edgar read so avidly, particularly the early dime novels, were not welcome in Quaker households. Although they had a lofty moral tone unlike the later sensational ones, they were scorned as trashy literature. Consequently, as Edgar in later years revealed, he hid his "yellow-backs," as they were called, in a knothole of an old maple standing on the edge of a deep wood behind his grandmother's house.

Young Edgar also read all he could about Indians. And he observed the descendants of Red Jacket when they camped next to his grandmother's property on their semiannual trip from their new reservation in Cattarugus to their old home on the Seneca Reservation. From then on Edgar was a student of Indians and Indian ways. He was fascinated by them as matchless woodsmen. Most of what his uncles taught him about hunting were Indian techniques. And he had planted corn on his relative's farms in the Indian manner, a fish buried with each few grains of corn. He began to develop a lifelong respect for the Indian in his natural setting before the white man came. As an artist, many years later, he portrayed them this way almost without exception.

Edgar's formal schooling consisted of regular attendance at the log schoolhouse at Websters Corners followed by two years at the Friends Institute close to his home. There is conclusive evidence that he never had any formal art training.

But he showed an interest and natural ability to draw remarkably early. At age four his father discovered him with pencil and paper hard at work sketching. The man was astonished to see a barn and barnyard complete with chickens taking shape. In the foreground was a grove of fruit trees and beyond the barn grazed a fat cow.[3] One of Edgar's schoolteachers, who knew him many years later when he was a successful artist, remembered that as a schoolboy Edgar "did marvels" in reproducing the colorful woodland birds and flowers. She also remembered an exceptional drawing young Edgar made of a friend of his father dressed in the uniform of adjutant of the State Militia and mounted on a fine gray horse.[4]

In 1861, when Edgar was only nine, an uncle aware of the boy's talent proposed an arrangement whereby he would be an apprentice to a scenic painter in Pennsylvania. In those days "scenic painter" was the title given to an artist who designed and painted backgrounds, stage wings and curtains for theater productions. Often the work was very elaborate and consisted of several backdrops for a single play. It was not uncommon for exceptional scenic artists to be given attention by the theater critics in their columns. The best artists were occasionally even billed above the actors.

But the apprenticeship was not to be. The Civil War intervened and its terrible effects were felt in Erie County. Nearly all able men volunteered or were conscripted. Edgar's father became a member of the 67th Volunteer Infantry. Ten-year-old Edgar served as a drummer boy for new recruits. It was a solemn time for Edgar and affected him greatly. By early summer of 1863, the war was ominously close to home. On July 1 the residents of Websters Corners—women, old men and children—gathered together in fear and excitement as news came that Lee was advancing on Gettysburg, Pennsylvania. The family feared that Edgar's father was there. The sounds of big guns could be heard on July 4, but no news reached the village. Although just a boy, Edgar felt he might soon have to fight for his life. It was a trauma he would never forget. But Lee got no farther and began to retreat. The family was spared. Edgar's father had been at Harrisburg during the Battle of Gettysburg and ultimately survived the war.

Peaceful rural life returned to the Erie County village but was shaken again in 1865 by another incident that affected Edgar greatly. On April 14, Edgar and his brother Everett were cleaning out the cellar, when through a window they heard the cry, "Lincoln is shot!" A few days later, Edgar's father took him to Lincoln's bier in the "arcade" at Buffalo. After they struggled through the crowds, Edgar's father held the boy up to view the slain president. Forty-five years later, Edgar wrote in his journal, "That face in the casket I never shall forget." Young Edgar had seen Lincoln once before, also in Buffalo, on the way to the inauguration in 1861. The boy had been awed by the man's height and heroic bearing. Then to see the great figure in death had a profound impact on the impressionable youth. He repeatedly recalled the incident in his journals of later years. It helps to explain Edgar's unbounded patriotism, his willingness to volunteer for service in the Spanish-American War at the age of forty-six and his determination to portray heroism and nobility in his art.

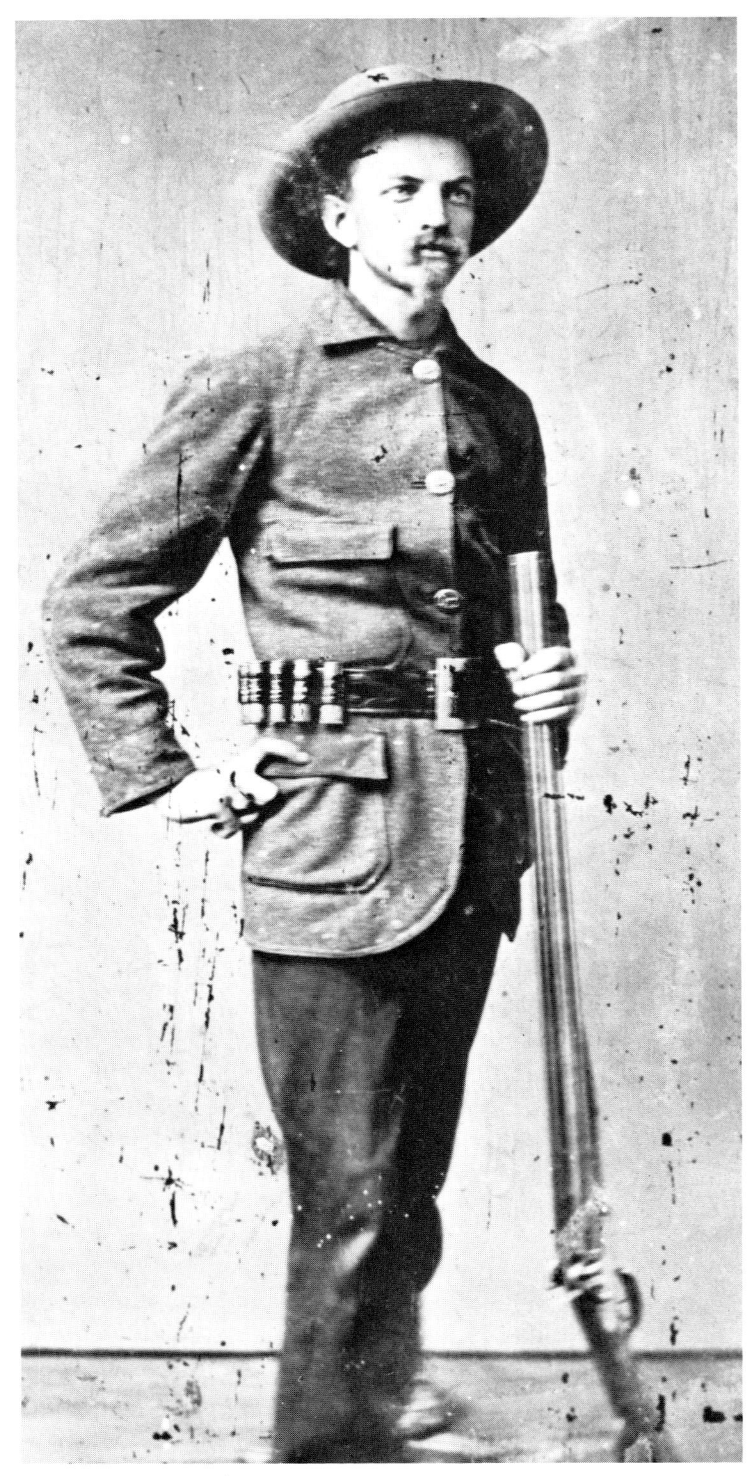

Edgar S. Paxson in 1874 at age 22.

2

Going West

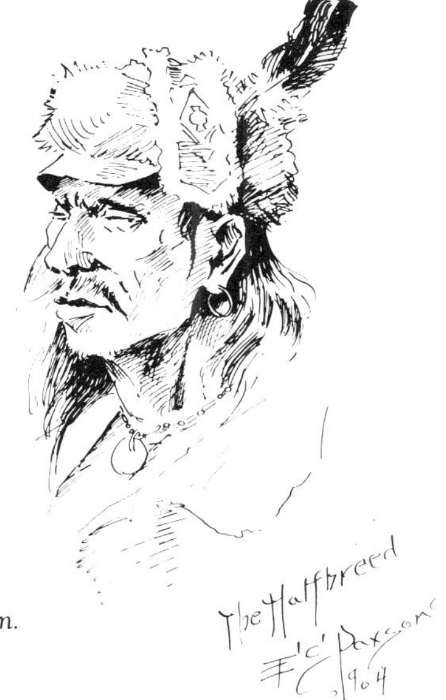

"The Halfbreed," ink, 1904. *Private Collection.*

In 1849, Edgar's uncle Orlando Hambleton traveled by wagon train to California, lured by the gold rush. He remained several years, established a successful sawmill near Sacramento, then sold out and returned to the East. When Edgar was a boy, Uncle Orlando visited the family in Erie County and told of his experiences with Indians, grizzly bears and the long trek through the plains and mountains. For years after, Edgar longed to make that overland passage. At age sixteen he met and conversed briefly with Kit Carson, the famous old scout, in Buffalo, New York, just a few months before Carson's death. And in 1872, also in New York, he met Captain Jack Crawford, "the Poet Scout," who told him much about the West and who became a lifelong friend. So by the time Edgar had completed his studies at the Friends Institute, he was undoubtedly yearning to go west. What transpired in the Paxson household at that time can only be surmised. There was very possibly some disagreement within the family. Edgar's father operated a successful carriage-building shop. The logical step for Edgar would be to begin an apprenticeship there. Perhaps a compromise was reached, for at age twenty, Edgar began traveling, but returned in several months and took up the apprenticeship, specializing in painting and fancy scroll work on the carriages. But his urge to see the West was great: after a little more than a year he was traveling again.

The sequence and extent of Edgar's travels, from 1872 until he arrived in Montana in early spring 1877, is not well documented. It is known that he returned to his home more than once, being there on June 4, 1874, to marry Laura Millicent Johnson, who had been a classmate in the old log schoolhouse.

In 1872, on his first trip, Edgar spent some time in Michigan at his cousin's home in Saginaw, which was at that time 300 miles deep into the forests. He also ranged as far south as Kansas where he was first introduced to Buffalo Bill Cody at Fort Hayes. Edgar recalled the time in a 1916 newspaper interview: "A lot of guides, scouts, hunters and trappers met about the fort and we were all introduced much the same as we meet friends in a hotel lobby today. We talked awhile, mostly about the country. He [Cody] was just getting the title of 'Buffalo Bill' then."[1] This was the first of many meetings of the two and developed into a continuing friendship.

At some time during the early '70s, Edgar traveled with his brother Everett, but little is known of their adventures. There is mention of them visiting Fort Vincennes, Wisconsin, and Fort Niagra and Hamilton, Canada. During these travels he worked occasionally, once reportedly as a lumberjack and another time as a guide for hunting parties.

Apparently Edgar spent most of 1874 at home with his young wife, but in the spring of 1875 he determined to go west with the idea of establishing a home, then sending for his wife. Shortly before he departed, Laura gave birth to their first child, Loren.[2]

Edgar picked a turbulent time to go west. The word had not long been out that there was gold in the Black Hills. Large numbers of settlers were heading for the Dakotas. But this was the heartland of the Sioux; the Treaty of Laramie in 1868 had set it aside as their reservation. They were deeply offended and alarmed by the 1874 exploratory expedition commanded by Lieutenant Colonel Custer through the Black Hills which had confirmed that extensive gold deposits existed there. Tensions increased and General Sheridan ordered federal troops to keep all white persons out of the Black Hills. Meanwhile a commission was appointed by the secretary of the interior to get the Sioux to sign away the right to mine the gold. The reservation Sioux were near starvation due to lack of supplies promised by the government. They said, "Pay us what the gold is worth and give us buffalo country." The commission refused and the troops failed to keep the gold hungry whites off the reservation. In the fall of 1875, many hungry and angry Sioux left the reservation to hunt buffalo along the Powder River to the

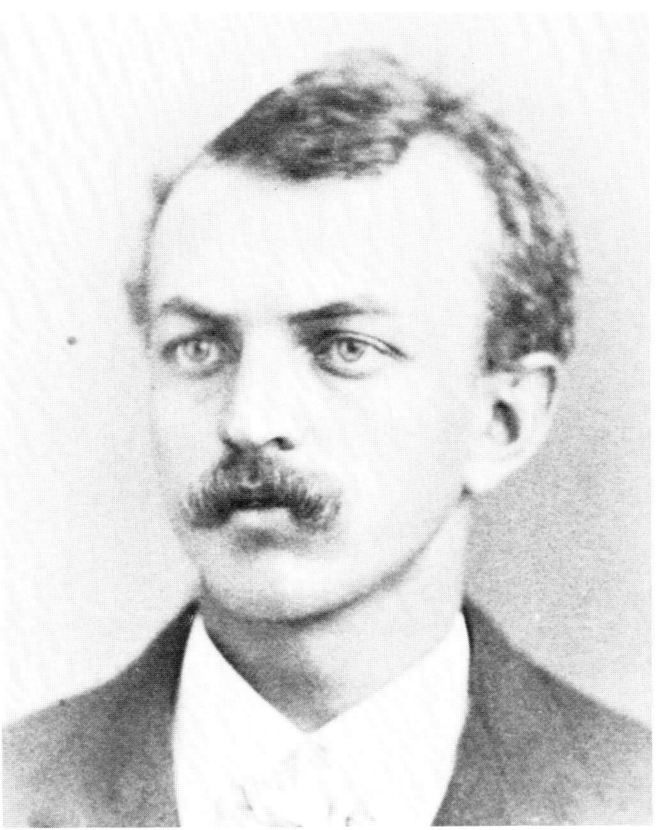

Paxson and his bride, Laura about 1875.

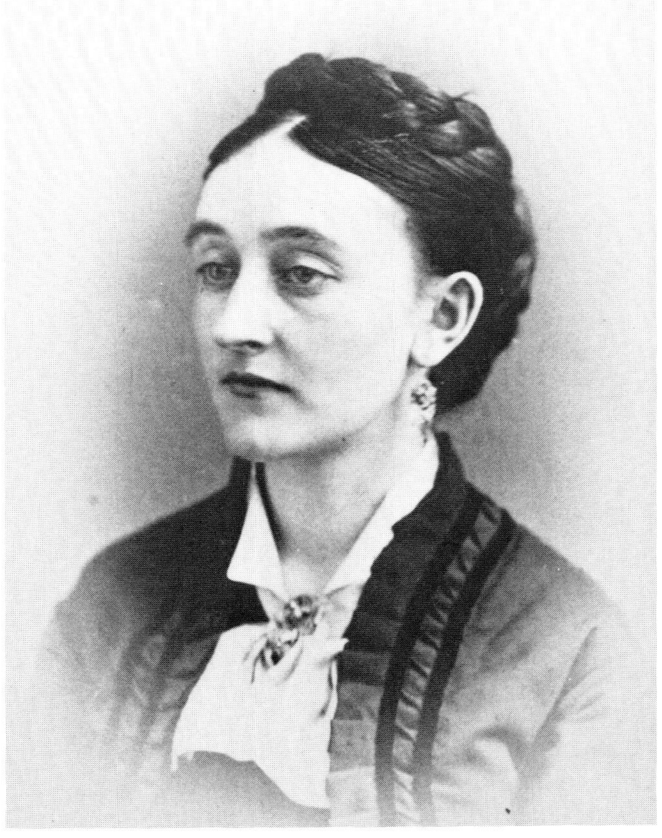

west. Winter came early that year. They could not or would not return to the reservation as ordered by the federal government and were declared renegades. The War Department made plans to subdue and drive them back to the reservation in the spring. The army devised a plan in which three columns of troops would converge on the Indians in the buffalo country. Lt. Col. George Custer and his 7th Cavalry were part of one column.

Meanwhile Edgar and Everett were working their way west. As a boy Edgar had learned to handle a heavily loaded wagon and team on trips to and from a mill with his grandfather, and so was able to sign on as a freight driver to Wyoming in that spring of 1876 when the military was to move against the Sioux. It is uncertain whether Everett accompanied him although both brothers ended up in Montana about the same time.

As Edgar was making this overland passage, or shortly thereafter, about 250 miles to the north Custer's scouts discovered the tracks of a large band of Indians. Anticipating that he could intercept the Indians on the banks of the Little Bighorn River before the other columns converged, Custer divided his command for a three-pronged attack, himself leading one contingent and Maj. Marcus Reno and Capt. F. W. Benteen leading the other two. Custer's strategy and the events that followed are still the subject of great controversy. What is certain is that Custer and the 263 men in his contingent were wiped out by an overwhelming number of Indians on a hill above the Little Bighorn River on June 25, 1876, while Reno and Benteen's troops were dug in about four miles away.

Soon afterward Edgar returned to St. Louis where he again met William Cody and Captain Jack Crawford.[3] Everywhere in the city the topic of conversation was the Little Bighorn battle. The most outrageous stories spread through bars, hotel lobbies, livery stables and freighter-outfitting establishments. Every man who had just arrived from the West (and many who had not) had his version and the newspapers printed every one.

Edgar was fascinated. The sense of history that ruled so much of his life took hold. He determined then to someday paint the Custer fight as truthfully as was humanly possible.

Another who frequented the St. Louis haunts of cowhands, scouts, trappers, prospectors and hunters at that time was a youngster about twelve years old who had a fascination for cowboys and Indians. Cutting school or slipping away from the home of his well-to-do family he walked the dusty streets seeking out old-timers with stories of the wild West. Perhaps he overheard Texas Jack Humbolt telling Ed Paxson what he thought about the Custer battle. No one will ever know, but many years later the lad, Charlie Russell, would become a close friend of Edgar, share the desire to paint the Old West as it really was, become known worldwide as "the Cowboy Artist" and write a stirring tribute to his fellow artist at Edgar's death.

Having the Custer battle on his mind, Edgar's destination on leaving St. Louis was clearly Montana Territory. In the spring of 1877 there were signs that Montana had plenty to offer the emigrant from the East. New mining techniques brought a resurgence of activity around Butte, the mining camp which had been very quiet after the decline of the 1860s gold rush. The Sioux Nation had been quickly subdued in a winter and early spring campaign following the Custer battle. This opened the trails to fertile land such as the Bitterroot and Deer Lodge valleys to homesteaders. And with the buffalo nearly wiped out and Indians on the reservations, the cattlemen could now begin to establish themselves on the grasslands.

Edgar set out overland in early 1877. He soon viewed the rolling hills and prairies surrounding the Little Bighorn for the first time. In the years to come he would return several times, going over the battlefield with the Indian participants and soldiers who were close to the tragedy, until, as he put it, "I became as familiar with the ground and circumstances as with my own home."[4]

But there was no immediate future for Edgar on the stark plains of central Montana. The Rocky Mountains to the west beckoned.

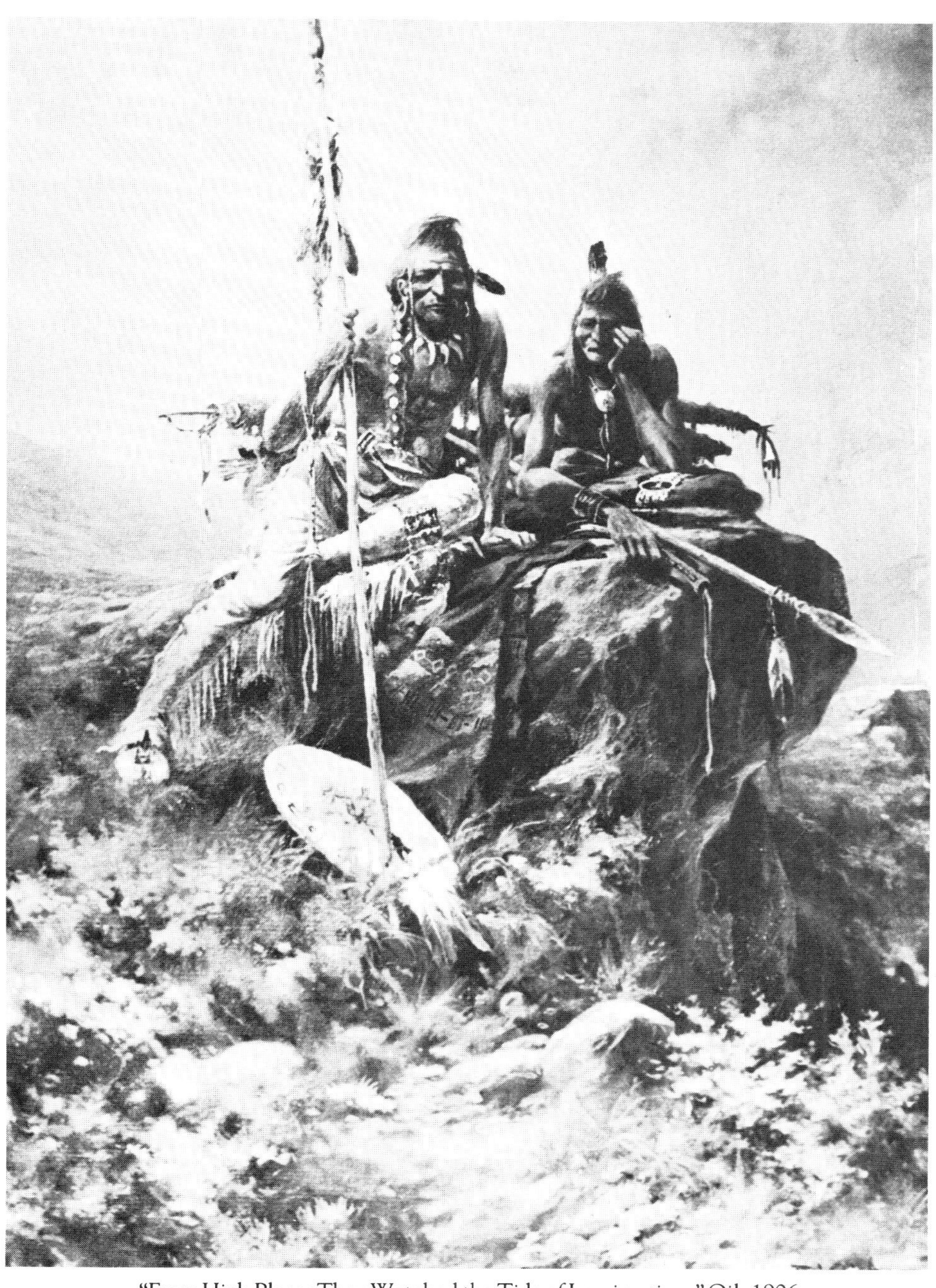

"From High Places They Watched the Tide of Immigration," Oil, 1906.
Reproduced from a photograph in the artist's album.

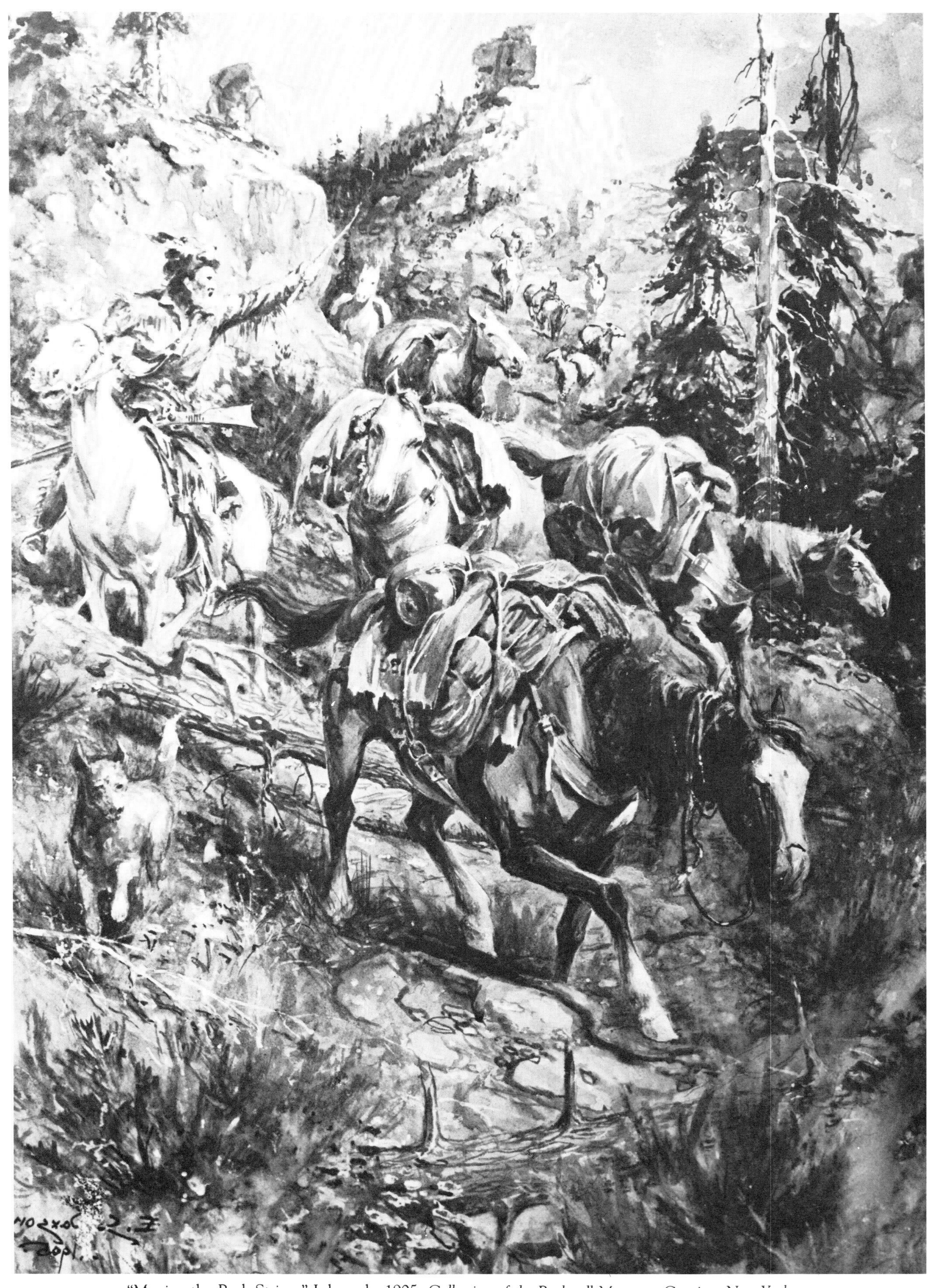

"Moving the Pack String." Ink wash, 1905. *Collection of the Rockwell Museum, Corning, New York.*

3

Frontier Days

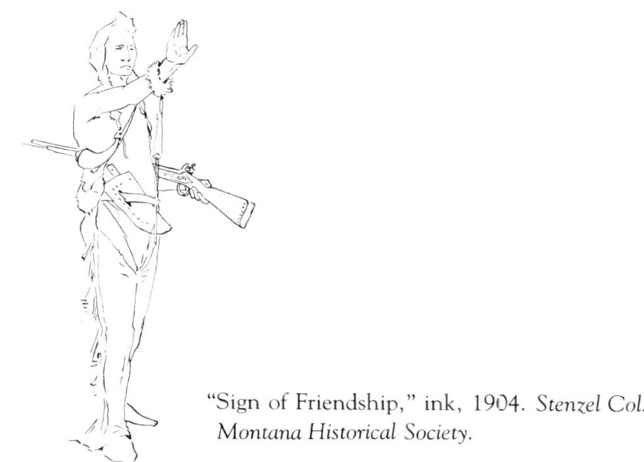

"Sign of Friendship," ink, 1904. *Stenzel Col., Montana Historical Society.*

Edgar had talents that the cattle ranchers in the foothills of the Montana Rockies could use. He had no inclination or special skills for cowpunching, but he was at home on a horse and he was a crack shot, skilled hunter and knew how to live on the trail. In his quiet, self-assured way, he soon proved he was not a tenderfoot. He found employment first in southwestern Montana, working for cattle ranchers around Ryan's Canyon. His job was primarily to provide meat for the cowboys by hunting wild game, and to hunt down wolves, bears and mountain lions that attacked the cattle.

Coincident with Edgar's new employment was the reappearance of Indian trouble, this time from the Nez Percé and Bannock-Shoshone in Idaho. Owing to this, Edgar was called on to perform two new and very risky duties for the ranchers. They asked him to scout for Indian bands who slaughtered cattle and to act as a messenger between the isolated ranches and the nearest settlement, Iron Rod. Being small and wiry (5' 8" and barely 140 pounds), Edgar was a natural choice for procuring mail, newspapers and light supplies in a hurry on a fast pony. And being trail-wise and reliable, he proved his worth as a scout.[1]

For Edgar this was the beginning of a three-year period of adventure and drama in a territory as raw and dangerous as any in the Old West. He would feel the stomach-churning menace of a proximate war and see men die in violent confrontation between Indian and white and between white and white. He would know long, anxiety-filled nights while camped in Indian country and would live through face-to-face encounters with renegades in the wilderness. But also he would know the comraderie of high country hunts and shared campfires with both Indian and white companions. All the while he would be absorbing the detail and essence of the frontier which through his genius would reappear in his paintings after the Old West had passed away.

The new Indian trouble developed first with the Nez Percé Indians. In 1876, a commission instructed that they be moved to the Lapwai Reservation near Lewiston, Idaho. A large number of the Indians insisted that they wanted to remain in the Wallowa Valley in what is now eastern Oregon, as it was their ancestral home. Hostilities began in June 1877 when a few braves killed a white man on the Salmon River during a dispute. White Bird, a chief of importance, declared war and ten more white settlers were killed. The Nez Percé, always known previously as a peaceful tribe, had never before warred against the whites. Chief Joseph, their leader, had repeatedly stated his peaceful intentions. Now he determined to lead his people to the buffalo hunting grounds to the east in Montana, along the Lolo Trail which the Nez Percé had used annually for hundreds of years. Word reached Montana settlements and outposts by telegraph that the Nez Percé were on the warpath. The army was reported in pursuit, but behind and unable to keep pace. In Joseph's command were several hundred braves and as many women and children.

With Joseph approaching Montana and less than 100 federal soldiers stationed in the territory, settlers were extremely anxious. There were only about 500 settlers at that time in the Bitterroot Valley, which lay just south of Missoula and through which passed the Lolo Trail. Calls for help from Missoula were answered from throughout the territory. Men hurried there singly and in groups. Ranchers in the outlying areas were put on the alert. They sent out scouts to warn of the approach of the Indians. Edgar was one of these scouts.

On July 25, 100 citizens of the Bitterroot Valley, forty army regulars from Fort Missoula and 350 men from other sections marched a few miles up Lolo Creek and hastily constructed fortifications, as the Nez Percé were then camped only four miles farther upstream. Truce flags were raised and Captain Rawn, leader of

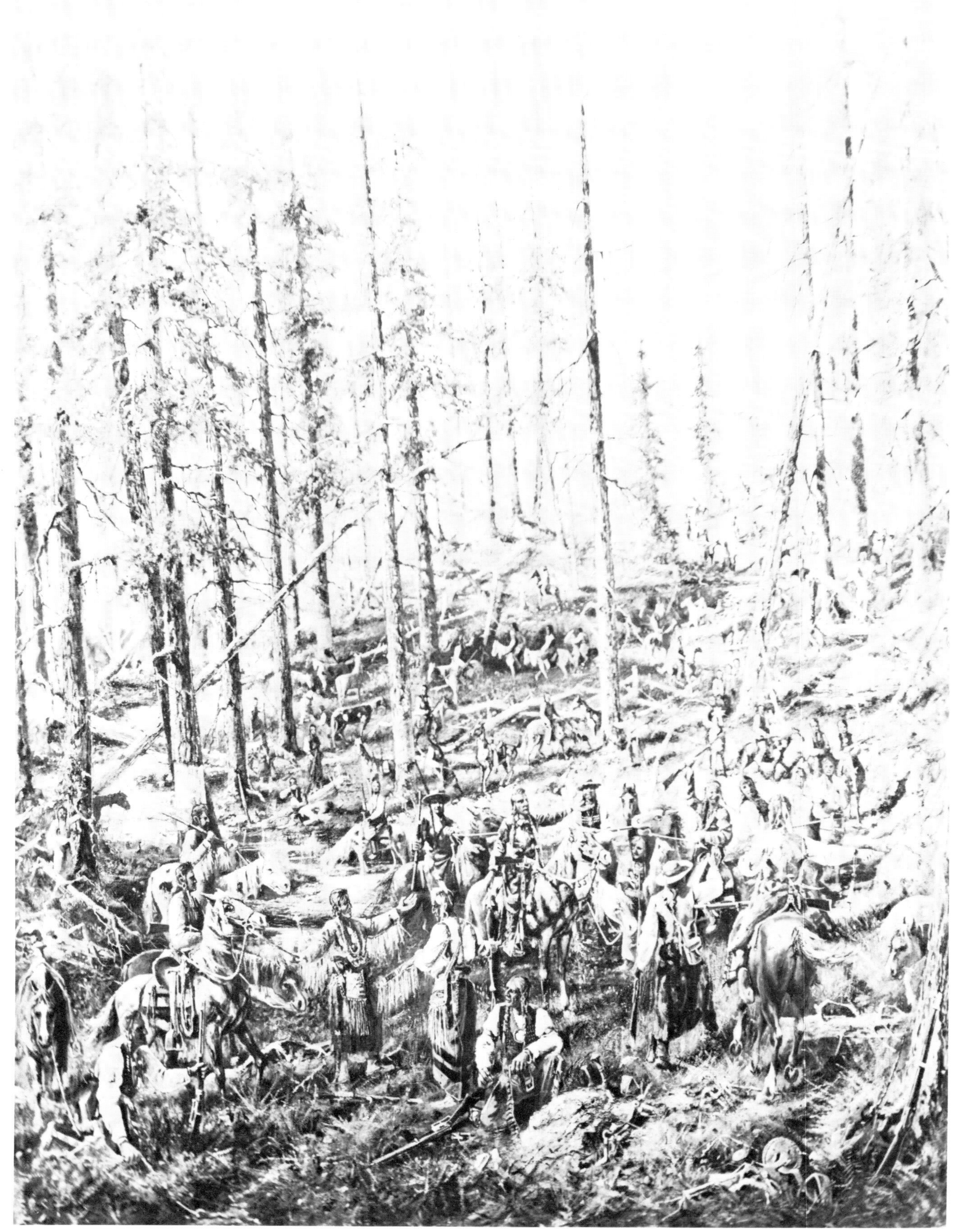

"The Lolo Trail." Oil, 1893, 56" x 42". This is one of Paxson's early efforts at frontier subjects. *Reproduced from an early photograph of the painting courtesy, Montana Historical Society, Helena, Montana. Whereabouts of the painting is unknown to author.*

the forty Missoula regulars, sent a message to Joseph demanding surrender. Joseph insisted that he did not want to fight and would pass peaceably through the valley toward the Yellowstone River headwaters where he hoped to make a new home for his people. He could not be persuaded to do otherwise. He would not surrender.

Edgar, being occupied in the employ of the ranchers southeast of the Bitterroot Valley, was not at the confrontation on Lolo Creek. But he later painted an ambitious oil depicting Chief Joseph receiving the message from Captain Rawn. The painting, entitled *The Lolo Trail*, is evidence of Edgar's intense interest in historic fact down to the finest detail. Many of his friends in later years were participants in the Lolo Creek incident, and he sifted and resifted their stories until he was satisfied that his depiction was as close to the truth as he could make it. In a pamphlet he wrote a description of the painting:

> Chief Joseph is represented in the center ground, sitting on his horse, consulting a scout who has been informed by Rawn that they must surrender or go back to the reservation. "Say to Captain Rawn, I shall go in two days" was Joseph's reply. Wal-lit-za, with his gun upraised, endeavors to prevent this, aided by his friends Tap-sis-il-pilp (on the ground to his right), and Um-til-elp-coun (on horse to his left), who are in favor of an immediate attack. White Bird, with his hand raised, upbraids them and succeeds in quieting them. Immediately behind Joseph is Hush-Hush-Cute, who seems to be taking in the big talk. He was a young man, a good friend of Joseph, and was greatly in favor of going through the country peaceably; but after the fight on the Big Hole he was one of the most cruel and relentless. Watering his horse can be seen Sin-che-la (Little Wolf), one of the most inveterate horse thieves of his tribe. He was afterward killed on the Joco reservation. Looking Glass, a sub-chief, is sitting on the ground, filling his belt with cartridges which he has emptied into his blanket. He seems to listen to the conversation of Too-hul-hul-sote (Medicine Man) and Ollicut (Joseph's brother) who is holding his horse, these two favoring Joseph's instructions to the messenger. Pe-con-na, a Blackfoot renegade, is on his knees holding his horse which is evidently tired out. Crossing the creek on the white horse is Indian Samiah. He evidently has been acting as a flanker and has ridden in to find out the cause of the delay.... In the distance is seen Lolo Peak.[2]

The Nez Percé, true to their word, detoured around the fortifications of the settlers by passing, partly concealed, over a ridge nearby and descending into the Bitterroot Valley. Several hundred of the Indians were in the valley before most of the disorganized settlers had realized what had happened. Valley residents, who had always had good relations with the Nez Percé, considered it wise to take Joseph at his word and let the Indians pass unmolested. During the next week, the Indians moved slowly through the valley and passed through the mountains to the basin of the Big Hole River. Meanwhile, General Gibbon's troops had been sent from Fort Shaw in the north to intercept the Indians. With the Fort Missoula regulars and some civilian volunteers, they attacked the Indians on the Big Hole. It was a surprise attack and desperately fought, much of it hand-to-hand. The Nez Percé, outnumbering the attackers two to one, succeeded in finally driving them off and retreating in an orderly way, although casualties were heavy on both sides. The troops were too decimated to pursue, General Gibbons himself being wounded. Edgar, having been informed of the Indians' progress away from Ryan's Canyon and of the battle on the Big Hole River, rushed to the battle scene. He arrived the day after the fight and set about caring for the wounded. He stayed with them on the arduous wagon trip sixty miles to the nearest hospital in Deer Lodge.

Edgar said more than once that he took no active part in the fighting against Chief Joseph and the Nez Percé. Indeed he many times denied he had ever been an "Indian fighter." But he did affirm that he acted as a "scout in the campaign," as he put it. Whether this was wholly in the employ of private interests is uncertain. Laura Paxson mentioned briefly in a 1932 interview with Montana historian Albert Partoll that her husband had spent three days "around the stage station in Dillon" looking for Indian signs "as a volunteer" during the Nez Percé troubles.[3] But no other specific information is known.

It is known that Edgar returned to his duties at Ryan's Canyon shortly after he left Deer Lodge, and very soon, with the consequences of war still fresh in his mind, he got quite a scare while on a scout. He related the incident in *Outdoor Life* in 1901. Characteristic of his preference to not draw attention to himself, he referred to himself as "Sam":

> About ten days after the fight on the Big Hole, Old Bob, Dick W. and he who I will call "Sam" (who were on a private scouting trip for cattlemen) made a camp on a small willow-fringed stream north of Market Lake, Idaho. Just in the edge of evening a "heap big" dust was seen to arise in the south. Dick, picking up his rifle, went to a rise of ground and took a long and cautious look. Turning suddenly he came down on all fours, exclaiming "Injuns!" All scattered for high ground to reconnoiter. As near as could be made out the strangers were a party going toward the lake, having evidently come in from the valley to the west. Knowing "Major Jim" to be a renegade Bannock and that some of his followers were on the prowl, it was thought to be him, as Joseph and his Nez Perces were still supposed to be to the north. As the country is here low and flat, with broken ridges leading to the range of mountains on either side, a change of camp was deemed advisable by the trio of whites. The little white mare was therefore quickly packed with tee-pee, tin pots and kettles, and leading the saddle horses by the long lariats through the low willows to the north for about two miles, a halt was made. "Jersy Lil" was unpacked, while the other horses, with loosely cinched saddles, were left to stand at the picket pin. They remained on guard for shifts of three

hours each through the night. The camp was disturbed only by the occasional howl of wolf or bark of coyote.

As morning dawned each went on a still hunt alone. Away down in the valley was to be seen a great commotion. Indians on their ponies were flitting here and there, with flashes of light darting from their arms and equipments, sending a halo of dust, which tipped by the brightly rising sun, looked like a golden mist against the dark shadows of the distant mountains. Soon, in a long continuous line, they moved off toward the northeast, and were finally lost amid the rolling hills.

After a consultation of some length, the little party decided on keeping to the hills to the north. After traveling about fifteen miles they came out on the stage road where, upon a small stream, a camp was made. While eating the remains of an antelope, a lone man who was a scout separated from his command, came in. Through him it was learned that Joseph had crossed the stage road north of the divide and that a fight had followed on Camas Creek. The Indians seen the night before proved to be S. G. Fischer, chief of scouts, and his Indians who were then on their way to join General Howard, which they did on the north fork of the Snake.[4]

So the scare was a false alarm, but the next day the scouts experienced a genuine confrontation with hostile Indians when two renegade Bannocks chased Beaver Dick into their camp, the incident related in the introduction to this book.

Edgar had closer scrapes with renegades while he served as lone messenger for the Ryan's Canyon ranchers. One incident he recalled in his journal in 1908 upon the death of his "old pard," Joe Shineberger. Through some tactic not fully explained, Shineberger helped Edgar escape when, in Edgar's words, "Poker Joe's and Bannock Jim's band tried to round me up."

Another incident is described by Franz Stenzel in his monograph on the artist published by the Montana Historical Society in 1963. In it Edgar is said to have related the event in an interview many years later. According to the account, Edgar was actually captured by a band of about thirty Indians while he was on his way to town to pick up newspapers and mail for the ranchers. While the Indians were holding council to determine his fate, he pulled out paper and pencil and sketched the brave who seemed to be the leader. The Indians soon noticed what he was doing and gathered around, astonished at the excellent likeness. Obviously the Indians thought this was "strong medicine." Perhaps it saved Edgar, for he was later released unharmed.[5]

Records are sketchy as to Edgar's whereabouts after he left the Ryan's Canyon ranchers. Many of his recollections in his journals, on the back of old photographs, and in the margins of books are cryptic and tantalizing to the historian. For example, in his 1916 journal he wrote no more than, "in '78 with Nat Evans, had a mixup with Indians." The details no doubt have gone to rest with Edgar and his "old pards."

In the margin of a book, Edgar noted that he had traveled the Lolo Trail in 1877. He described it as unchanged since Lewis and Clark traveled it, worn four feet deep in places by the lodge poles dragged by the Nez Percé and Flatheads as they went to the buffalo country east of the Bitterroot Mountains. He mentioned that many times over the years he saw hunting parties pass along the trail. As an artist, this was one of his favorite subjects.

In October 1877, Edgar turned up in Watson, Montana, a village in the hills about thirty miles east of Helena. This is documented by an old leather billfold neatly inscribed "E. S. Paxson, Watson, Montana, October 1, 1877." Eight days later, a little over 100 miles to the northeast at Bearpaw, the Nez Percé finally surrendered to Gen. Nelson A. Miles. Joseph had led his people from the Big Hole Basin east through Yellowstone Park, then north hoping to reach Canada. He had eluded and beaten back federal troops along 1,400 miles of trail.

Shortly after Joseph's defeat, Edgar interviewed and sketched the chief and other Nez Percé leaders.[6] In 1913, he painted his conception of Joseph's dramatic surrender in one of six documentary murals he did for the Montana capitol building in Helena.

It was in Watson that fall of 1877 that Edgar was asked by anxious townspeople to help them keep the peace with a band of Bannock-Shoshone known as Lemhis. For one or two previous nights, Simon Estes' store had been entered and robbed of money, whiskey and a few other items. The next night a clerk lay in wait with a gun. He fell asleep but was awakened by the gurgling of whiskey being poured from a cask. The burglar was commanded to halt but made for a window and was killed instantly. He was found to be one of Chief Ten Doy's band of several hundred Lemhis on their way from the reservation to hunt buffalo near the Yellowstone River, with permission from the Department of Indian Affairs. Having recently been alarmed by the heretofore peaceful Nez Percé, the edgy settlers were worried that the Lemhis would respond violently to the discovery that one of their number had been slain. Edgar was sent with the message to the Indian camp on nearby Blacktail Creek. Ten Doy, always a peaceable chief, quieted the settlers fears. He said of the thief: "He was a bad Indian. Put him under ground."[7]

Ten Doy and Edgar became good friends over the years. Perhaps they were friends prior to this incident, which would have been good reason for Edgar's selection as messenger by the settlers. Edgar once noted that he had spent three months hunting with Bannock. Presumably this was Ten Doy's band. During this hunt, they procured 1,000 deerskins in one month which they sold to Simon Estes.

In describing in his journal the country in which they hunted, Edgar showed his ever-present awareness of its history. It was near the head of the Jefferson River in the Bitterroot Mountains where a steep, rocky cliff shaped like a beaver's head rose 150 feet above the water. It was here, noted Edgar, that the Indian woman Sacajawea was kidnapped from the Shoshones by the Minnatarees; and later it was here she was to return as interpreter and guide for the Lewis and Clark Expedition.

Edgar's next employers were Gilmer and Salisbury, proprietors of the Overland Stage Company. His experiences working for them proved to be just as risky and exciting as had been those while working for the ranchers. His first job was to drive 240 horses from Ogden, Utah, to Fort Benton, Montana. Much of the trail passed through Bannock country. Since the earliest days of John Jacob Astor's fur trading, frontiersmen had regarded the Bannocks as skilled horsemen, fierce warriors and consummate horse thieves. Now they were again becoming worrisome to the settlers around their reservation at Fort Hall, Idaho, a situation which deteriorated into war in 1878. As the winter ending 1877 came on, the Bannocks faced starvation on the reservation, owing to insufficient government rations. Their alternative was to leave the reservation and attempt to survive the snows and cold, hunting in nomadic bands. Many chose to do so. The winter proved to be unusually severe. Edgar himself was snowed in en route to pick up his charge of horses, again finding himself at Ryan's Canyon. For ten days he could not travel due to a raging blizzard. Stranded with him were a detail of soldiers en route to Fort Missoula. A number of them had been in the Big Hole battle. Undoubtedly many stories of that fight and others were exchanged those cold nights while the men huddled around campfires. No one could blame Edgar for some trepidation as he began driving the herd of horses north that bitter cold December in the vicinity of desperate Indians. On the trail the drovers and horses passed several small camps, smoke curling from the teepees, but there was no sign of hostility. The worst enemy, as it turned out, was the cold. Once, Edgar feared he had frozen his foot. One particular night he recalled in his journal—it was near Melrose, the driving almost completed. He wrote that he "slept on the side of the river...with not a sign of civilization in sight. Gosh! It was cold." Nevertheless, he delivered the entire herd safely.[8]

Still in the employ of Gilmer and Salisbury, Edgar then began "riding the telegraph line," reporting fallen and broken lines and making repairs. Again he chanced upon renegades. This time he was cornered at some cliffs on the Little Blackfoot River north of Deer Lodge. When he didn't report in, a party was sent out to hunt for him, but whether they were instrumental in his escape is not clear from the brief account of the incident in his journal.

Hostile Indians weren't the only renegades in Montana Territory in 1878. The lack of law enforcement on the frontier drew many outlaws and social misfits to the Montana frontier. Edgar witnessed more than one episode of violence involving white against white. One time an acquaintance of his was murdered after which Edgar saw the murderer turn the gun on himself and commit suicide. Much of this type of violence centered in the mining settlements rather than out on the trail. One such place where Edgar spent some time in 1878 was Emmettsburg in Henderson Gulch. In Edgar's 1914 journal he remembered the settlement as "a wild camp of about 100 cabins and shacks." He wrote: "Life was cheap in that camp. There were many shooting frays. Many died by the gun there."

Crime in the territory often required volunteer law enforcement from law-abiding settlers. Once Edgar provided his services as a scout, trailing an escaped murderer from Deer Lodge in the wilderness around Mount Powell. Edgar found the trail and caught up with the escapee only to lose him again. Two days later the man was captured by another search party.

To combat lawlessness, citizens formed what they called "vigilantes," short for Vigilance Committees, who took the law into their own hands and many times performed lynchings in their zeal. A central figure in the organization of the vigilantes was the famous U.S. marshal, X. Beidler. Edgar had occasion to act as guard with Beidler on a stagecoach carrying a large payroll in gold from Dillon to Iron Rod, a distance of forty miles. Edgar had been regularly employed as "shotgun" for Gilmer and Salisbury's Overland Stage Line. This time it was suspected that road agents were privy to the particularly large payroll shipment so the stage company had taken extra precautions to protect the cargo. Beidler rode up on top with the driver as "shotgun." Edgar, being small, was concealed in the boot, covered with a buffalo robe, and one "Shotgun" Brown rode in the coach as if he were a passenger. They rode all night. Edgar in his cold, uncomfortable and claustrophobic position was jarred repeatedly as the stagecoach bounced through ruts and potholes, the driver pushing the team to go faster than usual. They expected to see a roadblock around every bend in the trail, but just before dawn they safely pulled into Iron Rod station.[9]

So it can certainly be said that Edgar was familiar with the old stagecoaches inside and out. He later wrote a nostalgic description of one in *Outdoor Life*:

> The blushing red sides of the old stage-coach "Helena" were...seen to glitter through the grinning and dusty sage. Then the alkalai dust arose, leaving a long white snake like trail behind the old coach, with its jerky, bobbing hulk swinging and swaying from side to side. There she was, loaded to the guards with...messages of love and sorrow, and thirteen passengers hanging on to the edges. "Little Dock" was "slinging the braid" with "Gov" on top, his bald head glistening in the declining sun, swinging his old sombrero and whooping 'em up like a wild man. Those were great days, indeed."[10]

In 1912, artist Paxson immortalized that old stage, portraying it in one of the eight murals he was commissioned to paint in the Missoula County courthouse.

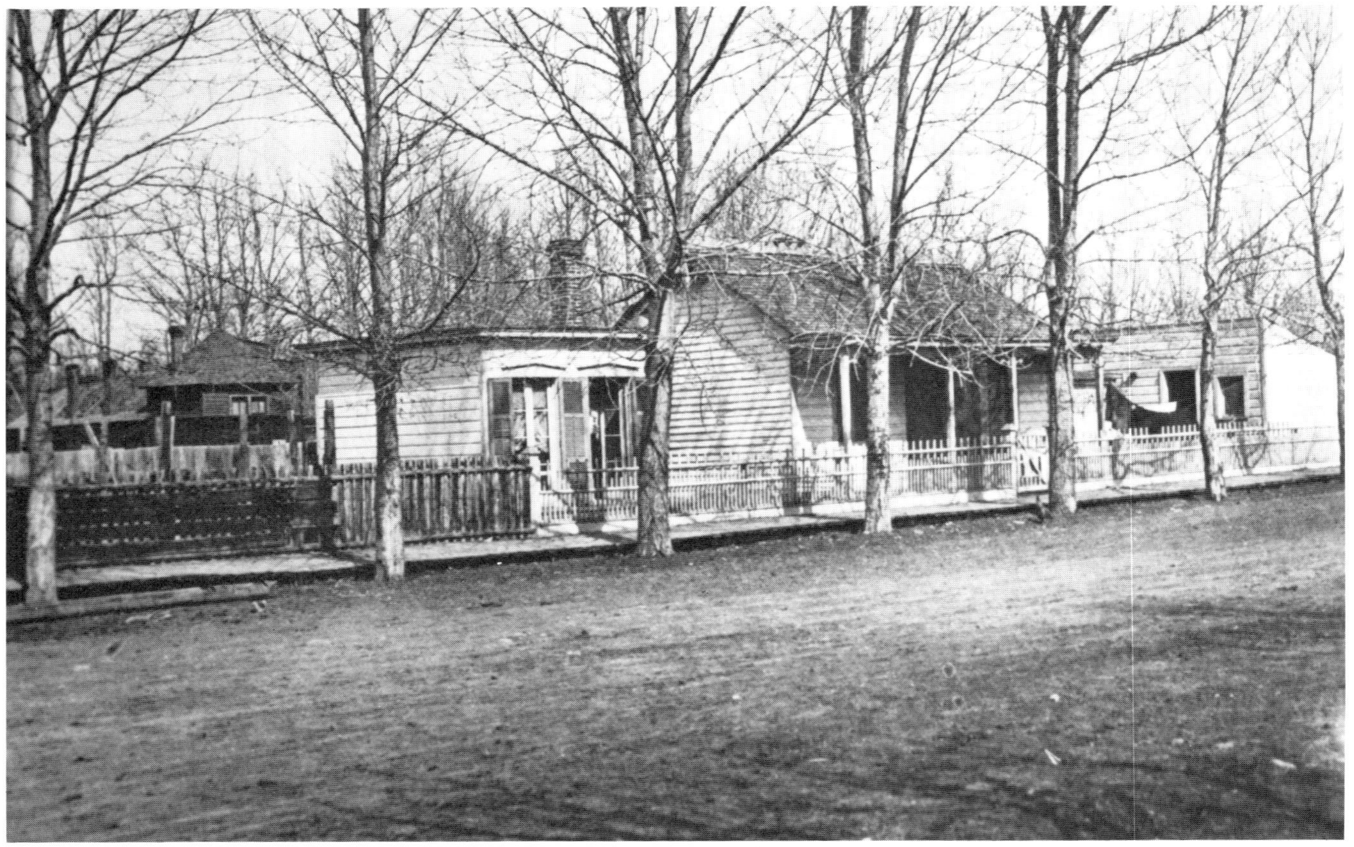

The Paxson home in Deer Lodge, 1878-1880.

It was just such a stagecoach in which Laura Paxson and three-year-old Loren arrived at Deer Lodge in the spring of 1878. Edgar had sent for them, feeling that Deer Lodge was a good and relatively safe place to raise a family. The Indian troubles appeared to be nearly over. The Bannocks were on the warpath but the fighting was moving far to the west into Oregon.

In the 1932 newspaper interview with Albert Partoll, Laura recalled the long trip to Montana. With Edgar's brother Robert, she traveled by the Union Pacific Railroad from New York to Ogden, Utah, then by stage to Deer Lodge. Laura had led a relatively sheltered life up to this time, having never been out of New York State. The stagecoach trip was a new experience for her. It was a long time to sit on thinly padded, stiff-springed seats bouncing over a trail that looked impassable to her. The wilderness passed slowly by between the tiny settlements. On the leg to Warm Springs, Montana, the stage driver was drunk. He shouted and ranted at the six horses, driving them on. The other passengers, four Chinese, kept up a constant banter in their native tongue all night long as the stage crashed through the darkness. But Laura withstood the trip. She was a determined woman and took readily to life in Montana. In a short time she had made herself and her family at home in a house Edgar had rented in preparation for her arrival.

But Indian hostilities were not quite over. When the Nez Percé had surrendered in October 1877, a few hostile bands had escaped to Canada. Not long after Laura had arrrived, reports that these Indians were threatening in northwest Montana caused consternation around Deer Lodge. Furthermore, small bands of renegade Bannocks were reportedly entering Montana Territory from the west after their main body was defeated by federal troops in eastern Oregon and Idaho. The Paxson family quickly packed and was prepared to go on short notice to Fort Owen in the Bitterroot Valley for protection.[11]

During that time, the summer of 1878, Edgar had yet another close call with renegades when he attempted a trip alone on horseback from Deer Lodge to his brother Everett's sheep ranch in Beaverhead County. While camping en route near McKay's Gulch, he was awakened when his disturbed horse, Old Sol, loose except for his "trail rope," ambled through camp upsetting equipment and snorting. Laying low, Edgar soon found himself nearly surrounded by Indians, although remarkably, they were unaware of his presence. There were about twenty young braves, mounted and well armed. The absence of pack horses, women and children alerted Edgar to a very real danger. Quietly, Edgar broke camp and concealed himself and Old Sol in some rocks until the Indian party passed by. Then when it was safe he returned to Deer Lodge to warn the townspeople. As he had thought, the Indians were indeed renegade Nez Percé. A miner, who had been placer mining in McKay's Gulch, confirmed it. He had successfully fled for his life after the renegades had killed his two companions, stole their supplies and passed into the mountains toward Idaho.[12]

In 1902, Edgar painted his experience at McKay's

Gulch. The painting, done in oil *en grisaille*, depicts the artist in buckskins peering into the gulch, his horse nearby. Edgar, not forgetting that it was the horse that saved his life, entitled the painting *Old Sol*.

Old Sol was Edgar's favorite horse and longtime companion on the trail. In the 1880s Edgar often traveled and hunted alone on Old Sol. One time he rode him through a blizzard from Helena to Deer Lodge, a distance of fifty miles. Edgar had purchased him from Crow Indians who had captured him from Sioux in a fight while buffalo hunting on the upper Yellowstone River. When Edgar got him he was, in Edgar's words, "all done up in Indian fashion." He was painted, his mane was ornamented with red cloth trimmings and his tail was beautified with colored streamers. His former Indian owners termed him "buffalo wise," and he had the so-called "iron jaw" of the range cayuse, which meant that a string of rawhide tied around his lower jaw served as bit and bridle. A length of rope added to this made a "trail rope" which had the advantage that when dropped, the horse remained where it was for a time as though tied to a post.

In Deer Lodge, Old Sol, held only by his loose trail rope, was free to graze on the prairie which began at the Paxson's back door. Edgar's first studio, improvised in the Deer Lodge house, had a big open window facing out onto the prairie. In later years, Edgar recalled wistfully how Old Sol would occasionally amble up to the house and put his head in the window for some affection or a lump of sugar. He recalled, too, that Old Sol could be a cagey old cayuse. He frequently evaded Edgar when it was time to hit the trail. He ran just far enough ahead so Edgar couldn't catch the trail rope. One time there was a bridge over a stream to be crossed and as the horse approached it, Edgar quickly forded the stream. As the pursuit seemed to have stopped, Old Sol slowed up and Edgar caught him on the other side. The bewildered horse might have had more respect for his master after that, but he never gave up his antics when it was time to hit the trail.[13]

Having his family with him, Edgar was no longer inclined to roam through the territory looking for adventuresome employment. For a while he worked as a telegraph operator, but not forgetting his promise to himself that he would someday paint the Custer fight, he looked for employment that would give him a chance to wield an artist's brush. He soon found that he could make a living as a sign painter in Deer Lodge, which was just big enough to sustain one member of that trade if he was especially clever and willing to supplement his income with a little hunting on the side. Edgar, of course, did not need much of an excuse for a hunting trip into the mountains he loved. Throughout the rest of his life, as long as he was physically able, he would make time to roam the high country for deer, elk, antelope, bear and bighorn sheep. He was happiest in the wilderness. He always said that his health improved when he got out on the trail. And in his years as an artist, his hunting trips were not only a source for subject matter but, most importantly, a source of inspiration.

Edgar had many exciting hunts through the years, but the one in the fall of 1878, just after he had become settled in Deer Lodge, developed into a life and death situation. Edgar, brother Everett and their "pilgrim" (another frontier name for tenderfoot) friend Carrol Smith who was just arrived from New York, had headed for the high country in good spirits. Soon after they made a camp on a small creek, Smith had foolishly struck out alone late in the day despite Edgar's warning. He had tracked a deer into the waning light

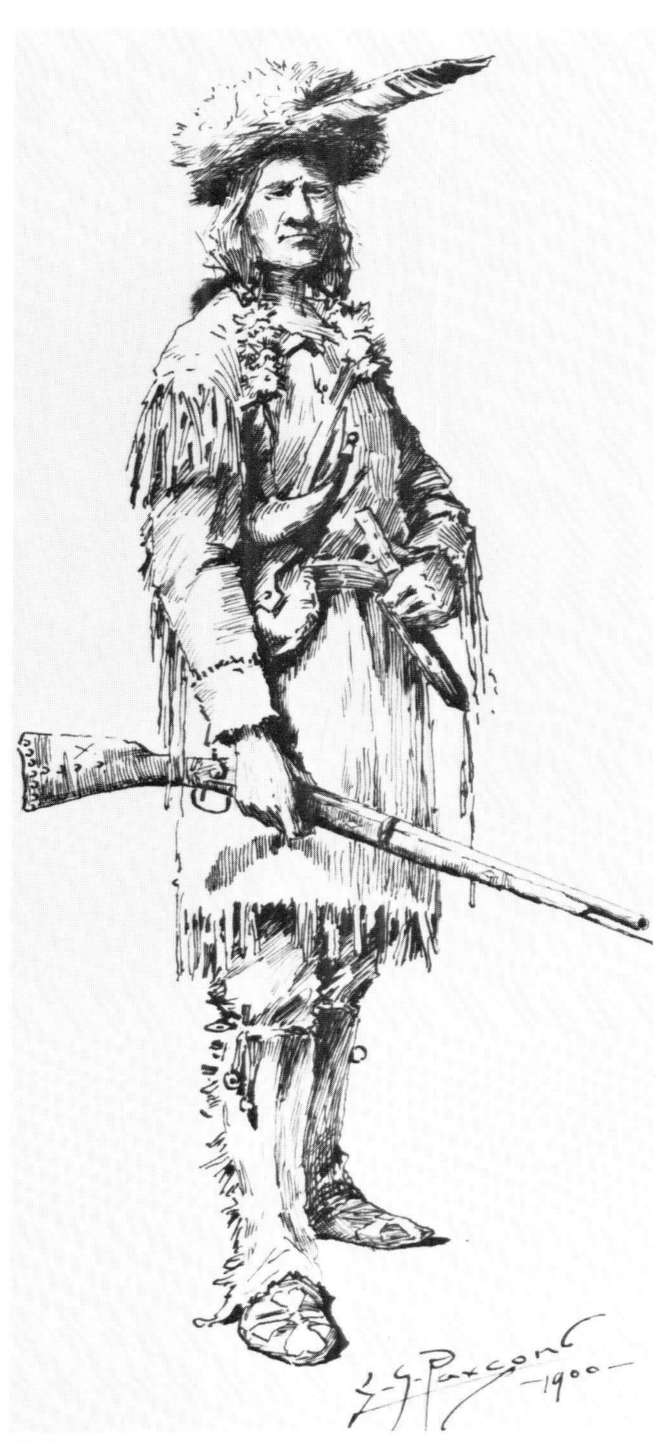

Title unknown. Ink, 1900. *Montana Historical Society, Helena, Montana.*

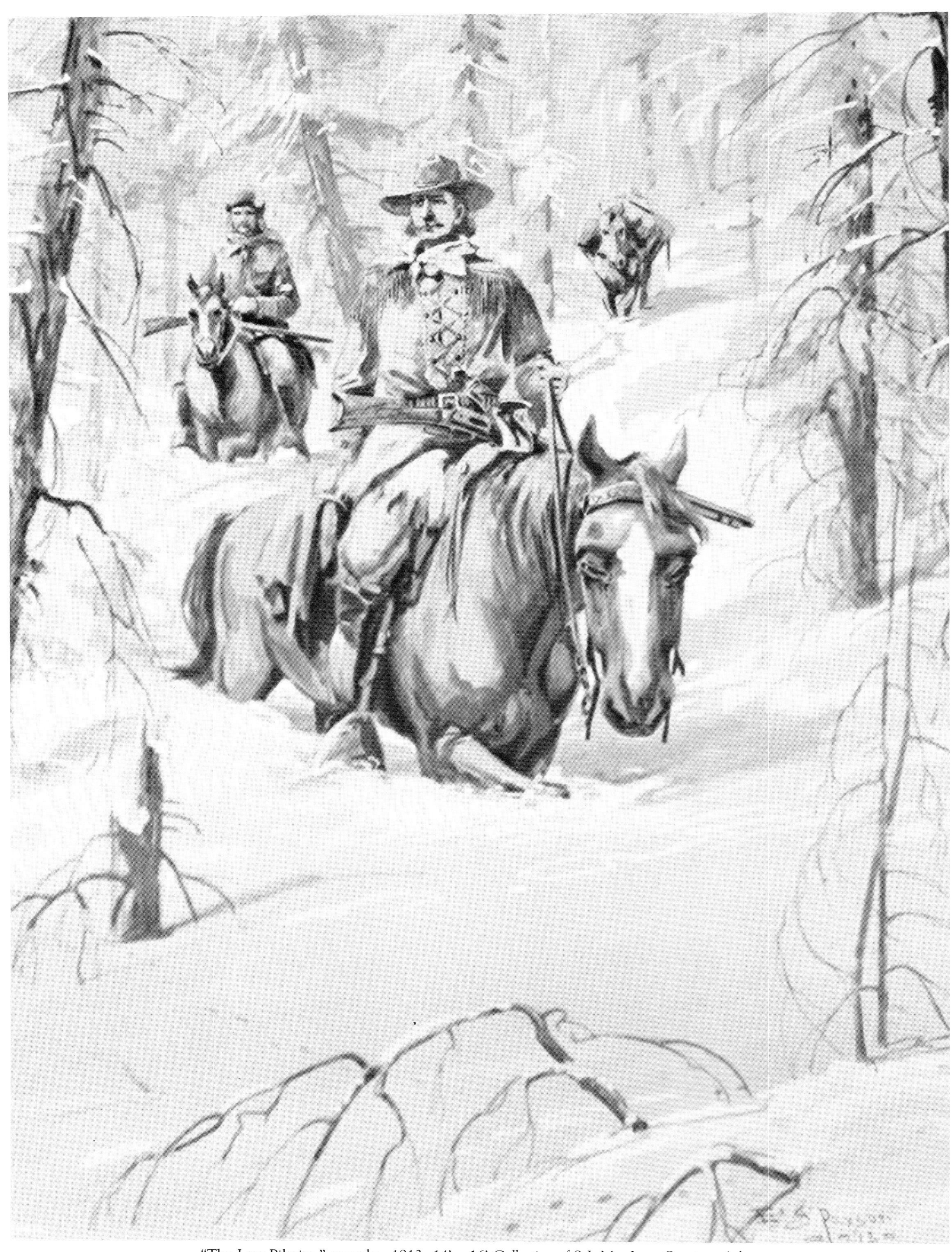

"The Lost Pilgrim," gouache, 1913, 14' x 16' *Collection of S.L.M., Inc., Corning, Arkansas.*

and, suddenly aware that it would soon be dark, had become disoriented in his haste to return. As darkness came on, the brothers became thoroughly alarmed. A drizzly, freezing rain was falling. The two men built a giant bonfire and fired shots into the air to attract their lost friend, but without success. By morning there was a foot of snow on the ground and more snow falling. The brothers searched all day on horseback with no luck. By nightfall there were two feet of snow and no let up expected. The horses could no longer find grass to feed. It was obvious that help was needed. The necessity of breaking camp and traveling through the snow-covered wilderness now put the brothers' lives in danger. Early the next morning they started the thirty-mile ride to Deer Lodge in four feet of snow. The snow obliterated every trail and veiled every landmark so that they had nothing to guide them but Edgar's experience and instinct for direction. Once they were out of the mountains, the rolling hills and benchlands presented a vast unmarked expanse devoid of signs of human habitation. Snow continued to fall without a break. Edgar later said it fell so thickly that often "it was impossible to see much beyond the ears of our horses." At times the men were forced to walk in order to rest their mounts. Finally, exhausted and nearly frozen, they stumbled into the inn at Deer Lodge long after dark with the news that Smith was lost. Great concern was shown by the men there, but only two would brave the cold mountains for a search. So early the next morning Edgar and Everett, with a little sleep and some warm food, started out with fresh horses and the two willing comrades, Nat Evans and Bert Hawley. The continuing snow had already filled their tracks, but Edgar unerringly led the group back to the camp. They searched the region until, on the eighth day since Smith had been lost, they gave up. Sick at heart, they returned to the inn at Deer Lodge. There, to their astonishment, they found Smith. But he was delirious and barely alive. He had groped his way sixty miles downstream, stumbling at last into a settlers cabin, crazed, starved and frostbitten, not even aware of his own name.

For the next three weeks, Smith lay in a semiconcious state, nursed by Edgar and Everett, but he finally regained his health.

In 1913, this story was written in detail by Merle Kettlewell as told to her by Edgar. It was published in the Missoula newspaper and then, as "The Lost Pilgrim," in *Following Old Trails*, a book by A. L. Stone. Edgar painted the searchers on horseback in the snow-choked wilderness for an accompanying illustration.[14]

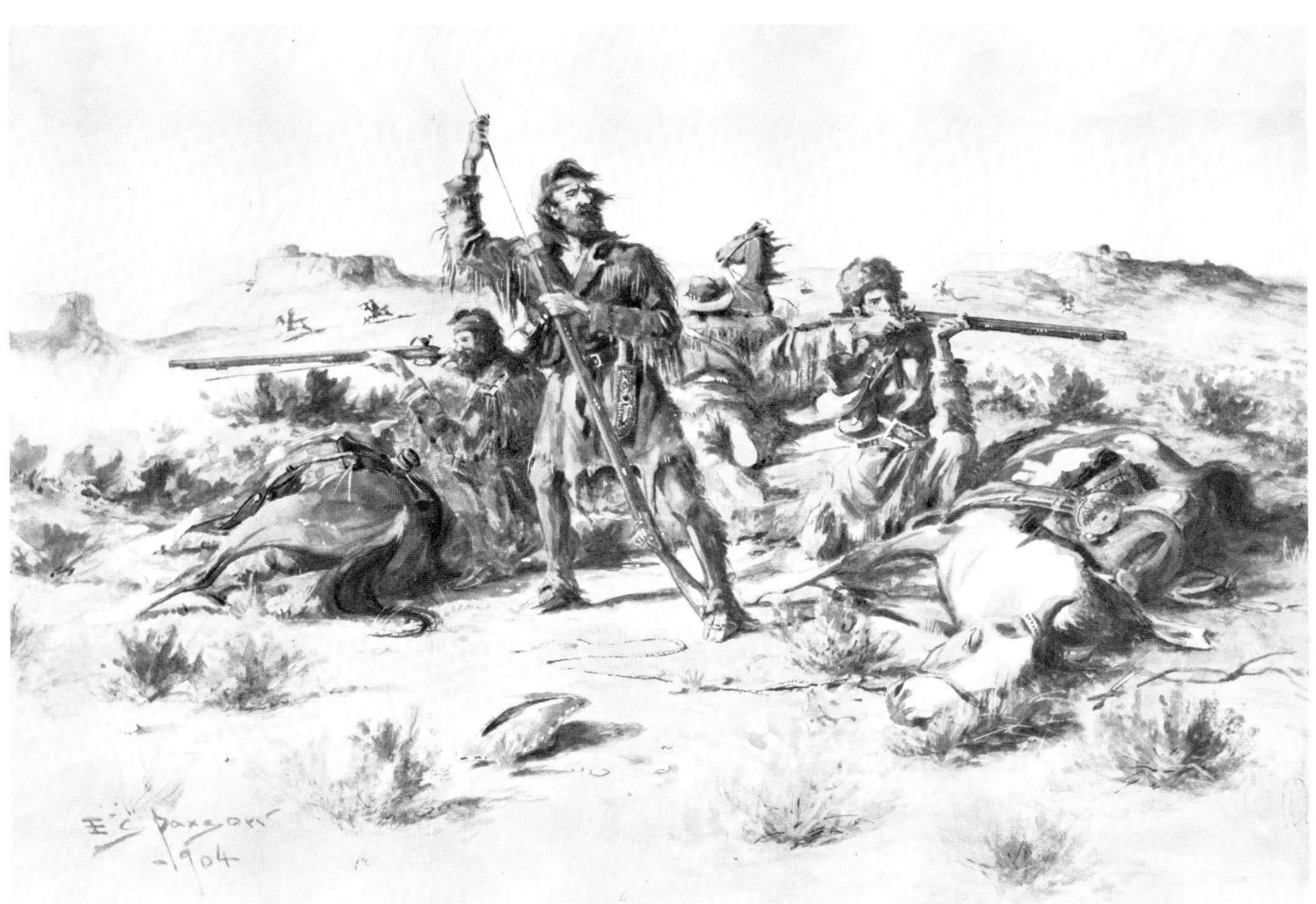

"Four of a Kind," watercolor, 1904, 14' x 20'. *The Thomas Gilcrease Institute of American History and Art, Tulsa, Oklahoma.*

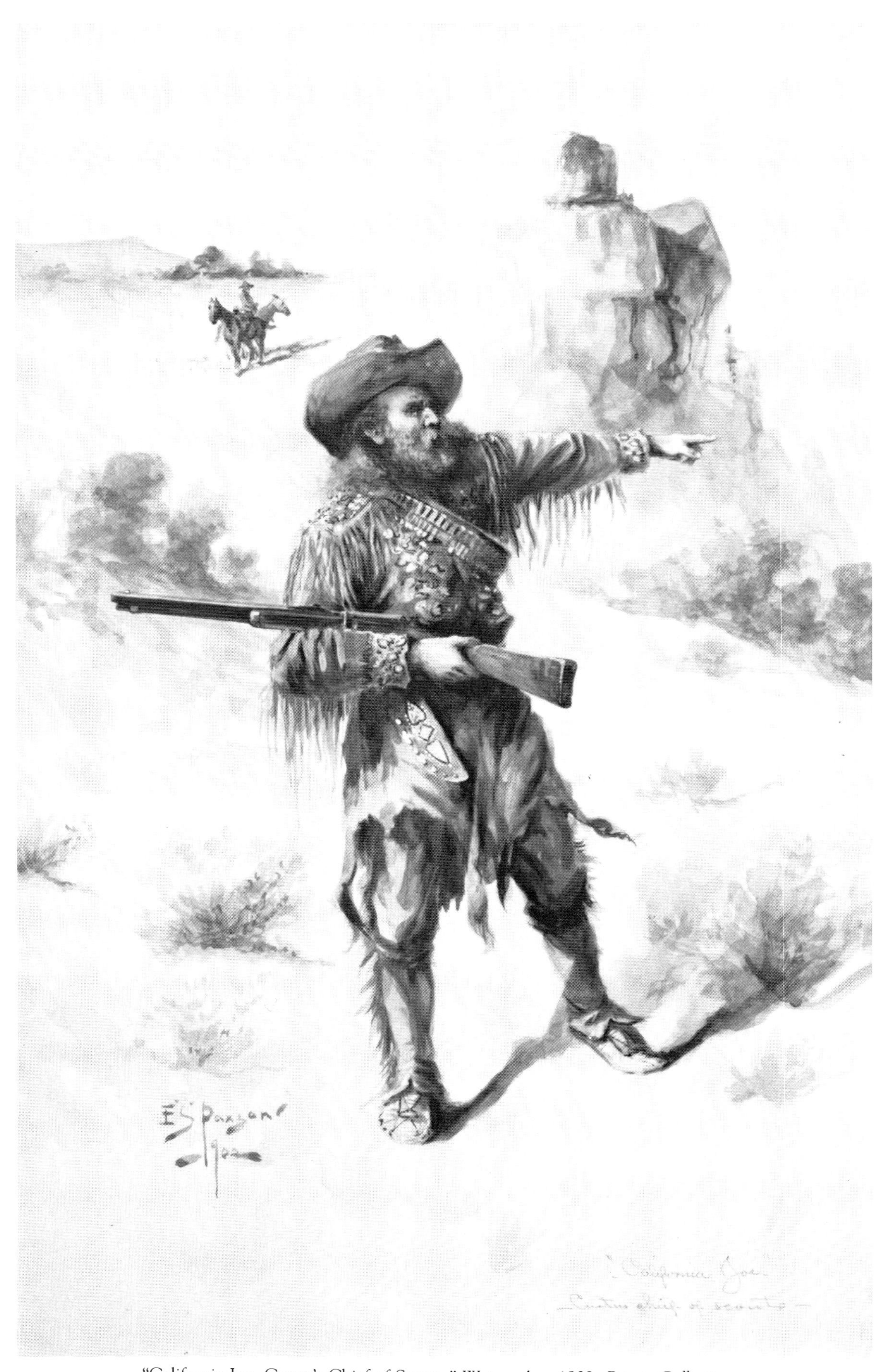

"California Joe, Custer's Chief of Scouts." Watercolor, 1902. *Private Collection.*

4

Beginning Artist

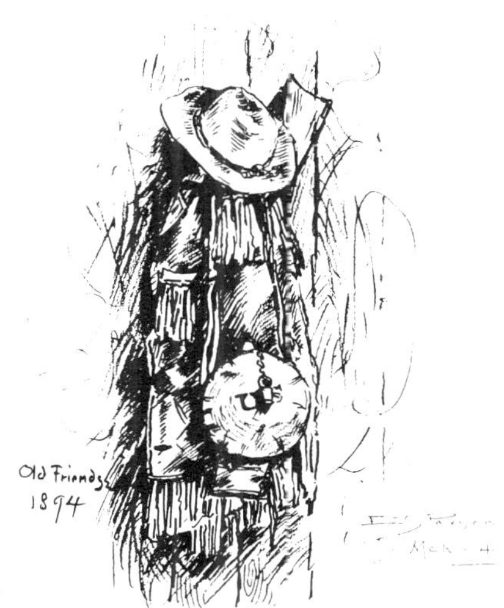

"Old Friends," 1894, pencil. *Private Collection.*

Whenever Edgar was asked what started him working toward a career as an artist, he always said it was the desire to paint the Custer battle. As early as 1877 his saddlebags carried artist's supplies. Even in those wild early days during the Nez Percé War, Edgar spent his leisure hours sketching with pencil or brush. In his own words, "I kept dabbling with the brush; each day I saw some improvement."[1]

Very soon Edgar's drawing talent was noticed by the cowboys he bunked with at Ryan's Canyon. On quiet evenings in the bunkhouse when the cowpunchers were playing cards or telling stories, Edgar would sit back and sketch what he saw. Sometimes he made sketches, caricatures and cartoons at the request of his comrades. Once he sketched the boss for their amusement. Friendly Indians that hung around the ranches and funny occurrences were also subjects. The drawings were passed around, tucked away to be forgotten and lost, or sent east in letters to show relatives what life in Montana Territory was like.[2] Edgar was never without a sketch pad and stub of pencil in his pocket, a habit he maintained throughout the rest of his life; and a habit that perhaps saved his life that day near Ryan's Canyon in 1877 when he impressed his Indian captors with his quick sketching.

Edgar attained a boost to his local fame as an artist by a humorous incident that happened while he was riding the telegraph lines for Gilmer and Salisbury. The stage line superintendent and his brother from the East had been out in a buckboard wagon looking over the countryside in southeastern Montana for a possible new stage route. They noticed a cloud of dust rising in the distance, so the superintendent climbed a nearby telegraph pole to get a better look. He yelled down, "Indians are coming!" and his brother reacted by jumping excitedly in the buckboard. The surprised horses bolted, carrying the buckboard away across the prairie, leaving behind the superintendent, still up the pole. The "Indians" were in fact Edgar and his fellow telegraph line repairmen, who were approaching on horseback. Edgar realized the humor in the situation and drew the scene, showing the superintendent clutching the top of the telegraph pole and the buckboard moving away in the distance. The drawing, entitled *Indians Are Coming*, was posted in the local stage office and passed among the drivers, agents and telegraph operators with much approval.[3]

There is no record of Edgar ever being paid or soliciting money for any of these early sketches. They were for the entertainment of his comrades and more importantly, to develop his artistic ability. But as early as 1877, Edgar put his brushes to work commercially as a sign painter. He noted in his 1912 journal that he did his first sign in Butte, gold leaf on glass, in 1877 for George W. Newkirk. And in Deer Lodge the same year he lettered a "prescription case" in gold. This case was in use into the 1950s when it was apparently destroyed.

It wasn't long after Edgar settled down with his wife and son in Deer Lodge that everyone there was aware of his special talents. Even in the wild West, daily life in a town with a population of less than 1,000 was fairly uneventful. A man lettering a sign was an event that often drew an audience. Edgar recalled one old-timer who would sit puffing on a long pipe and watch him work all day long, day after day.

It was in Deer Lodge in 1879, at age twenty-seven that Edgar made his first attempt at formal painting of a western scene. In 1902, the Butte Women's Club prevailed on him to give a talk on himself and his art. In his talk he gave an account of this first attempt, laced with his characteristic low key wit:

> I remember well and with some amusement my first attempt to portray upon canvas life in the West. It was 26 (*sic*) years ago when Capt. James H. Mills suggested my doing a picture for the territorial fair to be held in Helena. After considering the matter for some time I concluded to make the attempt at least.

I procured my canvas from the relic of an old stagecoach, which had long before ceased its lonely rambles through the alkali dust and dingy sage—for a palette I used the colors from diverse and sundry cans and tubs containing housepaints for at that time I was an artist (?). I wasn't satisfied to paint one picture, so must paint two. Uh! I remember them well, one a "Buffalo Chase"—at least many old-timers said they looked some like buffaloes—the other a freight outfit, with its long detachment of bulls and nondescript horses. After long and trying struggles I knew they were "pictures, all right." But the frames! Well, here was a quandry! After some search I found in the cabinet shop of John O'Neill a piece of gold molding about one inch wide and with some pretty blue ribbon for a lining succeeded very well.

In due time they were boxed and put aboard the coach and sent on their way. I procured some new "store clothes," and with buckskin leggins, gun and lunch stowed away in the saddle pockets, mounted my pony, and after a lonely ride of fifty miles arrived safely in "Last Chance," [Helena] tired and hungry. The fair was there all right, so were the pictures, big as life. I remained several days and saw all the sights (for Helena was a big place) and returned to Deer Lodge. I had a horseback ride of over 100 miles, paid for expressage to Wells & Fargo $20, and for dressing up $15, and after waiting patiently for two weeks received as a first premium $2.50 I never have been so fortunate since.

The pictures are now, and have been for twenty years, in the home of Joseph McDonnell of Philadelphia. They were the envy of Deer Lodge for a long time; people came from afar to see them. (I refer wholly to the frames.)[4]

But there was still little or no demand for fine art in Montana Territory. Indeed commercial art barely earned Edgar a livelihood. Then fate, which had many years before denied Edgar a career as a scenic artist, gave him a new opportunity to take up the trade. The man that made it possible was John Maguire, a pioneer of theater in the West. He had begun giving one-man shows in the small towns, camps and settlements in the territories after a career as an actor in San Francisco and other western cities in the late 1860s and 1870s. Edgar probably met Maguire when he brought his one-man show to Deer Lodge in 1879 or 1880. Edgar later recalled traveling from "camp to camp" throughout Montana Territory with Maguire. That was the beginning of a twelve-year association between the two men which, through those years, developed into a big business for Maguire.[5]

In 1880, Edgar and family moved from peaceful Deer Lodge to Butte, the notorious roaring copper camp. Undoubtedly they were sorry to leave their friends and lovely valley home for the smoke and noise of bustling Butte. But it was obvious to Edgar that patrons and businesses needing his artistic talents could only be found in a city; and Butte was the fastest growing city in Montana Territory, while sleepy Deer Lodge was on the decline.

When the Paxsons arrived in Butte, it claimed 3,000 inhabitants. It had just begun a population explosion ignited by rapid improvements in mining technology. In the early 1870s, after the placer boom of the '60s, the camp had become a ghost town of as little as 60 residents. But by 1890, metropolitan Butte boasted 25,000 and by the turn of the century, 50,000. There would be plenty of signs to paint for an energetic commercial artist.

Fortunes were being made in Butte. This meant wealthy art patrons. In fact a patron was the main reason Edgar decided to move. He was commissioned to paint a large panoramic view in Butte and was promised $800 for the job. But apparently, fortunes were being lost as well as made in the camp because Edgar was never paid although he completed the painting to the satisfaction of his client.[6]

This was only a temporary setback for Edgar. His work as a scenic artist quickly became a major source of income. From the first, John Maguire had been enthusiastically received everywhere he went. People in the territories were starved for entertainment and many of those who had recently come from the East felt culturally deprived on the frontier. In the 1880s westerners, Montanans in particular, became sensitive about their backwoodsman's image. Many felt it was time to embrace the more cultured way of life of the eastern cities. So Butte, often said to be the toughest town in the West, became one of the leading cities in cultural pursuits. It was said at the turn of the century that Butte was second only to San Francisco as a western cultural spot. All the major theatrical companies made it an important stop on their tours. And John Maguire was the prime mover in this development, keeping Edgar busy with his brushes.

In 1881, the Renshaw Opera House, the first in Butte, opened with Maguire as manager and Edgar as scenic artist. Maguire simultaneously managed theaters in Anaconda, Bozeman, Deer Lodge, Phillipsburg, Livingston and Helena; and Edgar painted curtains and backdrops for them all with success. It has been said by Deer Lodge old-timers that Edgar painted a curtain for the Cottonwood Theater in Deer Lodge that was so impressive many people came to the theater simply to see the curtain alone. It depicted a scene in Venice with a gondola, a beautiful woman descending some steps and two other figures in ancient Roman attire. In later years, Butte theater owners tried to buy it, but it was ultimately destroyed when the Cottonwood Theater burned down.[7]

The Renshaw Opera House, although just a second floor hall in a Butte office building, drew celebrities such as Nellie Boyd and Henry Ward Beecher. Because of this early success, Maguire was able to convince Butte's leading citizens to build a real theater, and in July 1885, Maguire's Grand Opera House had its opening night performance. Edgar was provided with his own studio in the theater building. In the succeeding

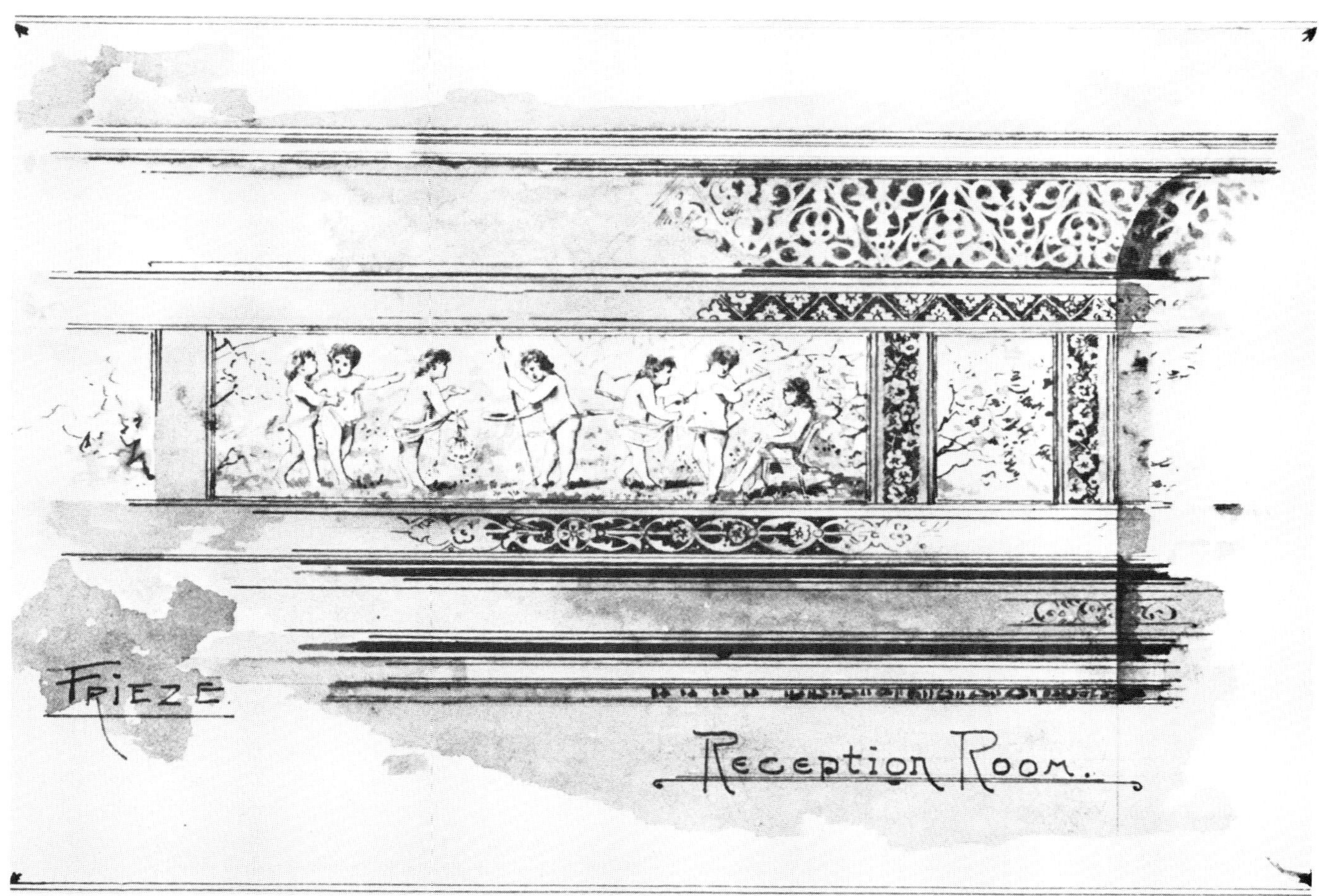

Watercolor drawing for a frieze in the reception room of a Butte copper baron's mansion. 1892, 9 x 13. *Montana Historical Society, Helena, Montana.*

three years many big names in theater including Sarah Bernhardt appeared there and Edgar created elaborate scenery for them. He diligently painted scenes along the Rhine, snowy London by gaslight, docks along the Mersey by moonlight and exotic far eastern palaces. He was repeatedly credited in the newspaper theater reviews, often in grand terms like this in the *Butte Miner*:

> The third tableau was a scene on the road between Chatham and London in mid-winter. This scene was one of the grandest stage pictures that could be conceived. It was a scene that if produced in New York the audience would show their appreciation by calling for the artist. Paxson, our local artist should have received this recognition last night. The scene was loudly applauded but he deserved a call.[8]

On the evening of July 24, 1888, the actors were in their dressing rooms getting ready for the night's performance. A few early theatergoers were already in their seats and John Maguire was on stage. Backstage a breeze blew in through an open window and across a defective gas jet. A flame flared up, igniting some flimsy stage props. Instantly backdrops and curtains were aflame. Maguire ran backstage and turned on the overhead sprinkler system, but it failed to work. Everyone in the theater escaped, but within an hour the theater had burned to the ground, taking with it all of Edgar's tools and artist's supplies.

A new theater was quickly built, opening in February 1889, but not long afterward Edgar and Maguire had a falling out. Exactly what happened is unknown, but Edgar did not open a studio in the new theater. he had bought a home at 30 East Woolman Street and remodeled a building on the property to make a cozy studio. In 1889, he still listed himself as a scenic painter in the city directory, but substituted 30 East Woolman for Grand Opera House as his address. And in 1890, he listed himself only as "painter." Edgar still did some work for Maguire until 1891, but he also did work for other theaters not managed by Maguire. Maguire died in 1907, a few months after retiring in California, still owing Edgar $1,800. Edgar never got his money, but he later described Maguire as "a good man and the pioneer of theatrical life in the Rockies, despite his faults and business troubles."

Throughout his time as scenic artist, Edgar actively sought sign-painting jobs too. His business card while at his studio at the Grand Opera House carried the note, "Traveling Commissions supplied on short notice." He not only did many fancy gold leaf signs, but large advertisements on the sides of buildings in uptown Butte. Perhaps some of the old and faded signs on still existing turn-of-the-century buildings there are his work.

Judging from the dates on existing paintings, it is clear that Edgar increasingly devoted time to his real interest, painting western subjects, after he ended his career as a scenic artist. Paxson paintings dated before

1890 are very rare. But throughout the 1890s Edgar could not make ends meet by selling paintings alone. He continued to solicit sign-painting jobs until 1898, when he served in the Spanish-American War. He clearly wanted to devote himself solely to fine art but, as he later said, there were many discouragements and difficulties.

In 1893, Edgar made his first attempt to promote his work outside Montana. He took three paintings, all of Indian subjects, to the world's Columbian Exposition in Chicago, where they were displayed in the Montana building. One of them was *The Lolo Trail*, the large painting of Joseph and the Nez Percé discussed in chapter three. The descriptive pamphlet he had printed was handed out to viewers of the painting. Edgar's efforts, however, brought him little more than short articles in Montana newspapers. When Edgar returned to Montana, he stuck the rolled up canvas of *The Lolo Trail* away and forgot about it. Many years later C. E. Simons, proprietor of a store in Missoula that provided Edgar with artist's supplies, discovered the painting dust covered and still rolled up under a dormer eave in the artist's Missoula studio. At first Edgar could not identify it, but then recalled what it was. He made a gift of it to Simons who restored and framed it. In 1951, it was loaned to the University of Montana, but since has passed to private ownership and its whereabouts is unknown to the author.

Apparently, in 1897 Edgar's efforts began to show some good results financially. Instead of a one-line description in his city directory listing, he took out a quarter page display calling himself "Artist and Sign Painter." He began getting a few commissions, at least one of them for portraiture. In 1896, he painted a life-sized portrait of a local resident, a Colonel Lloyd. In 1898, he had two oil paintings hanging in the state building in Helena. They were described in an 1898 newspaper article.[9] One was *Chief Looking Glass Leading His Nez Percé on the Trail to the Big Hole Basin*. The other painting entitled *Me*, showed an Indian brave gazing at a photographer's showcase where he discovers his portrait. Edgar was also commissioned by the state in 1890 to design the seal of the state circuit court.

But what fame Edgar had was still strictly local, not unlike Charles Russell's reputation at the time. The two artists were both as yet "undiscovered."

A man who admired the talents of both Edgar and Russell from the beginnings of both their careers was Charles Schatzlein, who later became friend and agent of several Montana artists. Schatzlein owned a paint and art supply business in Butte through which he received interior decorating commissions. Edgar apparently worked for or with him as early as 1881, as implied by this 1903 entry by Schatzlein in Edgar's studio guest register: "It is 22 years since we have done our first work together. You are alright when it comes to camping out in the snow, with the thermometer 14 degrees below zero. But your greatest gift is with brush and canvas."

It may well have been Schatzlein who introduced Edgar and Charles Russell. According to an old newspaper story in the now defunct *Butte Evening News*, the three men went on several camping and fishing trips together.[10]

Schatzlein proved to be a good friend to both artists. He provided a few dollars of income when they sorely needed them by selling some of their paintings, or by buying them himself. In a typical instance, Schatzlein received a letter from Russell in 1897 saying: "Friend I send by express a picture I wish you would sell for me the price is $25 pleas (*sic*) pay the express on it and hold out when you sell it as I haven't sent (*sic*) your friend C M Russell."[11]

Edgar was often just as hard-pressed. By 1889 he had three children to feed. For a time his Woolman Street home did not even have running water.

Schatzlein had some sound advice for his artist friends that seems to have been largely ignored by the artists themselves. He told them they were by far underpricing their paintings. Russell had little regard for the dollar value of his pictures, but his wife Nancy listened carefully and in the years to come put Schatzlein's advice into practice with her innate business acumen, showing dramatic financial results. Edgar kept his prices comparatively low. He was selling few paintings and most likely assumed that he would sell even fewer at higher prices. He chose instead to continue diligently pursuing his commercial art business for the bulk of his livelihood, meanwhile working on his large Custer battle project and his other paintings when he had the time. He also contributed articles under the pen name "Pistol Grip," along with cartoons and decorative scrolling used as fillers, to *American Field*, an outdoorsmen's magazine.

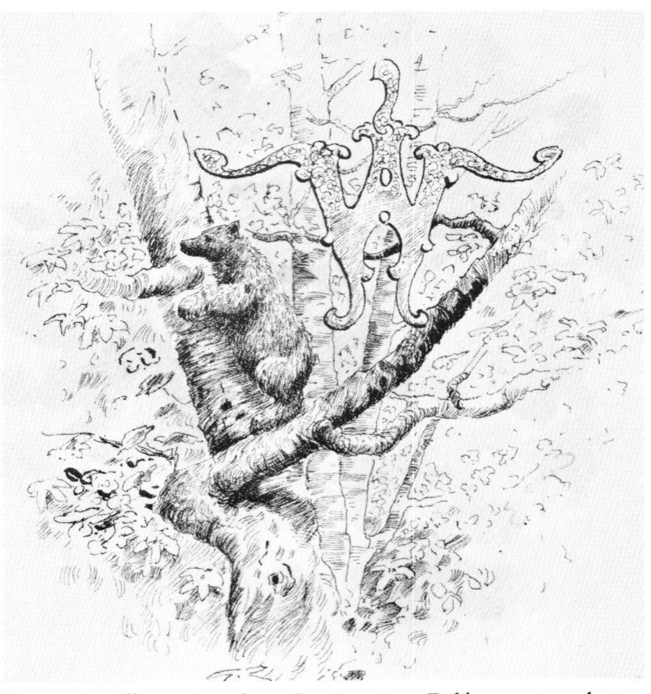

Decorative illustration done for *American Field* sometime during the 1880s. Ink. *Montana Historical Society, Helena, Montana.*
The artist about 1887.

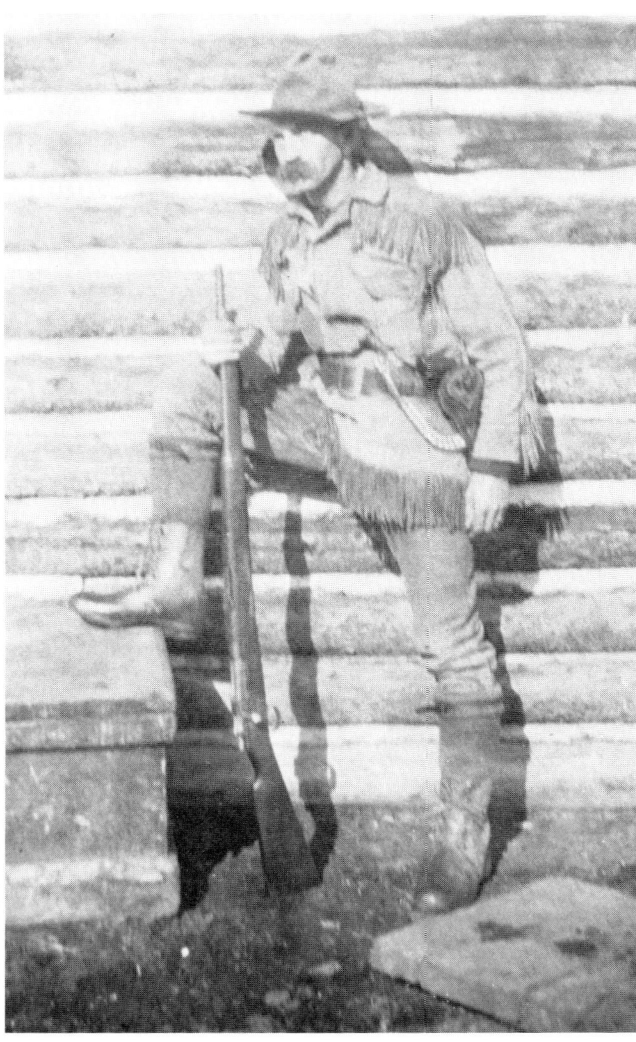

The Artist about 1887.

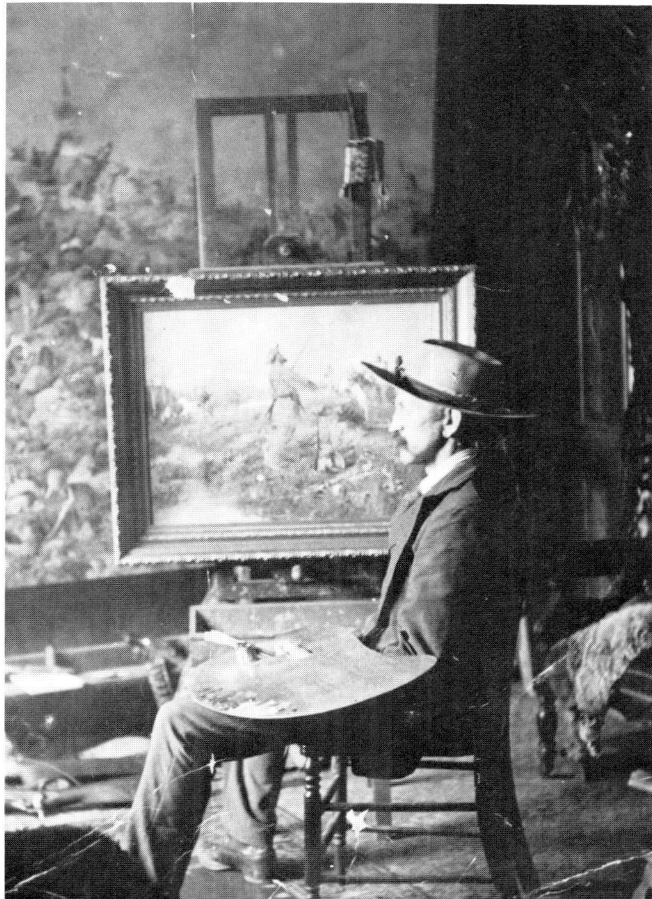

The artist in his Butte studio, 1898. On the easel is "The Death of John Bozeman," and behind it is the nearly completed "Custer's Last Stand."

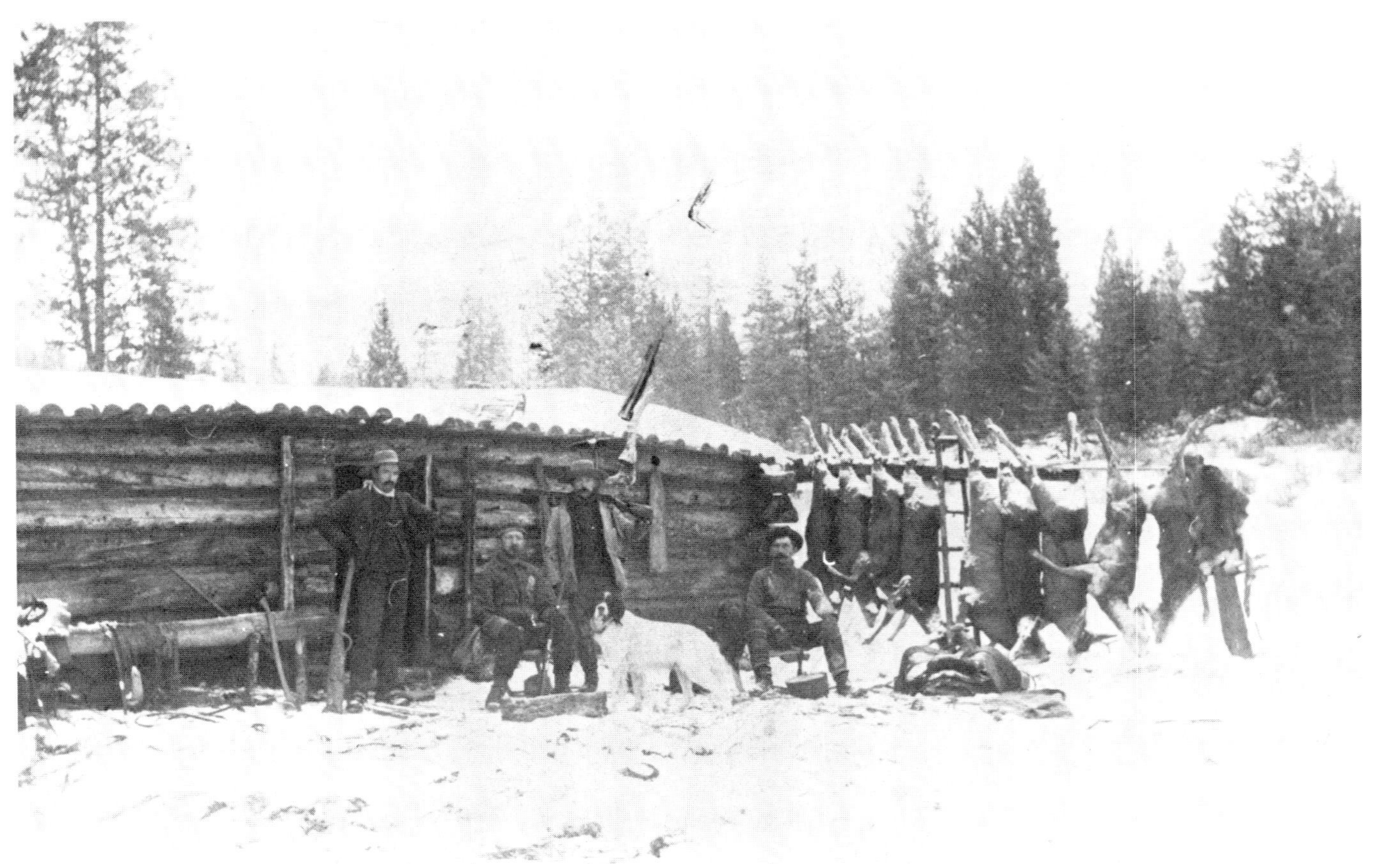

At brother Robert Paxson's hunting cabin at Big Hole, Montana, late 1880s. The artist is third from the left.

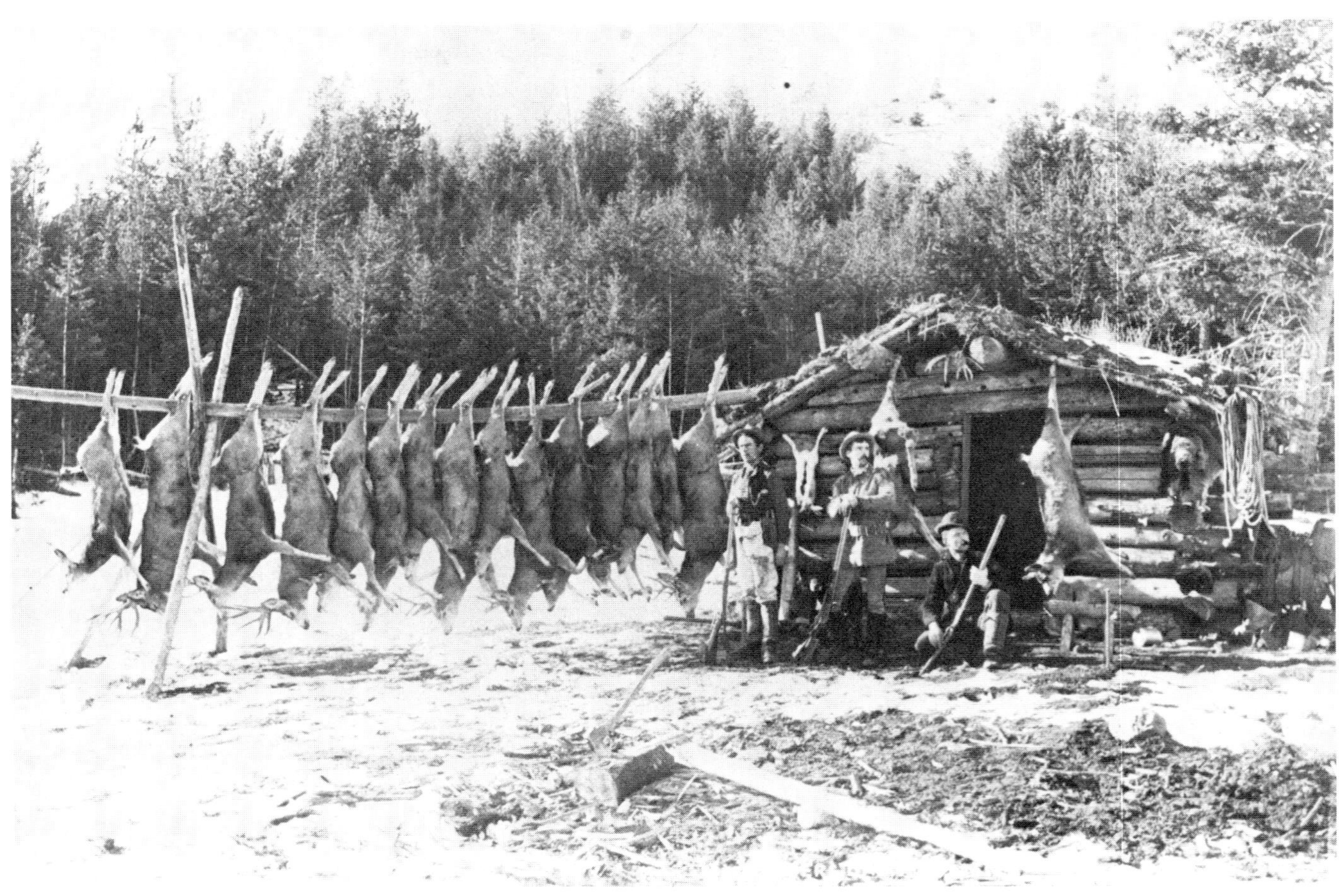

Paxson's hunting cabin on Boulder Creek, late 1880s. The artist is at the right.

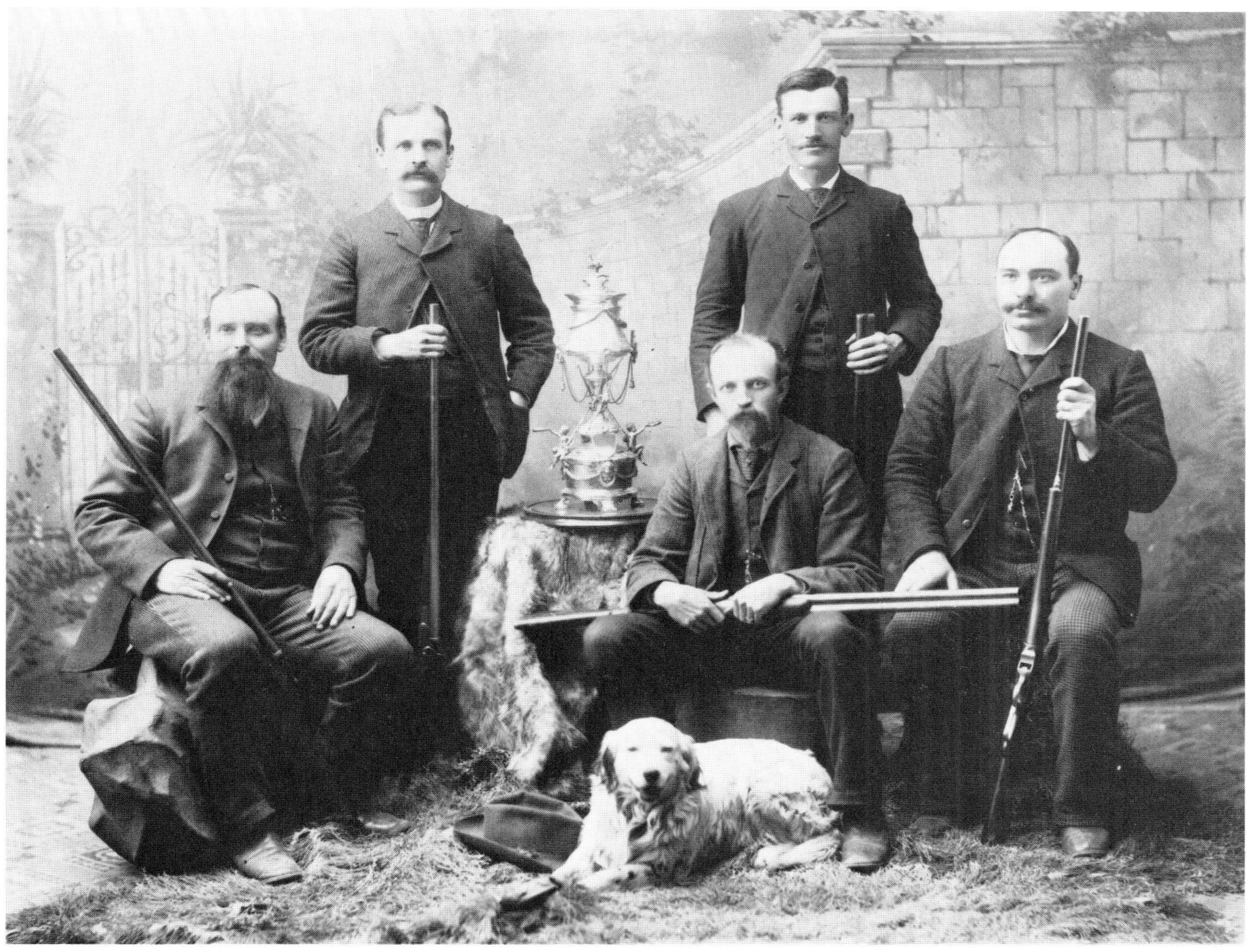

Paxson (seated, center) poses with his favorite dog, Highland Chief and members of the Butte Rod and Gun Club, 1887. The five-man team had just won the championship in a state-wide competition. *Montana Historical Society* and *Butte Trap and Skeet Club.*

Aside from Edgar's money problems and his relatively undiscovered status as an artist, the 1880s and '90s in Butte were happy times for him. He derived great pleasure from his family. Besides his four children, his two brothers and sister also lived in or near Butte. Also during this time, his father and mother and Laura's widowed mother moved to Butte from the old home in Erie County, New York. There were many happy get-togethers of the close-knit clan. Family dinners were a favorite. Edgar's enjoyment of them shows in this entry from his journal: "All the family was here for dinner, which consisted of chicken, cranberry sauce, mashed potatoes biscuits and butter, mince pie, etc. One can live on these things when there is nothing else, you know."

All the Paxsons were very well respected in the community. Brother Robert was a pharmacist and Everett, who had sold his sheep ranch, became a teacher and eventually a school principal. Laura was very active in several women's clubs devoted to cultural pursuits and community service. The Butte papers of the time had frequent notes in the social columns of Mrs. Paxson's dinners, teas and parties given for visiting artists and dignitaries. Edgar's name was often found in the papers among the trapshooting scores, usually among the top scorers. He competed regularly and had many ribbons and medals to show for it. He was a member of the original Butte Rod and Gun Club organized in 1879. He decorated the old clubhouse with his drawings and sketched a number of his fellow club members, who had a high regard for him as an artist as well as a sportsman. He was, however, far from immune to having a "good time" with his fellow sportsmen. He was no stranger to serious drinking and card playing and it was not unknown for him to "tie one on with the boys."

Edgar's happiest hours were still those on the wilderness trail. He rarely missed the annual fall hunt, when two or three of his friends would join him for three or four weeks in the high country. And often several members of the family, grandparents and children alike, would camp for one or two weeks in the mountains during the summer. Laura loved to camp, too. In 1882, she and Edgar along with their two sons, Loren and Harry, packed in on horseback to country never before visited by a white woman.

Sometimes Edgar took long canoe trips on the Missouri. In 1883, he passed through "the Gates of the

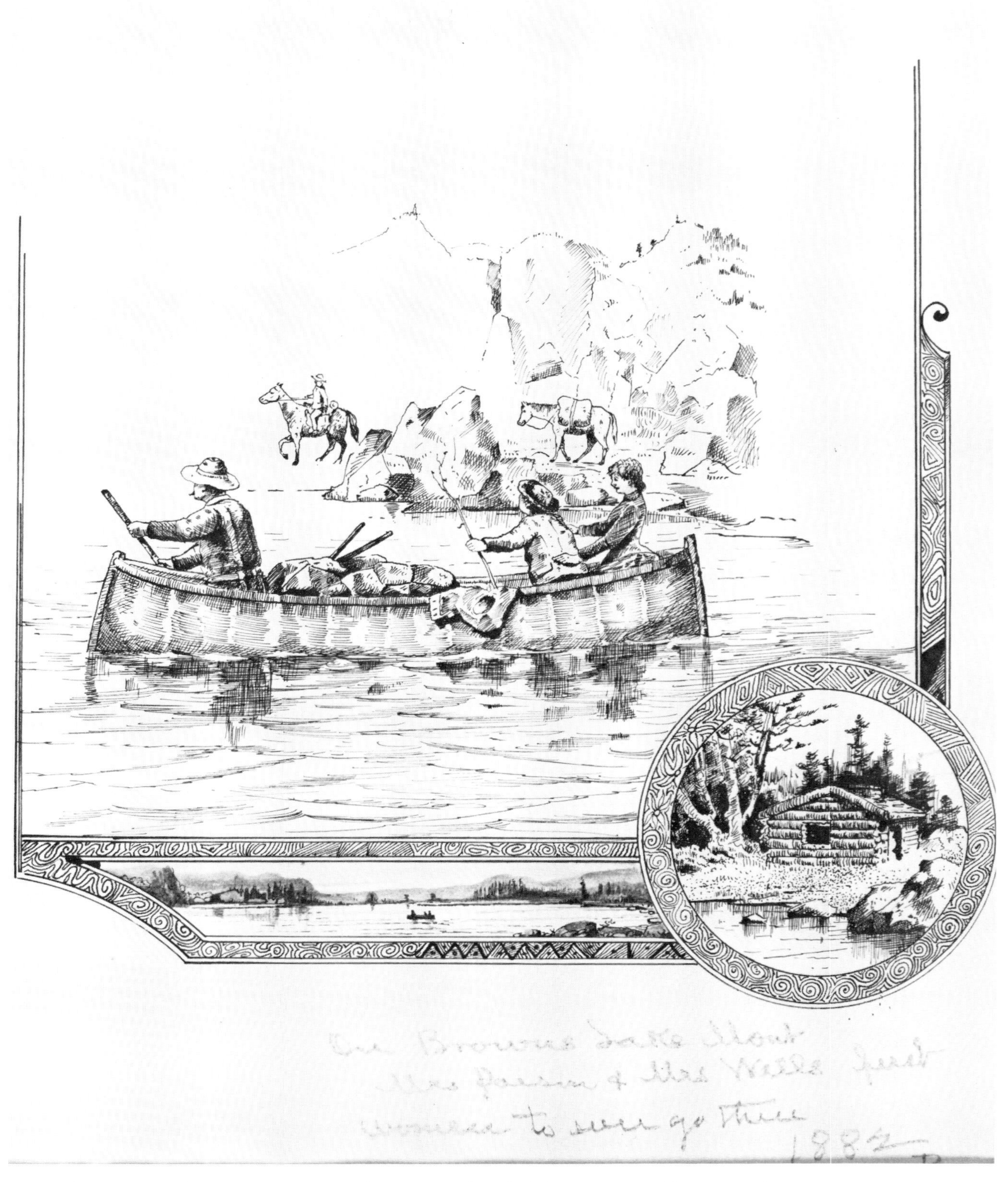

"On Brown's Lake, Montana, 1882." Ink drawing and wash. This was presumably done to illustrate an article for *American Field Magazine*.

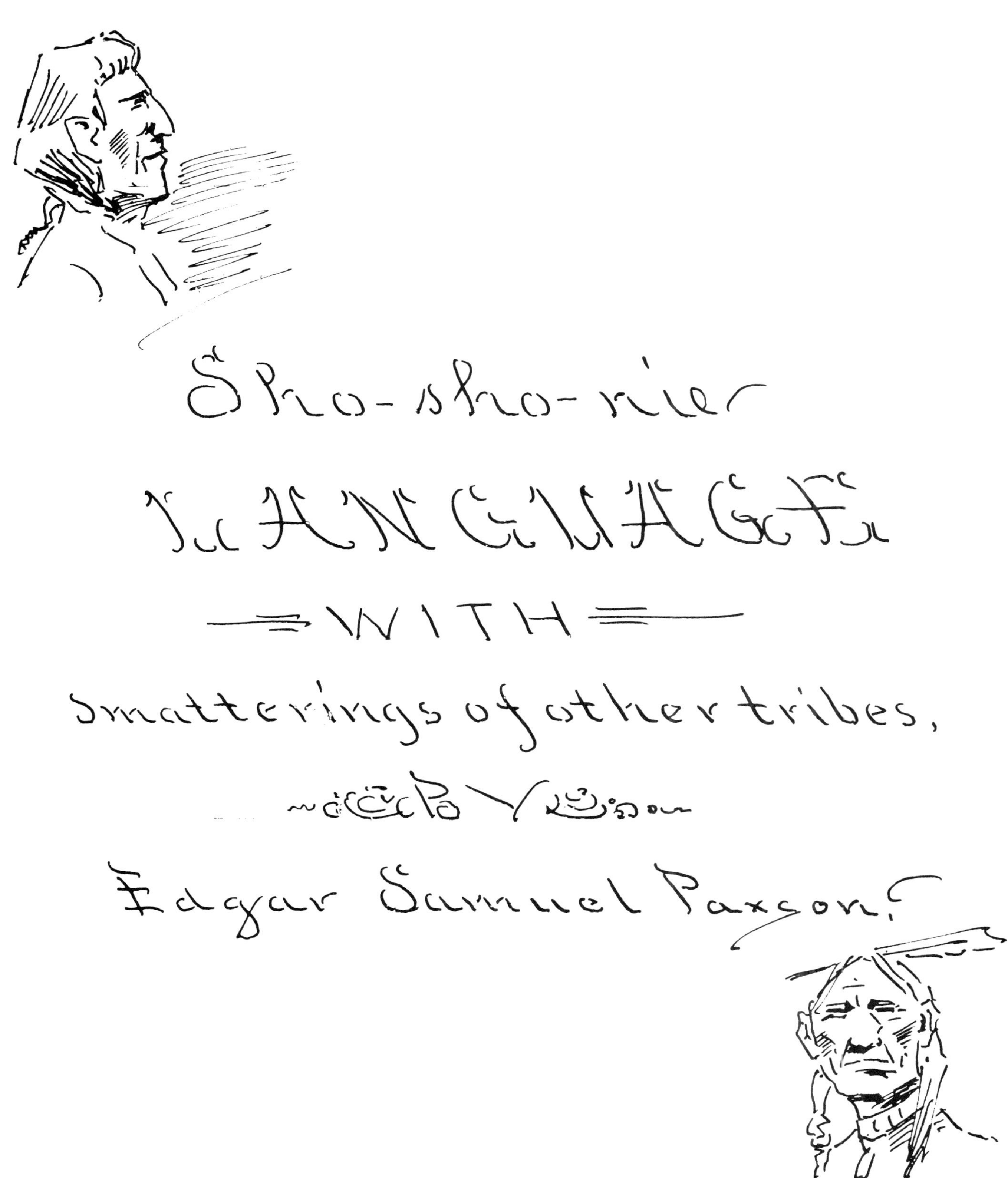

Sho-sho-nier
LANGUAGE
WITH
smatterings of other tribes,
BY
Edgar Samuel Paxson

Above and following: Title page and first page of one of Paxson's two handwritten Indian dictionaries.

a

Antelope-	Quar'-ree.
" (Buck)	Wānty.
" (Doe)	Quar'-ree em-bee'-ab.
Ax.	Ho'-han.
All.	O'-yoke.
Awl.	Wee'-yok.
Arm.	Boor'-rak.
Aunt.	Em-bah-hah.
Afraid.	Mer-ree'-yeu.
American	Ŝoo-yah'-pe.
Across (other side)	O'-nung-wa.
Awkward.	Maw'-wat.
Arrow.	Ho'-pog-gau.
Arrow Case.	Ho'-coon-ah.
Already.	Him'-besk.
Ashamed.	Nash'-u-i.
All gone.	Cay'-wot.
Ants.	An'-ning-qwuts.
Ant eggs.	An-ne-no'-yo.
Ausk, or asking.	In-dib'-bin.
Alive.	Kwidge'-o-ni.
Again, (Also)	A-tee'-is.
Always.	Ard'aps.

Mountains" where the Missouri breaks through the Belt Range in western Montana. He found it a place of incredible beauty. Through the deep and dark canyon the river ran narrow, rapid and clear. From canyons joining on either side came shafts of light, the smell of pine and the roar of waterfalls. As Edgar guided his canoe downstream, he knew that Lewis and Clark had done the same four decades before and nothing had changed there since. Edgar surely returned to his studio afterward filled with inspiration and enthusiasm. In 1891, Edgar took another canoe trip on the Missouri. This time he and his party were shipwrecked. They were marooned for two days on a sand island in the "Cascades" and experienced a little of the privation of earlier days.

For many years Edgar and his friends hunted in the region of the Three Forks of the Missouri where nearly all the major Indian trails in the region converged. Not long before, the Blackfeet passed there on their raids against the Shoshones, Bannocks and Crows. The Shoshones passed back and forth on their annual hunt on the Yellowstone and Snake River plains. The Flatheads and Nez Percé came there, too, to hunt. Even the Piegans and Gros Ventres from far to the north came to that favored spot. No tribe lived there but Edgar saw signs of many. During Edgar's hunts, small bands still passed through the area, and Edgar visited them in their camps. This is the country so often portrayed in his paintings.

In those days many Indians still spoke no English, but Edgar gradually acquired knowledge of their languages. His degree of fluency is not known for certain. From the bits of evidence available, it appears that he had some knowledge of several dialects but was not fluent in any. He relied often on a working knowledge of Indian sign language. In 1932, Laura, in reference to Edgar's Indian friend Nag-a-shaw, commented that the Indian "could not speak English and Mr. Paxson could not speak 'Indian,' but they understood each other."[12] Edgar's daughter wrote in a paper presented in 1946: "At about the age of five or six I remember being called in and of having to sit in the lap of, perhaps, some famous Indian chief. Through a meagre knowledge of their language dialects and by signs my father was able to converse with these friends, but to me the sessions were a series of gutteral grunts and ughs."[13] Perhaps the best evidence of Edgar's knowledge of Indian languages are the dictionaries he compiled. One, entitled "A Dictionary of the Shoshonee Language with a Smattering of other Dialects," contains nine hundred entries, including phrases and numbers. The other contains 450 words and twenty-six phrases of other dialects. Both dictionaries are in Edgar's longhand, presumably for his own use.

There are several references regarding Edgar's knowledge of sign language in his journals. On hunts or when visiting Indian camps, he often referred to "talking by signs." In his later years he occasionally complained in his journal of being out of practice, implying an earlier proficiency.

By the early 1890s, Edgar had nearly finished researching for his Custer battle painting. After considerable preliminary sketching, he began to paint but the work went slowly. He set the canvas aside many times, not only because of the demands of his commercial art business, but because he could only work on it when inspired. Slowing the project further was the necessity of adequate sunlight for so large yet so detailed a work. Cloudy days and the smoke from Butte's smelters many times frustrated him when he was ready to work. So many were the discouraging delays that the painting was still unfinished when Edgar went away to war in April 1898.

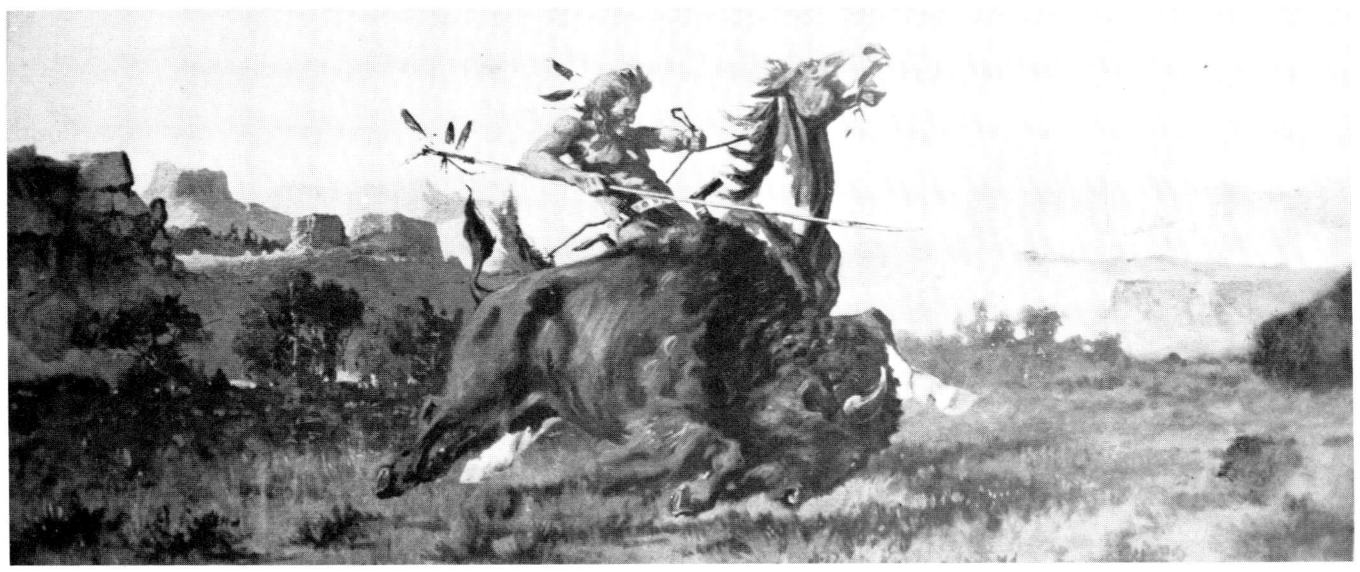

"Breaking the Pony." Oil, 1900. Reproduced from a photograph in the artist's album.

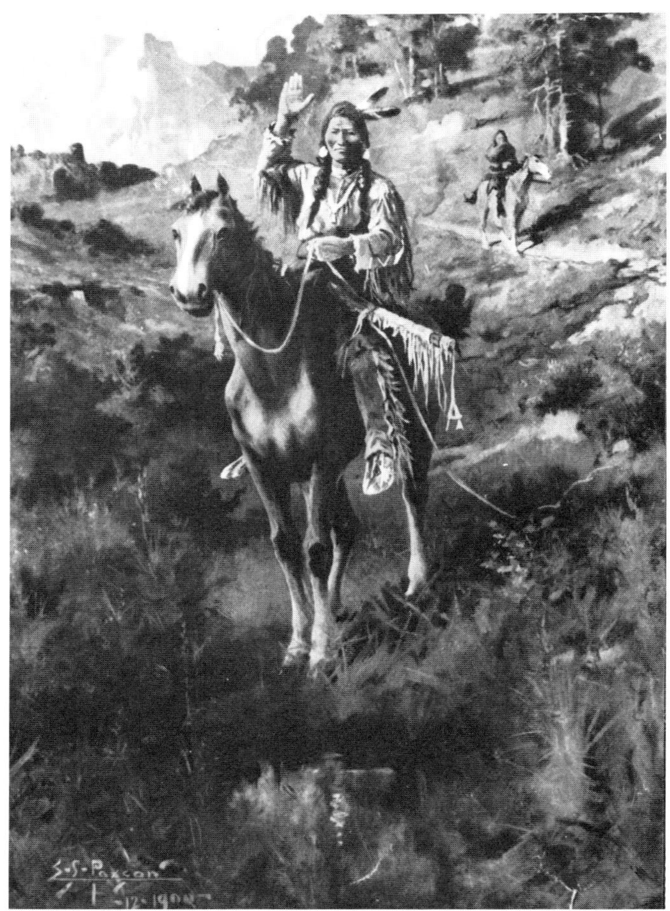

"The Greeting." Oil, 1900. Reproduced from an early lithograph.

From the artist's sketchbook: "'Robbie' Mch. 8-1902." Pencil. Robbie was the youngest of the Paxson's three sons. *Private Collection.*

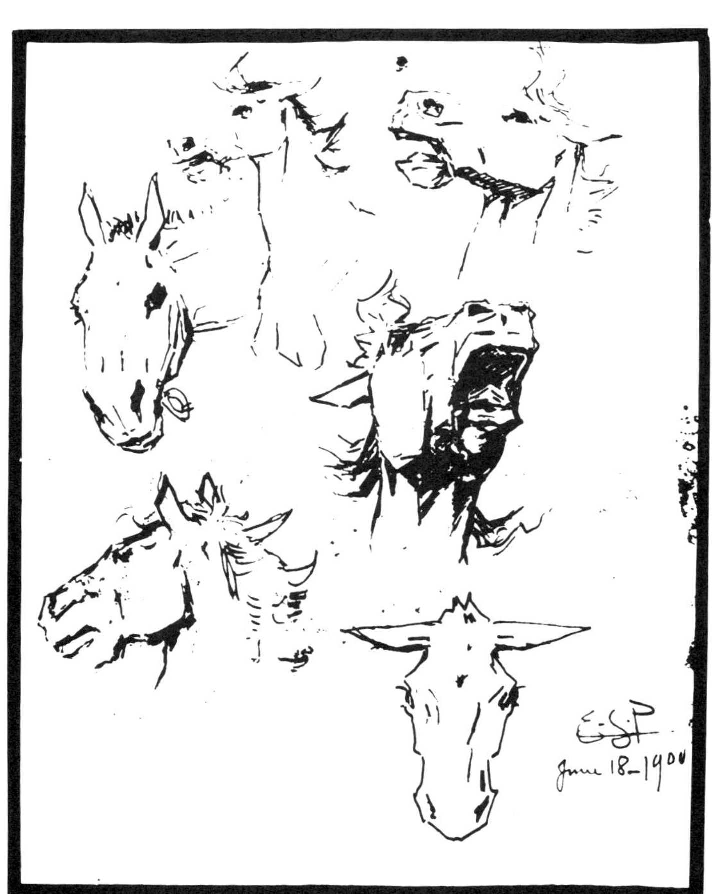

From the artist's sketchbook, dated June 18, 1900. Pencil. *Private Collection.*

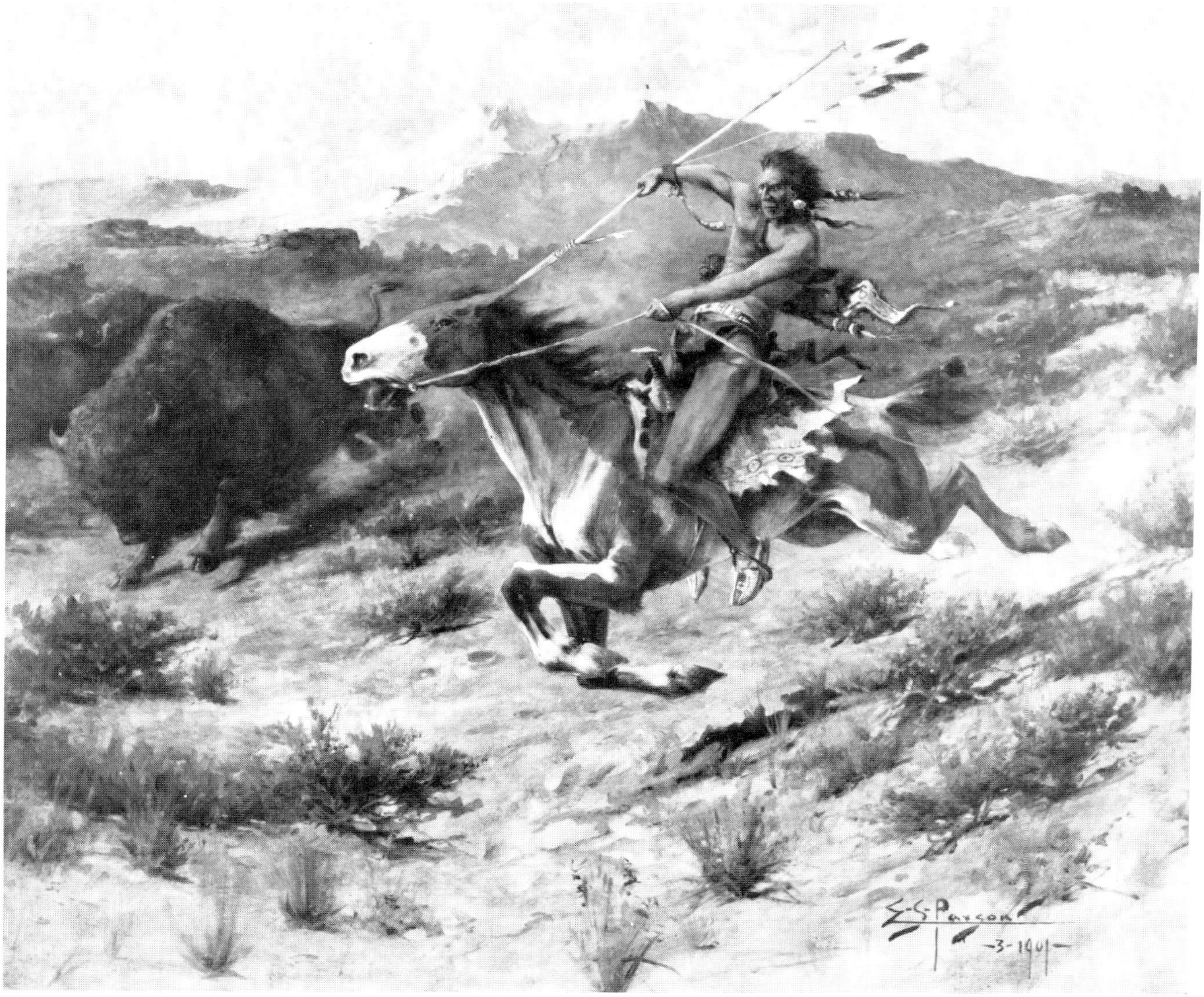

"Buffalo Hunt." Oil, 1901. *Private Collection.*

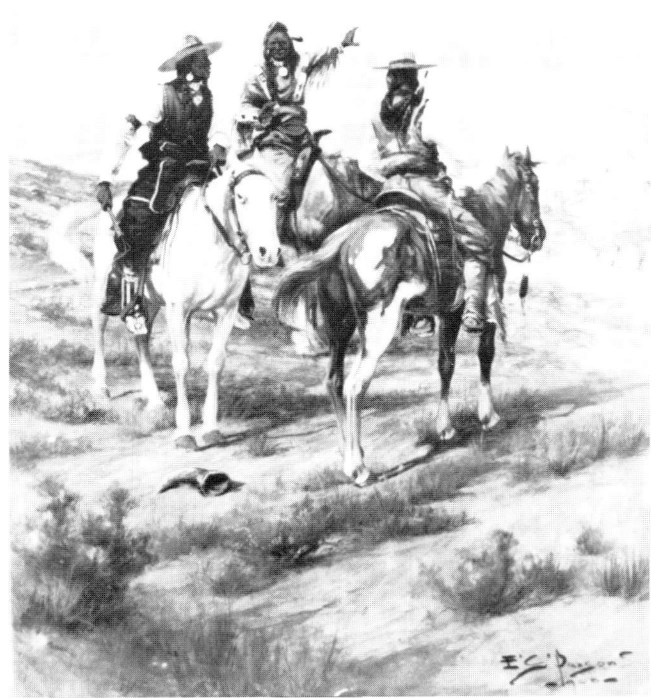

"A Story of Other Days." Oil, 1900. Reproduced from a photograph in the artist's album.

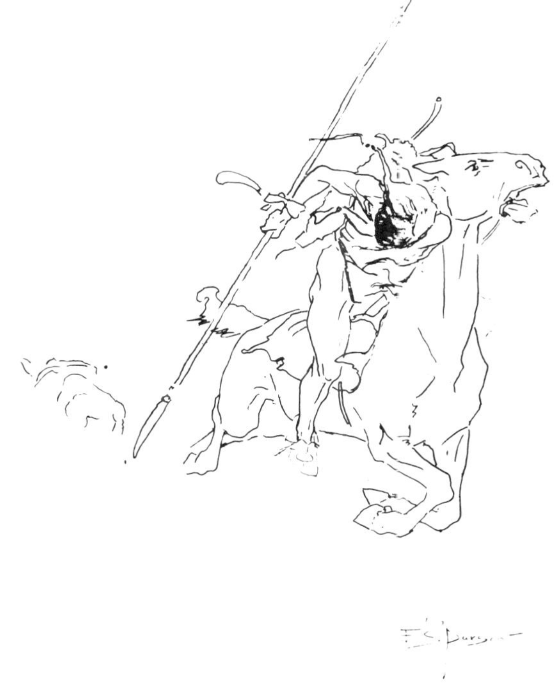

Working drawing. Ink and pencil for oil painting, "Winning His Coup." *Private Collection.*

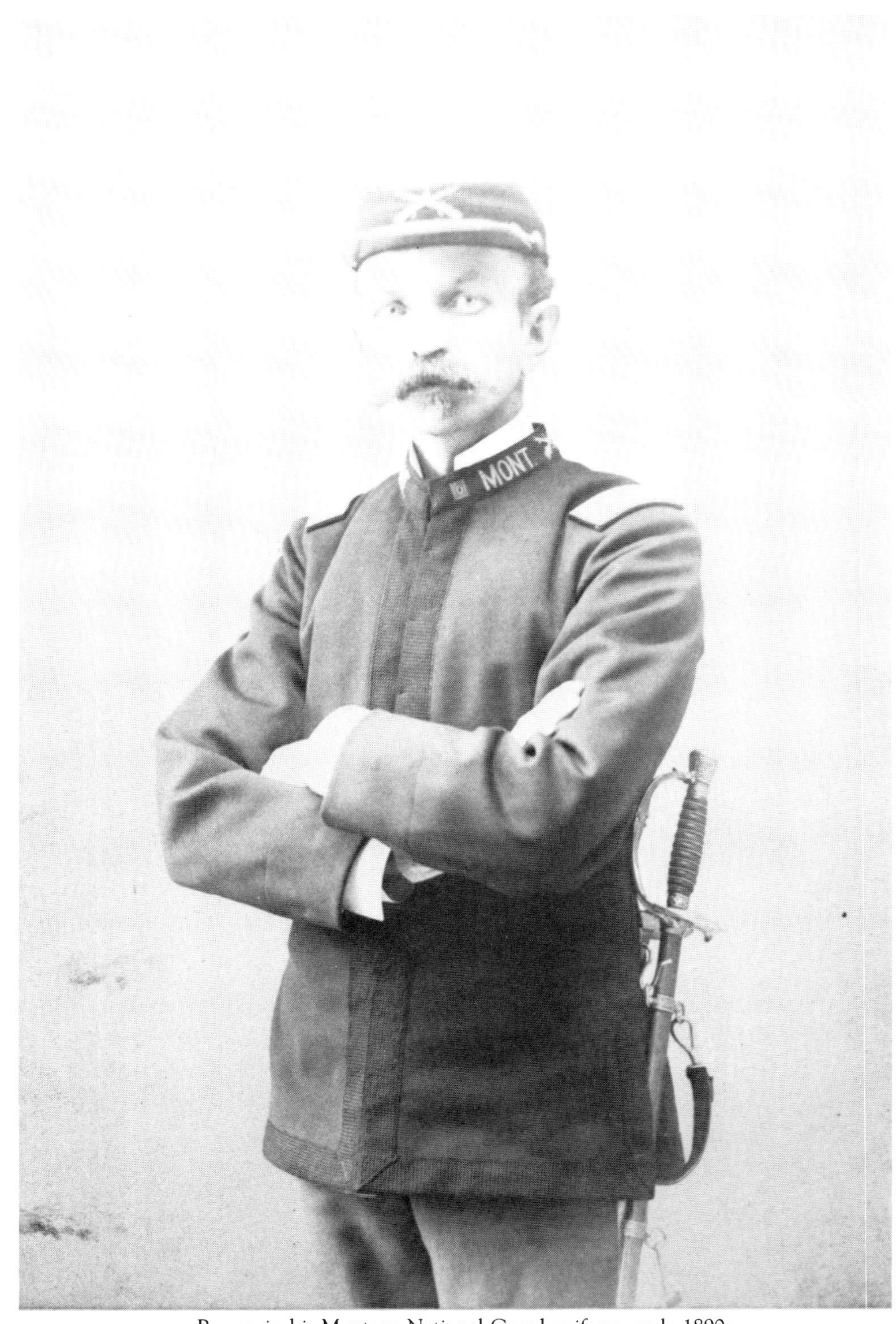

Paxson in his Montana National Guard uniform, early 1890s.

5
Soldier

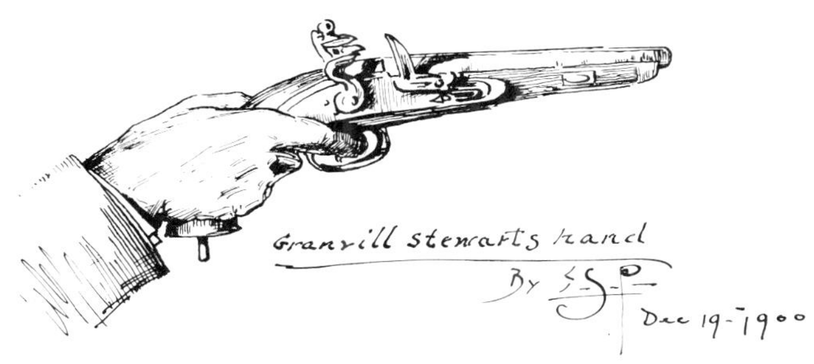

"Granville Stuart's Hand," ink, 1900. *Montana Historical Society.*

In early 1898, Edgar was the happy father of four. His Custer painting was well on the way to completion. He had hopes that, once completed, he could show it in major cities around the country, generating enough interest in his work so that he could devote his energy solely to painting. Yet he was compelled to leave his promising future, his family and his beloved mountain home to volunteer to fight a war in the malarial jungles of the Philippines.

This remarkable decision was only obvious and appropriate for a man like Edgar. Although his community would not have lost any respect for a forty-six-year-old family man who did not enlist, Edgar was determined to do his part, as he liked to put it. He had a patriotic zeal rooted in those early days as a drummer boy for recruits in the Civil War and in his youthful admiration of Abraham Lincoln.

Edgar wasn't new to soldiering when he was mustered into the First Montana Volunteers in May 1898. In 1889, he had enlisted in the Montana National Guard. In 1894, he was called out to quell a Fourth of July riot in Butte. It was the first of many major riots in Butte during its peak years as a mining center. The later riots were due to union-management squabbles but this first, which achieved national attention, was a street fight between hundreds of Irish Catholics, who comprised a large part of the Butte population, and the members of the American Protective Association (A.P.A.) The A.P.A. was an anti-Catholic, anti-immigrant national organization which had become popular. Some of its members had decorated two Butte saloons with their association flags along with the usual Independence Day decorations and, during the afternoon of the Fourth when plenty of liquor was flowing, someone dynamited the front of one of the saloons. This set off a melee in the street between A.P.A. sympathizers and the fighting-mad Irish. The entire city police force entered the confusion swinging nightsticks. Over the next two hours, men battered each other as new recruits with pickhandles and the like joined the fray. Many were seriously injured. A thunderstorm slowed down the riot briefly, and the mayor mounted a packing case to try to quell the fighting but was forced to flee by a shower of stones. He had no choice but to call in the militia. Eighteen armed militiamen, one of them First Sergeant Paxson, charged the crowd of 4,000. Guns appeared among the rioters and shots were fired. At least two people were killed, a policeman and a bystander. But the shots sobered the crowd. In twenty minutes the street and saloons were cleared with the help of the fire department wielding high pressure water hoses. The area was roped off and Edgar and his fellow militiamen stood guard until 10:00 A.M. the next morning.[1]

Edgar never mentioned in his writings what he thought of the incident, except that he was bound to do his duty and he did it. He many times did allude to the high esteem he felt for the humble soldier serving his country. He felt the privations of the ordinary soldier's life were ennobling. His soldierly attitude soon had him promoted to first lieutenant in the National Guard and many officers in both the guard and the regular army came to have a high regard for him. For a lieutenant, he seemed to have an unusual number of high-ranking officers as friends. In fact when Edgar was found to be slightly under the minimum weight at the mustering of the First Montana Volunteers, a colonel intervened in his behalf.

Edgar joined in the national enmity toward Spain aroused by Spanish oppression in Cuba. When the U.S. warship *Main* was blown up while in Havanna Harbor on a peaceful mission, he, like most Americans, wanted to avenge the deaths of the 261 men lost in the explosion. He wrote the oft repeated words in his journal: "Remember the Main! End Spain's four century curse on the world!" He and 103 other members of the Montana National Guard formed the Butte

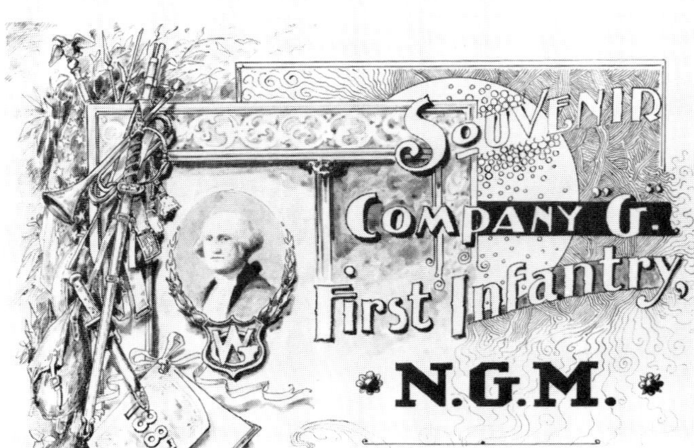

Title page illustration done by Paxson for his National Guard company's 1896 yearbook. India ink.

contingent of the First Montana Volunteer Infantry soon after the *Main* went down. They drilled every day for six weeks without pay or any real prospect of being recognized by the War Department. Then in the first week of May they were ordered to Helena to be mustered into the army. Edgar, with a commission of first lieutenant, was made second in command of company "G" of the Butte Volunteers. In the company was Pfc. Harry Paxson, his seventeen-year-old son. Edgar's brother, Robert, the pharmacist, was mustered in as a steward in the medical corps.

So began a curious interlude in Edgar's artistic career. It had little or no effect on his art—when he returned he took up where he had left off. But it is a dramatic story in itself—a story of the harsh realities facing a soldier overseas in the tropics. Although Edgar and his comrades served primarily as an occupational force, they suffered greatly from many privations and from disease. Edgar himself returned in broken health and took years to recover completely.[2]

But that May of 1898 in camp outside Helena, spirits of the new recruits were high. There was much good-natured joking, comaraderie and the excitement of impending adventure. Edgar wrote in his journal that he felt fine, his enthusiasm undampened by a severe toothache and a bad cold.

The first days in camp showed little order or discipline. Drills were laughable—many recruits had no rifles; half didn't have uniforms; some had only bayonets while others had only scabbards. The camp was first located on low ground in a meadow, which turned into a swamp after a heavy rain. It was rumored that it had been placed there only to accommodate the local saloon and prostitutes, who were doing a brisk business. Tent floors turned to mud and many soldiers came down with colds. A number of soldiers had to stand guard duty in the rain without overcoats, as none had been issued. Camp was finally moved to higher ground, but not before cases of pneumonia were reported. By the end of the first week, men were complaining because uniforms and equipment were slow to arrive. Lice and other vermin began to invade the camp. But drinking and fighting diminished due to the removal of the camp from the meadow near the saloon, and by the time orders were received on May 17 to depart by railroad for San Francisco, the camp had attained a more military aspect.

On May 24, Edgar and his 1,144 compatriots boarded a Union Pacific train for the trip to the coast via Ogden, Utah. Along the leg to Ogden, Edgar recognized the familiar country through which he had driven 250 horses en route to Fort Benton in 1877. There were teepees along the river just as before. He recognized the site of Old Fort Hall, made famous by John C. Fremont and Kit Carson, and Harkness station of stagecoach days. But now the fort was gone and the station was no longer a few log buildings and corrals—it was a flourishing town, a sign of changing times.

West of Ogden, the train passed through country new to Edgar—alkalai desert, a wilderness of greasewood and sage. But he knew its history and recognized its few inhabitants—Piute Indians. When the train stopped for fuel and water, he talked with them.

Edgar's train was one of many bringing volunteers along the same route from several states. At each town, bridge and underpass, cheering people were lined up with signs and banners reading, "Remember the Main." Amid much fanfare the troops disembarked from their trains in San Francisco and set up their tents in a sprawling camp around the Presidio. There were 14,000 troops in the encampment and more arriving daily. Hundreds of civilians wandered through the camp adding to the commotion. Many were friends of the soldiers, many were ladies from local service organizations bringing gifts—food, blankets and even flowers—to the officers and men. The first several nights many soldiers took advantage of the commotion to sneak past the guard for, as Edgar quaintly put it, "a moonlight ramble through Golden Gate Park" on "French leave." His Quaker-bred morality surfacing, he noted with some disapproval that there were many young girls walking the streets at all hours with an eye out for "anyone in brass buttons." When on duty as officer of the guard, Edgar often had to fight to keep rowdy prisoners at bay in the guard tent after they were caught drunk on their return to camp.

But as the days passed, the camp calmed down. Hours of drilling, war games and long tramps with heavily loaded packs wearied the soldiers. They increasingly used their spare time to rest instead of raising hell. And there was homesickness. Edgar, revealed his distinctly sentimental nature in this emotional description in his journal of an evening in camp after the boisterious first week had passed:

> The boys are tired out tonight and as I sit here by the candle and huge roses in a wash basin, they come to the tent and wish to be excused from roll call as they wish

to go to bed.... Away across the hills among the camps of the California, Penn., Minn., Texas and Missouri boys comes the familiar strains of "Home Sweet Home" and while sitting here it brings to mind a good wife, a little boy and darling daughter perhaps preparing to retire. And from the lips of the dear mother a prayer is breathed for the welfare of absent husband and son who in their humble way are doing their duty. May she have the strength and encouragement to sustain her and ours. Good night! Good night!

Camp life dragged on for six weeks. There were drills and more drills. Cold winds and fog kept the tents damp and uncomfortable. Guns and swords rusted. Fleas flourished. Clothes wore out and were slow to be replaced. Many soldiers suffered during drills and maneuvers from blistered and infected feet due to a lack of proper boots. Edgar, being an officer, occasionally got leave to go to town for a decent meal and a warm, dry room at the home of friends or in a hotel. He visited what he called "Mr. Gump's Art Store" (the now fashionable and famous Gump's) and dined at Mr. Gump's home.

But Edgar had problems too. He had had a painful toothache since he left Montana. He finally went to town and had eleven teeth pulled in one sitting. Four days later he painfully had impressions made for his "store teeth" as he called them. Then his regiment received orders to board the troop ship *Pennsylvania* bound for the Philippines. There was Edgar with no teeth amid the uproar and excitement of thousands of troops breaking camp. His dentures would not be ready until the afternoon of the day he was to board ship. That day was chaotic. He described it in his journal:

From the time we arrived at the dock at 10:15 until 5:30 pm, it was a constant rush and jam. The mass of people who tried all schemes imaginable to gain access to the interior of the long wharf is indescribable. Women fainted, children (were) tramped on and several were injured. The guard was equal to the occasion. One member of Co. F, Stanly, endeavored to use a knife on Sargent Marford of Co. G and was promptly knocked down by him. His jaw was broken and he was taken to the Division Hospital for repairs. He will not go to Manila. Many women and girls marched in the ranks and assisted their heavily loaded sons, brothers, or lovers. Some shouldered the rifle and many even their knapsacks which they carried bravely along amid cheers of the vast throngs who lined the streets. I met many old friends who grasped my hand in tears.

In late afternoon Edgar went ashore without permission to pick up his dentures. When he reached the dentist's office, he found they were not yet ready. He waited what he called the longest hour of his life. He knew it was possible that the ship would cast off at any moment leaving him as an apparent deserter. But he was able to reboard the ship, dentures in place, minutes before the whistle blew and the vessel steamed out into the bay to anchor and await orders. Again, from Edgar's journal: "It was a sight long to be remembered, the waving of handkerchiefs and the cheers and good-byes of thousands of voices.... The rigging was filled with men and the deck crowded with all (the rest) on board."

The next morning, July 20, 1898, the anchor was hove and the *Pennsylvania* sailed through the Golden Gate amid an escort of small vessels, with more cheering and a salute from the big guns on shore. Twenty-five miles out the pilot was taken off and the ship was alone on the ocean.

This was, of course, the first time Edgar had been to sea. He displayed a keen interest in everything around him—an interest that was so much a part of his personality; an interest that in concert with his sense of history, caused him throughout his life to record what he saw in his journals, sketches and paintings. During the passage he frequently pulled from his pocket his ever present sketch pad and sketched the ship's officers and some of the crew and soldiers. He learned about the use of a sextant from the captain and kept close track of the ship's speed and progress. In his journal he recorded changes in the weather and sea state and noted the various forms of sea life.

Edgar found almost immediately that he was not subject to the seasickness affecting nearly all of those on board. The first night was terribly rough, with mountainous seas and gale force winds. Below decks conditions were wretched with vomit, so Edgar made his way to the captain's bridge where he watched tremendous waves wash the decks and even break over the bridge itself. The next day as sea conditions calmed, and several days thereafter, Edgar helped serve meals to those who wanted to eat. His queasy comrades came to call him Jolly Tar. He became friends with the ship's officers, entertaining them with his version of the Custer battle. This first leg of the passage could hardly have been more enjoyable for Edgar. The weather in the trade winds was beautiful and warm. He regularly sat at the stern in the star-filled evenings puffing on his pipe, watching the phosphorescence in the ship's wake and contemplating.

In eight days the ship arrived in Honolulu, a stopover that was more like a holiday than war. The troops feasted on the grounds of the queen's palace and the officers were entertained by Mr. Dole, the pineapple tycoon, at the Hawaiian National Guard officer's quarters. Edgar toured the city in a carriage guided by a friendly Kanaka.

After a week in paradise, the *Pennsylvania* sailed for Manila. It was soon apparent that the vacation was over: heat became unbearable; water and food were rationed; thievery, fights and complaints became commonplace. After twenty-one monotonous, miserable days, the ship arrived at Cavite across the bay from Manila. The anchor was lowered among the U.S. fleet and the remains of the Spanish navy destroyed by Dewey in May.

While the *Pennsylvania* had been at sea, the Spanish had surrendered. Edgar and his comrades were to occupy the Philippines until a treaty was signed. Many Filipinos, however, were not in accord with that plan. They had welcomed the help of the Americans in defeating the Spanish, but now they wanted their immediate independence. They did not want to simply pass from the control of one foreign power to another. Consequently, the troops disembarking from the *Pennsylvania* were facing possible renewed warfare, this time against Filipino revolutionaries—"Insurgents," as the Americans called them. The first troops ashore were fired upon from the jungle, although shooting was scattered. They took up residence in the old Spanish barracks at Cavite. For the next several weeks, they suffered greatly from relentless humidity and heat, drenching rain, mosquitoes and disease. The cities were occupied by U.S. forces while some 5,000 insurgents held the countryside. Fighting was sporadic while negotiations went on. Nearly every night, soldiers on guard duty were fired upon. By the second day ashore, Edgar and his fellow soldiers were covered with mosquito bites. Dysentery and skin infections soon were widespread. By the end of the first week, many including Edgar had symptoms of malaria. But despite sickness, whoever was able was required to continue camp routine and the unloading of supplies from the *Pennsylvania*. Edgar described his day-to-day existence in his journal:

> I have had to be day and night with the company. Captain Wynne stays at officers quarters ¼ mile away and one officer must be constantly with the company (Lt. Knowlton, the only other officer in the company, is aboard the *Pennsylvania* supervising the unloading). [I get] up at 4 a.m., see that the men are up and bunks arranged, and that the 1st Sargent has special details for the day (which by the way he seldom has). Then to the mess department. Fall in for breakfast. Then morning drill. By this time (perhaps) the Captain arrives. Then the "fatigue call" sounds—men all fall in, those on special detail excepted. Then I march them to the landing, where we usually stay until noon in the hot sun unloading the "caskas." Then back to dinner. About two p.m. we again fall in. The company goes off to the boats—details here and there—all must be looked after...5 p.m., fall in for drill, 45 minutes. Then supper and clean-up. To say nothing of intervening duties which occur at all times.

On September 4, Edgar became so ill that he could no longer continue his duties. He admitted himself to the camp hospital. The medical staff advised a two-month leave back in the States. Edgar objected. It meant much to him to remain with his company until they all went home. By this time, over 1,000 of the soldiers were disabled by sickness. Edgar tried again to perform his duties as best he could. On September 27 he wrote in his journal that he could only keep going by "hard exertion of will." He found that his strength varied greatly from day to day. Some days he could barely get around with the aid of a cane. One day he could not finish inspection of the soldiers because he had not the strength to lift a rifle. Two days later he was able with some members of his company to chase off a few insurgents in a brief skirmish.

On October 1 Edgar determined to apply for sick leave. He hated to leave behind those who had suffered with him, but it seemed that the war was essentially over. He finally admitted that his health was at stake and his age was against him. He knew he should go home for the sake of his family.

He was assigned a room in the military hospital at Cavite but was free to move about at will. Since the troop ship back to the States was not leaving immediately, Edgar had the opportunity to see Manila and what remained of the Spanish reign. The sights from his hospital bed itself were interesting enough, as described in his journal:

> We are upstairs in a quaint old building of the real Spanish type, musty and damp. Ants and spyders play upon the walls and floors. Through the funny windows an occassional breeze finds its way driving the fumes of the drugs from our neighbors (who we can tickle with a fishpole so narrow is the street), the hospital staff. Down below us the natives flit here and there in their charming (?) way, their shoes going tick-tack, tick-tack on the rough tiles and the jabber of Spanish-Philipino constantly ringing in your ears. Ten feet away the sentinel hollers "halt" seventeen times per minute. Then an old cart with a buffalo goes creaking along—Then Huddla! Huddla! and a native with his little Cabalo and "Cadashe" goes flopping along in great hurry all humped up in the bottom while on the seat behind two sturdy men-o'-war's men go from side to side hitting only the high places. Up from the street comes that everlasting musty smell, which smells like Hell!...Such is the "Calle Del Arsenel."

In both Manila and Cavite, Edgar poked around the churches and fortifications, all of whitewashed brick, left behind by the Spanish. In dungeons he saw screws for torturing and guillotines. He saw human skulls and dried blood on the walls. He wrote of one dungeon, "It smells like and looks like the picture of a slaughterhouse."

Edgar sketched much of what he saw. There are over thirty sketches in pen or pencil and at least three watercolors extant. Several are of natives going about their daily tasks. Edgar noted in his journal that whatever the natives were doing, they always managed to be smoking at the same time. Several of his sketches show the ever-present cigarette.

On October 22 Edgar boarded the *City of Para* for return to the States via Japan. He was still not satisfied that his going was right. His fellow officers tried to console him and convince him that hostilities were over and there was nothing more he could do. There were many solemn goodbyes and the *Para* departed in

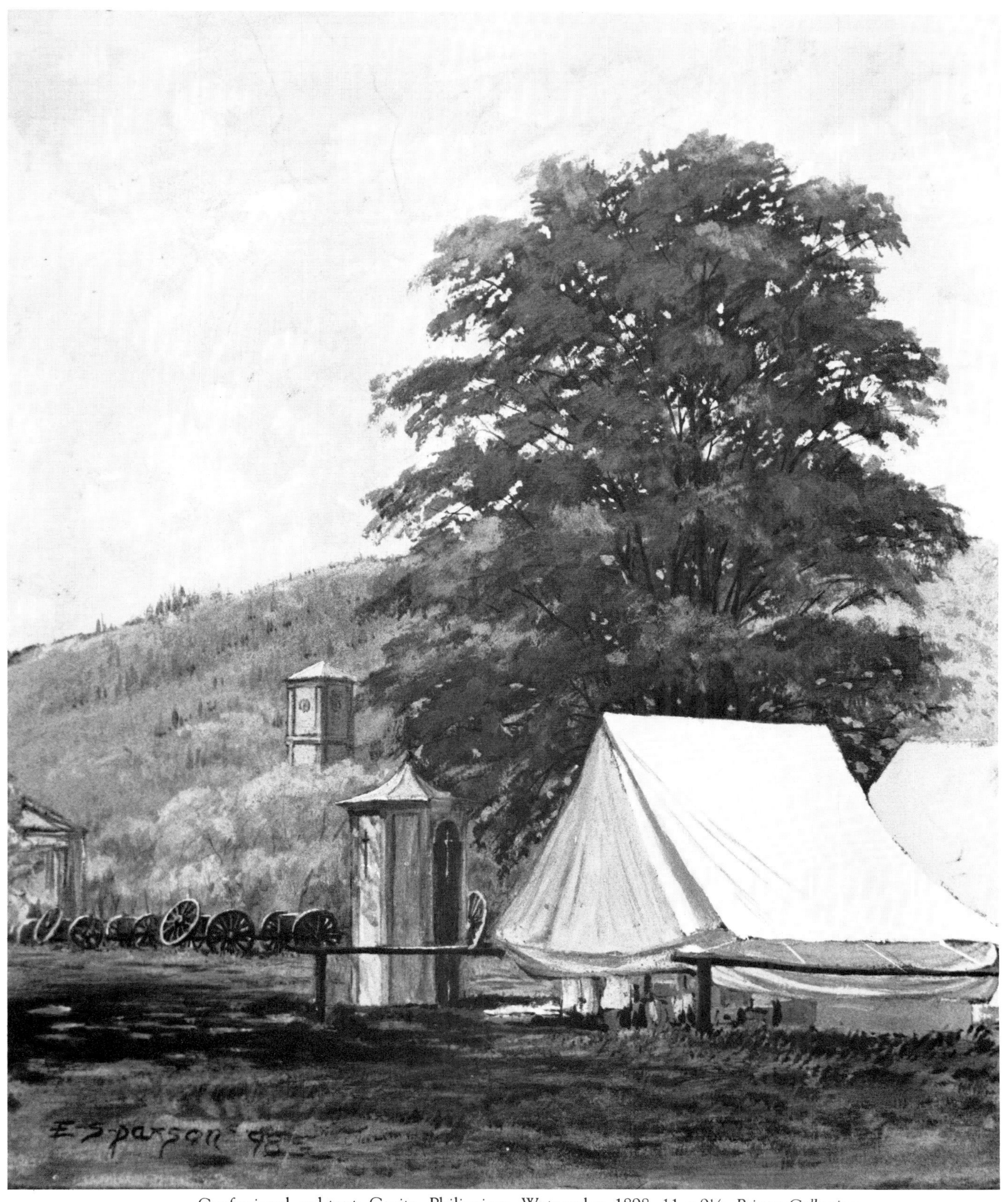

Confessional and tent, Cavite, Philippines. Watercolor, 1898, 11 x 9½. *Private Collection.*

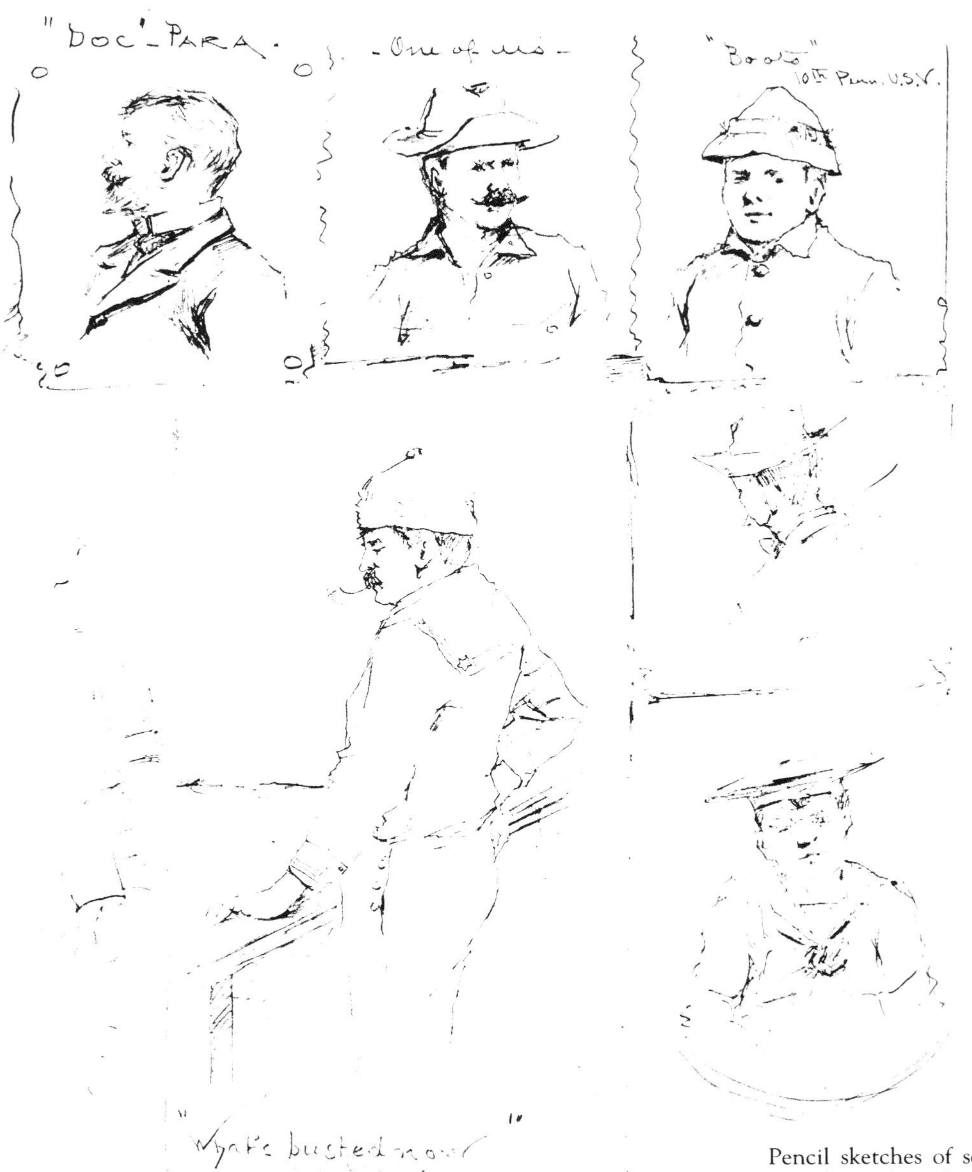

Pencil sketches of some of Paxson's ship-board companions en route home from the Philippines, 1898. *Montana Historical Society, Helena, Montana.*

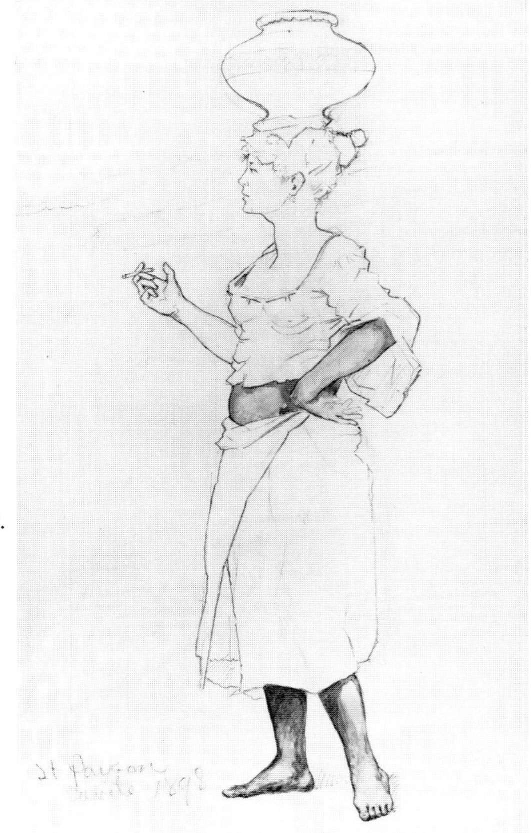

A Filipino woman sketched by Paxson at Cavite, 1898. Pencil and watercolor.

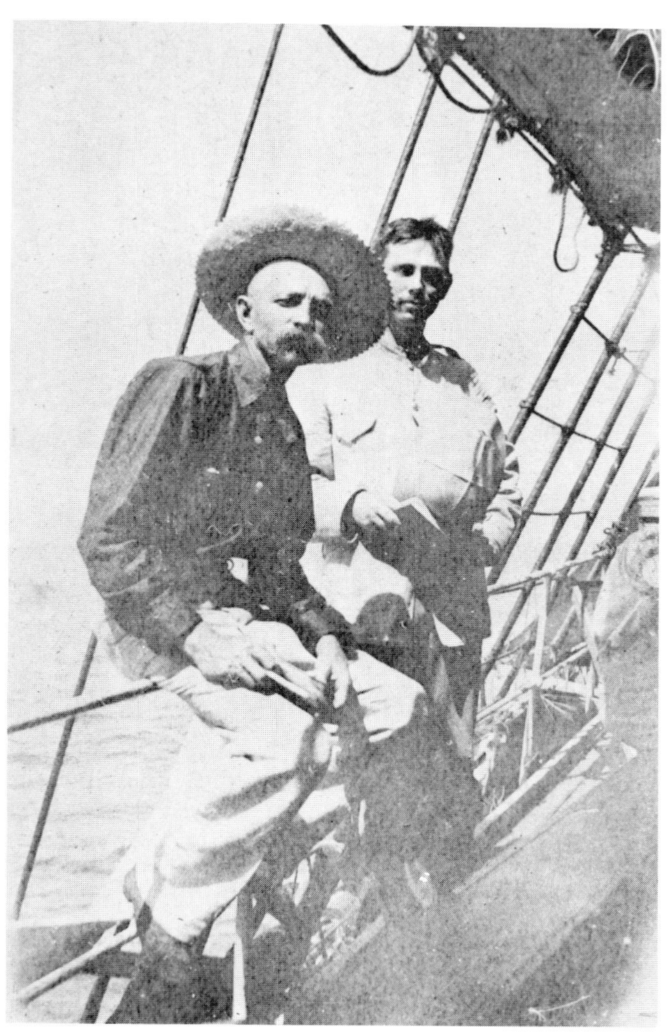

Left: Paxson (with sombrero) aboard ship on his return from service with the Montana Volunteers in the Philippines. Below: an emaciated Paxson (left), soon after his return from the Philippines in 1899. Paxson's wife Laura is standing. Also pictured are eldest son Loren and youngest son Bob.

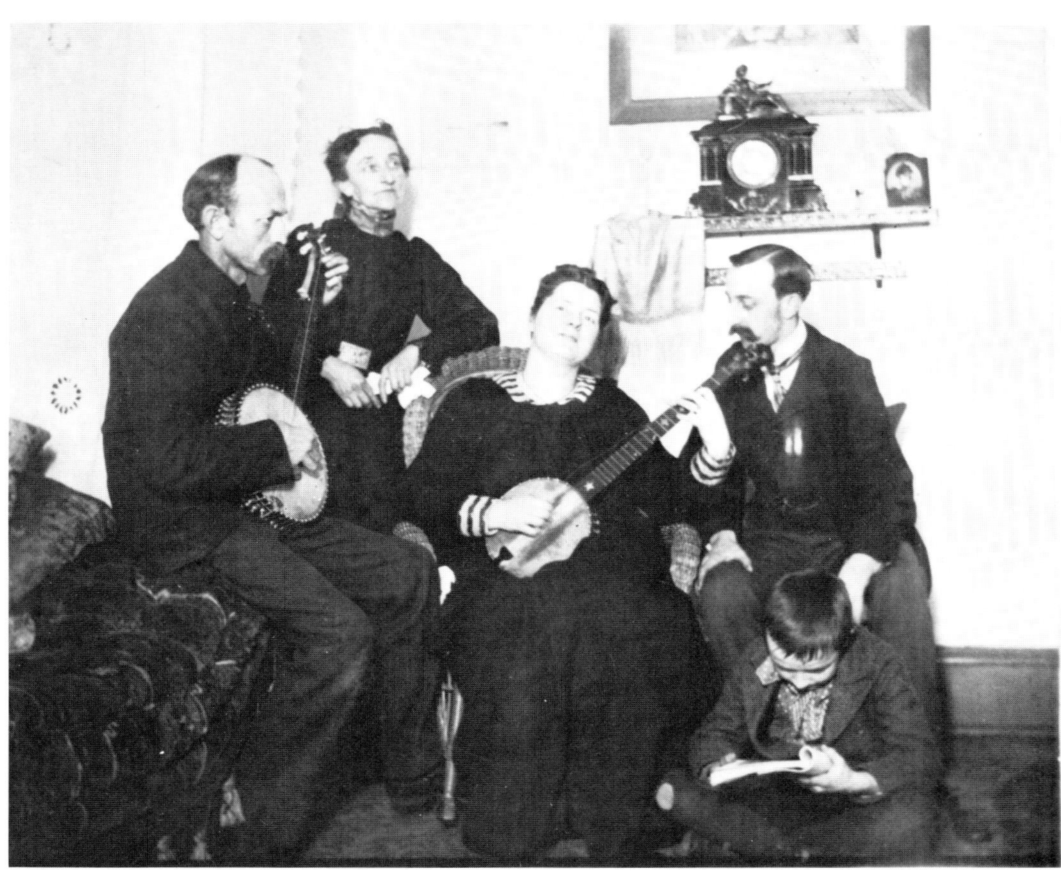

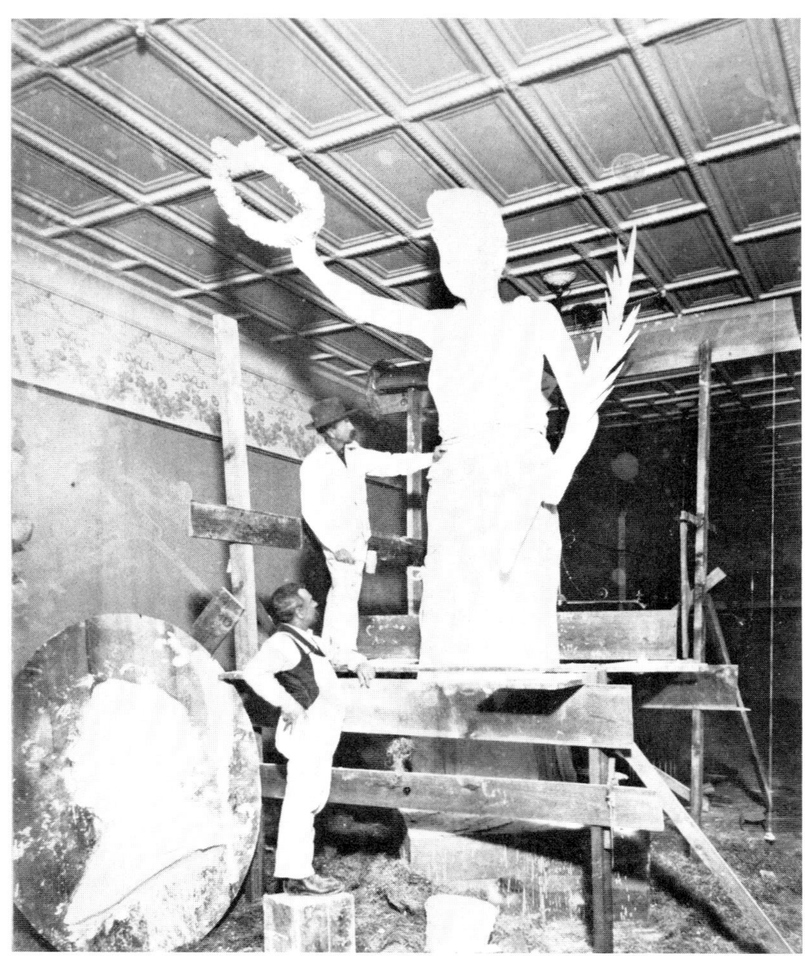

Left: Paxson (in hat) working on statue of "Peace," commemorating the return of the Montana Volunteers from the Philippines. The medallion at left is also Paxson's work. Below: the triumphal arch designed by Paxson for Butte's welcoming home of the Montana Volunteers who served during the Spanish-American War. The statue of "Peace," done by Paxson, can be seen atop the arch.

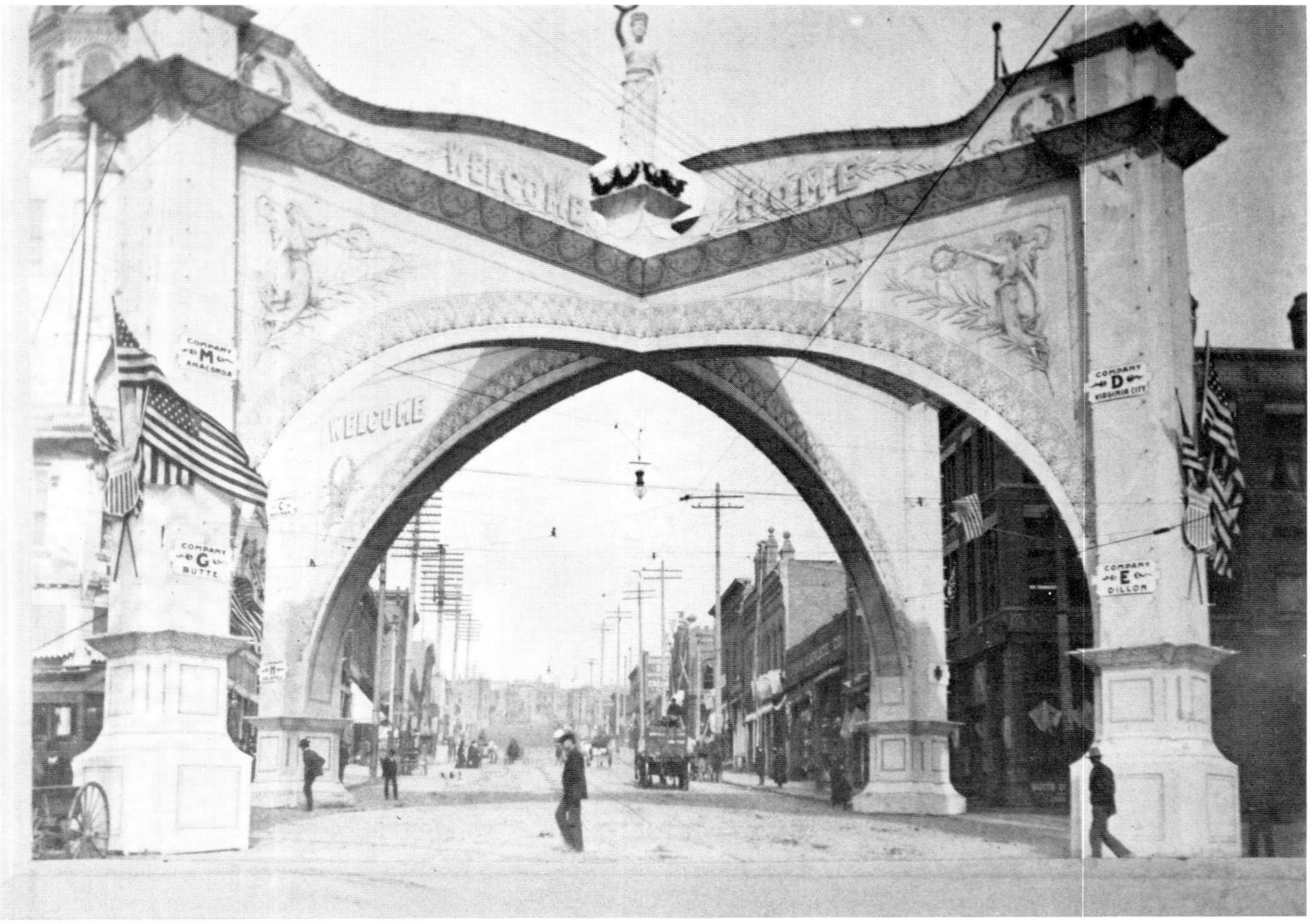

a gale with reports that a typhoon was at its height in the China Sea to the north. Brother Robert was also due to return home soon, but Edgar's son Harry stayed behind.

The necessity of sailing in the eastern seas during the typhoon season dismayed both crew and passengers on the *Para* and all were relieved when the harbor at Nagasaki hove into sight. The ship arrived after dark. Edgar wrote in his journal of the beautiful effect of hundreds of tiny fishing boats, each with a lantern in the bow. During a two-day layover, Edgar toured the city by rickshaw. He marveled at the cleanliness and neatness of the city. He traveled into the picturesque countryside and partook of Japanese hospitality. He was very much impressed. He wrote that Japan "was the one bright picture" of his wartime experience.

The *Para* then departed Nagasaki, traveled north the length of Japan's protected west coast, and then entered the open North Pacific on November 7. Within hours the ship was wallowing in the troughs of monstrous seas with the engines shut down for repair and hurricane force winds screaming through the rigging. For five days the sea raged and the ship was repeatedly stopped for repairs. It began to snow and sleet. On the thirteenth, Edgar wrote in his journal: "Last night was the worst of all...I never expect to see anything so grand but awful. About one this morning...the upper deck was swept clear of railings and guards. The stern bulkhead [was] crushed and swept overboard."

That was the peak of the storm. Over the next three days, the weather and sea settled. On November 26, twenty-four days out of Nagasaki, the *Para* passed through the Golden Gate, and on December 4, Edgar was again among family and friends in his beloved mountain home.

The ordeal was not yet over though. Edgar suffered repeated malarial attacks. At an annual G.A.R. meeting where he was given a seat of honor on the speaker's platform, one of the speakers pointed to him as evidence of a soldier just returned—"a physical wreck of a man whose whole life has changed."

In fact Edgar proved resilient and was eventually able to resume the life he loved. But for five months he was in no physical condition to work on the Custer battle painting. Besides his recurring attacks of malaria, he was hobbled by an injury to his hip sustained during the night the *Para's* decks were swept clean by the North Pacific storm.

But during these months of recuperation, Edgar was able to paint at times and completed several smaller new paintings. Then in May 1899 he resumed work on the big painting.

There was, however, one more delay. Fighting had resumed in the Philippines between the Filipino insurgents and the U.S. forces. Edgar's sons, Harry, served on the front lines, distinguishing himself as bugler and courrier for General Crook. Once he had the heel of his boot shot off, the bullet passing so near to the flesh that it raised a blister the size of a silver dollar. Owing to Edgar's desire to pay tribute to his son and his comrades, he was commissioned by Butte citizens to design a massive triumphal arch and sculpt a statue of *Peace* to stand atop it, welcoming home the volunteers in October 1899. Edgar fulfilled the commission admirably within a few weeks, a remarkable accomplishment, for Edgar had had virtually no previous experience in sculpture. He had made his first attempt at modelling in clay only a month before, when he modeled a medallion, also in commemoration of the returning soldiers.

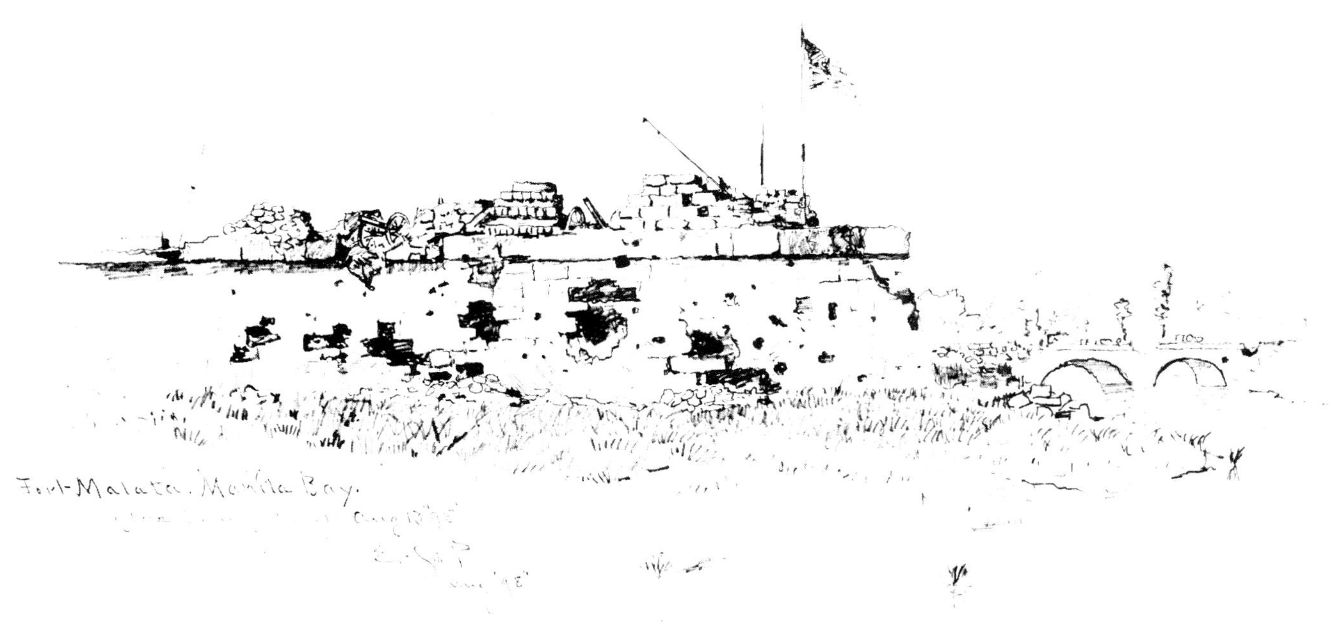

"Fort Malata, Manilla Bay After Bombardment Aug. 13 '98". Pencil sketch. *Montana Historical Society, Helena Montana.*

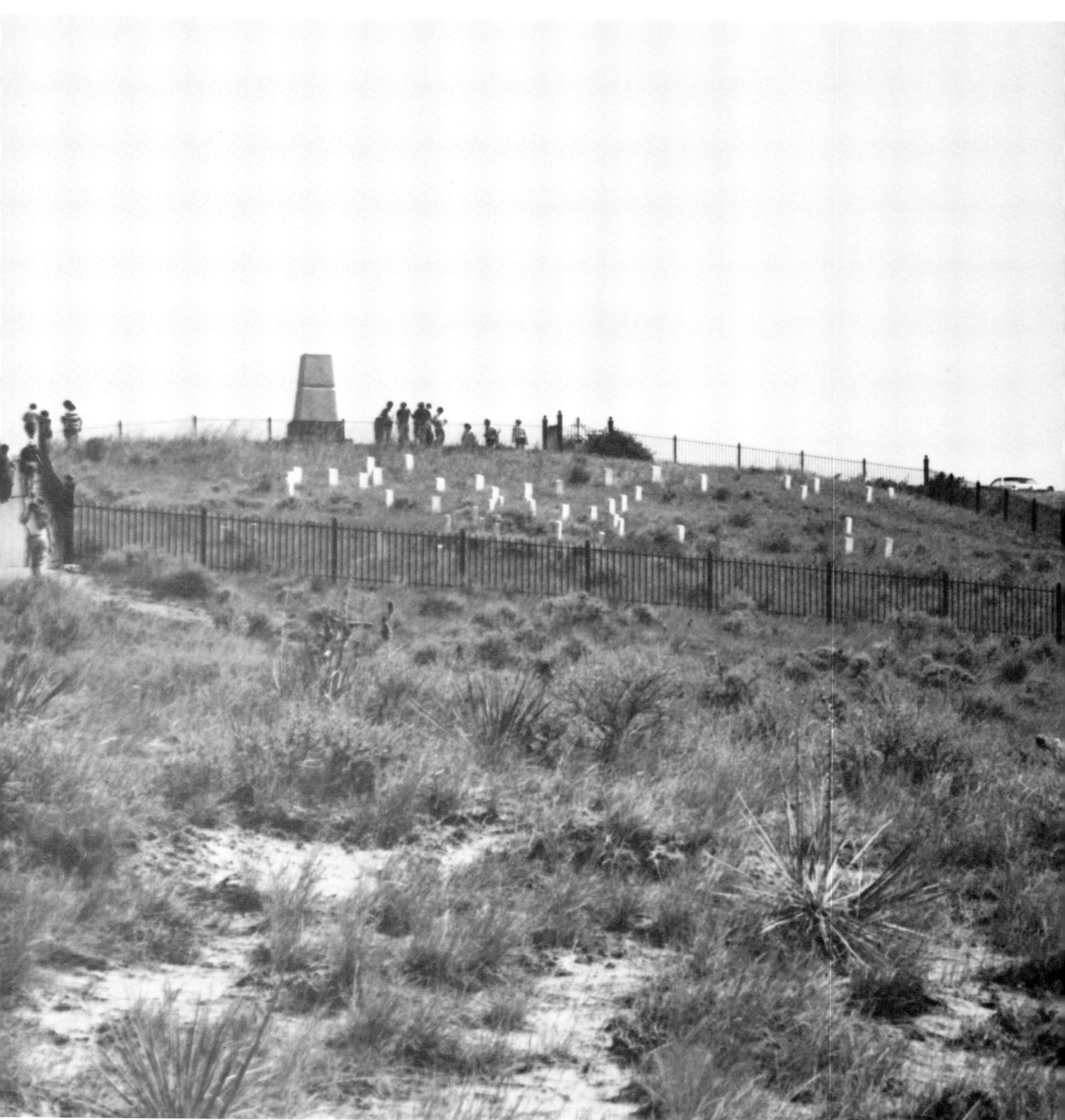

Custer Battlefield, *John Popovich.*

6

The Artist's Masterpiece: Custer's Last Stand

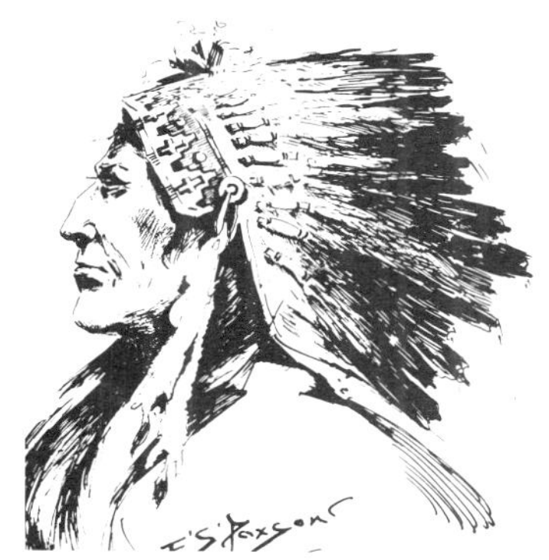

Title unknown, ink, 1903. *Collection of Connie Jo and Harry Lockwood, Midwestern Galleries, Cincinnati, Ohio.*

Edgar finished his documentary *Custer's Last Stand*[1] in December 1899.

The painting is central in two intimately related stories: the story it tells of the battle itself and the no less interesting story of its own creation and subsequent passages back and forth between the public eye and obscurity.

The annihilation of Custer and the five companies with him on Custer Hill above the Little Bighorn River is without a doubt the most famous and controversial of all confrontations between white man and Indian. This has been so since July 5, 1876, when the delayed and fragmentary news of the fight first hit the front pages of the nation's newspapers. Known facts, assumptions and outrageous fictions have been hashed and rehashed continually ever since. Still no one knows exactly what happened. Certainly no white man lived to tell about it. Indians who were there had plenty to say, but their often conflicting stories only added to the confusion. Why should the red man tell reporters, Indian agents, commissioners, and army officers what happened? Why would a man tell his captors how he killed their brothers on the battlefield? Why not fool them, mislead them, tease them? And later, when the captors have taken everything from the red man so that he has nothing more to lose, why not boast a little and embellish that one great victory that preceded the end?

Of the many who have presumed to describe the fight on Custer Hill in the face of these obstacles, Edgar was certainly one of the most suited to succeed in separating the facts from half-truths and outright lies. He knew intimately the ways and attitudes of both Indians and soldiers: he had lived with both. And, importantly, he had attained a mutual respect with both, certainly a rarity on the frontier. This plus his artistic talent and persistent researching make him unique among all those who have attempted portrayals of the Custer tragedy.

Edgar received the respect of the Indian leaders in the battle not only because he respected them, but also because of his artistic talent. It was much admired among Indians as "strong medicine." That he had been given the Indian name *Cot-lo-see* (he sees everything) is evidence of this admiration.

Edgar also had the advantage that he could communicate with the Indians without the aid of an interpreter. His son Robert, in discussing the artist's battle painting in later years, always stressed that Edgar avoided interpreters when seeking information because they invariably, whether intentionally or not, distorted the conversations in translation.

There are a number of references among Edgar's papers regarding his efforts at seeking out the Indian participants of the battle. Several times he went over the battlefield with them. He noted, in his journals and letters, his trips in 1877, '82, '84 and '96. The Sioux chief Gall and the Cheyenne Two Moon, who were two of the acknowledged leaders of the Indians in the battle, held Edgar in high regard and gave him many details of the actual fighting. It has always been said in the Paxson family that Edgar and Two Moon "shared a blanket" in camp on the battlefield. Edgar interviewed other Indian participants with varying degrees of success and made sketches of them at the same time. Custer's famous scout Curley, who was the closest "friendly Indian" to the annihilation, gave Edgar his story on the battlefield. At other times, not on the battlefield, Edgar interviewed other Indians who were army scouts during the Sioux campaign.

Edgar never mentioned specifically that he met the infamous Rain-in-the-Face at the battlefield, but he did meet him in 1893. Edgar was on a train returning to Butte after a trip east to visit relatives and see the Columbian Exposition in Chicago. Rain-in-the-Face and some other Sioux were also on the train, returning to the Standing Rock Reservation after a highly publicized trip to the East. Edgar wrote in his notebook at the time: "I had a talk with 'Old Rain' and he said he was glad to go home. 'Too much big houses. Too much Pow-Wow. Make big head—no like.' He is about forty-five years old, large and rather good looking. Straight as an arrow." Edgar also added, "He is a vicious and very shrewd Indian." Edgar knew well that "Old Rain" had had a grudge against Tom Custer previous to the Little Bighorn fight. While east the Indian persisted to boast that he had personally killed Tom Custer on Custer Hill and cut out and ate the soldier's heart. In Edgar's portrayal of the battle, the likeness of Rain-in-the-Face can readily be seen about to strike down Captain Custer with a war club.

Soldiers who fought in the Sioux campaign provided a wealth of fact and opinion about the Custer battle to Edgar. He usually had little trouble getting them started on the subject and Indian warfare in general. By Edgar's count, he interviewed ninety-six officers and men who were close to the battle. One old soldier, Jack Donaghue, had been a member of Major Reno's contingent of the 7th Cavalry at the Little Bighorn. He had been wounded in the knee during Reno's controversial retreat while Custer and his men were four miles away. Despite being hobbled by his wound, Donaghue had helped bury the dead on Custer Hill afterward. In 1898, he shipped out to the Philippines with Edgar. The two had many free hours to discuss the battle on the long voyage across the Pacific.

Another old-timer who helped Edgar greatly was Frank Server. He had been a sergeant in the 4th Infantry and was detailed from General Terry's command with scout Muggins Taylor to advance up the Little Bighorn to locate Custer. They were the first to find the dead on the battlefield. After reporting their grisly find to General Terry, they rejoined the command which then moved up and located Reno's and Benteen's battered contingents, all that were left alive of the 7th Cavalry.

Edgar wrote in his journal upon the death of his old comrade in 1911: "Server was among those who buried the dead. I spent many a long evening in converse with him. Often we rode over the battlefield with Two Moon and other Indians when I sketched for my battle picture."

The soldier who helped Edgar most to get a clear idea of the battle was Gen. E. S. Godfrey. He had been first lieutenant of "K" Troop in Captain Benteen's contingent of the 7th Cavalry at the Little Bighorn. Benteen's men had advanced very slowly. They had met with Reno after Reno's retreat and had dug in under heavy enemy fire. The sound of distant gunfire they heard proved to be from Custer's last stand. Godfrey was among the first to view and identify the mutilated dead bodies on Custer Hill.

Edgar became acquainted with Godfrey soon after the battle and the two corresponded during the years Edgar researched for his painting. Godfrey himself became an acknowledged expert on the Custer battle and wrote articles in national publications about it. He not only had an interest in the battle from a militarist's standpoint, but from an emotional one. The men who died on Custer Hill were his comrades—a number of them were close friends. He grieved that day he helped commit their mutilated bodies to shallow graves where they fell. He felt it proper that they be immortalized in a documentary painting and was keenly interested in Edgar's efforts. Because of its gross inaccuracies, Godfrey had been disappointed in Cassily Adam's painting of the battle which was presented to his regiment in 1895 by the Anhauser-Busch Brewery. He hoped to see these errors corrected in Edgar's portrayal. To this end, he wrote Edgar a letter in January 1896 detailing his firsthand knowledge and that of comrades still living with whom he had consulted. Answering Edgar's questions down to minutiae, he wrote:"1st: Gen.Custer rode'Vic'into the fight: Vic was a sorrel with four white feet and legs and a blaze in the face: he was not found on the field: I have heard that he had been identified in the possession of some indian in the hostile camp after they went into the British Possessions. The dogs were left with the wagon train. 2nd: General Custer carried a Remington sporting rifle, octagonal barrel: two Bulldog, self-cocking, English, white handled pistols, with a ring in the butt for a lanyard: a hunting knife, in a beaded fringed scabbard: and a canvas cartridge belt. He wore a whitish gray hat, with broad brim and rather low crown, very similar to the Cowboy hat: buckskin suit, with fringed welt in outer seams of trousers and arms of blouse: the blouse was double breasted, military buttons, lapels generally open, turned down collar, and fringe on bottom of skirt. 3rd: Captain Tom Custer was dressed about the same as the General. He was found near the top of the hill, North a few yards from the General, lying on his face; his features were so pressed out of shape as to be almost beyond recognition; a number of arrows had been shot into his face, several in his head, one I remember without the shaft, the head bent so that it could hardly be withdrawn; his skull was crushed and nearly all the hair scalped, except a very little on the nape of the neck.

"The General was not mutilated at all; he laid on his back, his upper arms on the ground, the hands folded or so placed as to cross the body about over the stomach; his position was natural and one that we had seen hundreds of times while taking cat naps during halts on the march. He was hit in the front of the left temple and one in the left breast at or near the heart.

"Boston, the youngest brother was dressed similar to the other brothers; his body was found about two hundred yards from "Custer Hill," between that and the Little Big Horn, at the foot of the ridge that runs up from the river, and as it were, forms the lower boundary of the battlefield. The body was stript except his white cotton socks, and they had the name cut off.

"4th: Yates, Cooke, Smith and Reilley lay on Custer Hill and in the vicinity of the General but nearer the top of the hill, the General was slightly down the slope, toward the river. Calhoun was in the vicinity of the hill but further removed from the others as if he had been killed going toward Custer, from the position of his troop, on the left. Crittenden was on the hill on the extreme left of the line when facing the river. Keogh was in the depression just north or below Crittenden Hill, and on the slope of the ridge that formed the defensive line furthest from the river; the body was stript, except the socks, and these the name cut off; in life he wore a catholic medal suspended from his neck; it was not removed.

"All the officers wore the dark blue shirt with rather wide falling collar, which when the blouse was worn, was over the blouse collar; most of them had cross-sabers and 7, like the old cap ornament, worked in white or yellow silk on the points of the collar.

"Yates, Cooke, Smith, Porter and Calhoun, and sometimes Keogh, wore buckskin blouses, but I don't think any of them wore other than blue trousers; Harrington wore the blue blouse and white canvas trousers, with fringes on the outer seams. The day was very warm and few had on any kind of blouse.

"In describing the dress, I give it as generally worn, for when the bodies were found, after the fight, they were stript.

"I found Porter's buckskin blouse in the village, while destroying the property, and from the shot holes in it, he must have had it on and shot from the rear, left side, the bullet coming out on the left breast near the heart. Dr. Lord and Lieutenants Sturgis and Reilley wore the blue. Dr. Lord wore eyeglasses.

"Sergeant Robert Hughes Troop K, who carried the General's battle flag, was killed near the General on the hill. Nearly all the men wore the blue, but many, perhaps most of them had their trousers reenforced with white canvas on the seat and on the legs from the knees half way up. Nearly everyone wore the short top boot (that was then uniform) not high like these now worn, although a few of the officers wore the Wellington boot and some had white canvas leggings.

"5th: The command was armed with the Springfield carbine and the Colt revolver; every officer carried the revolver. NO ONE CARRIED THE SABER. Nearly every illustration I have seen of that fight or campaign have officers and men armed with the saber. Adam's painting of "Custer's Last Fight," last winter presented to the regiment by Mr. Busch, has the men armed with the Winchester and the saber. In a historical painting, I think, if I may be allowed the suggestion, that the equipments, etc., should conform to those used at the time of the fight. The bridles were different from the present pattern; the carbine socket was a small leather ring, instead of the boot now used. Every saddle had a small canvas sack about 20 inches long in which was carried 12 pounds of oats, strapped on the cantel; there was no hood on the stirrup used by the men.

"6th: There were no 'good indians' left on the field at the time we saw it; they were all removed; our dead were alone! There were not so very many dead ponies on the field, nor many dead horses, indeed surprisingly few, and most of them were on or near Custer's Hill; it would seem that they were turned loose that the men might better defend themselves, or were wounded and broke away. The scene on the left, N & E of Crittenden Hill or near the point on the map marked 'spring,' where the indians stampeded the 'led horses' of Troops I and L, must have been a wild one; and their loss must have made their hearts very heavy and perhaps caused many a man to give up hope at the very beginning! A representation of that scene in the background would add immensely to the effect from a realistic point of view, whatever it might be from an artistic point!

"Troops F, I, and L had bay horses; Troop C had light sorrels, and Troop E had grays; the trumpeters rode grays; Cooke rode an almost white horse; as a rule the officers rode horses the same color as the troops to which they belonged.

"As to 'accessories' on the battlefield, there were none. The marble white bodies, the somber brown of the dead horses and dead ponies scattered all over the field, but thickest on the near Custer Hill, and the scattering tufts of redish brown grass on the almost ashy white soil depicts a scene of loneliness and desolation that 'bows down the heart in sorrow!'"

General Godfrey closed the letter with this emotional note:

"I can never forget that sight! The early morning was bright, as we ascended to the top of the highest point whence the whole field came into view, with the sun to our backs. 'What are those?' exclaimed several as they looked at what appeared to be white boulders. Nervously I took the field glasses and glanced at the objects; then almost dropped them, and laconically said: 'The dead!' Col. Weir who was near, sitting on his horse, exclaimed: 'Oh how white they look! How white!' No there were no accessories; everything of value was taken away: arms, ammunition, equipments and clothing. Occasionally, there was a body with a bloody undershirt, drawers or socks, but the name was invariably cut off. The naked mutilated bodies, with their bloody fatal wounds, were nearly all unrecognizable, and presented a scene of sickening, ghastly horror! There were perhaps a half dozen spades and shovels, as many axes, a couple of picks and a few hatchets in the whole command; with these and knives and tin cups we went over the field and gave the bodies, where they lay, a scant covering of mother earth and left them, in the vast wilderness, hundreds of miles from civilization, friends and homes— to the wolves!"

Yours Truly,

E. S. Godfrey
Capt. 7th Cavalry
Brevet Major U.S. Army[2]

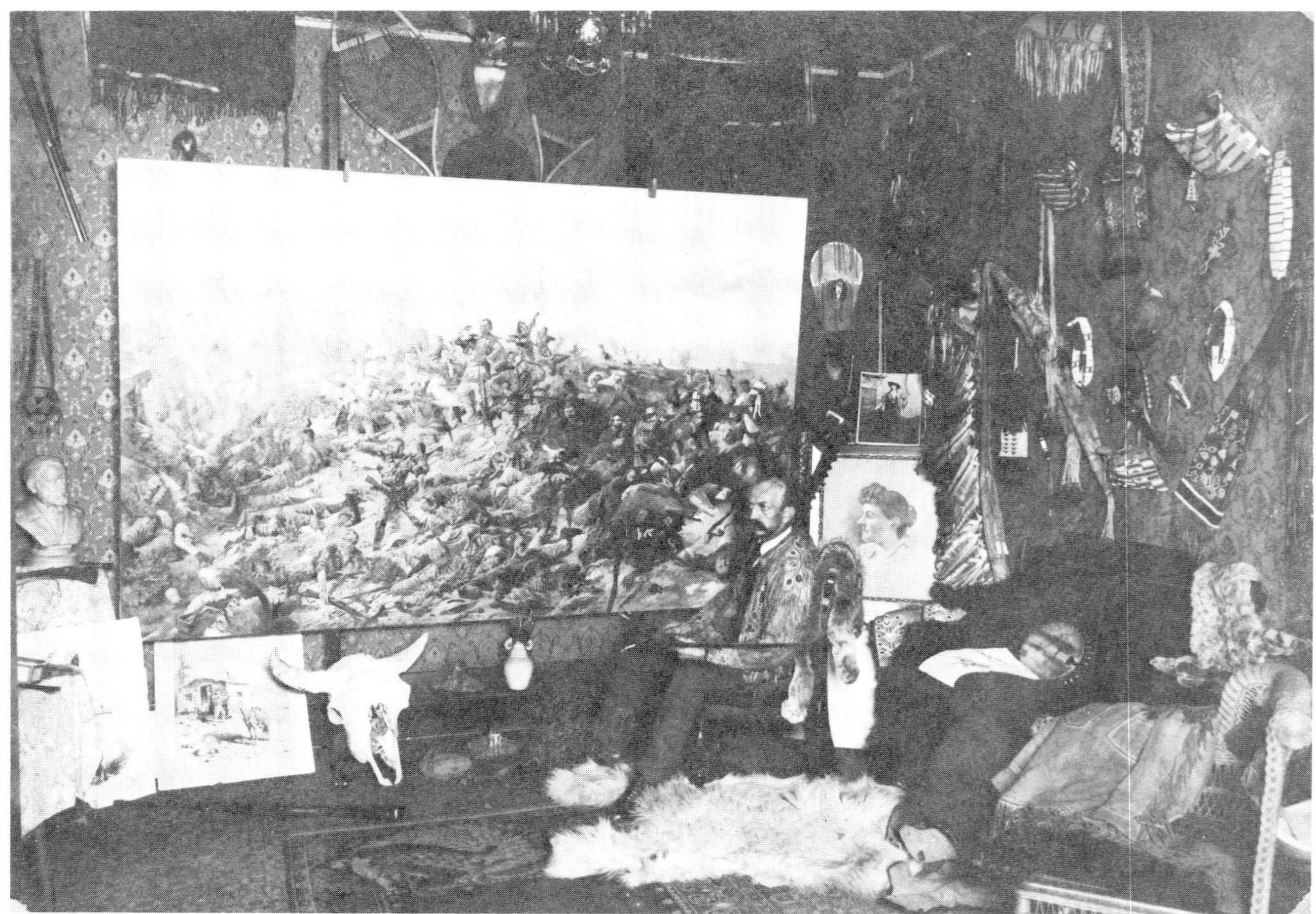

The artist in his Butte studio with his nearly completed masterpiece, 1898.

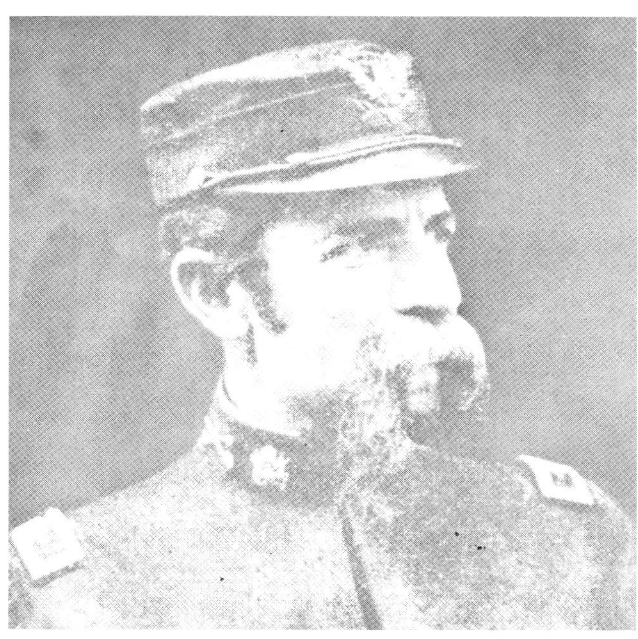

Gen. E.S. Godfrey about 1898.

Godfrey did not have an opportunity to see Edgar's painting until 1908 when he viewed it in Edgar's Missoula studio. When he first saw it he was overcome with emotion. Edgar wrote in his journal: "He seemed to stand in amazement for a long time. Tears came to his eyes and he appeared to be in deep thought. When he did speak he said, 'It is wonderful. The detail is perfect.' He could not leave it and was much depressed during the remainder of our interview. We later had a long talk in the studio."

An interesting footnote is that Godfrey noticed that Custer's personal flag of elaborately embroidered yellow silk—the flag he had acquired at Appomattox—was not in the painting although he had it with him at the Little Bighorn. Edgar had known about the flag's existence but had omitted it because he had not known its whereabouts the day of the battle. Eight years later Godfrey viewed the painting for the second time. There fluttering in the smoke and dust of battle was the yellow silken flag, which Edgar had carefully painted in.

In addition to gleaning all the information he could from the Indians and soldiers involved in the Sioux campaign of 1876–77, Edgar procured photographs of the participants of the Custer fight from many sources. He mentioned in his journal once that L. A. Huffman, post photographer with the army under Custer and General Miles, was an old friend. He was very likely a source of photographs of many of the soldiers.

Edgar looked to his Indian curios collection to assure accuracy of detail regarding the dress and weapons of the Indians in the painting. Since arriving in Montana, Edgar had been collecting all manner of Indian paraphernalia. He was aware of the distinguishing characteristics in the dress and accessories of the various tribes at the Little Bighorn encampment and made sure the warriors in his painting were properly portrayed. He sketched and painted accurately from his collection of Sioux and Cheyenne war shirts, war bonnets, clubs, lances and the like. His collection even contained several items found on the Custer battlefield itself, among them rawhide stirrups and an old Winchester rifle with Sioux marking on it. He also had a Brule Sioux war shirt and leggins, heavily beaded and fringed with scalp locks and weasel skins, which had been worn in the Battle of the Rosebud eight days before the Custer fight.

Preceding the actual painting, Edgar made numerous pencil sketches. Each figure in the finished painting was the subject of one or more studies done on roughly eight-by-twelve-inch paper. Then, Edgar sketched a detailed but scaled down pen drawing of the entire work to be. This was roughly eighteen-by-thirty-six-inches. Finally he began painting in 1895 on a canvas measuring six feet by nine feet. Slowly each major participant in the battle appeared on the canvas as a recognizable portrait, but in dramatic action. There were Lieutenant Colonel Custer, his brother Capt. Tom Custer, Lieutenant Calhoun, Adjutant Cooke, Lieutenant Porter, Captain Yates, Sergeant Ryan, and half-breed scout Mitch Bouyer. There, too, were Crazy Horse, Rain-in-the-Face, Hump, Two Moon, Crow King and Gall. In all, over 200 figures came to life in seething action.

Occasionally, while Edgar worked on the big canvas, Indian friends would drop in to the studio and study it intently. Some were Sioux whose brothers had fought Custer and some were Crow whose tribesmen had served as scouts with the army, fighting against the Sioux, their traditional enemy.

While Edgar was working on his massive painting, he had only a vague idea about what he was going to do with it when it was finished. Its size and weight (7' x 10' and over 1,000 pounds including frame) limited its possibilities for transportation and display. He only hoped that it would somehow be instrumental in making his work nationally known.

Shortly after completing the painting, Edgar found what appeared to be a solution to his problem in Col. William S. Brackett. Brackett was an old army man who had been familiar with the West since 1862 when, accompanied by Jim Bridger as guide, he had escorted the first two federal judges in Utah from the East to Salt Lake City. In May 1899, he was planning what he called a geological and scientific exploration of northwest Idaho, at that time a little-known wilderness, and while in Butte, visited Edgar to ask him to accompany the party as artist and hunter. Edgar had to decline because of his health and commitments, but the two men took an immediate liking to each other. Brackett bought a painting and admired the Custer battle picture. When he returned from his exploration he wrote Edgar desiring to lease the painting for showing in the East. This seemed a timely opportunity for the artist and plans were made to arrange a contract. On December 11, they signed the agreement which stated that Brackett would display the painting at his own cost in North America and Europe and pay Edgar for the priviledge $250 down payment plus $25 per month for the first four months, $30 per month for the second four months, and $35 per month for the remaining four months of the first year. The agreement could then be extended by the year at $50 per month to the artist. The contract further stipulated that the painting should be displayed in a main exhibition room as the sole painting, surrounded by Indian curios, photographs and other appropriate accessories, and that another room or extension be provided for display of other Paxson paintings offered for sale, their prices being determined by the artist.[3]

In early 1900, Brackett shipped the big painting east after showing it briefly at B. E. Caulkins Bookstore and Gallery in Butte. His plan was to tour the major cities, charging admission to view the painting. He had a brochure published entitled "Custer's Last Battle of the Little Bighorn in Montana, June 25, 1876." It contained an outline key to Edgar's painting, a history of the battle and a description and analysis of the painting. Brackett also wrote articles and news releases published in various eastern newspapers. He showed the painting in New York, Washington D.C., Chicago and other cities. There is no reliable record of all the showings. The painting achieved considerable recognition in Washington, D.C., where it was shown for several months in 1900. It was viewed there by many prominent army officers who had taken part in the Indian wars and had known Custer and his men. A guest register at the showing was filled with comments such as "I recognize the faces of all whom I knew," "True to every detail" and "I was present at the Battle of Little Bighorn...this is a great picture and true."

General Whitaker, Custer's chief of staff in 1865, was very enthusiastic over the painting. Gen. Nelson A. Miles wrote to Edgar especially to praise it. Elizabeth Custer viewed it and was moved to tears. She returned to see it several times.

But this modest success was the high point for the painting under Brackett's guidance. Brackett had personal and health problems which kept him from doing what Edgar had anticipated. In January 1901, the painting was put in storage in Washington and Edgar was concerned that it was not being shown. He apparently pursued other means of gaining revenue from the painting. He noted in his journal at that time that he had a prospective buyer and in February he discussed reproducing the painting with a firm in Chicago, but both deals fell through. In April he wanted the painting to go to the Pan-American Exposition in Buffalo, New York, but it did not go because arrangements were too late. Apparently the painting was neglected in 1902; there is no record of it being shown.

The situation culminated abruptly and unexpectedly in September 1902. On September 6, Edgar wrote in his journal:

> I was horrified to read in the morning paper that Wm S. Brackett had killed himself in Peoria, Ills. Though I had anticipated this, I had not thought it possible. Col. Brackett was a most warm and intimate friend. We had hunted, ate, slept together under the same blanket many a night in the wilds of the Big Horn and North Gallatin Mountains. It was he who gave me courage to finish my "Custer Fight" and place it before the world. Now he is gone! Where is he? I hope at rest, as he once told me by a roaring campfire one cold night far up in the mountains, when he was showing me a pair of Smith and Wesson Pistols. "They will do good work some day, then I will rest." I know not how he has left my affairs."

Edgar had, however, been having good success selling paintings both in Montana and the East. He was making enough money to devote himself solely to his art as an occupation.

But for nearly a year, Edgar's masterpiece suffered from lack of public exposure while he puzzled over what to do about it. In July 1903, still having made no decision, he had a long talk with B. E. Caulkins, who was having good success selling Edgar's other paintings. Soon thereafter eight Paxson paintings, including *Custer's Last Stand* were selected to be sent to the 1904 Louisiana Purchase Exposition in St. Louis as part of the Montana State Exhibit. Thousands viewed Edgar's paintings at the exposition, giving a substantial boost to his career. The Custer battle painting received more public exposure there than at any other time during the next sixty years.

Following the exposition, Edgar had his masterpiece shipped to Chicago with the assistance of Mrs. Marian A. White, the editor of the *Fine Arts Journal*, where it was displayed with modest success. Then in 1907 Edgar had it shipped back to Montana. En route back by train, it was snowed in on the Dakota prairies, within rifleshot of the trail Custer and his men followed to the Little Bighorn.

Once back in Montana the painting was displayed for eight months in Helena, the state capital, before being returned to Edgar's studio in Missoula. From then on Edgar made little effort to promote his masterpiece. It resided in relative obscurity for many years. He displayed it at the local Presbyterian Church on two occasions and once at the local "Apple Show." It hung for a time in the Florence Hotel in downtown Missoula, and incidentally, was unknowingly saved from destruction when it was removed, for in 1913 the hotel suffered a serious fire.

In 1910, Edgar moved the painting to the library of the University of Montana in Missoula. Sometime after his death it was moved to the Science Building where it remained in dimly lit seclusion until 1954. Then the Paxson heirs moved it to the Missoula Elks Lodge which perpetuated the painting's obscurity.

Through the years there were a number of attempts to sell the painting. In 1909 and 1915, several state legislators, urged by women's clubs and other service organizations, gave Edgar some hope that the State of Montana would buy it, but in the end the legislature failed to appropriate the funds. Just before his death in 1919, Edgar had correspondence with parties in Minnesota interested in the painting at $15,000. Then in 1920, the Montana State Federation of Women's Clubs tried to raise money to purchase the painting for display in the state capitol building. They were joined in their effort by school children and the Society of Montana Pioneers. Edgar's widow Laura offered the painting for $20,0000 the price her husband had set just prior to his death. A newspaper at the time reported that the states of Minnesota and Illinois had submitted offers of about $15,000. But no purchase was consummated. The Women's Club was only able to muster $1,000. This was finally used to buy a smaller Paxson, *Scouting for Custer* (20" x 31") in 1937.

Why Edgar's masterpiece did not achieve widespread fame is as debatable as the battle itself. It is apparent that Edgar himself was neither very adept nor exceptionally motivated in promoting his painting. There were Montanans who had a high regard for it, but they were few. Most Montanans were unaware of its existence. Curiously, most of its celebrity was outside the state. In 1920, Montana newspapers noted this irony in their efforts to publicize the Federated Women's Clubs' drive to buy the painting. By 1919, Edgar had what he called "a portofilo of comments from all over the world" on his masterpiece. In 1954, a featured article in the *Minneapolis Tribune* stated:

> It has been said that Montanans have been the slowest to recognize the worth of the painting. Elsewhere it has been acclaimed a masterpiece. Carveth Wells, explorer, author and lecturer, passed through Missoula a number of years ago when the painting was still hanging in one of the buildings of the University. He expressed indignant surprise that the famous painting was hanging in the "dimly lighted recesses" of the science hall. "In Lapland," continued Wells, "reproductions of the Paxson painting are seen frequently; in Africa the fame of the painting long has been spread; in London a man might raise his eyebrows when asked what a Minuteman was, but they all knew the Paxson painting of *Custer's Last Stand*. I have driven nearly 1,500 miles to see it, and to find it in such an obscure place seems pitiable in the face of its undeniable fame."[4]

Mr. Wells apparently was somewhat confused, because at that time there were no reproductions of Edgar's *Custer's Last Stand*. This suggests, perhaps, another reason why Edgar's painting suffered obscurity. The widely known Cassily Adams version of *Custer's Last Stand* was made so by the Anheuser-Busch Brewery which made lithographs based on the painting available to bars, saloons and restaurants around the world

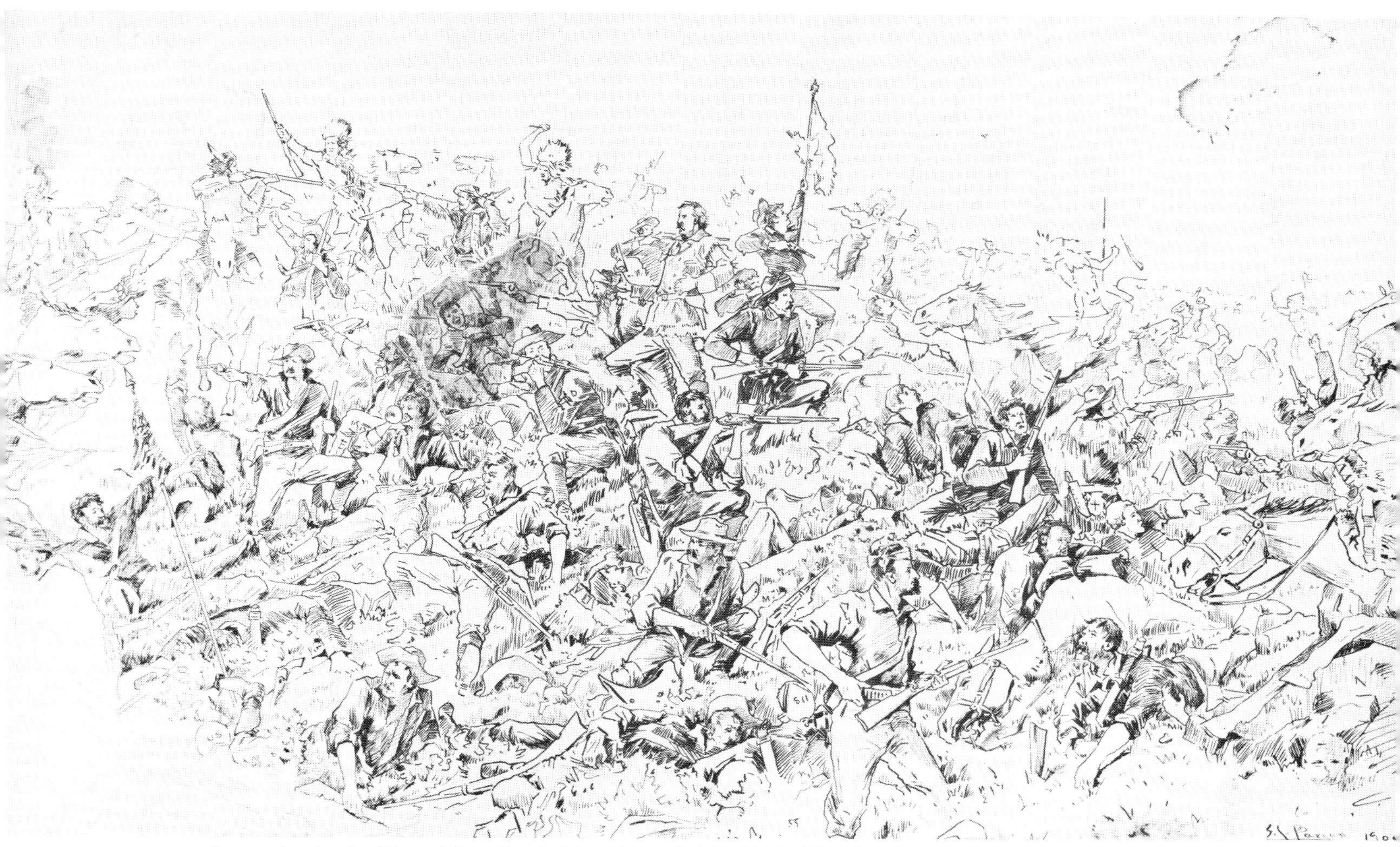

Layout drawing for "Custer's Last Stand. Ink and pencil, 16 x 24. *Buffalo Bill Historical Center, Cody, Wyoming.*

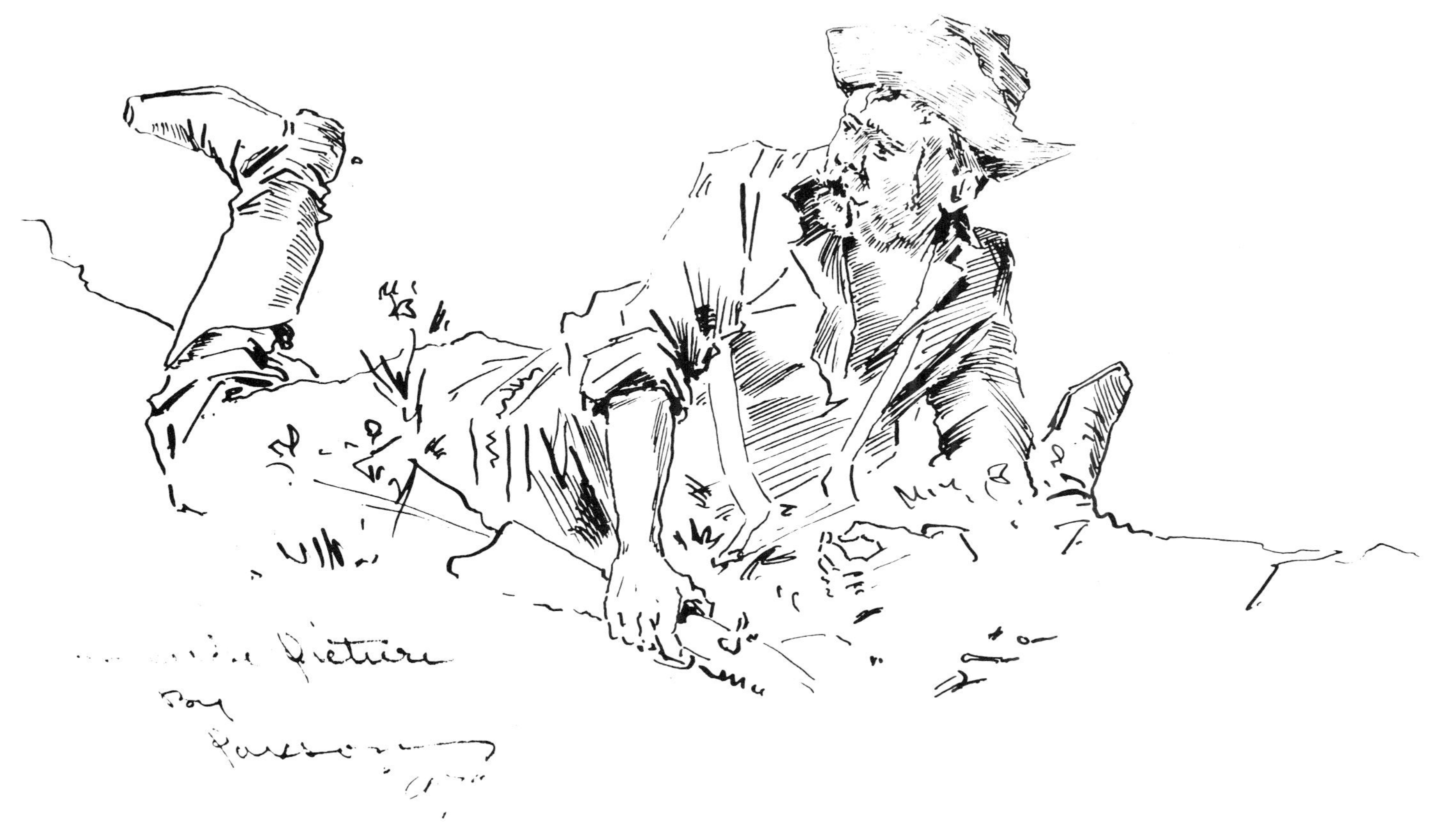

Preliminary study of figure in lower left of "Custer's Last Stand." Ink, 1897. *Buffalo Bill Historical Center, Cody, Wyoming.*

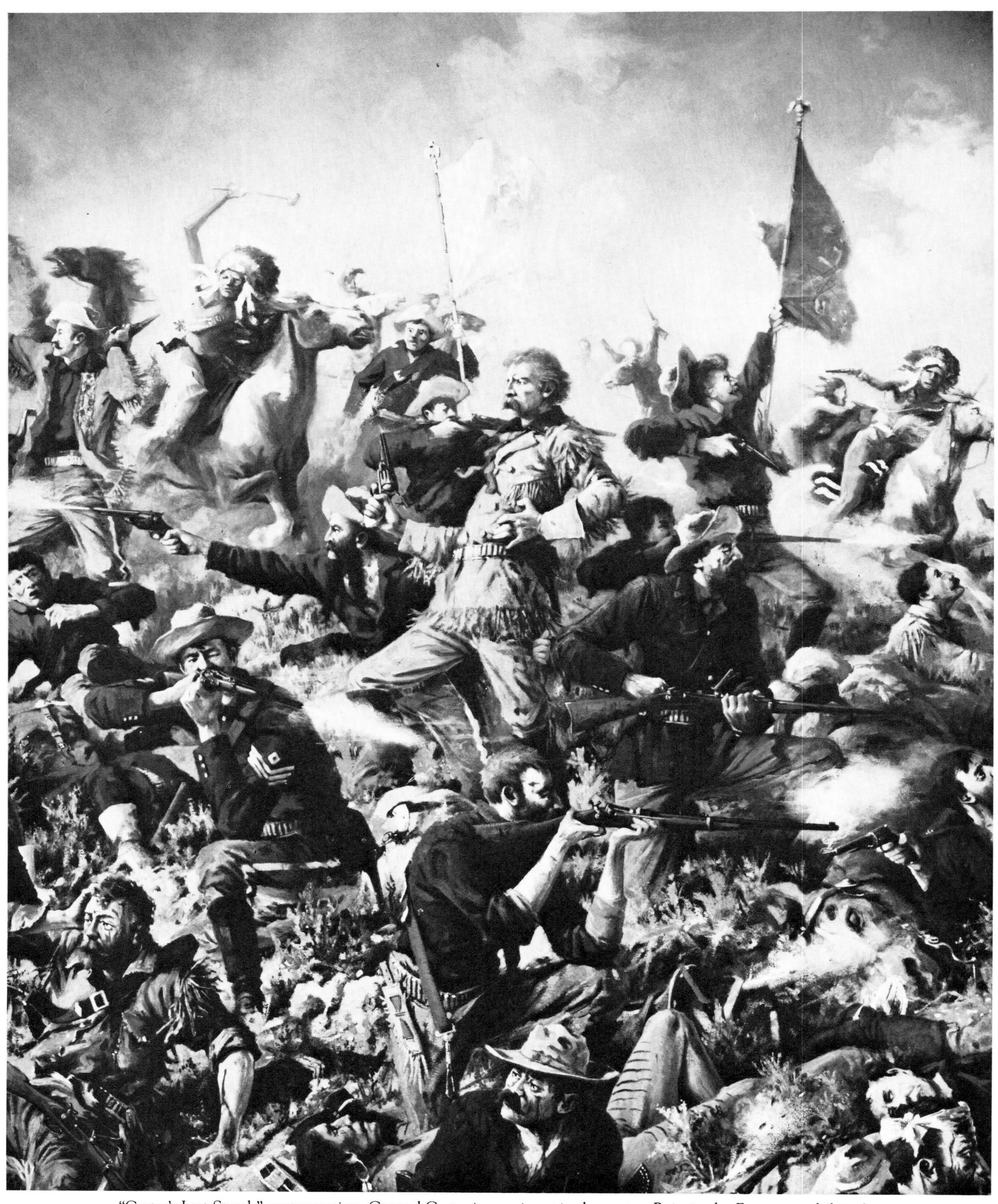

"Custer's Last Stand," center section. General Custer is prominent in the center. Rain-in-the-Face, upper left is about to strike Captain Tom Custer. *Buffalo Bill Historical Center, Cody, Wyoming.*

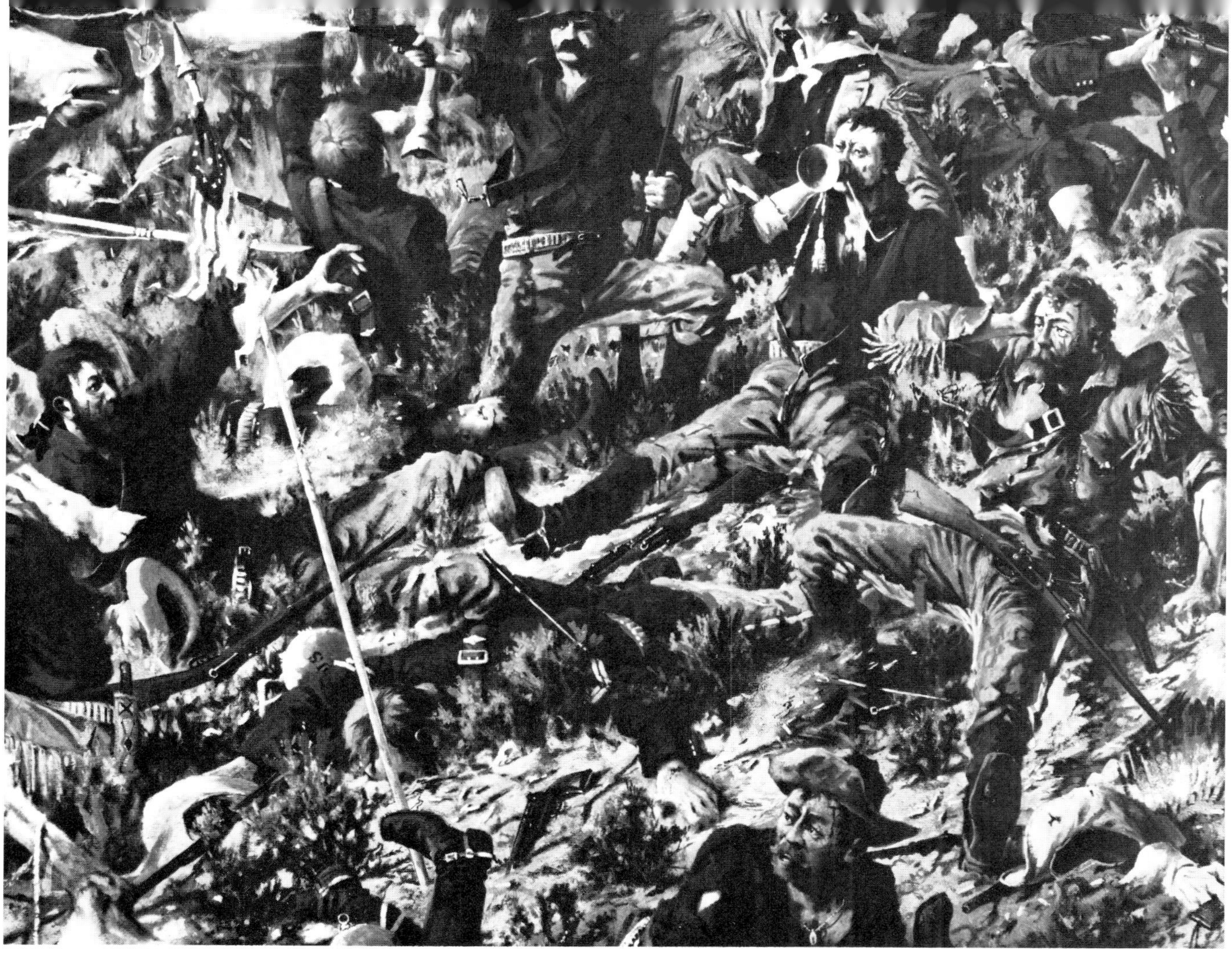

"Custer's Last Stand." Above: left-center section. Below: right-center section. *Buffalo Bill Historical Center, Cody, Wyoming.*

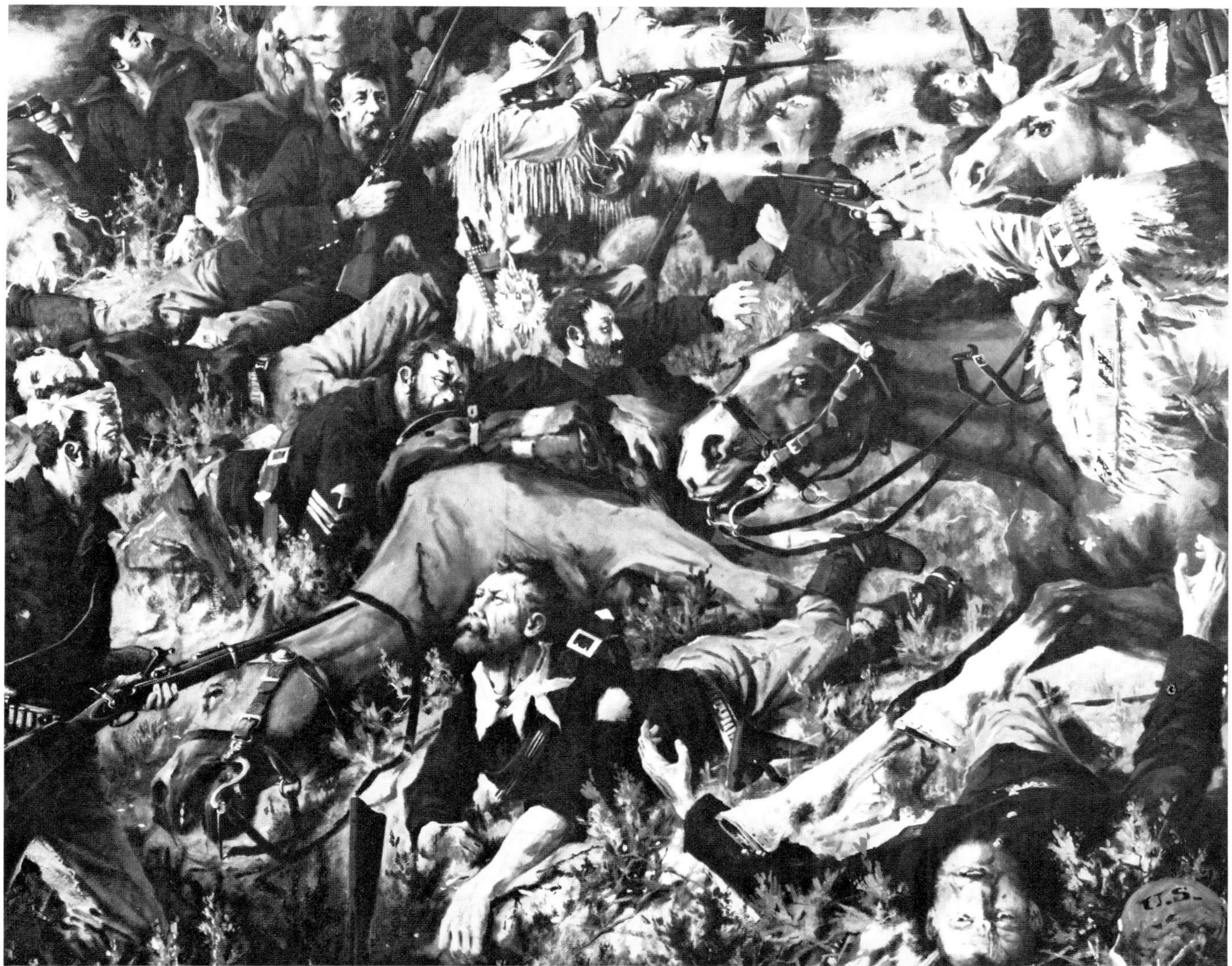

beginning in 1896 and continuing for many years. Despite the painting being both artistically and historically flawed (and destroyed by fire in 1946), it was the most publicized version of the battle. Edgar's is one of the many other versions which have hung in its shadow because of an advertising masterstroke by the beer company.

In 1962, the Paxson heirs loaned the painting to the Montana State Historical Society and appealed to the state to purchase it. They hoped for a sale because of a recent increase of interest across the country in western art and especially because of an increase in value of Paxson works. Many Montanans also hoped to see the state in possession of the painting, but it wasn't to be. The heirs learned that the legislature would appropriate only $9,500. Funds for such expenditures were an object of competition. A number of state officials and influential people preferred to reserve funds for purchases of Charles Russell's works, he being generally acknowledged the single greatest Montana artist. The Paxson heirs were dismayed not only by this but by disparaging comments about the Paxson painting made in public by the then director of the Montana Historical Society. The heirs felt that Edgar's reputation, which had just begun to grow, would be damaged severely if they did not reject the state.

The heirs then offered the painting to the Whitney Gallery of Western Art at the Buffalo Bill Historical Center Museum in Cody, Wyoming. Gallery director Dr. Harold McCracken, the noted author, art expert and historian, said that the Whitney Gallery would be most pleased to have the painting. He gladly agreed to the Gallery's purchase of the painting at the heirs asking price of $50,000. At the time he released a statement to the press and other media stating in part:

> Edgar S. Paxson's heroic size painting "Custer's Last Stand," is, in my opinion, one of the most important pictures in Western history...
>
> In my opinion, the Paxson painting is the best pictorial representation of all the pictures which have been created to immortalize that dramatic event.
>
> From a purely artistic standpoint, in my opinion, the Paxson painting is one of the best, if not the finest, by an artist who has long been recognized as one of the West's best historical painters. The fact is conclusively evident by a comparison which anyone can make by viewing it alongside lithographs of the other noted pictures which will be shown along with the Paxson work in the Whitney Gallery of Western Art in Cody next summer.

So in 1963, Edgar's documentary masterpiece was placed in a preferred position in the Whitney Gallery. Today the painting is valued at many times its 1963 purchase price and is seen by thousands of Americans annually.

A Descriptive Key to the Most Prominent Features in Custer's Last Stand

Edgar positioned the officers and cavalryment in the painting according to where they fell on the battlefield. To do so he referred to his correspondence with Gen. Edward S. Godfrey and markers on the battlefield itself.

GENERAL CUSTER stands prominently in the upper center of the painting, He wears the buckskin suit described in detail in General Godfrey's letter of January 16, 1896, to the artist. His gauntleted hand clutches a wound in his left side. His right hand holds a pearl-handled revolver that Godfrey described. His hair, which he commonly wore long, is shown cropped short, a precaution he took shortly before the battle, presumably to make his scalp less attractive to the enemy.

ADJUTANT W.W. COOKE kneels on one knee immediately behind General Custer. He fires a revolver with his right hand while making an effort to support the wounded general with his left.

To the left and a little farther up Custer Hill is the general's brother, CAPT. TOM CUSTER, in a buckskin shirt open in front. He fires one revolver while cocking the other over his shoulder. Godfrey noted in his descriptive letter that all the officers carried revolvers while no one carried the saber. Edgar armed his figures accordingly, with the correct Colt and Springfield weapons. Edgar also portrayed the unreliability (reported by Godfrey) of the 7th Cavalry's rifles. In the lower center of the painting can be seen a soldier anxiously trying to eject a jammed cartridge from his rifle with a knife.

Near Tom Custer, the mounted likeness of the young Sioux RAIN-IN-THE-FACE is about to strike the captain down from behind, avenging a long-time, and later much publicized grudge. Edgar is known to have met Rain-in-the-Face at least once, that in 1893.

To the right of Rain-in-the-Face is *GENERAL CUSTER'S PERSONAL BATTLE FLAG* of yellow intricately embroidered silk—the flag he had gained at Lee's surrender at Appomattox. Edgar did not paint this flag into the picture until 1908, after General Godfrey remarked on its absence from the painting during a visit to the artist's studio to see the completed work.

Farther right is the 7th Cavalry's purple satin banner.

In the distant right is a cavalryman mounted on a light gray horse and receiving a bullet. This is LT. JAMES CALHOUN, Custer's brother-in-law, who, according to General Godfrey, had apparently been riding toward Custer Hill from his initial position when shot. None of the other soldiers is shown mounted because it was the considered opinion of General Godfrey that Custer had ordered a dismount and removal to the rear of the horses at the outset of the battle.

Custer's half-breed scout MITCH BOYER is at right-center, clad in a buckskin suit and with a feather

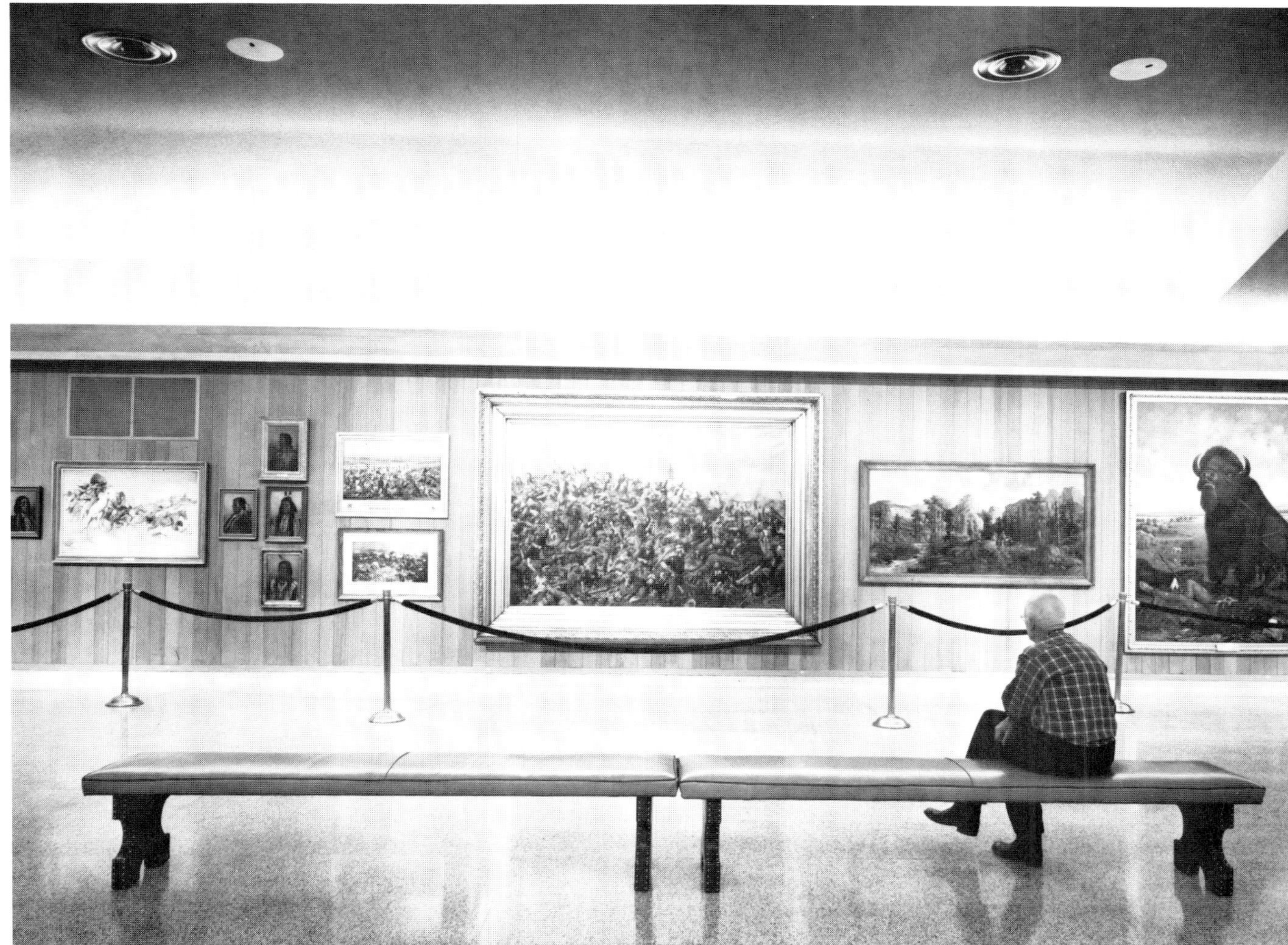

Dr. Harold McCraken, Director of the Buffalo Bill Historical Center, Cody, Wyoming, views "Custer's Last Stand" on display in the Whitney Gallery of Western Art at the Center, 1963. Paxson's "The Last Gleam" hangs to the right.

in his hat. He cooly fires his rifle at the on-coming figure of CRAZY HORSE, who, bearing the well-known scar on his cheek, raises a three-pronged war club.

Below Crazy Horse, crouched low on a captured mount bearing the brand of the U.S. Cavalry, is the Uncapapa Sioux chief, CROW KING.

CAPT. GEORGE YATES is immediately behind the trumpeter, center-left, having just fired a revolver with his right hand. He also wears a buckskin shirt. Godfrey noted the buckskins were popular among the officers, though most wore blue cavalry trousers, as shown in the painting.

TWO MOON , a Cheyenne who later befriended Edgar and described the battle in detail to him on the battlefield while they camped there together, is at the far left. Only his war-bonneted head and right hand holding a lance can be seen as he forces his pony into the fray.

In the left background, mounted on a white horse and directing the battle with an upraised right hand holding a rifle, is the Sioux war chief, GALL. He, too, in later years discussed the battle with Edgar at the scene of the tragedy.

On first viewing this documentary masterpiece, one anticipates finding many manifestations of blood and gore—arrows protruding from limbs and torsos, gaping skull wounds from scalpings, and war clubs imbedded in flesh. In fact, there is an absence of this dime novel sensationalism. What is manifest is a sense of action and anticipation. The drama of conflict is heightened to a marvelous degree by a prodigious yet careful use of detail and believably vital postures and expressions of the figures. Especially impressive are the horses.

Much of documentary western art has been criticized for extravagance of detail by "main-stream" art critics. They contend that detail detracts from the overall statement of a painting. And so Edgar's documentary painting with its two hundred figures has been called "too busy." Yet the documentary nature of Edgar's monumental work would surely suffer from a lessening of detail. Is there indeed always a trade-off between these two aspects? Or can detail be handled with such genius as to enhance rather than detract from the impact of a painting? If it is true that "a work of art is great in ratio of its power of stirring the highest emotions of the largest number of cultured people for the longest period of time,"[5] then Edgar's CUSTER'S LAST STAND, now that it has been recovered from obscurity, may well prove in time that documentary detail, brilliantly handled, is a means to achieving greatness in painting.

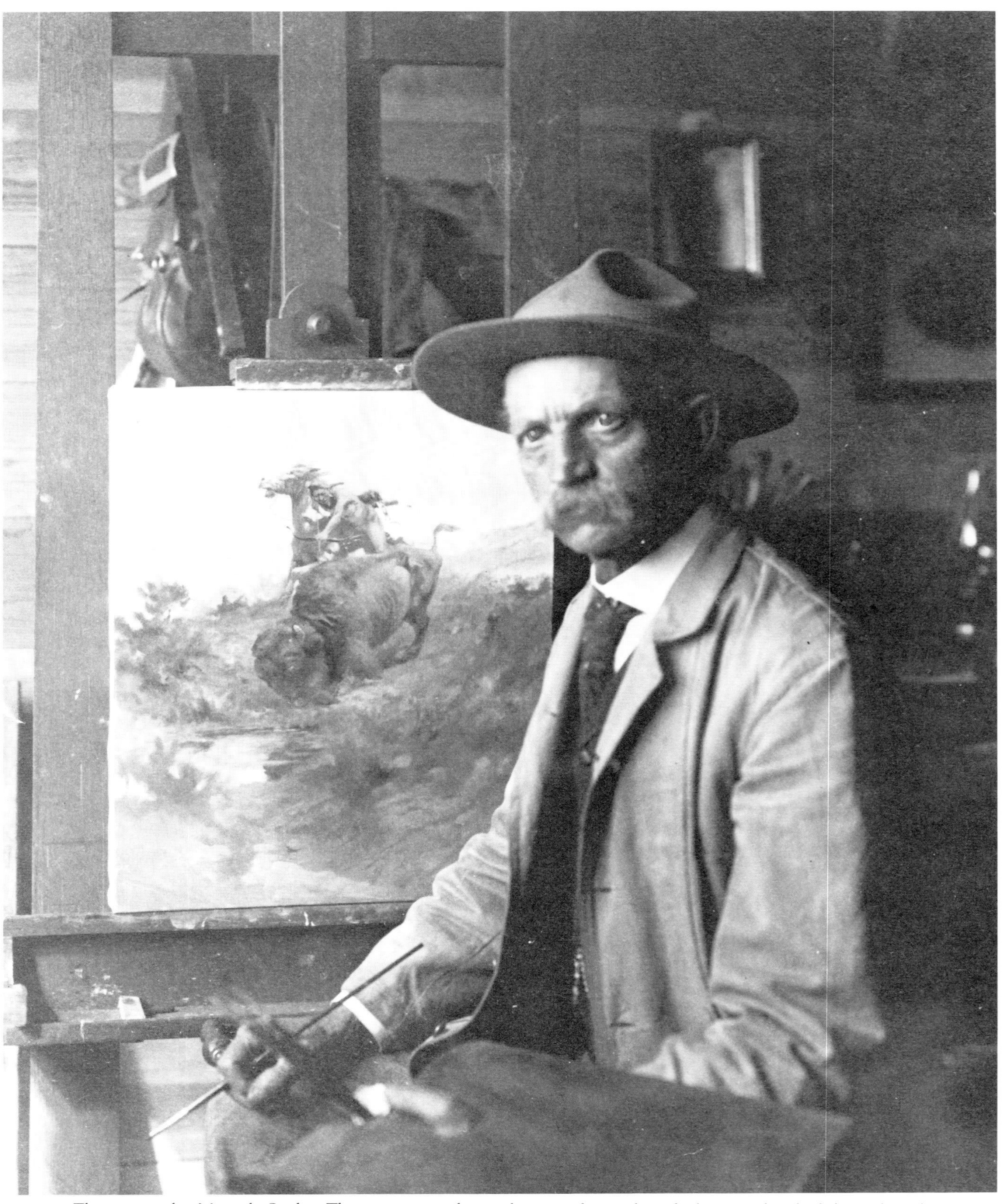

The artist in his Missoula Studio. The painting on the easel is one of a number of Edgar's works which have slipped from public view over the decades. Its title and whereabouts are not known to the author. *Montana Historical Society, Helena, Montana. Photo furnished by Dick Ettinger.*

7

Successful Artist of the Old West

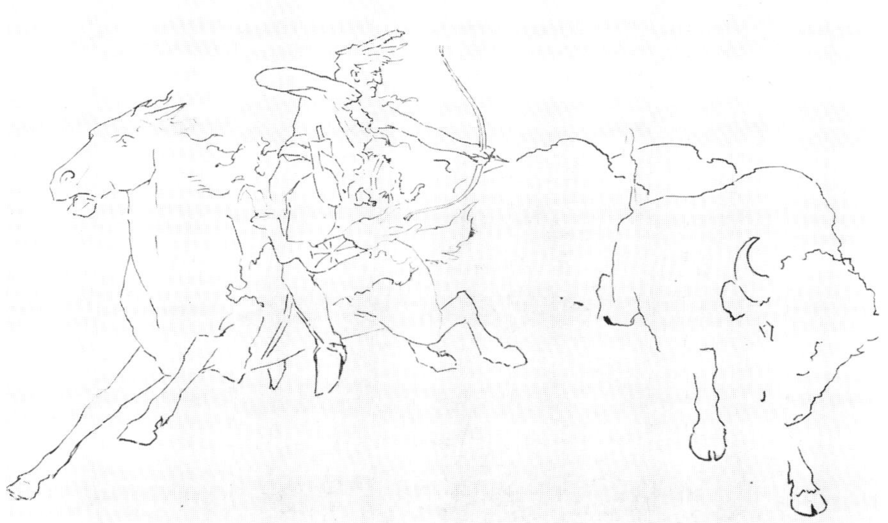

Working drawing in ink for oil painting. *Private Collection.*

In 1899, as Edgar was recuperating from his service in the Philippines, he found that his war experiences had contributed to his already considerable celebrity around Butte. After the fighting resumed against the Filipino insurgents, many of his son Harry's letters were published in their entirety in local papers, which kept the Paxson name in the headlines. And Butte citizens were impressed by the pretentious triumphal arch and statue Edgar had created to welcome home the troops. Edgar soon found that local people were enthusiastically buying his paintings of western scenes. He painted as much as his unstable health would let him, displaying his works in the window of B. E. Calkins Bookstore. In April, just four months after his return to Montana, he reported in his journal that several of his paintings displayed at Calkins' were sold. In May he wrote "I can hardly paint them fast enough for the demand." He even neglected completion of his Custer painting for several weeks to devote his time to smaller works for immediate sale. He worked determinedly and with success. About this time, he began painting his now well-known and coveted watercolor Indian "heads" for which he received five to fifteen dollars each.

In August Edgar displayed his just completed *Grandpa's Luck* at Calkins' store. A tribute to the "mountain man of the old school," it is one of Edgar's finest works and attracted considerable attention from passersby while in Calkins' window.

Perhaps painting *Grandpa's Luck* was somehow curative for Edgar. Certainly the inspiration to portray such a captivating scene must have also quickened Edgar's desire to be again trailing game in the high country. Shortly after the painting appeared at Calkins', Edgar set aside his brushes and took his family on a ten-day camping trip by horse drawn wagon. It was a wonderful rejuvenation for Edgar. Although he had needed a cane to get around only two months before, he and his young son, Bob, tramped as much as ten miles at a time on day hikes. On the seventh day a snowstorm descended on their camp. Far from being dismayed, Edgar was overjoyed, for this laid down an ideal "tracking snow," something that stirs the blood of every ardent hunter. Off went Edgar and his ten-year-old son on another ten-mile tramp into country mantled with snow just like that portrayed in *Grandpa's Luck*. They saw plenty of "sign" left by deer and bear, and they shot some grouse for dinner. On return to Butte, Edgar happily reported in his journal, "I feel much improved in health." By the fall of 1900, he was back in his old hunting form. He went on two extended hunts in November and December of that year in the region at the head of the Boulder River and Powder Horn Creek. His old friend, Granville Stuart, the famous Montana pioneer, accompanied him on one of the trips. That winter the Paxson larder was well stocked with venison.

Occasionally travelers from the East would buy a Paxson painting to take home with them, but up to 1900, Edgar was still virtually unknown outside Montana. In July 1899, a representative of Kleckner and Co. of New York City, one of the nation's largest art dealers at the time, requested several of Edgar's paintings to be offered for sale in the East. Edgar supplied him with at least four. There is also some evidence that Edgar had sent paintings east to be sold by Kleckner as early as 1897, but there is no other indication of his work being known in the East before the showing of *Custer's Last Stand* by Brackett in mid-1900.[1] Despite the difficulties owing to Brackett's personal problems and subsequent suicide, the big painting's showings were undoubtedly the primary reason for Edgar's work becoming known nationally. Throughout 1901, Edgar found his work, particularly his Indian scenes, to be the object of widespread publicity in the East.

The first development occurred in late 1900 when Edgar received a letter from Marion A. White, editor of the Chicago-based *Fine Arts Journal*, inquiring about his life and work. The result was an article in the January issue of the magazine giving a glowing description of his work and a somewhat romanticized biographical sketch. The paintings Edgar had recently sent east to Kleckner and Co. were reproduced in the article as was a photo of Edgar clad in his hunting clothes. Edgar's work was also illustrated and reviewed in subsequent issues and generated so many reader inquiries that the October issue was published with a supplemental matted two-color reproduction of *The Parting Shot,* one of the paintings shown in the January issue.

The substantial reader response to Edgar's paintings was just one manifestation of the prevalent curiosity of Easterners about "Wild Indians." This was at a time when Buffalo Bill's Wild West Show and several imitators were still drawing crowds. Captain Jack Crawford, the "Poet-Scout" packed them into his vaudeville show of poems and tales of Indian warfare. Edgar's realistic Indian action scenes were what the public wanted. Soon after Edgar's work first appeared in the *Fine Arts Journal*, many eastern newspapers took advantage of the continuing Indian craze by supplementing their Sunday issues with reproductions of Edgar's paintings. Even though the newspapers often acted without Edgar's authorization, he was thereby provided with a free means of becoming better known to the general public. Edgar first became aware of the situation in April 1901 when Marian White sent him a newspaper clipping from the *Chicago Herald-Record* saying "In next Sunday's issue, we will publish a full page supplement, *A Race for Life* by the famous Indian painter S. (*sic*) S. Paxson. If you want a fine picture...now is the time to subscribe."[2] Edgar was quite certain he had never painted a picture by that name. When he secured a copy of the Sunday issue, he discovered that the print was of one of three figures in *Jumping the Game* which he had recently sold through a dealer in Pennsylvania. Edgar learned three months later that the dealer had sold the painting to a firm in Boston which had had it copyrighted and reproduced. Yet Edgar had still not received payment for the original. That same year, again without permission, the *Boston Sunday Journal* and the *St. Louis Globe-Democrat* published three-color reproductions of the *The Chase*, depicting a mounted Indian spearing a buffalo. Over the next two years, the *Chicago Tribune, Chicago Chronicle* and the *New York Journal* offered Paxson prints in a similar manner and the *St. Louis Globe-Democrat* offered a second print, *Injun's B'Gosh*.

Edgar began selling paintings across the country as a result of all the publicity. In 1901, dealers in San Francisco, Chicago, Boston, New York and elsewhere wrote him requesting to be his agent. He sent paintings as far as Portland, Maine, on consignment. Dr. Everett Culver, son-in-law of Montana mining pioneer Senator W. A. Clark, became very interested in Edgar's work and took several paintings to New York City, dispersing them among his wealthy friends there. Kennedy-Robjohn Art Company, Edgar's agent in San Francisco, sold several paintings in a short time. Edgar himself sold the sizable *Sitting Bull in the Big Horn Mountains* to a buyer in Ohio, sight unseen. Some paintings were even sold to buyers in Europe and South Africa.

At the same time Edgar received several requests by prominent authors to illustrate their new books. He quickly completed seven black and white paintings for *By Order of the Prophet—A Tale of Utah* by Alfred H. Henry and at least three paintings for *Glengarry School Days* by Ralph Connor, both books being published in 1902.

Edgar's work also appeared in magazines devoted to hunters and outdoorsmen. He wrote and illustrated the story of "Beaver Dick" for the national magazine *Outdoor Life* and did a cover drawing for *Roughrider.* In 1902, *Outdoor Life* published an illustrated article of his life and work and a long article about him appeared in a New York newspaper.

Montana newspapers regularly ran articles about Edgar's latest work along with anecdotes about his early years in the state. Many were illustrated or supplemented with color prints. Usually when a new Paxson painting was displayed in Calkins' window, the Butte newspapers would report on it. It was not unusual for the street in front of the store to be blocked by a crowd of people at these times. One time Edgar had fun painting the walls surrounding the display window to represent the interior of a log cabin complete with fireplace. He hung up Indian curios on the walls along with old rifles and pistols; set snowshoes by the fireplace; spread bear and mountain lion skins, blankets and Indians pillows on the floor; and draped his buckskin coat over an old bench. On an easel he put his latest painting and hung his old hat on the easel's corner, as was his custom in his studio. He reported in his journal, "When they took down the screen (hiding the window) a hundred people were soon assembled. Soon they were (overflowing) out in the streets." Each day for a week afterward, Edgar did a little on a painting and placed it on the easel in the window each evening. That the people of Butte as well as visiting Easterners enjoyed and purchased his paintings was most fulfilling for Edgar. He had the satisfaction of being paid for what he loved to do.

But Edgar's recognition across the country did not make him wealthy. Many times he did not get the remuneration for his work that he could have. Sometimes it was due to his own lack of effort or business sense, sometimes to unprincipled business practices by his associates, and sometimes to plain bad luck.

He certainly should have protected his major works from unauthorized reproduction by copyrighting them. In addition to those aggressive business types who copyrighted his paintings themselves and those who simply borrowed them from their new owners to make prints, some were so unscrupulous as to have prints made from Edgar's paintings on consignment but as yet unsold. In one instance, a Chicago agent received

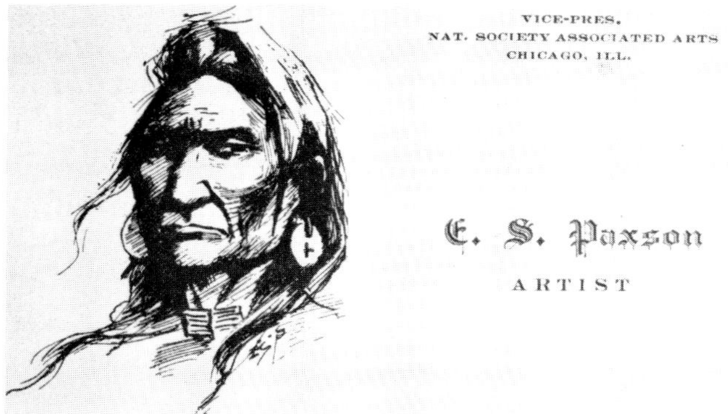

The business card Paxson used from 1903-1906.

a fee for allowing several of Edgar's consigned paintings to be reproduced without the artist's consent. Some agents were also delinquent in paying Edgar for paintings sold. One in particular owed Edgar several hundred dollars for a number of years, from paintings sold in Portland, Maine. By chance Edgar saw him on the street in Missoula and collared him. As for the others, Edgar was not willing to chase them across the country.

Perhaps one of the most important reasons Edgar did not become rich is that he did not raise the prices of his paintings significantly when demand for them increased. He held to his old prices even when he could not paint fast enough to satisfy the demand. In 1903, a small watercolor Indian head by Paxson could be had for $10–$20, only a couple dollars more than a similar head in 1900. His large oils did not bring more than $400, under $200 was more usual.

Luck has always played some role in financial success of artists. Perhaps Edgar's worst luck was the untimely death of Colonel Brackett. But successful businessmen contribute to their own good fortune. Edgar could have capitalized on his battle masterpiece had he gone east and applied himself to the mundane activity of generating dollars. But clearly his personality was not suited to promotional work. Edgar was a simple man with simple wants. He loved his home and family. Whether consciously or unconsciously, he opted to continue as he had done in past years: painting regularly, camping with his family every summer, hunting with his old comrades in the fall and spending quiet evenings at home reading histories of the early West or exchanging yarns with old-timers. In so doing he provided adequately for his family. He never indicated that he wanted more.

Edgar's reticence about discussing himself publically appears repeatedly in his writings. In 1906, he wrote in his journal, "I hope there will be no more interviews soon as I don't like them." He was especially sensitive to overstatements about his adventures in the early days. In one brief biographical sketch submitted to him for correction, he struck out, "He became known as one of the best scouts in the Northwest." Upon receiving Enos Mill's article for editing prior to publication in *Outdoor Life* in 1902, Edgar mentioned in his journal that he would "tone it down some." Of an article by old friend "Sandbar" Brown in the *Daily Missoulian*, Edgar wrote: "[He] gives me some romantic stuff. The 'Indian fighter' is all rot."

There are other examples of Edgar's distaste for drawing attention to himself. A former resident of Butte once recalled that as a boy of about twelve, he met a man while fishing near town. The two became fishing companions, meeting at local ponds and streams. The youth developed a tremendous admiration for his older companion owing to the man's ability to catch fish and tell stories of frontier days. The man was, of course, Edgar, but the two fished together many times before the boy knew his friend was the well-known artist.[3]

A similar instance happened in 1907 when James A. Garfield, then secretary of the interior, came to Missoula and spoke during the local Fourth of July celebration. Afterward the secretary had to hurry on to the Flathead Reservation and was unable to visit Edgar's studio as had been planned. Garfield did, however, take a few minutes after his speech to shake hands with several local citizens, among them Edgar and his elderly father. Edgar (who had never before met Garfield) wrote of the meeting in his journal: "Mr. Garfield mentioned [to Edgar's father] his regret that he was unable to see me and the studio. I did not make myself known."

In 1903, Edgar made his one important trip east to further his career. The trip occurred in response to an invitation by Marian White who was then president of the Society of Associated Arts in Chicago. She informed Edgar he had been elected a member of the society and was therefore eligible to show his work at the annual exhibit. She also opened up her home to him, even providing him space for a temporary studio. He spent seven very fruitful weeks there. He received excellent reviews of his work at the exhibit, sold several paintings and illustrated another book, *The Man on the Edge of Things* by Ella Peattie, a story of life on a California sheep ranch. He also delivered sixteen black and white paintings completed just prior to his trip for use in *On the Trail of Lewis and Clark* by Olin D. Wheeler, published in 1904.

While in Chicago Edgar went to the fine arts museums. There he saw originals of celebrated artists of the day and perhaps even some old masters. This was one of the few brief instances in his life that he had such an opportunity. He also visited the Art Institute of Chicago and the Chicago Academy of Fine Arts. At both, the facilities were made available to him. At the academy, the head instructor offered Edgar the opportunity to attend the life study class at any time, where there was a young woman posing in the nude. Edgar stayed only long enough to be polite. He did not feel at home in that atmosphere. In fact his stay in Chicago was to him something to be endured. He became aware of that at the very beginning—at the exhibition's opening day reception of 1,000 patrons, critics and artists. After two weeks he wrote in his journal: "I have been longing for home all day. I am tired of this noisy whirl." And a week later he wrote: "I would not give a week of Montana for the whole of Chicago. I am so sick and tired of it all. As soon as I get through I will hit the trail for home."

To fortify himself against the "noisy whirl," Edgar often arose early for a long walk through the woods or down to the shores of the lake near the White's home on the outskirts of the city. As always, he was intimate with the history of the ground he trod. He noted in his journal obscure events involving Indians and whites along the trails he strolled. And he noted the geese flying north overhead, which made him long even more for his mountain home.

But for his career, the trip was a success: he was elected a vice president of the Society of Associated Arts; the newspapers had given him considerable favorable attention; and he went west with more orders than he could complete in several months.

On his way home he stopped to visit relatives on their farm in Wisconsin. He proved he had not gotten a swelled head from his recent success: he went out in the fields planting corn and potatoes, fed the chickens, made butter and separated cream. Then he and his Uncle Orlando, the old forty-niner, went fishing and had a good gam about the old days.

Once back in Butte, Edgar went back to work immediately at his easel. He liked to put in eight to ten hours a day if possible, weekends included. But he was often handicapped by lack of good light. He insisted on painting by sunlight so whenever it was cloudy or smokey he had to set his brushes aside. He frequently wrote in his journal of frustrating days when "flying clouds" would intermittently block the sun. But the smoke of Butte's smelters was his worst nemesis. It blocked the sun like fog. Often it was impossible to see more than fifty feet on the street. On one gloomy winter day in 1901 Edgar wrote in his journal: "Smoke dam thick—it has for four weeks been so smoky that it is a task to live. Three hours of pure daylight is about all we get. The balance is damned smoke." Edgar was most frustrated when he received an inspiration—the "ghost," he called it—to paint but there was not enough light to work. He hated to set aside a large oil for lack of light because often the ghost would leave him and when he resumed work on the painting, a new ghost would take hold and force him to redo much of what he had done before. For this reason he worked little in oil during the short winter days, concentrating instead on small watercolors he could dash off when the sun broke through.

Sometimes the ghost would flee overnight while Edgar was working on a large oil. Then the work became what he called a "hoodoo." No amount of thought, study or work would bring about the effect he wanted. Sometimes he had ten or twelve unfinished hoodoos in the studio at once, but he invariably worked through them, even if they sat untouched for months.

At those times when the ghost was elusive, Edgar would often sketch new work to bring the spirit forth. At other times he would persist working on a problem in a painting the more it puzzled him. Once he wrote, "I am having more trouble with a little measely yaller dog than with anything I ever introduced into a picture." The next day he added, "I worked all day on that cur and finally rubbed him out." But the third day the ghost appeared. He wrote, "[I] put the cur in in five minutes, so I think he will *stay*."

Sometimes the ghost would embrace Edgar in the midst of his various day-to-day business. Then out would come his sketch pad. His grandson William remembers numerous mealtimes when the artist would suddenly excuse himself and rush to the studio to sketch out an idea.

Even when the ghost was attending, it was unusual for Edgar to complete an oil painting without some reworking. He once quickly painted in the horse ridden by John Bozeman in a mural for the state capitol while visitors looked on. He did it so rapidly that his audience was extremely impressed. He noted in his journal, however, that it was really "a chance shot."

Edgar still had many opportunities to paint the Indian from life. There is a story that he would often bail an Indian out of city jail in Butte, sketch him, pay him a dollar for being a model and send the puzzled man on his way.[4] Whether or not this story is true, it was well known that Edgar's studio was open to any Indian. He once wrote in his journal, "Every Redskin knows my shop." Many of his Indian friends often visited him in the studio, bringing their friends to see Edgar's delineations of buffalo hunts and other traditional Indian activities which had become only memories. Edgar often sketched the Indians while they gazed intently at one of his paintings or studied some piece of curios. Sometimes he payed them to sit for portraits.

One of Edgar's favorite subjects was Nag-a-shaw, half-brother of Ten Doy, chief of the Lemhi Bannock-Shoshone band. Nag-a-shaw had served as a scout for Generals Terry and Crook against the Sioux in 1876–77 and for Generals Miles and Howard against the Nez Percé in 1877. Edgar had first met him during the Nez Percé campaign. He made reference to the Indian in a 1901 entry in his journal:

> I secured 3 sketches of him in a pose of "good intentions," and "an offering," also a good "head." He is very intelligent and knows just what is wanted. He often gets down a gun or a tomahawk, or some pieces of Indian dress or accoutrements and strikes a pose with such grace and dignity as to make one wish he could do him in each and every one. He will sit all day for $1.00/hr. I often give him two-bits for simply drawing him in a five minute sketch.

Nag-a-shaw also helped Edgar in his preparatory research for painting. For *Jefferson Canyon*, which depicts the old Indian trail to the buffalo country, Edgar

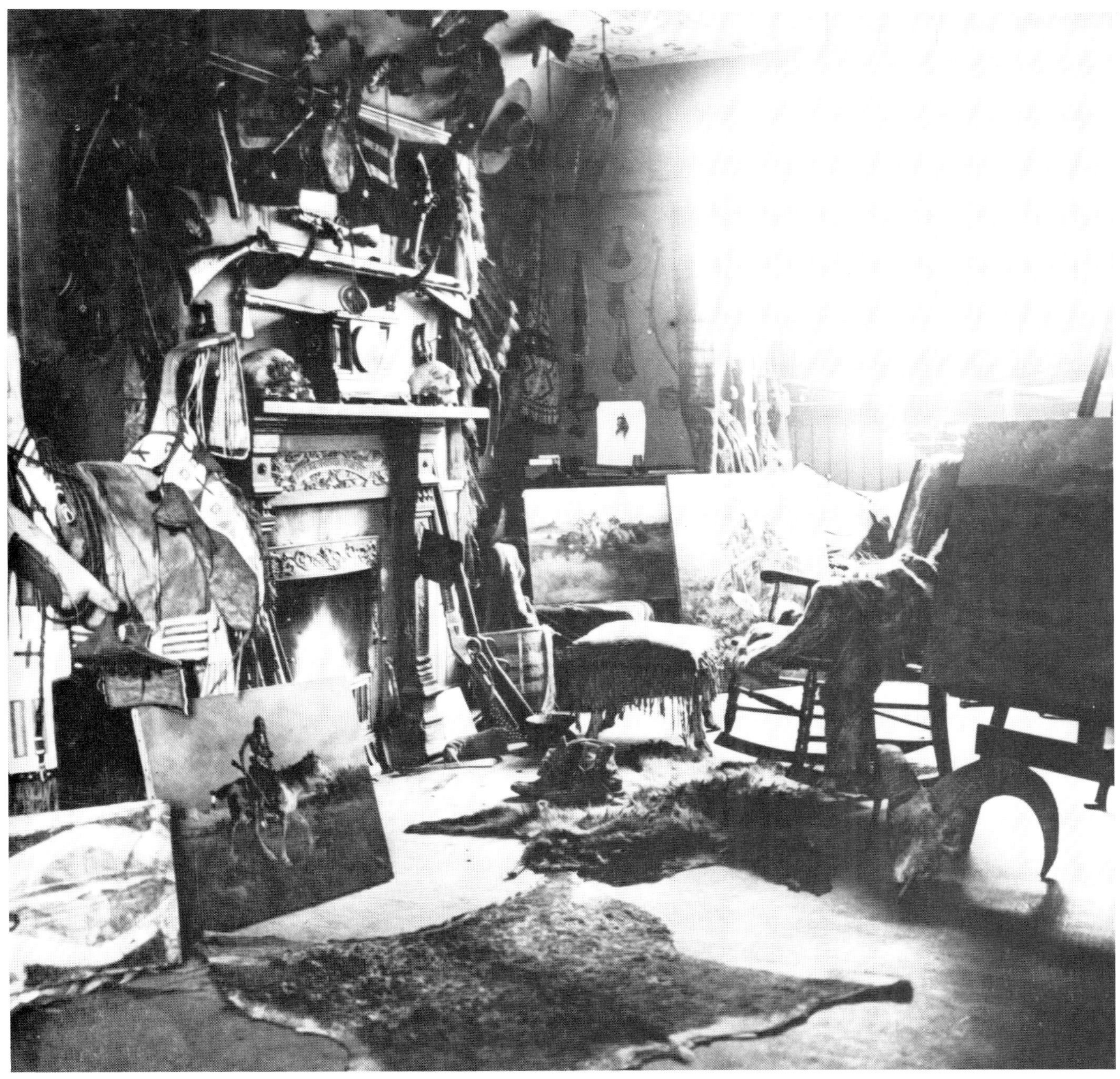

The Butte studio at 30 East Woolman, 1905.

noted that the Indian helped him "to define the trail and incidents which have transpired upon it."

Often Indian visitors brought Edgar gifts of Indian garb and accessories. By 1905, Edgar's collection had grown to over 600 pieces. His studio became a local tourist attraction, sometimes attracting 40–50 visitors a day on the weekend. Although the visitors often interrupted his work, he very rarely turned them away. Many times, when the ghost was with him, he kept on working while talking with his guests. In fact, his grandson William remembers that his grandfather talked incessantly while painting if there were visitors. One interviewer for a local newspaper found that stories of the early days flowed most easily from the artist while he was working at his easel.

Despite the hundreds of visitors over the years, for a long time Edgar never thought to charge admission to his "museum," until it was suggested to him by a tourist from the East. Not until 1919 did he finally put out a box marked "donations."

National recognition continued for Edgar. In 1904, his paintings, including his *Custer's Last Stand* brought excellent reviews at the St. Louis Louisiana Purchase Exposition and resulted in several sales. The Montana legislature passed a resolution of thanks for his contributions to the exhibit. He also received considerable press coverage for his display at the 1905 Lewis and Clark Exposition in Portland, Oregon. His *Saca-ja-wea* was especially well received there. Articles in national magazines on his life and work continued to appear. This was the time of his greatest national acclaim. For the first five years of the century he was very likely

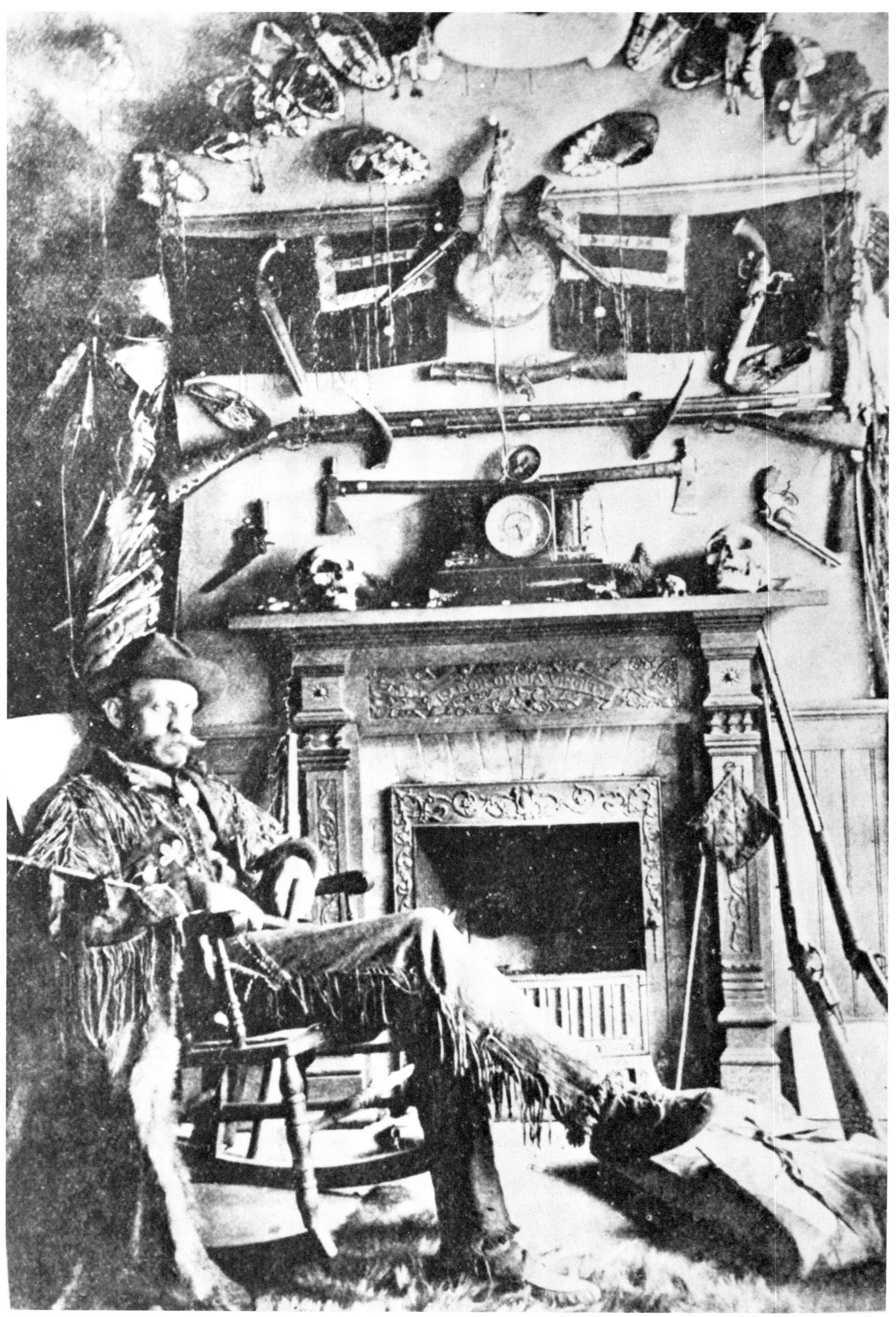

The artist in his Butte Studio, 1905.

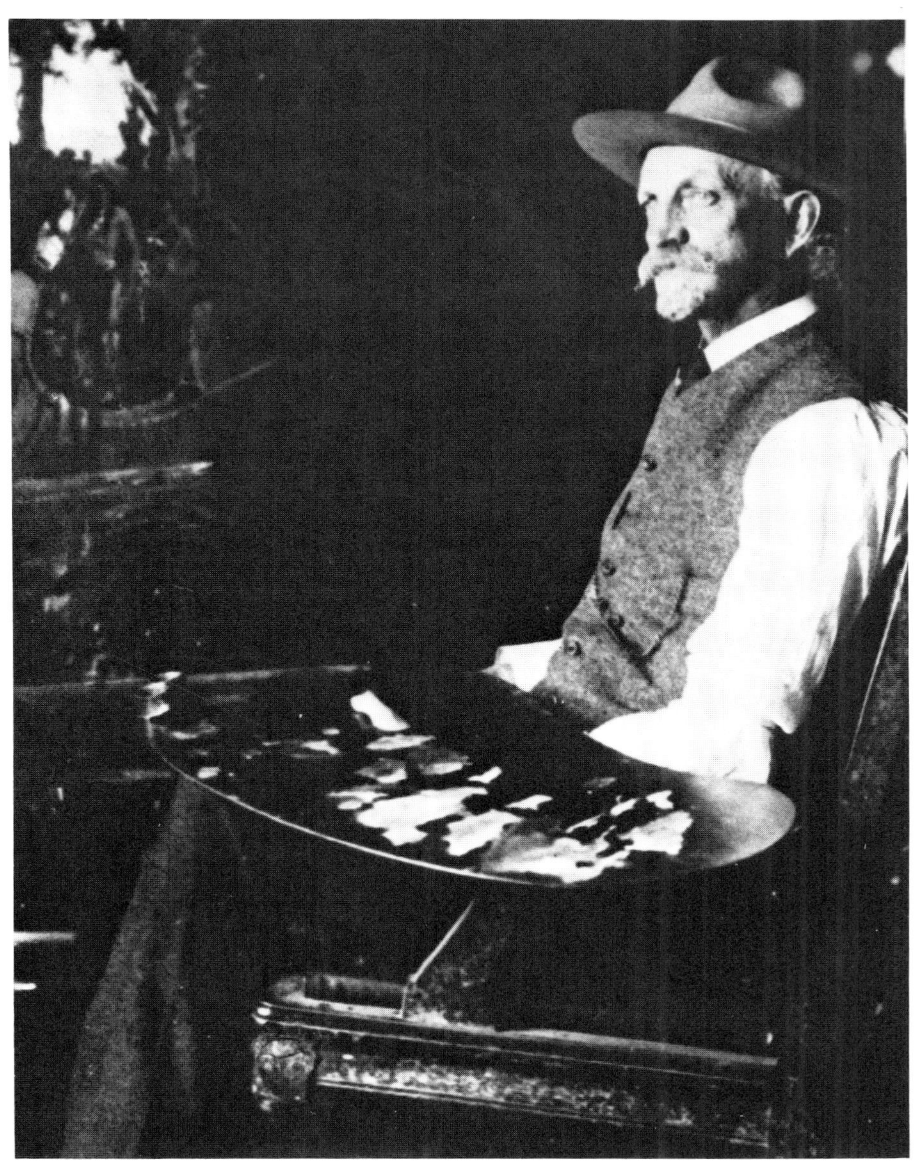

The artist at his easel, 1912.

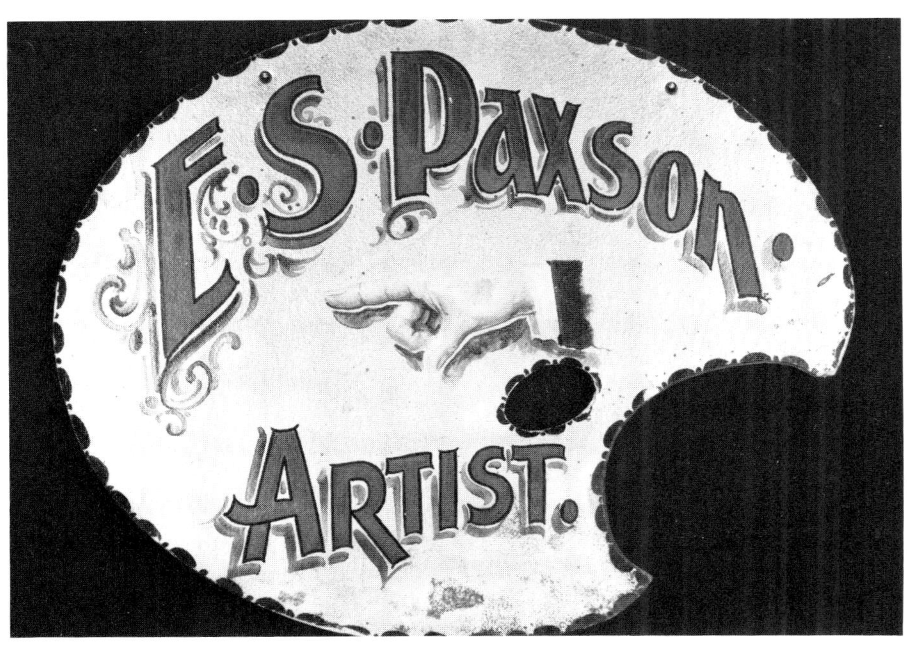

Sign done by Paxson, directing visitors to his studio.

the best-known painter of western scenes living in the West. Only Remington, who was an Easterner, had an undisputed greater reputation as a painter of the Old West during these years, though Charles Schreyvogle, also an Easterner, was achieving acclaim for his action paintings of Indian-cavalry warfare. But in 1901 the *St. Louis Globe Democrat* went so far as to call Edgar "the foremost Indian Painter of America."[5] In 1905 the *Fine Arts Journal* called Edgar, "the doyen of a group of clever and original painters in Montana—Paxson, Russell and Gollings."[6] Charles Russell's work did not achieve national acclaim until shortly thereafter when Brown and Bigelow "discovered" him by reproducing his paintings on thousands of calendars. But while Russell's career soared in the next ten years, Edgar's leveled off. In 1915, Russell oils were bringing several thousand dollars apiece while comparatively sized Paxson's continued to bring rarely more than $500. Schreyvogle paintings also were bringing more than that amount. In 1912, just after Schreyvogle's death at age fifty-one, his well-known *My Bunkie* brought $10,000. Yet Edgar continued to work as before and sold his paintings as rapidly as he painted them even with publicity of his work declining somewhat outside of Montana.

In 1906, Edgar and Laura could no longer stand polluted and noisy Butte. Laura's health was in jeopardy. Their home had become surrounded by mines and railroads and the streets of the neighborhood were overrun with young toughs. The week they sold their house a man shot and killed his wife three doors down and in a separate incident a policeman firing a pistol chased a youth past the house.

The Paxsons relocated in Missoula and immediately realized they had made the right decision. Laura's health improved and Edgar found good hunting and fishing within walking distance of their new home. It was situated on the outskirts of town with plenty of fruit trees surrounding it.

Edgar immediately set to work remodeling the house and turning an outbuilding on the property into his new studio. He felled trees in the forest and enlarged the building, using split logs with the bark left on to create a pleasing rustic effect. With the addition of a fireplace, the new building provided a studio and gallery comfortable the year around.

Edgar even made furniture for the house and studio. He always had projects underway such as a new chicken coop or cement walkway. He wrote in his journal in 1908, "I still love to use my tools as when a boy."

Throughout the transition period to his new home and studio, and afterward, Edgar continued to produce paintings with his usual skill and dedication, but the business end of his career was still distasteful to him. He continued to have trouble getting remuneration from agents who sold his paintings. In one instance he was paid seven years after the painting was sold. In another he received payment for a painting which he had completely forgotten about. He lost two oils and twelve watercolors in the 1906 San Francisco earthquake, all uninsured, and had several paintings lost or ruined during shipping. Finally, in 1908 he agreed to have B. E. Caulkins be his sole agent for one year so he would not be bothered with business for a while, at least.

During this time he did a few book illustrations and some cover drawings for *Overland Monthly Magazine*. Also some Montana firms paid him to use his paintings in advertising on blotters and calendars. One Butte company, McKee Printing, issued a series of postcards with some of his watercolor Indian heads as subjects. It is interesting that Brown and Bigelow, the company that made Russell famous, also wrote to Edgar ordering a picture for reproduction on a calendar. What became of the order is unknown and thought provoking.

For a little extra income, Edgar gave art lessons occasionally, a practice he began in Deer Lodge and continued in Butte. Sometimes he had as many as four or five students at once, but at other times, he discontinued the lessons completely for several months when he could not keep up with the demand for his work.

In 1910, Edgar suffered a personal tragedy. One January evening he received the news by telephone that his son Harry, only twenty-nine years old, had been electrocuted while on the job as electrician on a ruby dredge near Butte. The young man left a wife and two young sons—he had had much to look forward to in his life. Edgar was stunned; he seemed to have lost part of himself permanently. Thereafter he seemed to age more rapidly. Soon several increasingly severe health problems troubled him. But he was by nature an optimist and refused to succumb to his pains and periods of melancholy. He reiterated many times in his journal that he had indeed been a fortunate man overall despite his share of personal tragedies. He continued to paint, his determination to carry on overpowering his sadness and discomfort. He did some of his most important work over the next several years. And although he received little publicity outside the state, he was well known to collectors of western art as proven by undiminished sales of his paintings across the country. In 1911, he noted in his journal that he was having "the best sales" of his career.

During the remaining eight years of his life, Edgar traveled little outside Montana. In 1910, a few months after his son's death, he went to a family reunion in Oregon where he did some sketching. He returned for another visit in 1915, at which time he made a short side trip to San Francisco to see the Panama-Pacific Exposition where three of his paintings were shown.

Edgar continued to paint whenever he was physically able. During his last two years, he could work but a few minutes at a time, but he persisted until within a few days of death. Intermittent periods of impaired vision and partial paralysis from a series of strokes discouraged him by keeping him from painting for weeks at a time, but he always managed to return to his easel until the very end.

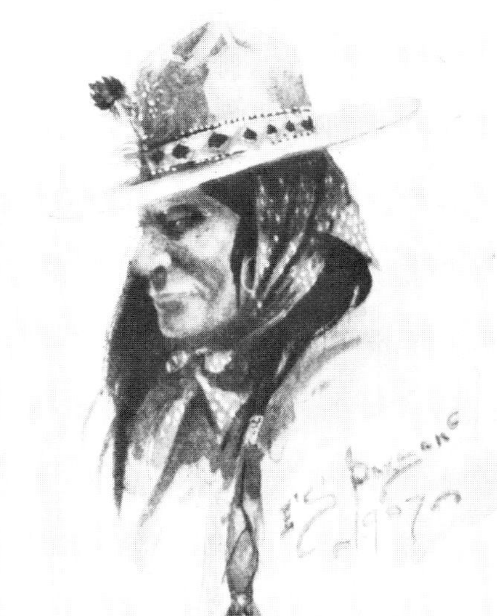

"Mis-sou-la"

PUT THE INDIAN SIGN ON POVERTY

**"For age and want, save while you may,
No morning's sun lasts a whole day."**

Metals Bank & Trust Co.
Metals Bank Building
Butte, Mont.

INTEREST PAID ON TIME DEPOSITS

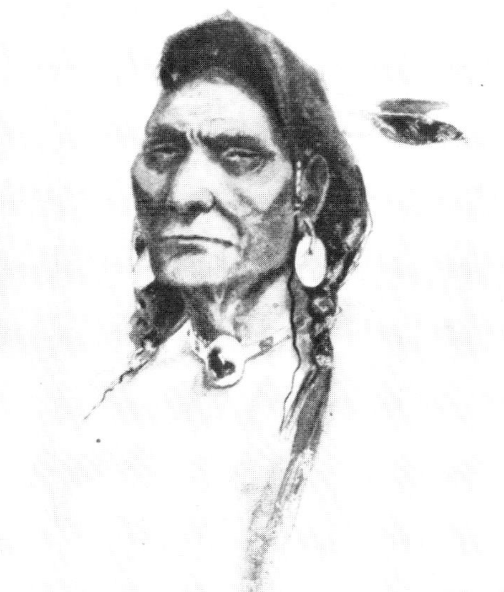

Crow

PUT THE INDIAN SIGN ON POVERTY

**"Put not your trust in money
but your money in trust."**

Metals Bank & Trust Co.
Metals Bank Building
Butte, Mont.

INTEREST PAID ON TIME DEPOSITS

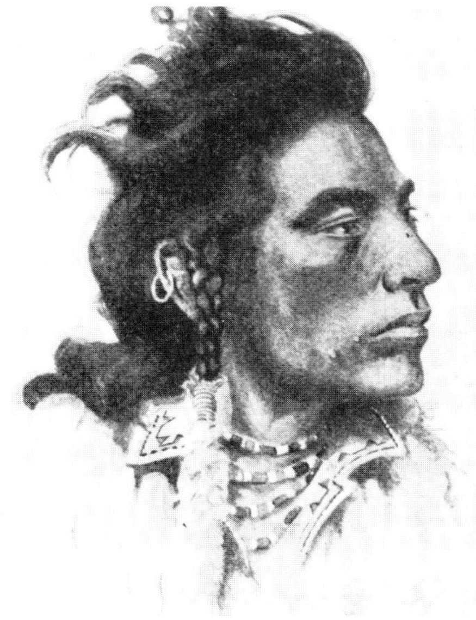

"Curley"

PUT THE INDIAN SIGN ON POVERTY

**The old proverb about
"a penny saved" is as pat
today as ever it was: —
START SAVING NOW!**

Metals Bank & Trust Co.
Metals Bank Building
Butte, Mont.

INTEREST PAID ON TIME DEPOSITS

Three of a series of several Paxson watercolors reproduced in color, on ink blotters by McKee Printing Co. of Butte about 1906.

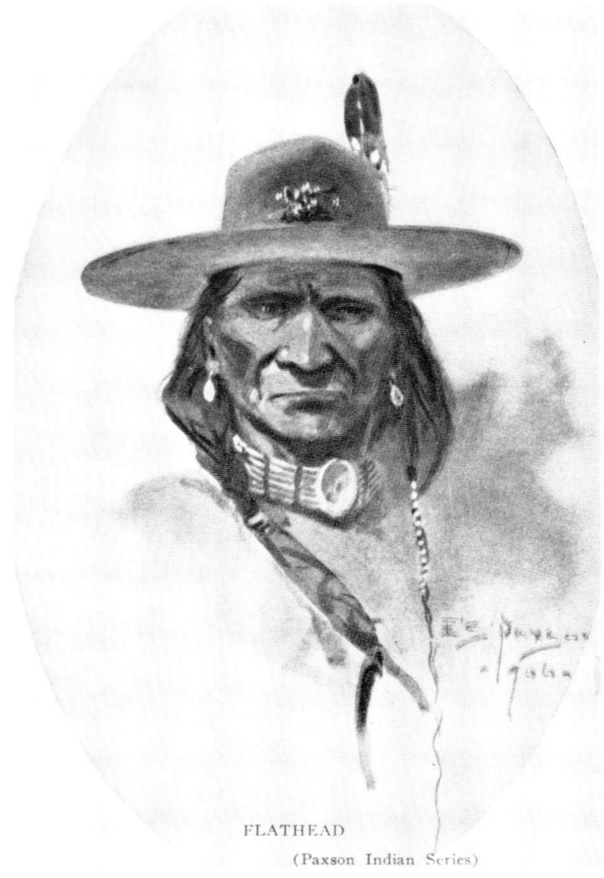

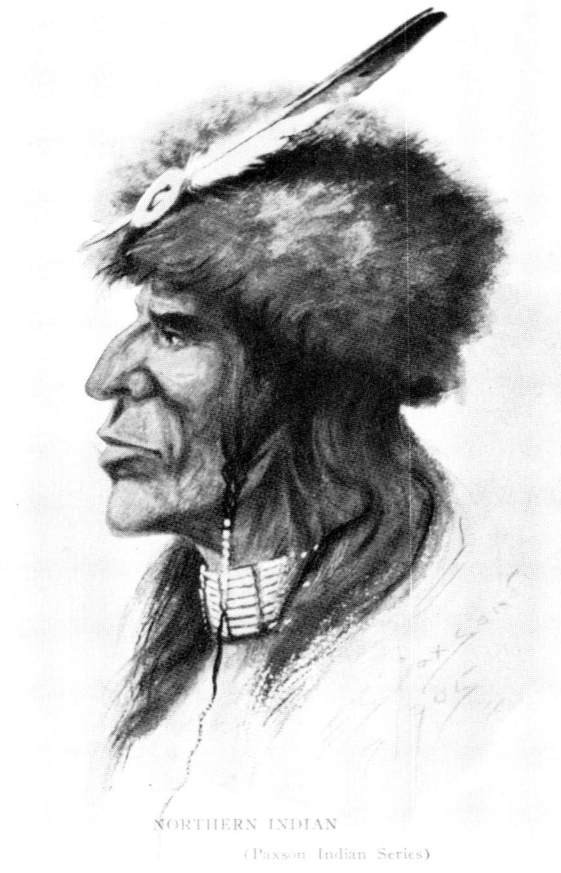

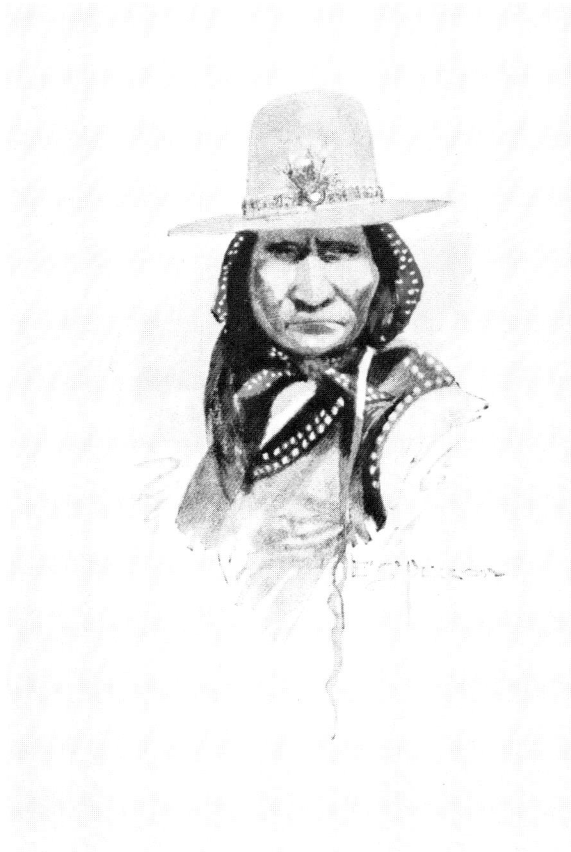

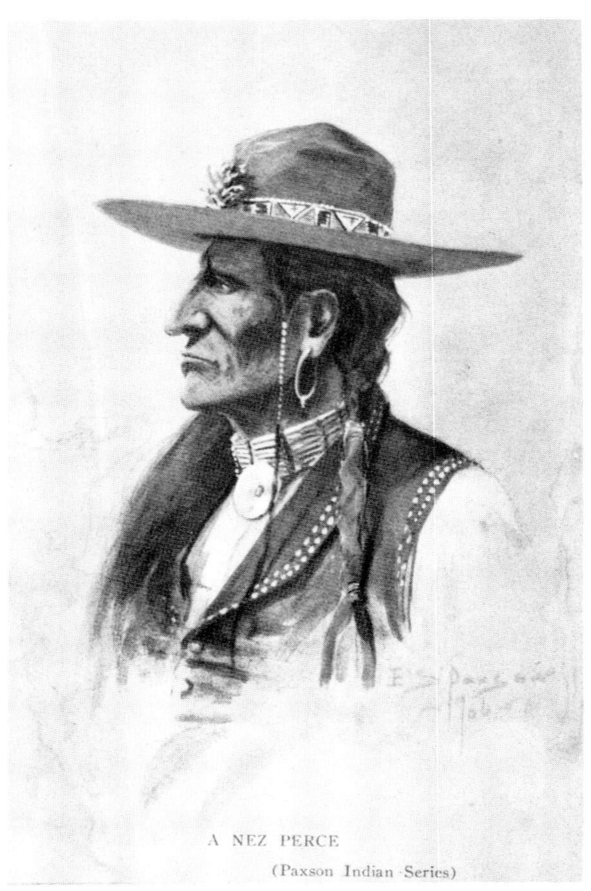

Four of "Paxson Indian Series" postcards issued in color by McKee Printing Co. about 1906, and later by Northwest Postcard and Souvenir Co. There were probably nine in the series. McKee also issued larger reproductions of a few other Paxson paintings. The artist received remuneration from McKee, in contrast to printers in the east who used his paintings without his permission.

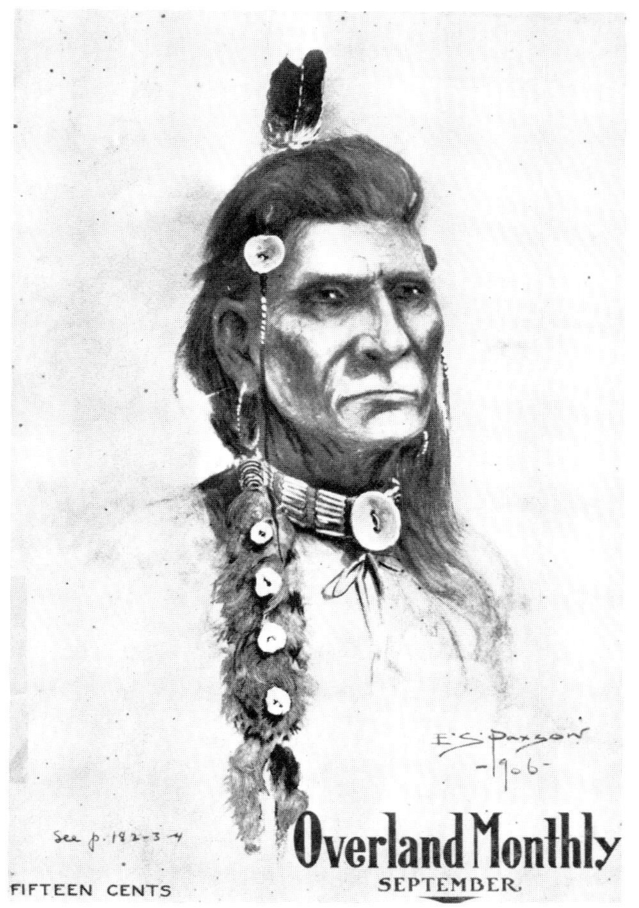

Cover of September, 1906 *Overland Monthly*. The issue also contained an article on Paxson's life and work.

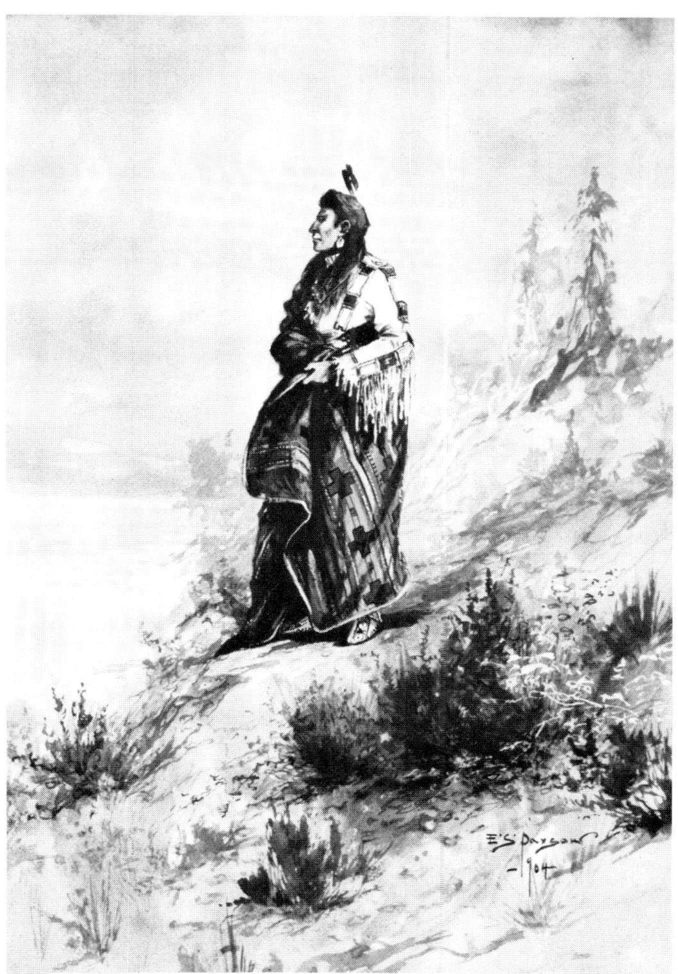

"On the Point of Placid Lake," black and white wash, 1904, 20 x 13. *Private Collection.*

Paxson's six murals hanging in the lobby of the House of Representatives, Montana State Capitol, Helena. Completed in 1912, they depict historic Montana events.

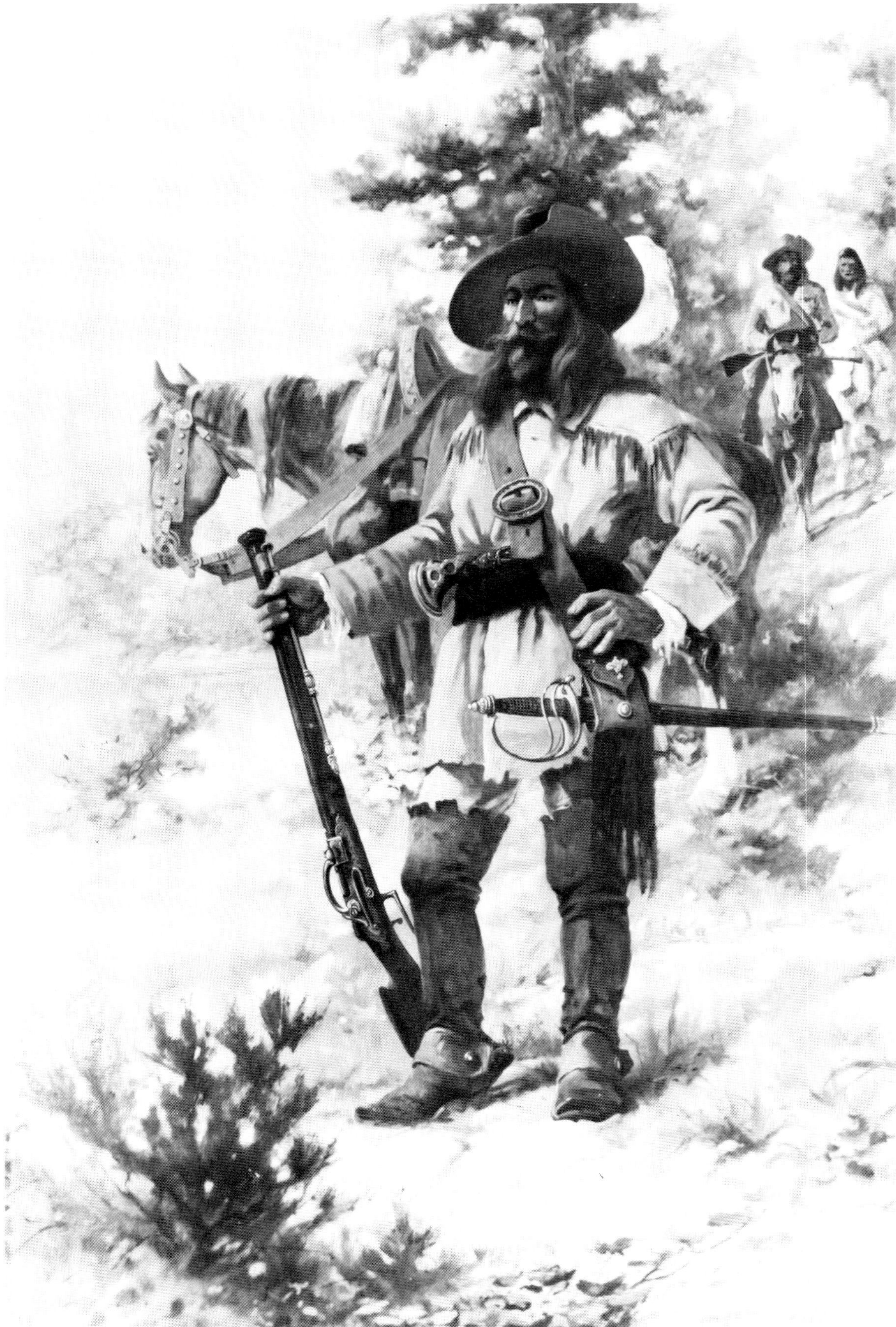

"Pierre de la Verendrye." 5' x 14' Paxson portrayed Verendrye as the first white man to enter Montana. In 1742 the French explorer, searching for the "Western Sea," travelled across much of what was to become Montana.

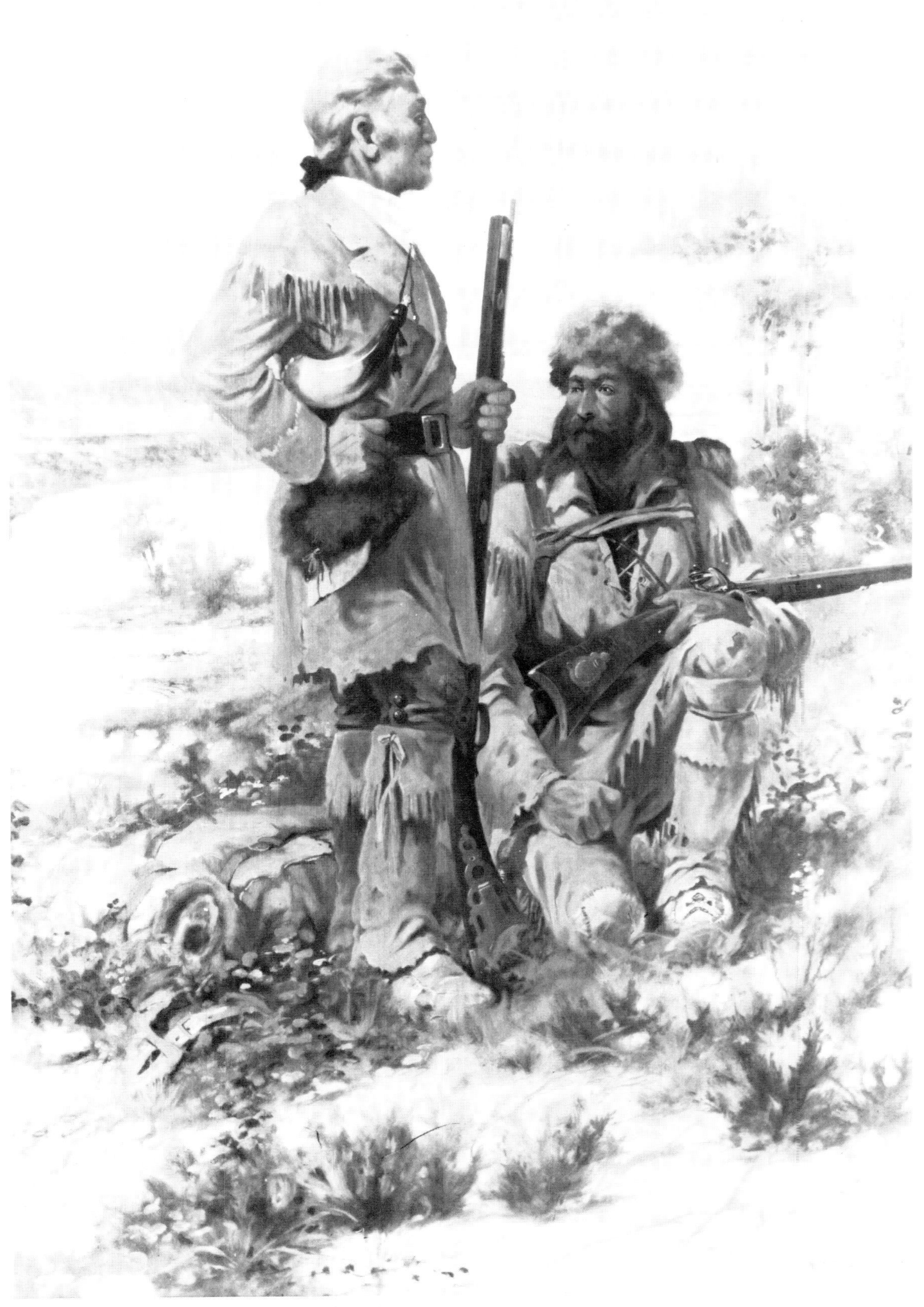

"Captain Lewis of the Lewis and Clark Expedition at Black Eagle Falls, June 14, 1805." 5' x 14'.

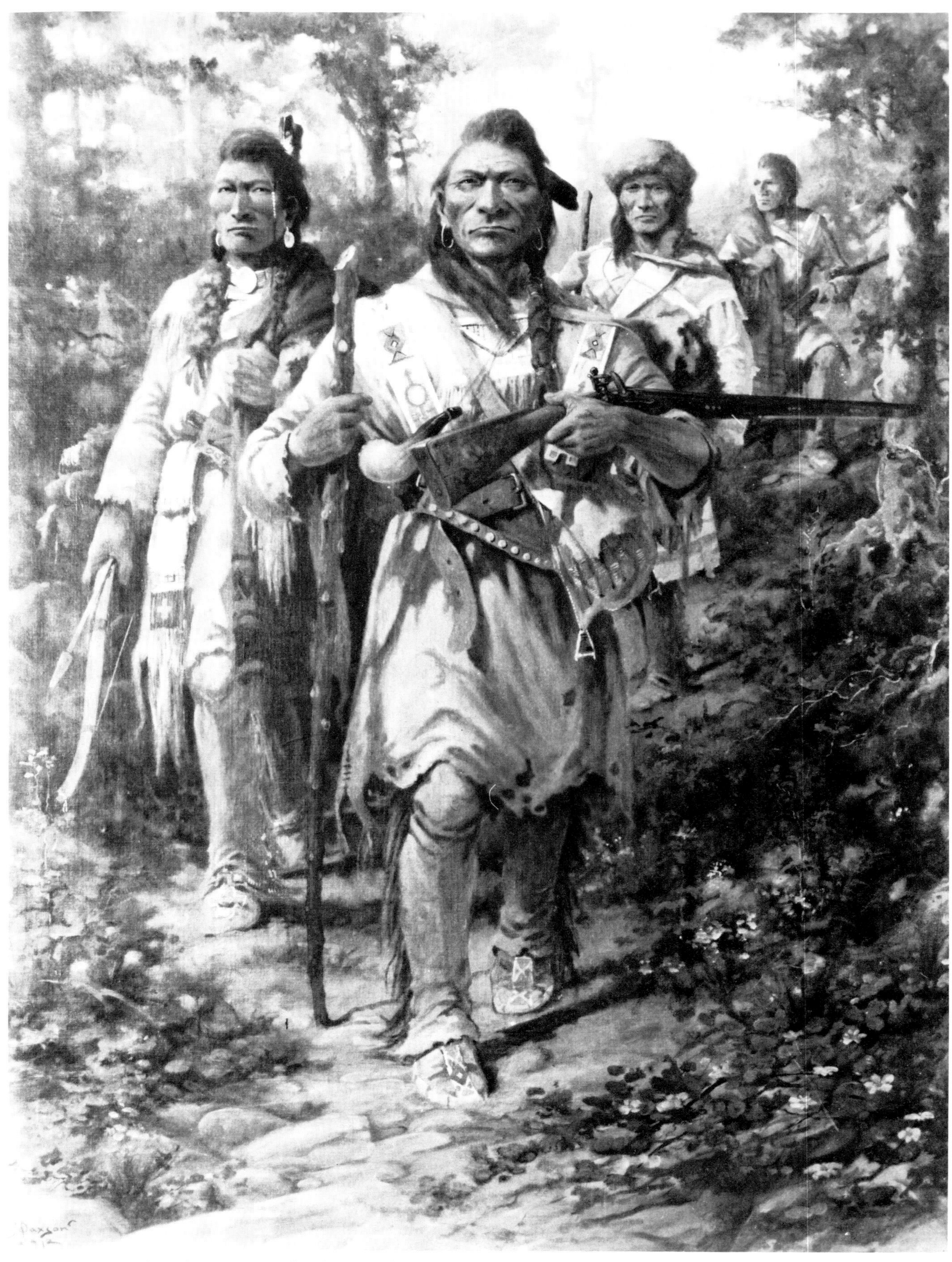

"Seeking the White Man's Book." 5' x 14'. The mural depicts Nez Percé and Flathead braves embarking on the long walk to St. Louis solely to acquire a Bible. The journey, which had a tragic conclusion, was begun shortly after the Lewis and Clark Expedition.

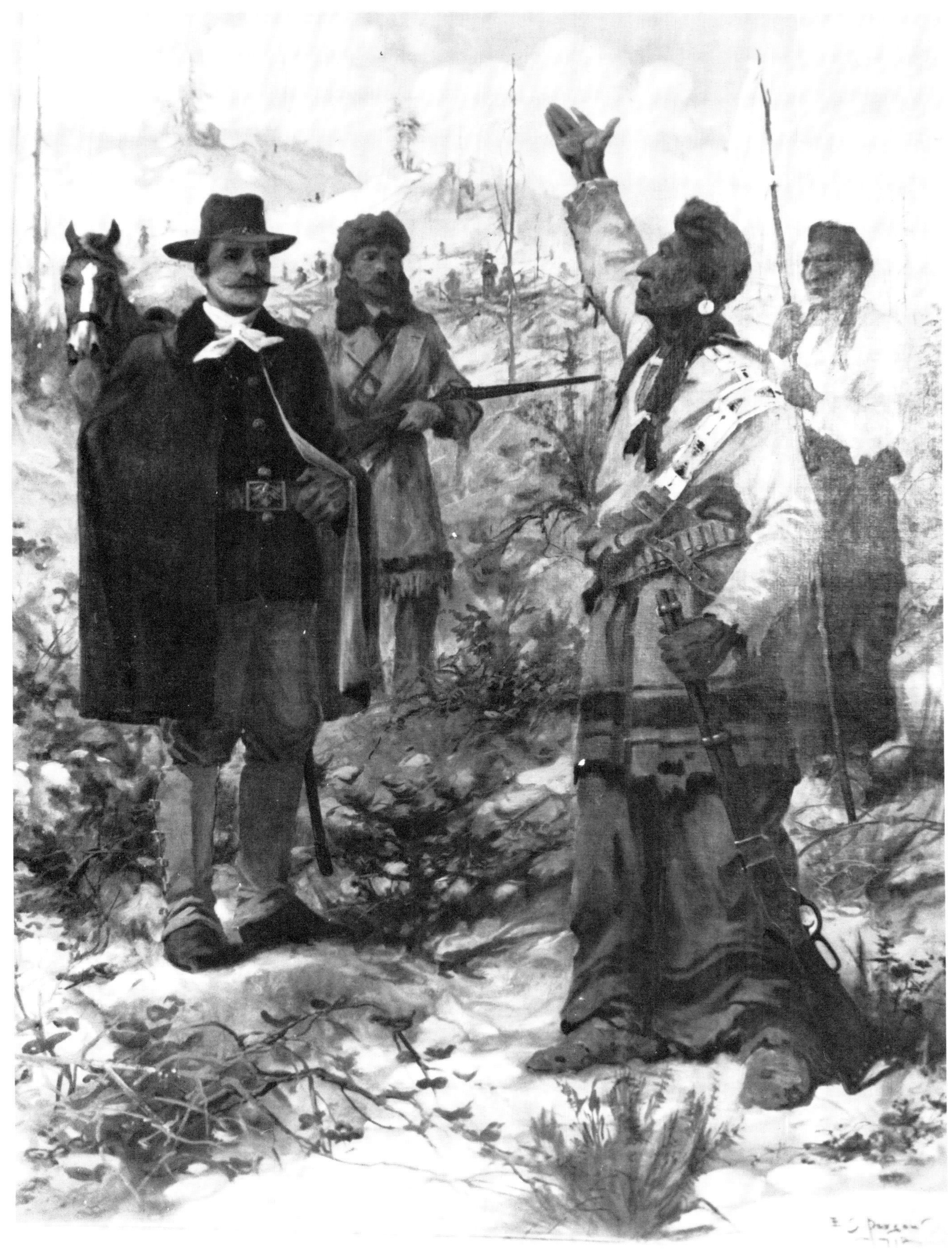

"The Surrender of Chief Joseph, October 9, 1877." 5' x 14'.

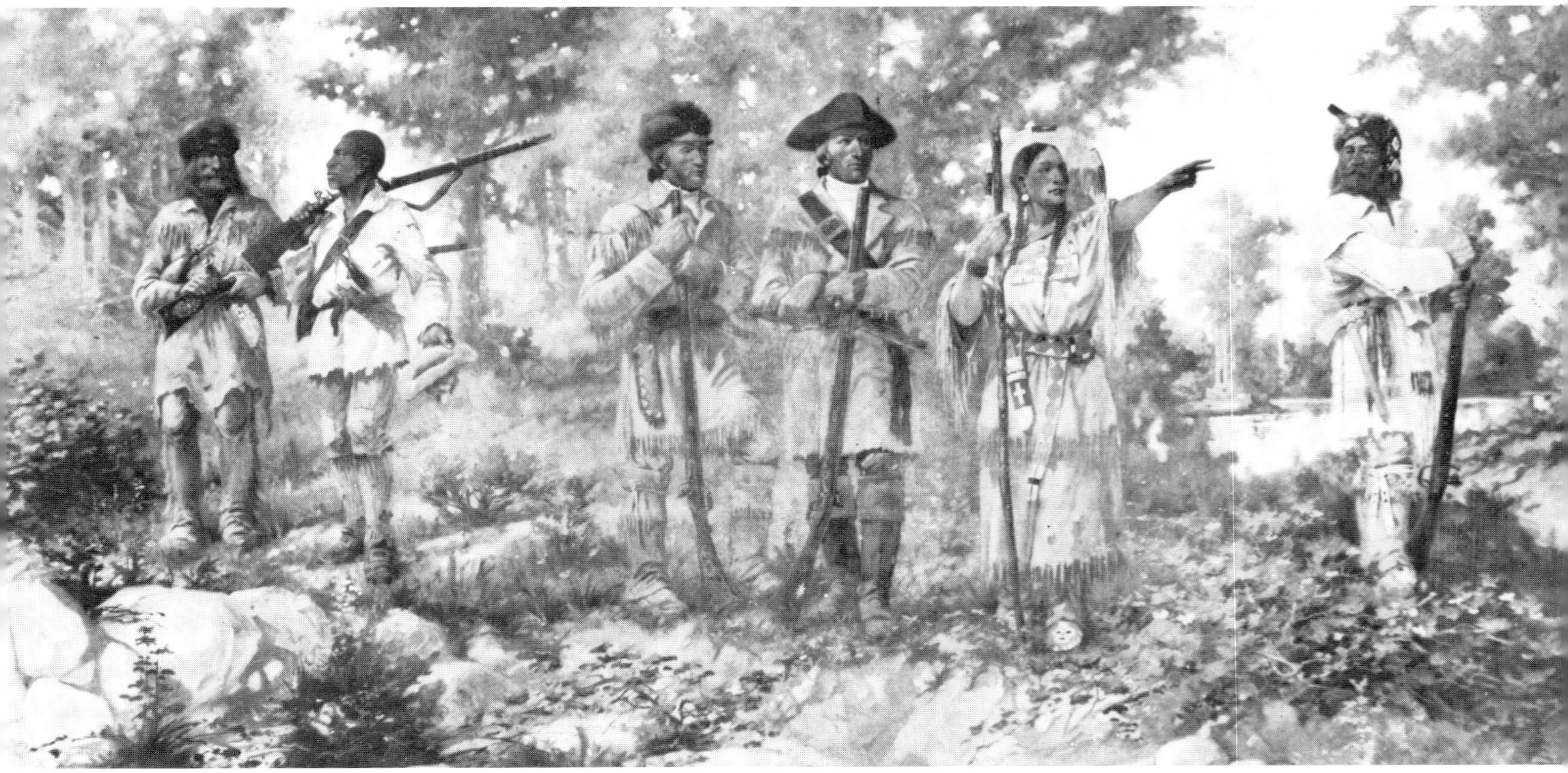

"Lewis and Clark at Three-Forks." 5' x 11'. Sacajawea, who at fifteen had been stolen from her tribe, the Shoshoni by Mandans, indicates her familiarity with the region by pointing out the spot where she had been captured.

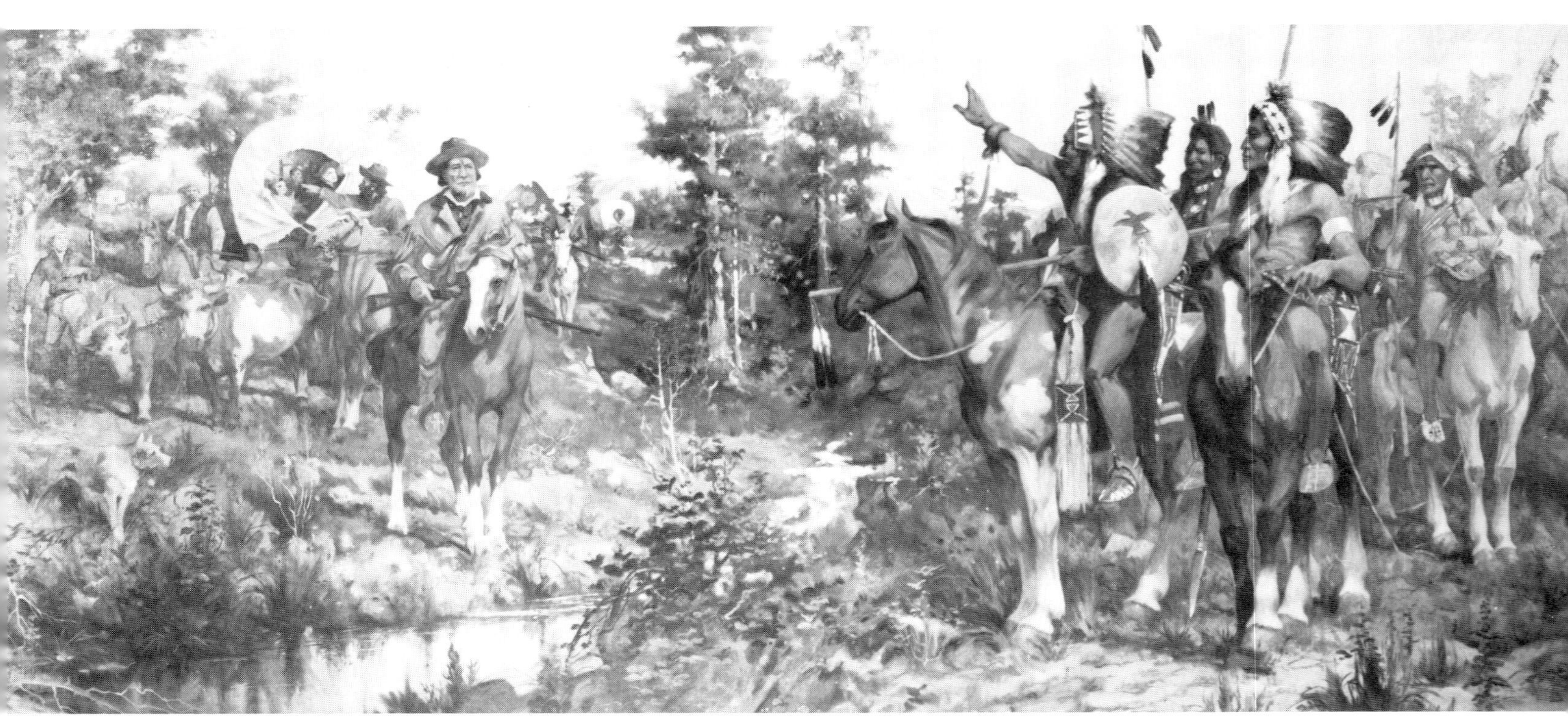

"The Borderland." 5' x 11'. Notable is that the artist has portrayed the foremost Indian giving the sign of friendship.

During the difficult years after his son's death, Edgar completed two of his greatest artistic achievements—six historical murals for the state capitol building in Helena and eight for the Missoula County courthouse.

Edgar began on the murals for the state in 1911. He, Ralph DeCamp and Charles Russell had been selected to do the work for the just completed wings of the capitol building. Edgar was commissioned to paint two, four-by-twelve-foot panels and four, four-by-four-foot panels depicting historic Montana scenes of his choice, these to be placed in the foyer of the chamber of the House of Representatives. He began with his customary dedication to historical accuracy, researching his selected subjects. Then he submitted watercolor sketches for approval. When he was given the go-ahead by the Board of Examiners, consisting of the governor, secretary of state, attorney general and the architect of the building, he plunged into an exhausting full year of painting, all done in his studio. As he worked, scenes from the Lewis and Clark Expedition took shape on canvas; Pierre Verendrye, an early white explorer of Montana, reappeared out of the past, standing in the foreground of a landscape that Edgar knew so intimately; Indian messengers *Seeking the Whiteman's Book* were portrayed as described by Edgar's Indian friends; settlers in their covered wagons and stoic Indians faced each other in silent confrontation across a stream symbolizing the frontier; and Chief Joseph was immortalized making his dramatic speech of surrender, "From where the sun now stands, I will fight no more forever."

Edgar drove himself hard despite severe headaches and kidney pains. Some days he worked twelve hours. As the project neared completion, he worked until exhausted each day. Upon completing the last panel, he wrote in his journal: "I have been almost constantly in pain and sometimes have thought 'Would I be able to complete them?' I feel that I have done something in the world."

That Edgar consented to paint eight more murals after so trying a project says much about his nature and commitment to pictorially recording history for posterity. He certainly did not do the Missoula County courthouse murals for monetary gain—he agreed to only $1,500 for the entire project. Even at that time, the eight magnificent paintings were worth nearly that much apiece. There is a story that Edgar turned down an offer by a wealthy patron of $1,000 for one of the murals.[7]

The courthouse had originally been decorated in 1910 by a firm from Clinton, Iowa. Edgar had submitted a bid including detailed sketches for the work, but the Clinton firm, although having provided no specifications, won the commission on the basis of a very low bid. The resulting work was sadly lacking in historical accuracy and artistic merit. Many Missoula citizens were very dissatisfied. Editorials in the local paper described the pictures as consisting of "wooden legged oxen and Irish Indians" and called them "a disgrace to Missoula County." The local Women's Club and leading citizens began a campaign to have the work replaced. Edgar's name was often mentioned in the newspapers as the most suitable artist for the job. In December 1912, after conferring with the County Commission on the project, Edgar consented to do the work. He began reading, studying and deciding on subjects. He interviewed old-timers and wrote inquiring for photographs of the historic figures to be portrayed. Using old maps and journals he puzzled out the exact locations around Missoula where the scenes he wanted to portray took place. Then he sketched and photographed the historic sites and became familiar with them. His determination in doing this background work is remarkable. He made three attempts at reaching the site of the Lewis party's (of the Lewis and Clark Expedition) crossing of the Clark's Fork River. It proved quite inaccessible, as he was not well enough to hike to the site. He made the first two attempts with his son Bob on the youth's motorcycle, but was thwarted by heavy timber, thick brush and marsh. Finally he succeeded by hiring a wagon and team and proceeding up a creekbed to the site.

The actual painting took Edgar sixteen months. Again he worked exclusively in his studio, beginning with small sketches which he enlarged on canvas. The large size of the canvases forced him to complete each mural before starting the next, thus not allowing him to change as he was moved by the ghost. Proper light to work by was also a difficulty in the confines of the studio—so much so that he ceased work completely during the short winter days. In the spring his work was interrupted by poor health. He complained of being in constant pain, having severe headaches and an enlarged prostate gland. Young William, his grandson who lived with him at the time and watched him work for hours at a time, remembers that his grandfather wore a rag as a headband, tightly knotted. Periodically he would tighten the knot, which seemed to give him a little relief from his head pain. In April 1914 Edgar collapsed from exhaustion. His doctor ordered him to rest, but he was back at work in two weeks. In July he completed the last mural. He was ready for a rest but, because he had a backlog of orders owing to the time consumed doing the murals, he continued to spend long days at his easel.

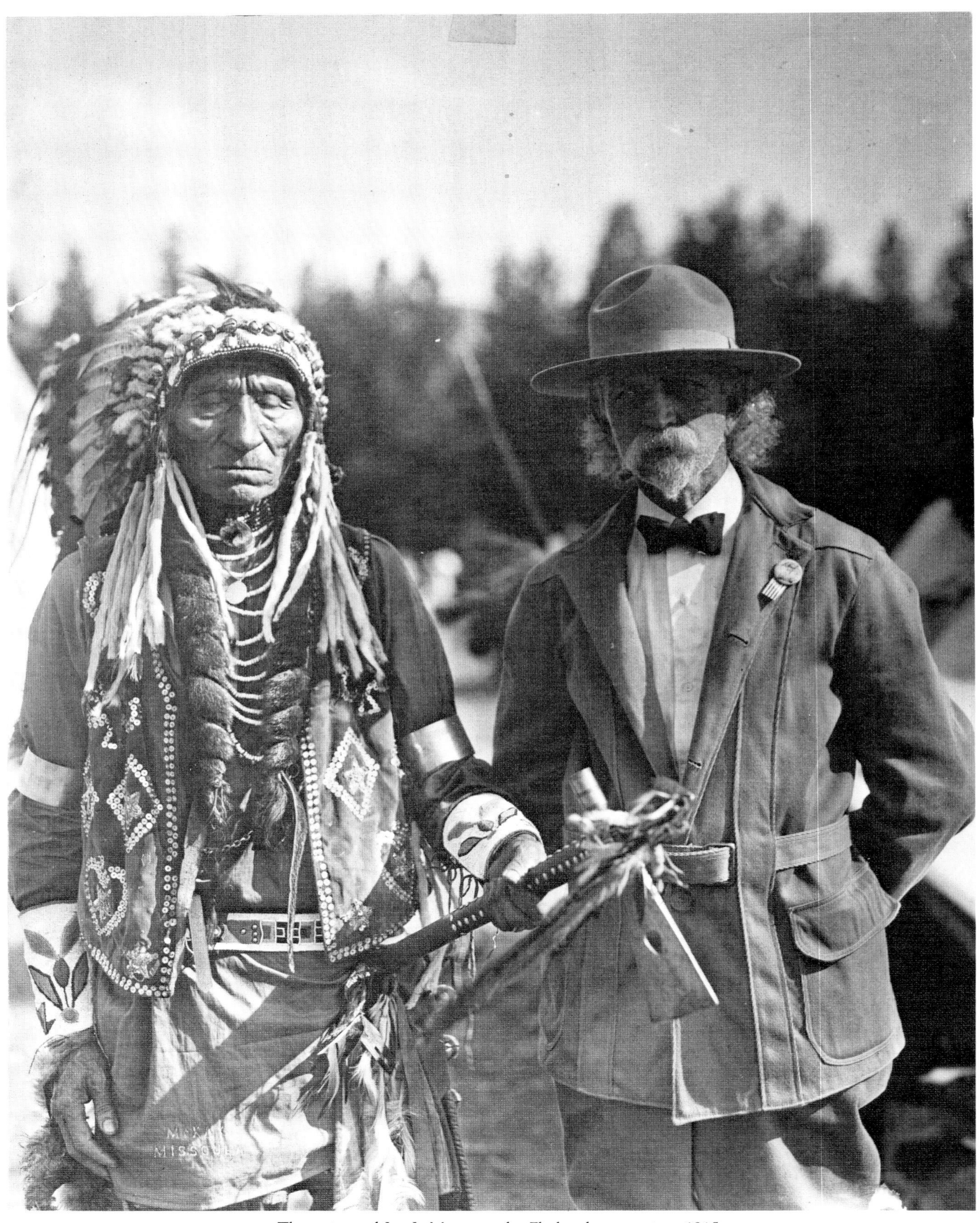
The artist and Joe LaMoose at the Flathead reservation, 1915.

8

One of a Dying Breed

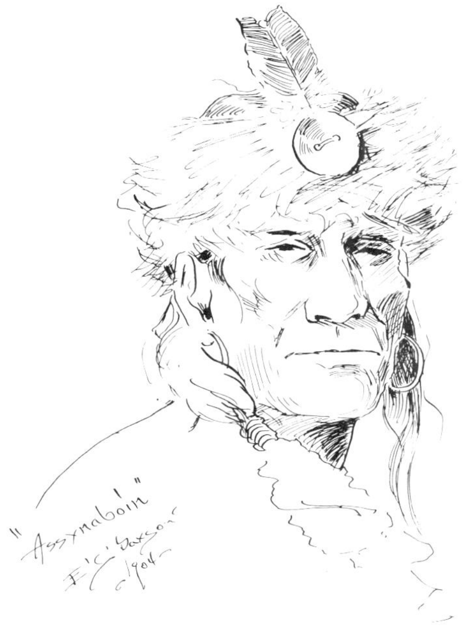

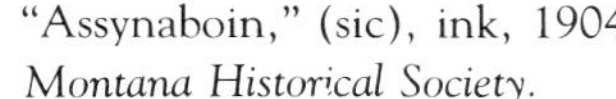

"Assynaboin," (sic), ink, 1904.
Montana Historical Society.

Edgar lived in the West during a time of exceptionally rapid transition. During his adult life the geographical frontier passed away and was replaced by a technological frontier.

Montana Territory was a wilderness when he arrived there. Missoula was only a trading post on the Lewis and Clark Trail. Indians camped nearby, jubilantly celebrating the success of a recent buffalo hunt. Butte was a mining camp of a few hundred hardy men and far fewer toughened women. The wilderness surrounding it was Edgar's hunting ground—the home of bear, deer and antelope.

In only a few years, much of all that had vanished, replaced by civilization. At the exact spot where Edgar once shot an antelope in the late 1870s, in 1904 the Montana School of Mines was situated, training men in the new techniques of extracting metals from the earth. Where Edgar had once stalked game, the smelters of Anaconda belched forth smoke and the towns of Livingston and Dillon thrived. In 1906, when Edgar moved to Missoula, the University of Montana was flourishing on the very site of the Indian encampment he had known in 1877. Edgar's home in Missoula was on the historic Lewis and Clark Trail. But the trail was no longer the familiar rutted track passing by the old trading post. In front of Edgar's home, the trail was now called Stevens Avenue. Edgar saw it paved. And he saw the coming of the telephone, electric lights, the automobile and the airplane.

But in the first decade of the new century, Edgar was not an old man—he was in his fifties. All this had occurred before he had even passed his prime. The time span to him seemed so brief since he had seen mule and bull teams pulling freight wagons into dusty Deer Lodge; since he had seen the telegraph gradually link the fledgling settlements of the territory; and since he had seen Henry Villiard at Gold Creek in 1883 drive home the gold spike completing the first transcontinental railroad through Montana.

Edgar had great admiration for the new age. "What changes!" he wrote in 1915, "Montana has grown to be a thriving and wonderful state." He marveled at the new inventions. Once he noted in his journal about reading in the daily paper of a murderer who had been apprehended aboard a steamer in mid-Atlantic by use of the "wireless." Edgar wrote in response: "We are living in a superior age. I doubt if ever there will be one to surpass it." In 1904, he wrote: "100 years

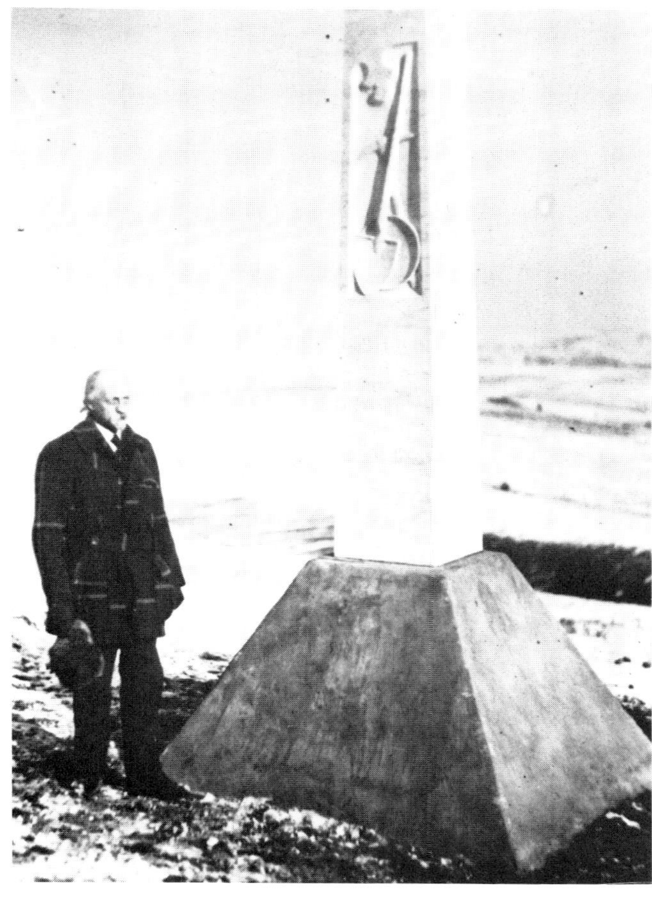

The artist at the Henderson Gulch Monument, 1914. He had known the wild mining camp in 1878 when it was in its heyday.

ago today at three p.m. Lewis and Clark set out from St. Louis upon their long and eventful journey to the 'Wild and Woolly' West. Could they see the change today they would gaze in wonder."

Edgar gazed in wonder in their stead. He was more akin in spirit to Lewis and Clark than to the pioneers of the new age. His mind was more in tune with the early nineteenth century than the early twentieth. He had grown up accustomed to the concept of a geographical frontier. Had he been a young man in 1804, he surely would have gloried in the opportunity to participate in the expedition through the Louisiana Purchase. But the new technological frontier was strange and occasionally unbelievable to him. Of airplane flight, he wrote, "It may be a success eventually, but I have my doubts." In 1913, he "guided and ran" (as he put it) an automobile for the first time, but never followed up the experience. He decided he didn't want a motorcar. He did, however, take to a bicycle and could often be seen pedaling down Missoula streets, giving the curious impression of a smallish Buffalo Bill on wheels.

So during the first two decades of the new century Edgar paid only passing attention to the changing world. He concerned himself with the remnants of frontier days—fall hunts, Indian and pioneer friends, his vast curios collection and, of course, his art. He took to wearing his hair long in the style of Buffalo Bill, with accompanying mustache, goatee and wide-brimmed hat. Occasionally he was even seen in town in buckskin shirt and leggins, or wrapped in a blanket Indian style. A recent article in a Montana newspaper claimed he sometimes let out a warhoop from a downtown street corner for the benefit of visitors from the East. This seems somewhat out of character for a quiet and reticent man, but his grandson William remembers his grandfather could issue a blood-curdling warhoop and often did to rouse the family at sunrise on camping trips.

Edgar's curios collection continued to grow and become more well known. He had several sets of authentic Indian deerskin suits which he loaned out on request to parties as far away as Europe. He had all manner of Indian artifact: saddles, pouches, sashes, leggins, moccasins, stone implements, war bonnets, bows, arrows, quivers, calumets, tomahawks, armlets, knives, clubs and tom-toms. He also had over sixty firearms including a fine matched set of flintlock pistols that had belonged to Granville Stuart and an old Kentucky flintlock rifle purported to have been the property of Lewis of the Lewis and Clark Expedition. Edgar wrote a detailed catalogue of his collection, describing the history of each item. Sadly, after his death most of his collection was scattered, lost and forgotten. The catalogue was destroyed by fire. All that remains is the first page.

Edgar's extended hunts were one means of immersing himself in the old days. He was never in want of companions for these trips. He had a reputation for being a good comrade on the trail and for his knowledge of the Montana wilds and the animals inhabiting them. He knew many of the mountain trails as well as a longtime city dweller knows the streets of his neighborhood. He could deduce an astonishing amount of information from animal tracks. He was even an expert at making buckskin hunting shirts, which he provided for his friends.

One of Edgar's most ambitious hunting trips was in the fall of 1905. With his old friends Fred and Will Orton and Ed Bennet, he traveled over 200 miles with saddle and packhorses through trackless wilderness, crossing the Kootenai Mountains in the process. During the four-week trip, they successfully hunted mountain goat, elk and deer, from which they dried and jerked meat and dressed hides. They saw recent signs of mountain lion, moose and bear, but the only humans they encountered were Indians, likewise on a hunt.

Crossing the Kootenais was an exhausting effort for fifty-three-year-old Edgar, but the thrill of adventure and the exhilarating view from the top of the pass made it worthwhile. Edgar described the crossing in his journal:

CATALOGUE OF INDIAN CURIOS
in the collection of
EDGAR S. PAXSON OF BUTTE, MONTANA

1. *Sioux Hunting Shirt, made by one of the daughters of Sitting Bull, the famous Sioux Medicine Man, who gave it to "Old Hoover," a Yellowstone trapper. Some years later, Sargt. Wilson of "K" Company, 4th Infantry, while on a scout up the Missouri, found him, "Old Hoover," with a broken leg; he was taken to their camp and, upon his recovery, he gave the shirt to the sargent. At the Battle of the Big Hole, Montana, August 9th, 1977, Wilson was wounded. He was the first to reach Deer Lodge with the news of the battle. Suffering from his wounds, he was placed in the Sisters Hospital with many other wounded, some of which died I often went up to the hospital to see and help, of possible, the sick and wounded. I often noticed the shirt, which hung on the head of Sargt. Wilson's bed, and took a great fancy to it. But upon his recovery, he gave it to a charming young lady. Twenty years later it was presented to me with the compliments of the donor.*
2. *Brule Siox War Shirt and Leggins, heavily beaded and fringed with scalp-locks and weasel skins. This outfit was worn in the "Rose Bud" fight, eight days before the lamented Custer and his gallant men fought their last fight with Crazy Horse, who was the leading spirit in both engagements.*

This is a duplication of the first page of Paxson's Indian curios collection catalog. The remainder of the catalog has been lost. After the artist's death, the collection was broken up, and a large portion, including the catalog, was destroyed by fire.

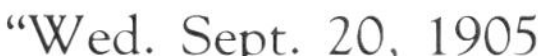

"Wed. Sept. 20, 1905

"We are perhaps the first white people to cross this mountain, and certainly the first to make a camp. As we neared the top, the view was the wildest and most grand I ever witnessed. We could see for hundreds of miles one vast forest dotted with numerous lakes glinting in the setting sun with silver threads turning here and there amidst the somber green forest while towering high above was the Mission Range clothed with pinnacled rocks trying to pierce the bright sky. And in all this vast virgin cloth of green not one sign of Civilized Man.... Fred and I after a jaunt of an hour and a half almost straight up reached a rim of rock surrounding one of the grandest scenes one could imagine. Below us with rock walls 3000 feet high, rough crags, in many places hanging far out, formed a canopy over the beautiful lakes and forest. The trees, monsters in size, seemed but toys while the lakes appeared like silver dollars. Fred says that the Yellowstone has nothing so wild and grand. As we crept around on the cone, the wind strong in our faces, we could see many goat tracks in the snow. Following the rim of rock for about a mile, we descended from a high towering dome of granite through a beautiful grassy slope fringed with timber and huge boulders. We saw many fresh bear sign and one of elk. In the rain we entered camp a little after dark. While we were making the fire, the other boys came in. They reported finding the trace of the Blackfeet trail we lost yesterday. If this is so we may be able to work our way out. Cold and raining tonight. To this point we have traveled 90 miles.

The artist ready for the trail, 1901.

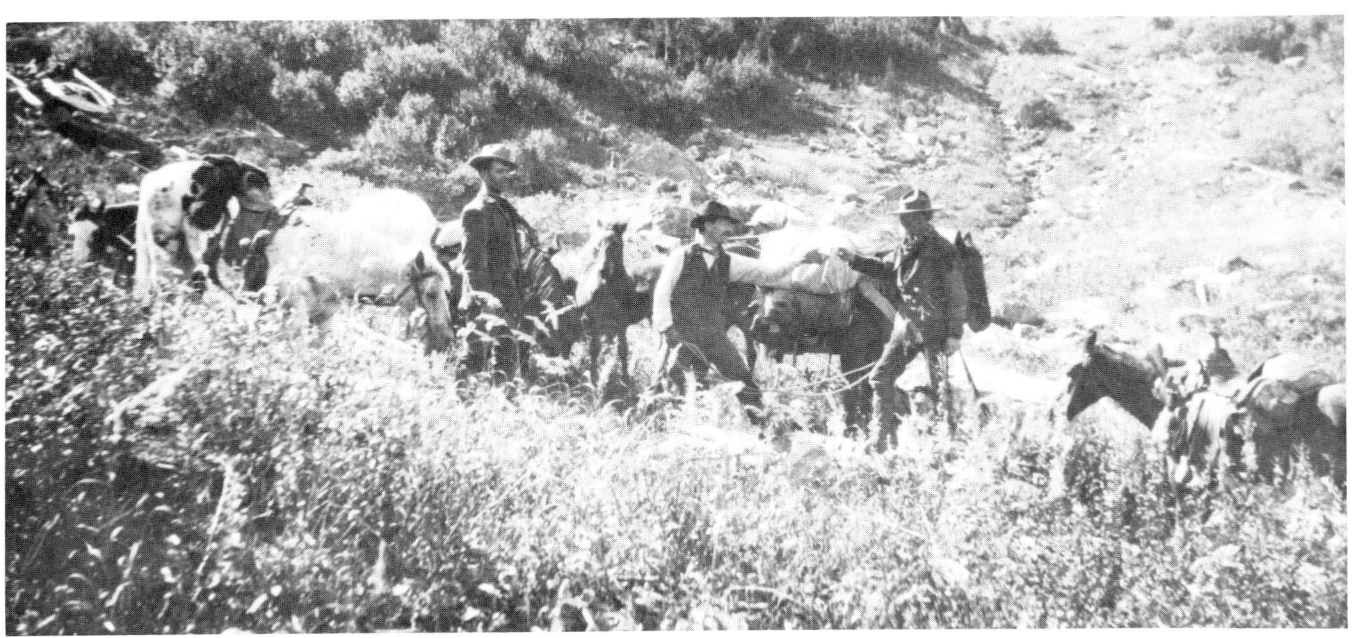

Edgar's extended hunts were one means of immersing himself in the old days, as in this shot taken at Young's Pass, head of Cottonwood and Lost Cabin Creeks about 1901. Paxson is at the right.

"Thurs. Sept. 21

"Broke camp early, discarded one pack and put all on four horses.... The ascent from here was very steep and rugged for about 1½ miles through dense timber and high grass. Arriving at the top to view the scene we took two photos. It looks from here like we could never get out—one vast stretch of heavily timbered mountains. On this side some 50 miles away the Kootenai range terminates in a high dome which was in view all day. Just as we began to come down the slope through a steep and ragged cut, Ed's 'Dollie' fell and got fast in the rocks. Will came up and cut her shoe loose with his hatchet. At a call from Ed I came down. When she got up we found an artery cut on the inside of her flank and spurting out a large stream. After much trouble Ed and I found the end of the artery and I tied it with a buckskin string. It was a most desperate thing to do, to attempt this crossing, but we stuck to it. Heavy timber lying in a tangled mass and steep rocky cliffs made a heavy trip. The trail was lost many times. Finally I went ahead and found it where we began to ascend again. Coming to an abrupt cliff it seemed impossible to go down it, but by taking one horse at a time we managed after an hour of hard work to make a landing 300 feet below without accident. The boys honored me with the distinction of being the first one to go down with my horse and named it 'Paxson's slide.' It was fearful to watch from below the decent of the others; they appeared to be coming head first. We came out on a meadow just before dark where we camped, after 14 hours of constant travel and only going 8 miles.... We are getting tired out and a long way to go yet without a trail."

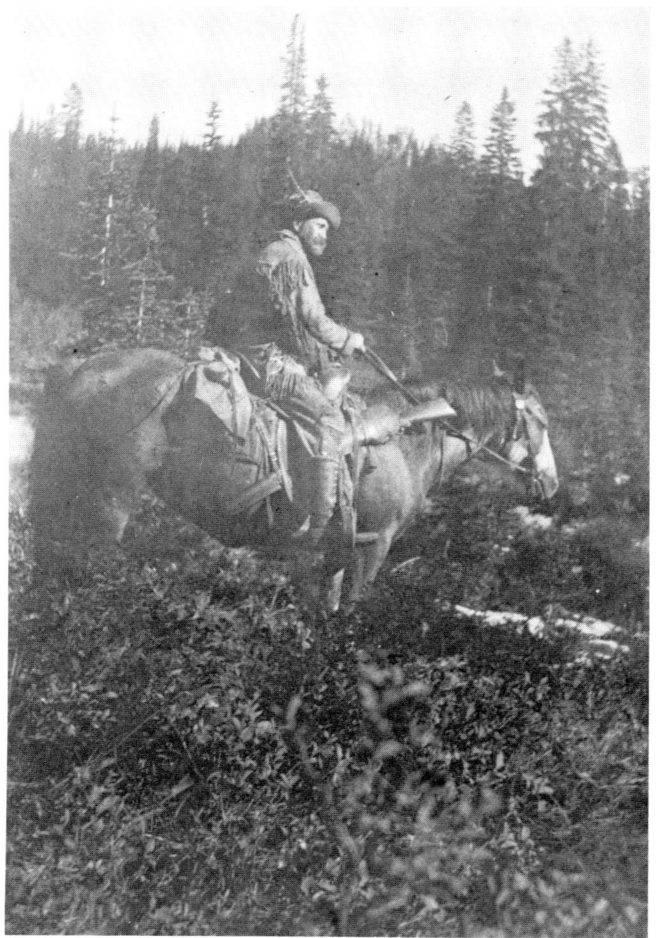

The artist on the trail: Continental Divide, Idaho, 1904.

The hunters intended to remain in camp for a few days to rest up, but they spotted mountain goat on the slopes above. They pursued the game amid craggy cliffs, Edgar getting one of the three goats killed. After four days, they continued their descent:

"Tues. Sept. 26

"Broke camp in a hard rain. This continued all day and the trail was very rough, sometimes lost entirely. Just at dark we made camp in a large meadow, well watered. In spite of the hardships and nasty weather everyone was content. We had one of the finest suppers on the whole trip, and were hungry enough to eat it. This camp...was a grand and impressive scene. A forest of massive pines surrounded our little patch of grass. To the north a rugged mountain's lofty peak pierced a white cloud stretching across the range from east to west. To the south a game trail led us to a dark swamp in the forest where lay a deep pool of clear sluggish water. Here many elk tracks freshly made and clear cut in the half dry mud were plainly seen. At some distance above we found recent sign of old bruin.

"Wed. Sept. 27

"Clear, cooler—rained most of the night. Everything was soaked, bedding and all but we felt refreshed and ready to move.... The trail was rougher than for two days. Fallen timber, steep, rough and rugged climbs were the feature of the day. About 3 p.m. we descended a steep rough bank and came out on the banks of the North Fork of the Flathead river. We forded it twice and from the opposite bank we saw two teepees. We recrossed and made them a visit. They were Flathead, hunting and preparing winter meat. I found a 'Ma-guts' or 'parflesh' which I purchased.

"Thus we made the crossing of the Kootnai Mountains after 9 days of hard and constant riding.... We made camp in a pleasant spot while Fred in 20 minutes caught 3 trout weighing 5 lbs. They were soon put to fry and we enjoyed them so much."

After a day's rest, the hunters struck the government trail with fifty miles to go to Ovando. On October 1 they entered the valley and were free of the forest for the first time in twenty-eight days. Edgar concluded:

"As we came out onto a wagon road, we were welcomed by meeting...a lady in a carriage. We doffed our hats decked with feathers, pieces of Indian blankets, etc. that we had found in the [Indian] camps. We presented a picture as we entered Ovando in tattered corduroy and dirty buckskins, but we were fat and sassy and proud of our conquests."

But because more "pilgrims" were crowding the mountain trails, as time went by, Edgar's hunts sometimes didn't measure up to the 1905 adventure. More than once he made camp only to have someone with no idea of mountain etiquette pick a site immediately upstream. And it became not uncommon to hear shots alarmingly close to camp. Edgar even had to endure the worst sort of tenderfoot in his own party. The party was camped in a deserted log cabin inhabited by rats. At night the rats invaded the camping gear and first one man and then another had to get up and

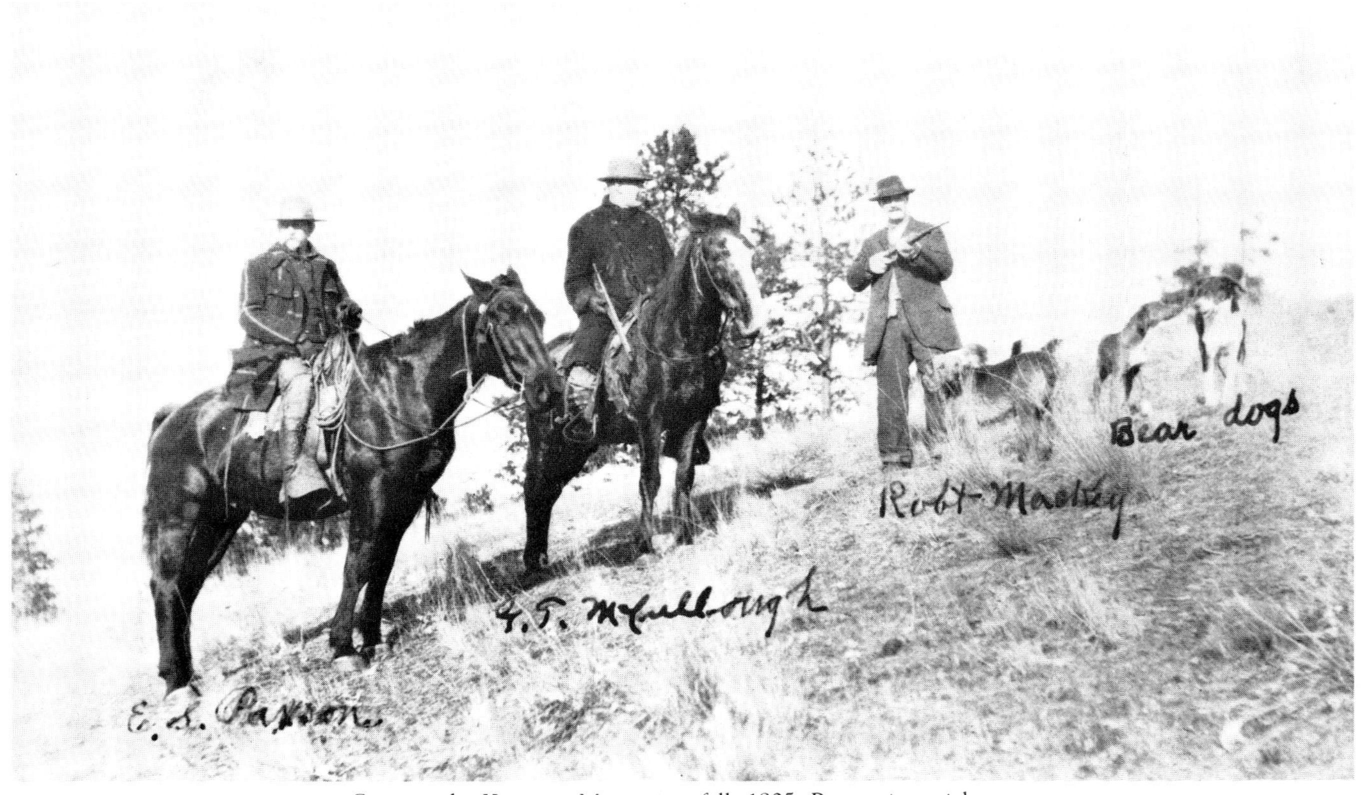

Crossing the Kootenai Mountains, fall, 1905. Paxson is at right.

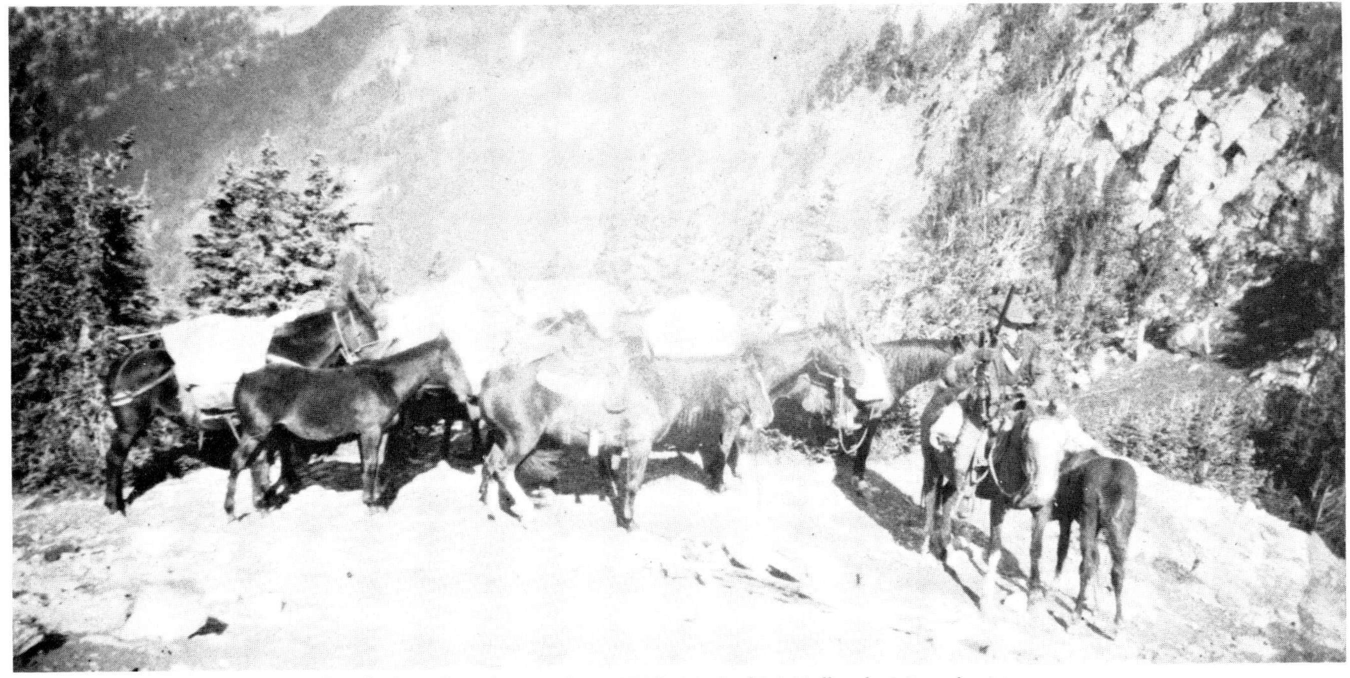
Ready for a bear hunt, about 1915. *Michael McCullough, Missoula, Montana.*

shoot a rat with a pistol. The tenderfoot, named Ogle, wanted his turn. Against his better judgement, Edgar handed over a pistol to him. In the darkness Ogle just missed shooting Edgar in the hand. Soon after on another trip, Ogle outdid himself. First he broke his rifle. Then he broke a borrowed shotgun, lost a hunting knife Edgar had loaned him, tore one of his leggins off and stepped on Edgar's glasses. Then he claimed to have seen nineteen deer, although no one else in the party had seen so much as a fresh track.

As Edgar aged and suffered ill health, his hunting trips became less ambitious, but he still managed to get out in the wilds. He felt a tramp in the woods was his best medicine. In 1908, he and a young married couple built a hunting cabin deep in the forest twenty miles from Missoula on Deer Park Creek. His young companions cut and hauled the logs and Edgar skillfully fitted them.

At sixty-three Edgar was still able at times to ride a horse, hike several miles cross-country and get his share of the game. One day in 1916, he took a twenty-two-mile ride on horseback through the forest. At one point along the way the horse bridled at shots and Edgar had to do some tricky riding before the animal found out "who was boss," as Edgar put it.

Edgar also enjoyed taking his young son, Bob, and his grandson, William, out on the trail to teach them the woodsman's skills. The boys eagerly learned to tie the diamond hitch and construct a teepee Indian fashion. Edgar's own tent was of his design, based on the teepee. In the summer when several family members joined in a camp-out, Edgar and the boys would happily fish for trout and grayling and hunt small game—grouse, pheasant, rabbit and squirrel. They pan-fried the fish for breakfast and made wonderful game stews for dinner on the open campfire.

It was undoubtedly saddening for Edgar to realize that his age and infirmities would no longer allow him to roam the mountain trails. Toward the end he persisted in making plans with his younger friends, only to bow out at the last minute. Bob Ward, who as a young man hunted with Edgar, remembered in an interview with the author that the elderly artist delighted in making elaborate preparations the night before a scheduled hunting trip. But invariably he would arise before dawn, look up at the sky and say when his fellow hunters arrived, "Well boys, looks like rain. I guess I'll pass this time." The young hunters understood the ritual and allowed its repetition without a word, for the sake of their venerable friend.

During the last several years of his life, Edgar's longtime pioneer friends "crossed the divide" one by one. Hardly a month passed that he did not mourn the loss of some old-timer in his journal. And as his own infirmities kept him off the mountain trails, he turned more to visiting with his old cronies still living. Gatherings of the Montana Society of Pioneers and Spanish war veterans were favorite times. Among his many friends with whom he kept in contact were several prominent Westerners: Granville Stuart, Major John Catlin, Captain Jack Crawford, author Frank Bird Linderman, Buffalo Bill Cody, Pawnee Bill (Major Gordon Lillie) Frank "Sandbar" Brown, Annie Oakley, and artists Charles Russell, E. L. Boone and Ralph DeCamp.

Granville Stuart and Edgar had been friends since

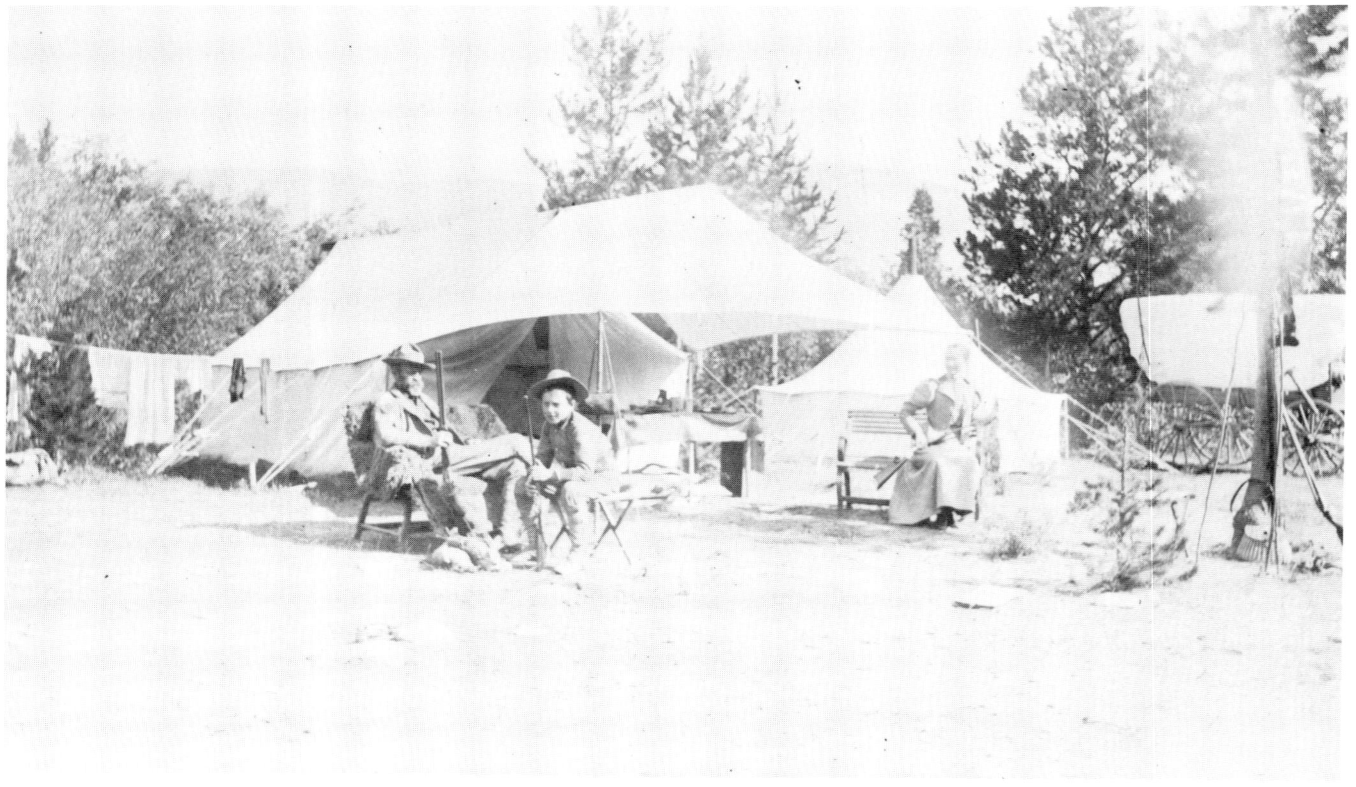

The artist camping with his family about 1905. *Montana Historical Society, Helena, Montana, and the Butte Trap and Skeet Club.*

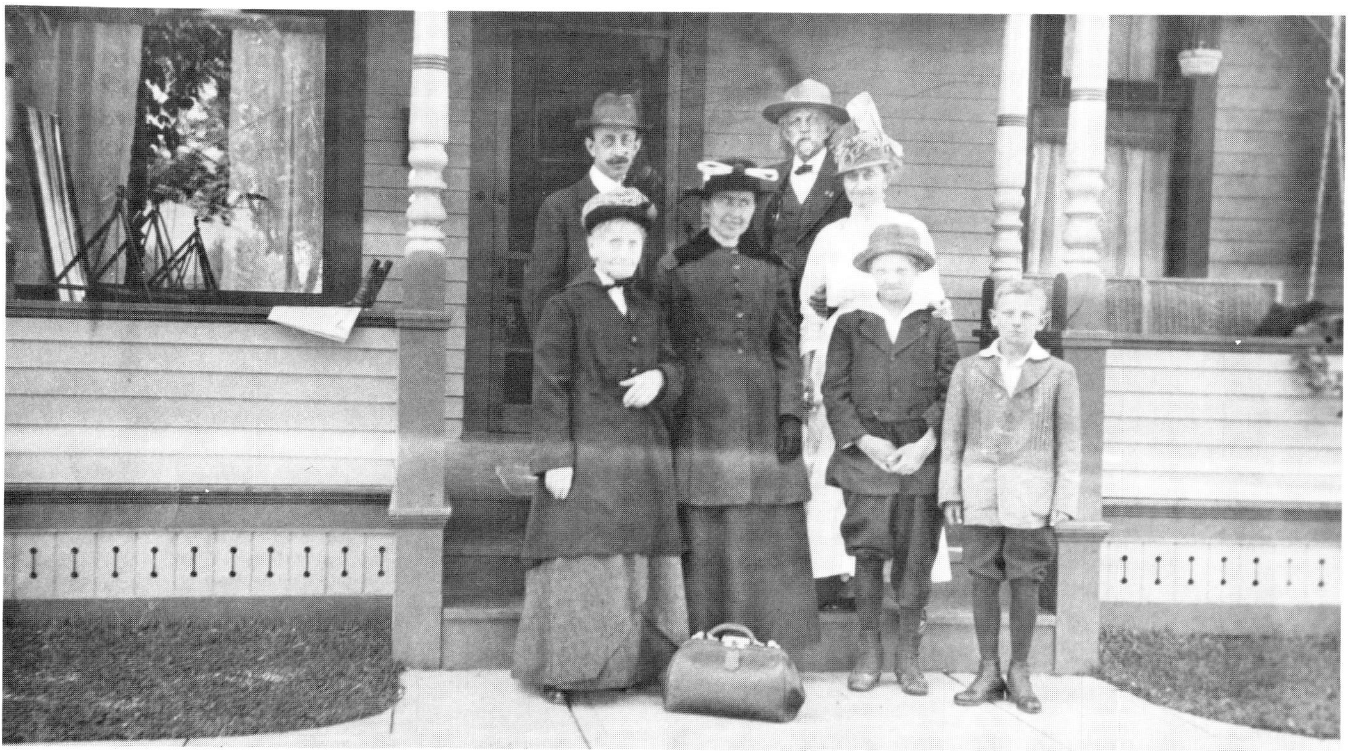

The Paxson family in front of the Missoula home about 1916. Far right is William Edgar Paxson, Sr., the author's father, and grandson of the artist.

the late 1870s. In Butte, Stuart was a frequent visitor to the artist's Woolman Street studio. Edgar wrote in his 1901 journal: "Mr. Stuart came over in the afternoon. I always enjoy his visits and take great interest in all he has to say of his early days here in the Rockies and on the plains. He is, one may say, the Daniel Boone of Montana. A gentleman and great student of nature and of men, once a mighty hunter and explorer. He is now growing old, but we often take a jaunt with the rifle which is always enjoyable." In 1918, Edgar wrote in the back of a copy of *Following Old Trails*:

> Granville and I were the closest friends and companions. It is now more than 40 years since we have been associated and in all that time we have always been dear to each other. We have rode together over mountain and plain, hunted and slept many a stormy night under the same blanket, chewed cold meat and "sower dough" when the snow was deep and the wind howled. Later with a rifle when the day was warm we would roam the mountainside only to pass the time and hark back to other days. Then we would shoot a "few lines," for he was famous with a "Hawkins." How things are different now. Not far from here in the Florence [Hotel] he is toasting his weary feet and casting his eye across the river. He can see where he sat in the snow and made a sketch of [Mount] "Jumbo," [Mount] "Sentinel" and the Hell Gate [Pass] near fifty years ago. At this writing he is eighty four years of age and still young.

Stuart certainly earned Edgar's appellation as the Daniel Boone of Montana. He came to Montana in 1857 and in 1859 was the first to find gold in the territory. Forseeing a great future for Montana, he sent word to Colorado of the strike. Stuart prospered, trading supplies to the gold seekers and becoming a prominent figure in the vigilantes' effort to eradicate criminals in the territory. In the 1880s when the great cattle ranchers flourished, he managed one of the

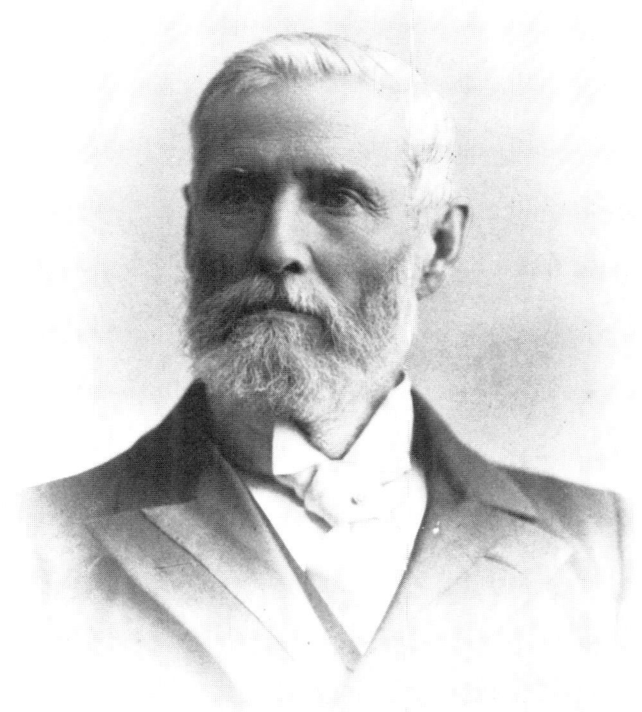

The artist's long time friend and Montana pioneer, Granville Stuart. *Montana Historical Society, Helena, Montana.*

largest and served on the Territorial Council and then the state House of Representatives. He later was appointed minister plenipotentiary to Paraguay and Uraguay by President Grover Cleveland.

During Stuart's eventful career, he acquired a vast fund of knowledge of Montana and its Indians and was a great help in Edgar's research preparation for paintings. Later, as librarian of Butte's City Library, he was able to provide Edgar with the best source books available. The likeness of Stuart himself appeared in at least one painting by Edgar. He is portrayed as a placer miner in *Injuns*, painted in 1903. Stuart was also fluent in Shoshone and other Indian dialects. Occasionally he would drop in to the studio while Indians were visiting and a long medicine talk would follow with many recollections of earlier days. Stuart moved to Missoula shortly after Edgar and with Major John Catlin, they formed an inseparable trio in their waning years. They could often be found in the lobby of the Florence Hotel or elsewhere downtown, reminiscing about their experiences. Catlin had much to tell, having been an officer in the Civil War, a civilian volunteer in the 1877 Battle of the Big Hole and later a Blackfoot Indian agent.

The colorful "Poet-Scout," Captain Jack Crawford, kept up a steady correspondence with Edgar as he toured the country with his vaudeville show. And when in Montana, he visited the artist's studio and joined Edgar on camping trips. Crawford had been chief of scouts for Generals Crook and Merritt during the Sioux and Cheyenne campaign of 1876 and for Generals Hatch and Buel against Victoria and Geronimo in 1881–85. He had always been a flamboyant and entertaining storyteller and later turned these talents into a successful career on the stage, giving readings of his poetry and dramatic narratives about the Old West. His recitals always had a moral, deploring especially the dime novel and alcohol as dangerous for young people. In 1902, while Captain Jack was a guest of Edgar's, he recited one of his "Cowboy Sermons" to visitors in the artist's studio. Edgar wrote: "His every movement and the play of his bright gray eyes glittered in harmony withs each word. He is a most remarkable man."

Edgar and Buffalo Bill Cody renewed their friendship in 1910. Their last previous documented meeting had been in 1893 in Chicago, during the Columbian Exposition, when Cody had provided Edgar with complementary front row seats to his Wild West Show. The occasion of the reunion was the show's engagement at Missoula. Edgar was bedridden from illness at the time and afraid he would miss his old friend. But Cody's partner in the show, Pawnee Bill, appeared at Edgar's door with a car to take him downtown. they had a long visit in the showman's tent. Edgar wrote in his journal afterward: "[Col. Cody's hair] is white as snow, but [he is] still strong and erect as ever. We talked of the older days and people we both knew."

In 1914, Buffalo Bill's show returned to Missoula and again the two old-timers got together. Edgar recorded the event in his journal:

> I was honored by Col. Cody, an old plains friend by riding with him at the head of the parade [seated between the two was Edgar's wide-eyed nine-year-old grandson, William]. Before this I introduced him to many friends who were pioneers. [We] went to the "U" library to see "Custer." This impressed him very much. At the Courthouse, he viewed the murals and remarked there was no building of the kind in all the country that could boast of anything so good. At the studio he sat down in perfect content and was loath to go. He will come again.

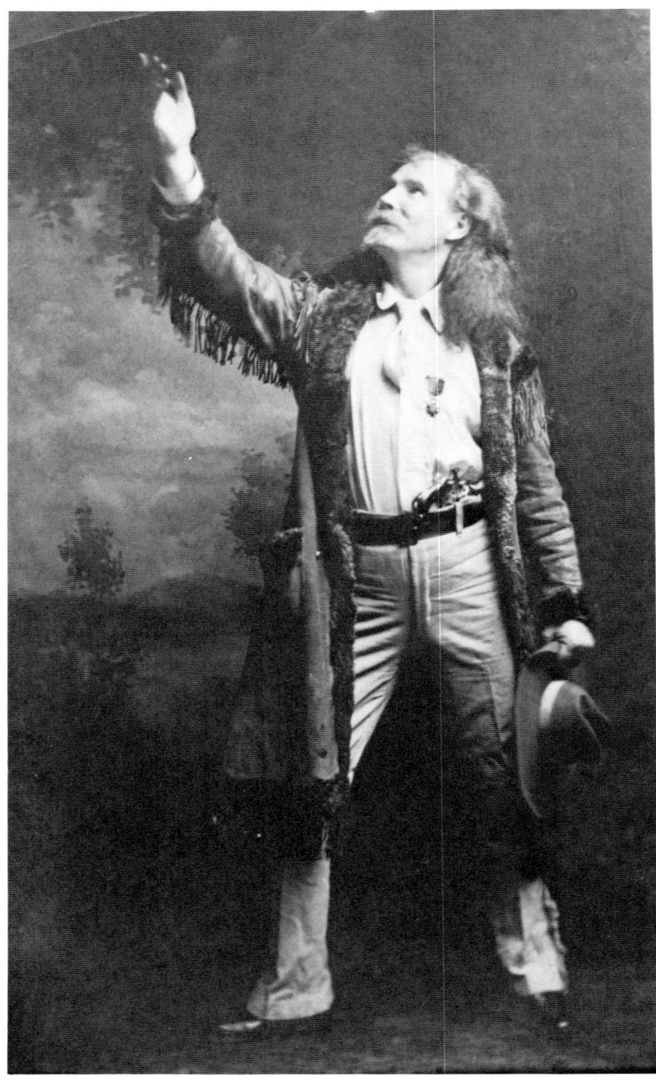

Paxson's long time flamboyant friend, Captain Jack Crawford, "The Poet-Scout."

But the famous scout never returned. He died seventeen months later. Edgar wrote at his death, "There will never be another like him and there will be no need."

When Charles Russell and Edgar first met is not known for certain. A 1901 entry in Edgar's journal notes that he had not seen his friend, "the Cowboy Artist," since 1891. This is the earliest documented date of their friendship, although no evidence conflicts with Albert Partoll's claim in a 1933 newspaper article that the two artists became acquainted in the early 1880s.[1] Russell came to Montana in 1880, the year Edgar moved to Butte from Deer Lodge. In 1902, Edgar did a watercolor Indian head as a gift for Russell. Charles Schatzlein delivered it to Russells home in Great Falls and returned with a Russell watercolor of a Blackfoot brave for Edgar. Thereafter the two artists renewed their freindship and the Russells, Schatzleins and Paxsons had several get-togethers. As the years passed, the artists were drawn together as kindred souls trying to retain what was left of the Old West. In 1908, Russell invited Edgar by telegram to join him at the annual buffalo roundup on the Flathead Reservation. Edgar grabbed his saddle and chaps and headed for the buffalo camp. The artists met at Arlee and took the stagecoach to Ronan, near the camp, and put up in a hotel room. They did not get to sleep until very late that night, for they lay awake in bed talking of old times, friends and art. The next day, as there was some delay in the roundup, Edgar and Charlie spent their time talking with and sketching the Indians and cowboys. In the evening they made themselves comfortable in the hotel lobby. Russell pulled out a lump of the beeswax he habitually carried and the two artists passed the time modeling. The next day they were up at dawn for a long walk on the prairie before breakfast. They spent most of the day out in the country contentedly sketching in watercolor, dipping their brushes in the clear waters of Spring Creek. But the roundup was further delayed by the escape of sixty saddle horses, so Edgar decided to return home to fulfill his commitments there. He left behind his saddle and chaps for his friend Charlie to use.

Whenever Charlie was passing through Missoula, he would always pay a visit to Edgar. One time he came at four A.M. owing to a delayed train. Edgar arose at six A.M., made a fire and sat down to read the paper. Over his shoulder he heard, "Hi there!" There was sleepy-eyed Charlie. He had fallen asleep curled up on a buffalo robe on the porch. The two friends had breakfast and went to visit Edgar's neighbor, George Falligan, who had been one of Charlie's "cow bosses" in the early days. There they swapped yarns until Russell's train was ready to depart for Great Falls. On other visits to Missoula, Charlie would put up in the kitchen of the Anderson family. Jack Anderson had also been a cow boss of Charlie's. On these occasions, Edgar would come over for the evening. In a newspaper interview, Anderson's son, John, recalled those times: "He [Russell] and Ed Paxson would sit up most of the night sometimes playing cards and having a big time.... He was always having friendly arguments with Paxson. He'd acuse Paxson of being unable to paint an Indian and Paxson would declare Russell couldn't paint a horse."[2]

In 1915, Edgar and Charlie led the Fourth of July celebration in Missoula. This year was particularly important for Missoula as it was also the fiftieth anniversary of its settlement. Accordingly, there was not only

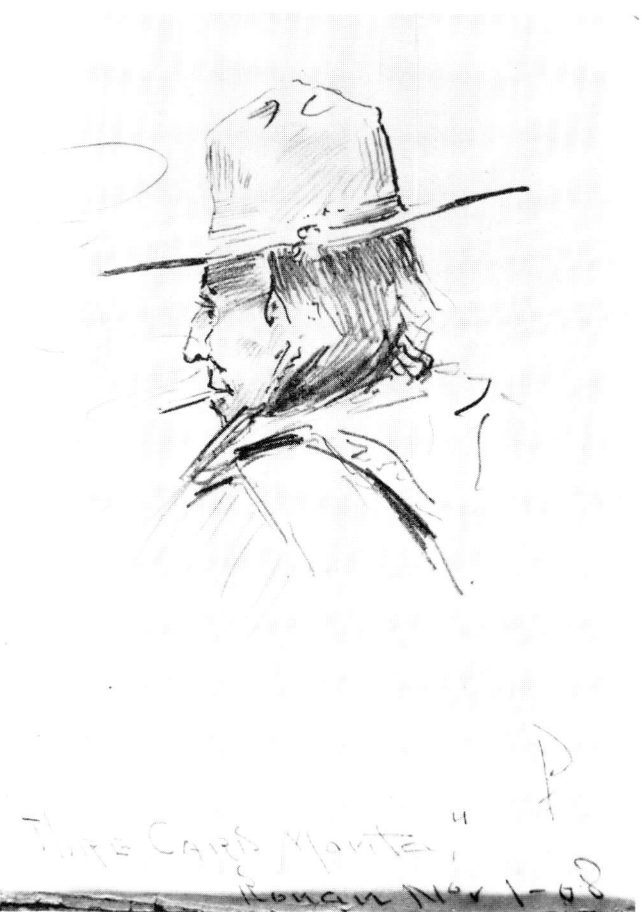

"Three Card Monte, Ronan, Nov. 1-1908." Pencil sketch done in the company of Charles Russell at the annual buffalo roundup. *Private Collection.*

the "Stampede" (fair and rodeo), but the usual parade was made into an "Historical Pageant." Elaborate floats were created depicting the famous events of Montana history. Edgar had the honor of being Grand Marshal of the Pageant. He rode a spirited pinto at the head of the parade. With him was Russell, whom Edgar had specially invited to share the honor. Twenty-five thousand people packed downtown Missoula to see the event. Edgar wrote in his journal that he was greatly pleased at the pageant's success in portraying the history he and Russell were endeavoring to preserve on canvas.

The same forces that drew Russell and Edgar together, drew many old Indian chiefs as well as young braves to Edgar's studio. There they would see visions of times gone by in Edgar's paintings and the graying warriors would often be stirred to speak proudly of buffalo hunts and Indian comrades long dead. Edgar wrote of one occasion in 1901:

> Two old Indians called on me this p.m. They were greatly taken with a picture I am finishing of a buffalo hunt. One of them through signs told me of the many times he hunted the "Moos-nea" with bow and arrow. He is 81 years of age. They all delight to sit and study pictures of wild Indian life. They are fine critics, going deeply into the minutist detail, attended with great excitement generally.

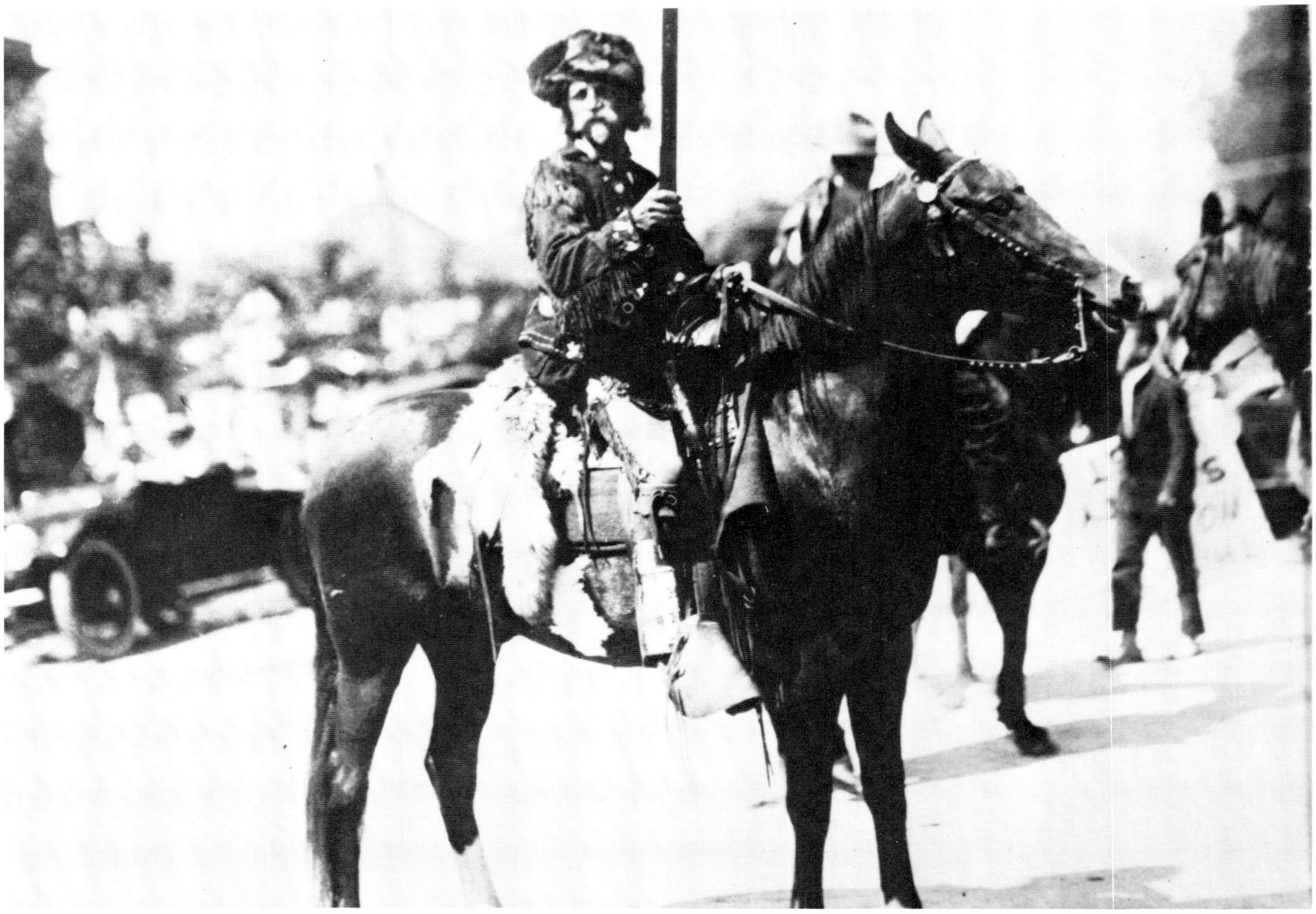

The artist as Grand Marshall of Missoula's 1915 Stampede Parade and Historical Pageant.

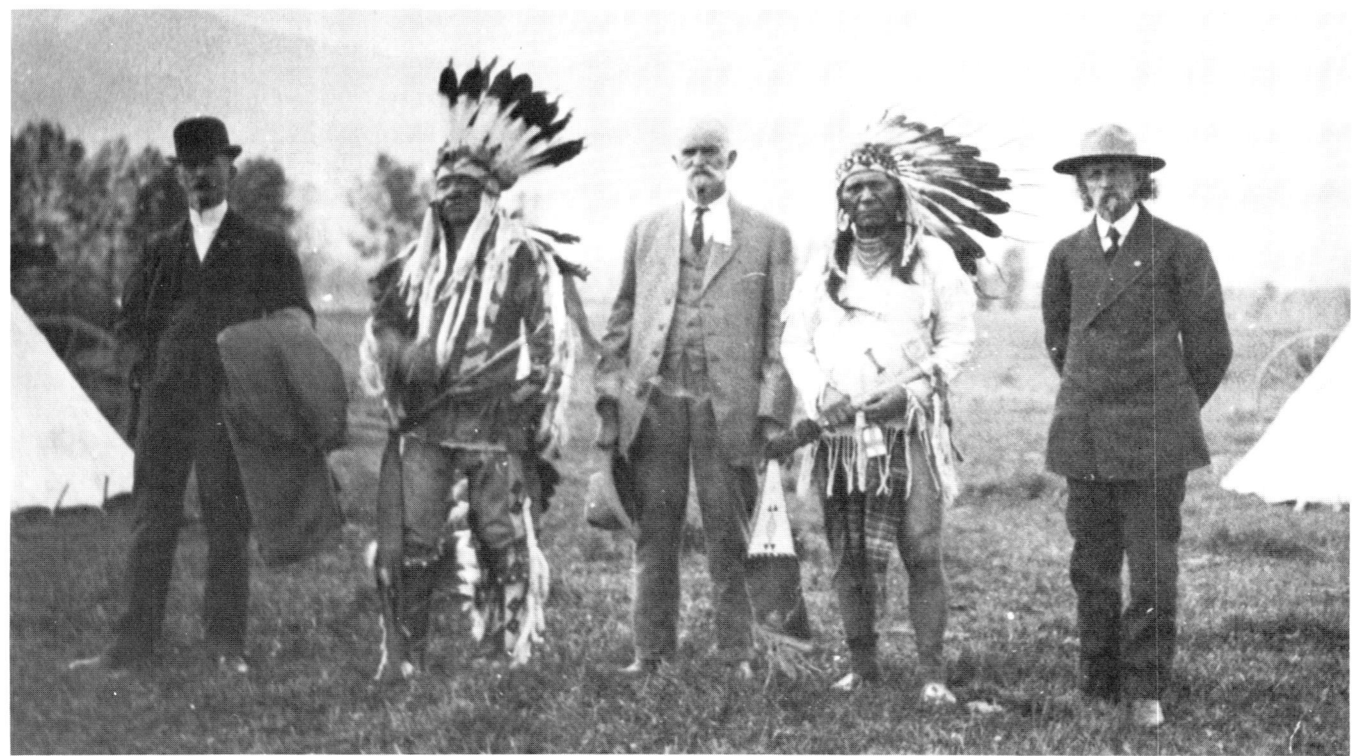

The artist with Flathead leaders at the funeral of Chief Charlo, 1910. Center is Major John Catlin, Paxson's long time friend.

Edgar noted another time that a son of Ten Doy was much taken with a buffalo hunt scene and sat silently studying it for twenty minutes, finally exclaiming: "Wagh! Much good."

The Cree Indians also camped outside Butte and Edgar occasionally visited to talk and play cards. He became a friend of a young brave of nineteen named Car-ne-con-yur who modeled for him many times. Edgar saw him participate in a sun dance in 1901, but five months later received the sad news of the young brave's sudden death from smallpox.

Edgar saw the passing of several of his Indian friends from the early days. Ten Doy, with whom he had spent several months hunting in 1877, died in 1907. Edgar noted at the time that at their last meeting, "The old chief took from his belt his pipe and pouch which he presented to me. I will ever keep it in remembrance of a fine old Indian."

In 1910, Charlo, the most famous Flathead chief, died. Edgar and John Catlin went to the reservation to pay their respects to his wife. In gratitude she gave Edgar a collection of rare photographs of the chief. Then they smoked the calumet with Louison, Moise and the other Flathead leaders, who were all gray and near the end of their years. Shortly thereafter Louison presented that historic tomahawk-pipe to Edgar. The old chief said it was given to his father, who was a chief of the Nez Percé, by Lewis and Clark on their return from the West in 1806. In 1912, Louison sat several times for a portrait, holding the calumet, but died as the painting was nearing completion. Edgar wrote in his journal at the time:

> My old Indian friend Chief Louison died last night. I hoped to see him again before he went on the long trail. I had little hopes of doing so when he last bid good bye to me after his last sitting for his portrait, which I finished with the exception of his dress. When he sent me the leggins he wished me well and said "Bye-n-bye me see you!" Louison was a quiet man always considerate for his people and did all he could to council them wisely in their affairs. In his younger days he was an imposing figure, tall and straight, and always proud of his Nez Perce blood. When Major Ronan appointed him judge he at once assumed that office and always with credit. It was he who gave me the name "Cot-lo-see," he-sees-everything. For many years we were the best of friends. Many is the story of his long life of 80 years he told me and I shall ever revere the kindly old man.

The Indian, the pioneer, the wilderness itself—Edgar mourned their passing equally. He had known them intimately and he knew that they were doomed. In 1907 he wrote: "In a few years the pioneer will be gone. There will be the last of a great people." Shortly after his 1905 hunting trip in the Kootenai Mountains, he wrote: "The day is not far distant when all that wilderness will be more accessible and the novelty will be gone. Then you boys will miss the wilderness trail and ride it no more."

There are dozens of references in Edgar's journals

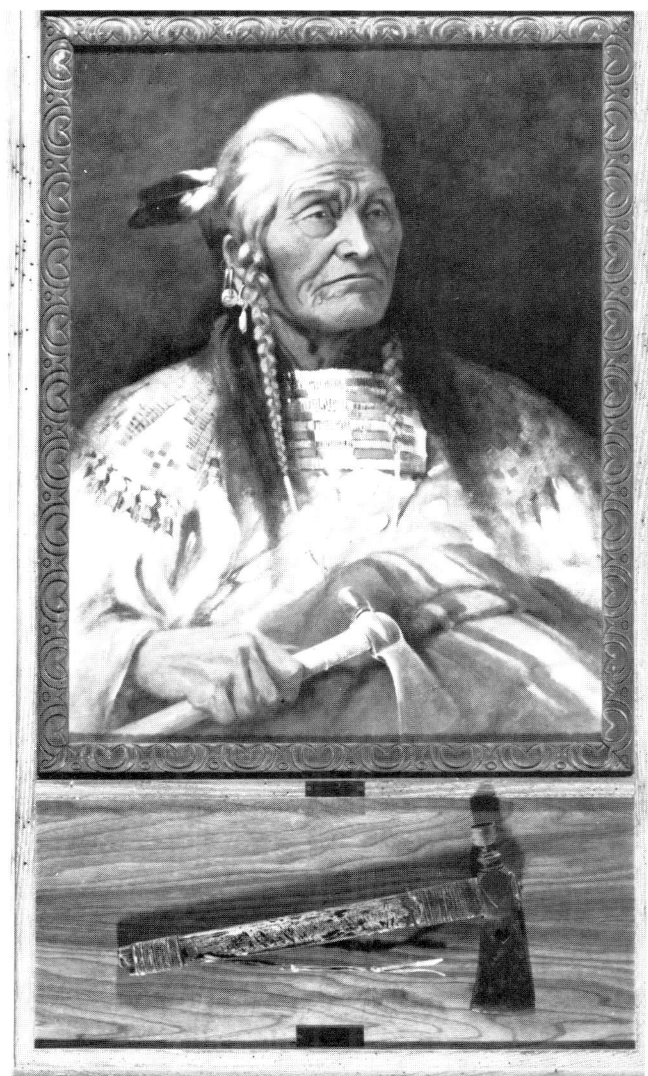

"Louison, Sub-chief and judge of the Flatheads." Oil, 1914. 27 x 20. *Los Angeles Athletic Club Collection.*

to Indians visiting the studio in both Butte and Missoula. Some of the Indians who called were Flatheads—Louison, La Moose, Moise, Creeping Bear, Many Bears, Aeneas; Blackfoot Chief Curly Bear; chief of all the Crees, Little Bear; and Bannock-Shosone Chief Ten Doy and his half-brother Nag-a-shaw. Sometimes Indians would come in a group for a medicine talk complete with passing the pipe. Other times individual Indians would enter the studio silently while Edgar was in the house. Later he would come in to find them quietly studying some painting or artifact. They also on occasion silently made themselves at home in the house while Edgar was out. His grandson, William, remembers that it was not uncommon for the family to come home and find Nag-a-shaw or Louison wrapped in a blanket, sitting at the kitchen table or in the parlor. One time Nag-a-shaw's brother, Wa-na-pee, stole quietly into the house and upstairs unbeknownst to the family while Edgar was in town. Laura found him quietly sitting on a bed and gave him a photo album to look at until Edgar got home. She knew Wa-na-pee, as he was often a guest for lunch, as were many of the other Indians.

Edgar often visited his Indian friends on the reservations and when they camped outside of town. One instance he recorded in 1901:

> I had Robbie get up the pony and having put a gun in my belt lit out for the hills. I had a delightful ride, after which I visited the Sho-sho-nie camp where I met Ten-doy after 24 years save a short time 8 years ago. He is looking hale and hearty in spite of his 58 years of hard life. He took me to his lodge where we had a visit of two hours, relating many incidents of long ago. Weather permitting he will be up soon to sit for his portrait.

That Edgar had the ability and knowledge to record for future generations the heroic and noble side of those who lived and struggled in the western wilderness, was a great joy to him.

Yet Edgar was neither discouraged nor bitter at the changes that civilization had wrought. He knew that he was part of a dying era, but he did not resent the changing world. He was able to reconcile his love for the Old West with his opinion that civilization had turned Montana into a "thriving and wonderful state." That he cared about future generations enough to paint *for them* is evidence of his optimism. This optimism made him able to accept the evolution to a civilized society as inevitable and desirable, in spite of the irreversible destruction of the wilderness he loved.

The Indian, of course, suffered most in the changing West. Despite Edgar's belief in the ultimate good of civilization, he roundly criticized the white man's wrongs committed against the native Americans. In the margins of many of the history books that were in his library, there are his notes deploring the duplicity of the whites. He was particularly severe in condemning Congress. He once wrote, "The usual Congress scandals are much in vogue, especially the robbery of the poor Indian." Edgar felt that this deceit was in a large part responsible for the Indian attacks on the white settlers. He did not at all agree with the widely accepted notion that Indians were innately treacherous. He judged both whites and Indians as individuals. And he believed that men were instinctively honest, but that, sadly, treachery bred treachery. He deplored men like Rain-in-the-face, who gave into treachery by committing atrocities; but he lauded many Indian leaders such as Red Cloud, Joseph, Charlo and Ten Doy, for facing treachery with dignity, honesty and strength. Of Red Cloud, who negotiated the 1868 Treaty of Laramie, Edgar wrote, "[He] was superior to any Indian Commissioner I ever knew." Regarding the story of the four Indians portrayed by Edgar in a Montana state capitol mural, *Seeking the White Man's Book*, he wrote: "This is my favorite.... Please tell me of a whiteman who would walk 2,500 miles for a Bible."

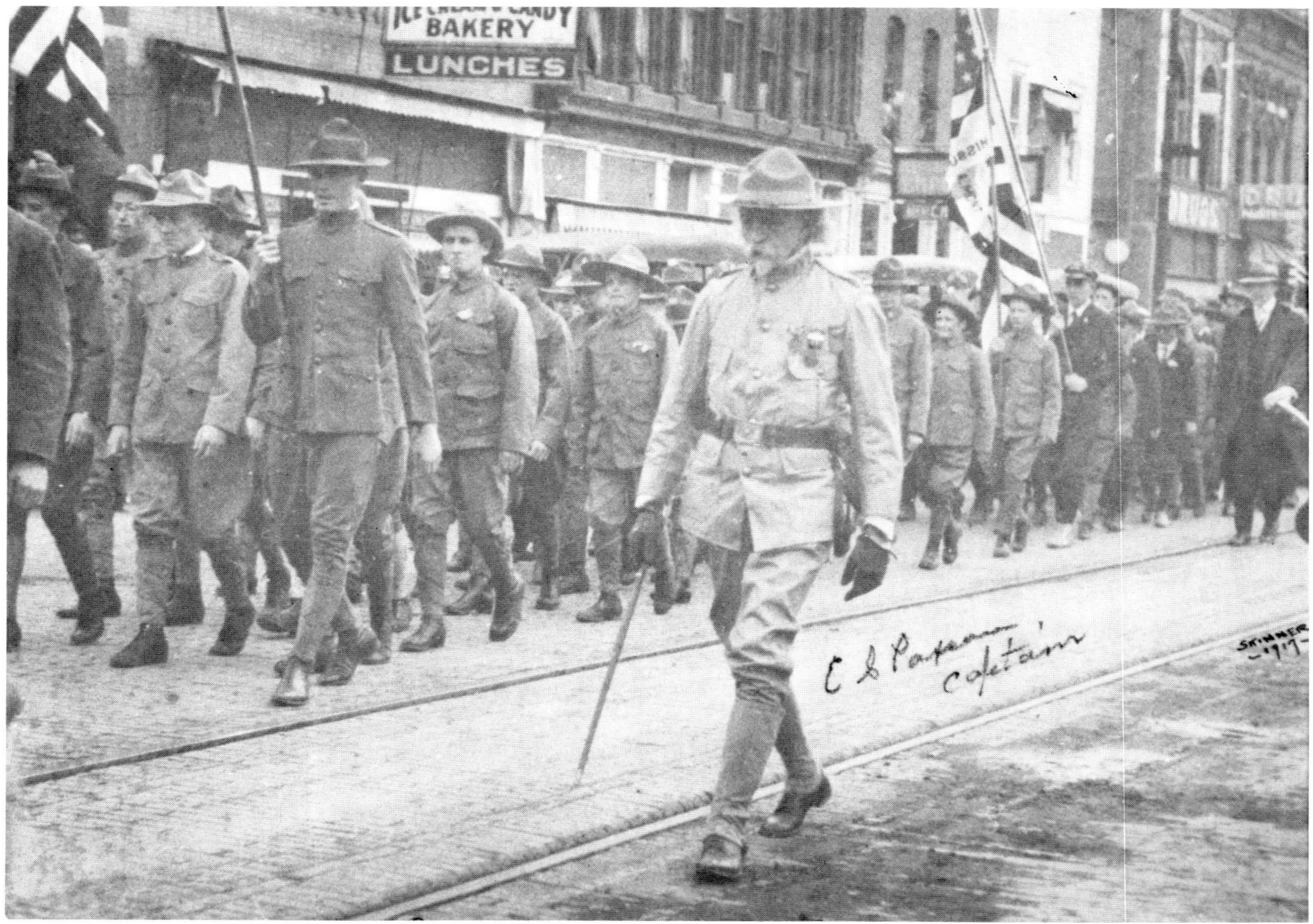

Drillmaster Paxson parading with his charges, high school and university students during World War I.

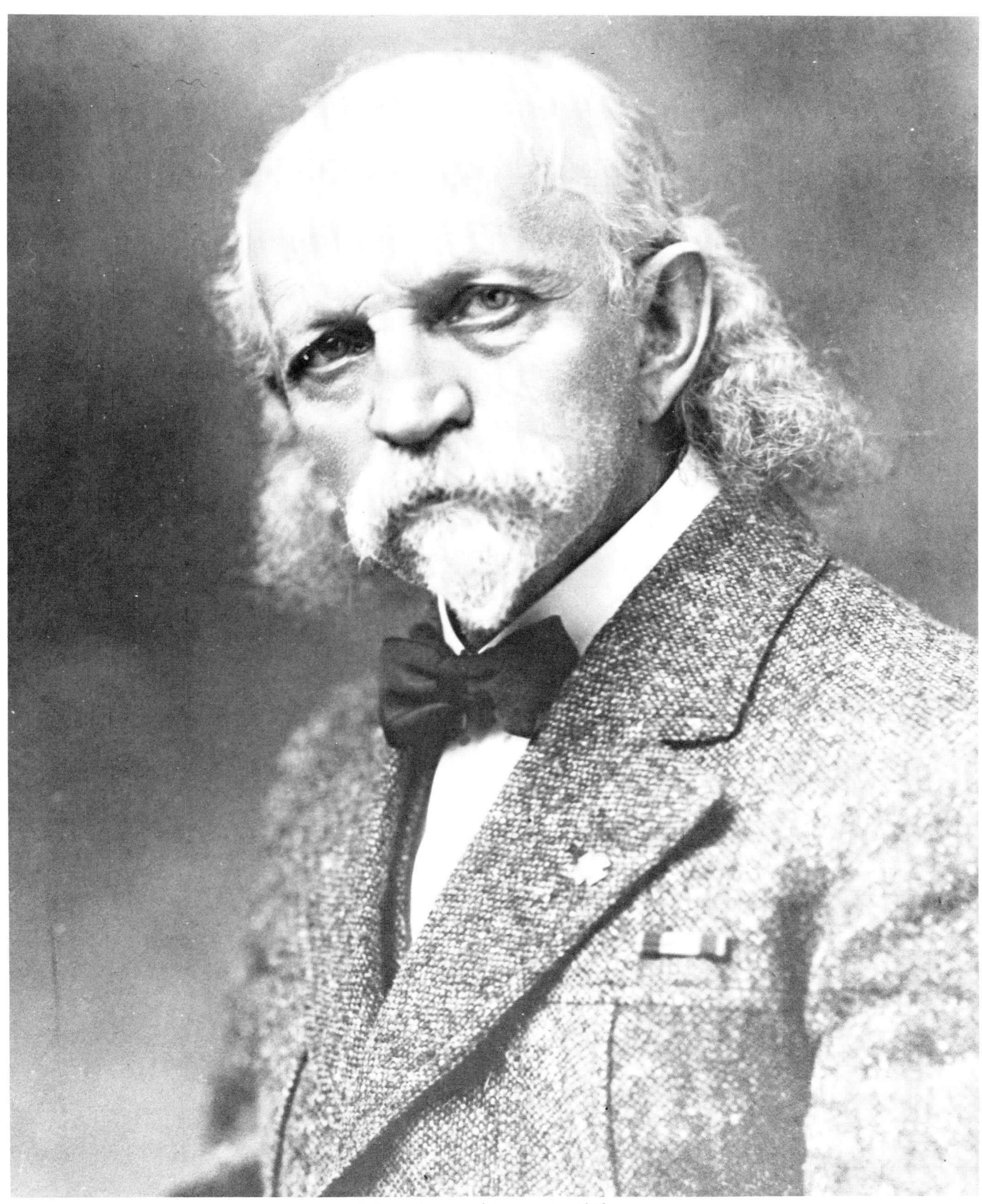

A final photographic portrait, 1919.

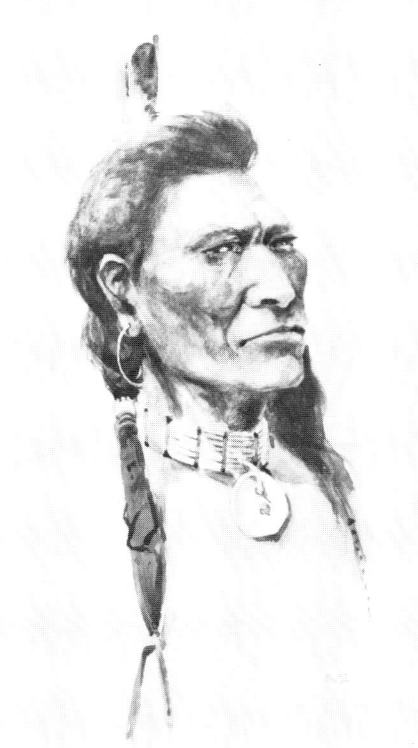

"Indian with Necklace," Watercolor on paper, 12 x 9. *Wunderlich & Company, Inc.*

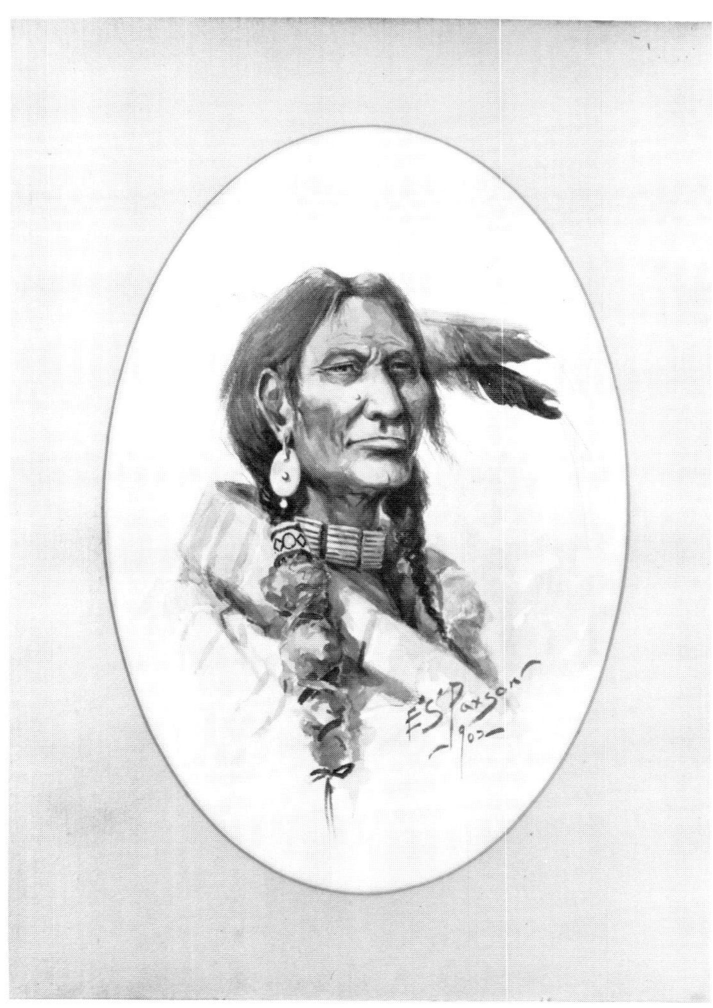

Title unknown, watercolor, 1902, 15 x 13. *Private Collection.*

Edgar was certain that "renegades and savages," terms used so often to describe Indians, were equally present in the white population. Once, at a site in the East where Indians wiped out a white settlement long ago, Edgar wrote in his journal: "How different today. Just a hundred years have passed. But yet! There are savages, right here yet!"

Edgar delighted in recording small incidents in his journal when Indian friends got the best of white "savages." On one such occasion Edgar reported that when a Cree acquaintance left a pony in front of a store, a white man tried to ride the Indian's property away. The brave quickly caught the thief and, as Edgar put it, "laid him out in fine style." In another incident, two whites snatched two dollars from a squaw and rode off in a wagon. Edgar reported that some Shoshones pursued on horseback "one plugging the hat of one [thief] with lead. They got away but not for long."

The "plight of the Indian" as well as everything else concerning the Old West was abruptly forgotten by the U.S. public with the advent of World War I. All attention was turned toward Europe and the new challenge. Even Edgar was diverted. As always he was patriotic and eager to "do his part." He dutifully wrote the War Department offering his services. He was a frail sixty-five when war was declared. Nevertheless, he donned his uniform again and drilled high school and university students and Boy Scouts, and helped out at the local enlistment and Red Cross offices. His son, Bob, enlisted and was soon sent to France where he fought on the front lines. During that period when Bob was overseas, July 1917 to July 1919, Edgar had little energy or inspiration to paint the western subjects he loved. Although he did produce some work of varying quality, he laid aside his brushes for months at a time. In the winter of 1918, he could not paint because coal was scarce—too scarce to heat the studio. In January he wrote, "I have pictures half over the world, I will depend on their sale." Sales of his paintings were, of course, very few during wartime, but he was apparently financially comfortable for at no time did he mention a shortage of funds during this period.

When Bob returned from the war, Edgar had only five months to live. His health was failing him. At times he was completely blind, but when he could see well enough, he returned to his easel. He did a watercolor of Fort Owens, Montana, and at least one oil depicting an Indian scene. Much of his effort went into a three-quarter-length portrait of Bob in uniform, which he had worked on a little at a time since his son had enlisted. It was nearly completed on November 9, 1919, when Edgar passed away at age sixty-seven.

His death was noted in newspapers across Montana, some with lengthy accounts of his life and work. The Montana House of Representatives issued a resolution "To the Memory of Edgar Samuel Paxson, Artist, Pioneer, and Writer."

But his greatest tribute came from his fellow artist, Charles Russell:

> A few days ago Ed Paxson crossed the big range. For several years the trail on this side was rough for him, so the Angel of Death, who is a friend to those who suffer, took his hand and led him to a smooth, well-worn trail that has been traveled since time began. He will not be lonesome, or a stranger, for many of his friends have gone before.
>
> Paxson has gone, but his pictures will not allow us to forget him. His work tells me that he loved the Old West, and those who love her I count as friends. Paxson was my friend, and today the west that he knew is history that lives in books. His brush told stories that people like to read.
>
> Civilization is nature's worst enemy. All wild things vanish when she comes. Where great forests once lived, nothing now stands but burned stumps—a black shroud of death. The iron heel of civilization has stamped out nations of men, but it has never been able to wipe out pictures, and Paxson was one of the men gifted to make them.
>
> I am a painter, too, but Paxson has done some things that I cannot do. He was a pioneer and a pioneer painter. He was also a soldier who fought under the colors of our country.
>
> Paxson loved Montana. May the land where he has gone be even more beautiful than the mountains that he loved.[3]

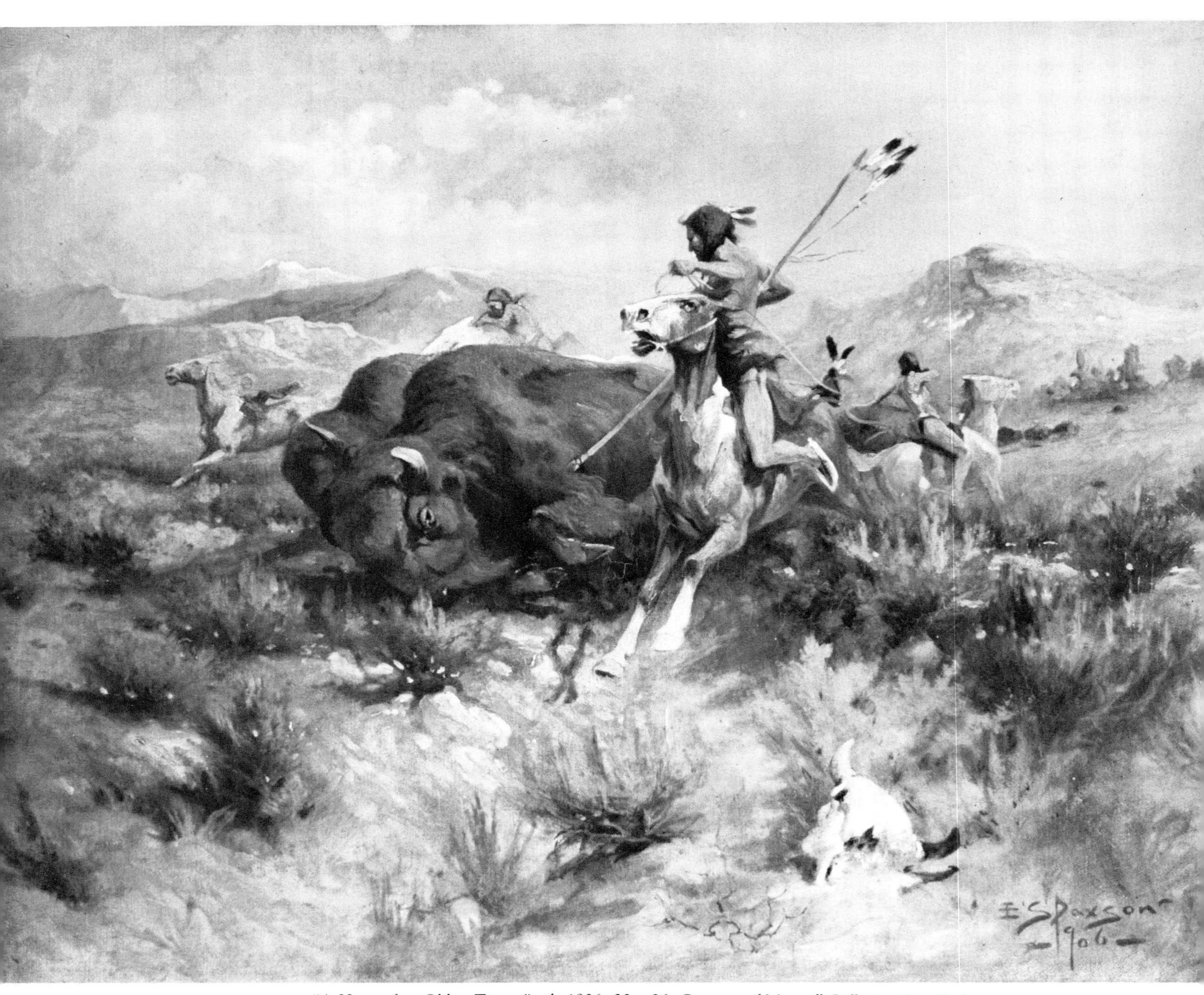

"A Hunt of ye Olden Times," oil, 1906, 20 x 26, *Courtesy of Maxwell Galleries, New York.*

9

The Art of Edgar S. Paxson

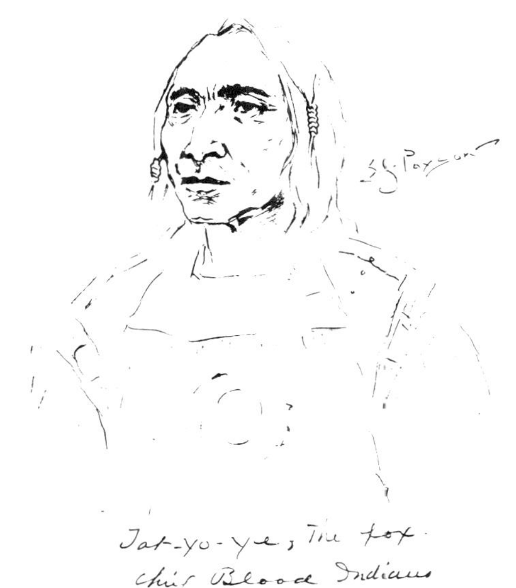

"Tat-yo-ye, The Fox. Chief, Blood Indians." Pencil. *Montana Historical Society.*

Edgar S. Paxson's art is of special interest because of his remarkably rich frontier experience. His early years on the frontier provided him with a store of subject matter matched by few western artists. Further more, Edgar truly became a part of the Montana frontier. He painted home ground—subjects he knew intimately through long association—in marked contrast to the perspective of the nineteenth century artists preceding him who painted the West. For them, the West was largely alien and bizarre, a mysterious wilderness to be explored by expedition and revealed on canvas in its awesome grandeur.

Edgar's work is also remarkable because he developed his genius for painting in what was then artistically isolated Montana. Of the many artists who have successfully portrayed the Old West, very few developed as Edgar did: without formal training and relatively unaffected by the prevalent styles, formulas and mannerisms of European and American art of the day. More than once, Edgar's contemporaries registered disbelief when he informed them that he was self-taught. When he visited the Chicago Academy of Fine Arts in 1903, the head instructor, who admired Edgar's work, was incredulous when Edgar told him of his lack of formal training. When a Swedish artist on lecture tour visited Edgar's studio in 1903, Edgar wrote: "He seemed amazed to know that I was my own teacher. He said he could not for a moment understand it."

More recently Franz Stenzel, in his 1963 monograph on the artist, doubted whether Edgar was in fact entirely self-taught. He interpreted some unsigned handwritten notes, found among Edgar's effects, to indicate that Edgar had studied for three months at the Art Institute of Chicago in 1903. Also mentioned in the notes was Edgar's first experience in drawing from live models at the Academy of Fine Arts.[1] But Edgar's journal, kept daily during his Chicago trip, provides conclusive evidence that he did not study there. His trip lasted only seven weeks and was spent primarily promoting his work. He visited both the art institute and the Academy of Fine Arts as a guest. At the institute the director gave Edgar a quarterly pass as a complimentary gesture. Perhaps this is the source of the mistaken notion about Edgar's three months of study at the institute. In fact, he spent no more than three hours in the institute's classrooms and visited the art academy twice with his own former student who had become a student at the academy. Again Edgar was given free use of the facilities as a complimentary gesture but stayed on each visit for only "a short time," as he put it in his journal.

Not only did Edgar lack formal art training, he had little opportunity for even informal training other than his own trial and error. In the lecture he gave at the Butte Women's Club in 1902, he said "I was never so fortunate as to be in a position where I could even acquire the rudiments of art."[2] Yet Edgar's early paintings show remarkable maturity in drawing and perspective. He, no doubt, developed these skills during his twelve years as a scenic artist, from 1880 to 1892. Because the verisimilitude of scenery in the theater of that time was especially important, Edgar must have directed his efforts from the first toward supplying the detail and illusion of reality that theater audiences expected.

According to a 1906 article about him in *Outdoor Life*, Edgar "absorbed technique by close observation."[3] But he had very few opportunities to view quality paintings. By the time he had determined to devote his full energies to his art in 1899, he had lived in the West for almost twenty-five years. There was precious little fine art there to observe. He could, of course, study lithographs and engravings in *Harpers, Leslies* and other periodicals, but these had limited value for the developing artist. A book of black-and-white Remington prints, which Edgar acquired in the 1890s, at least gave him some exposure to fine painting of western subjects, but it could help him little with oil and watercolor technique. The only instructional aids available to Edgar were the "How-to-paint" handbooks popular during the nineteenth century. A cover of one has been found among Edgar's papers.

Judging from the brief notes and comments Edgar left behind concerning paintings he observed during his lifetime, Albert Bierstadt's work made the greatest impression on him. In an interview with author Enos Mills for the 1906 article in *Outdoor Life*, Edgar recalled that during his youth—at the time he worked for his father painting carriages—he saw Bierstadt's *Laramie Peak* in a private gallery in Buffalo, New York. According to Mills, the painting, a grandiose depiction of a snowy peak, in the foreground of which spread a wide plain where Indians were hunting buffalo, "stirred [Edgar's] adventurous inheritances, and he at once started for the Rockies."[4] In 1915, Edgar again viewed some Bierstadt paintings at the Panama-Pacific Exposition in San Francisco. In his notebook he wrote at the time: "I still cling to Bierstadt who was my first love. His *Laramie Peak* still lingers in my memory, though 45 years have passed by." Also at the exposition were *Niagara Falls* by Frederick Church, *Burning Brush* by Edward Moran and a number of landscapes by William Keith. Edgar's comments on them were: "My ideal of what art should be!...Great!"

Edgar had a lesser opinion of works at the exposition by younger artists, some of whom, he noted, had recently returned from study in Europe. Apparently their work was quite different from the landscapists Edgar favored, for he dismissed them as "fads and freaks."

Edgar mentioned his admiration for his favorite landscapists as early as 1898. While returning to Montana after his service in the Philippines, he traveled by train through the Sierra range. He commented in his journal at the time that the views from the train renewed his appreciation for the paintings depicting the western mountains by Bierstadt, Thomas Moran and Thomas Hill.

When and where he saw the paintings is uncertain. He may have seen other Bierstadts besides *Laramie Peak* as a youth in New York. He chanced upon one Thomas Moran landscape in Minnesota in 1893. He visited galleries in San Francisco in 1898, but noted that most of the work displayed was by local artists. He wrote, "I failed to observe anything which would cause one to pause and reflect."

Edgar's only other opportunities, known to the author, to "absorb technique through keen observation" were on his trips to Chicago in 1893 and 1903. At the Columbian Exposition there in 1893 Edgar visited the fine arts building, and in 1903 he returned to the same building which had by that time become the Fields Museum. Unfortunately there is nothing revealing in his notes about what he saw. He only noted the names of a few leading painters in a matter-of-fact way, briefly commenting on drawing and handling.

Edgar's artistic isolation in Montana occasioned little contact with his contemporary western artists. There were none in Butte or Missoula. Charles Russell lived in Great Falls, over one hundred miles away.

Edgar probably had more contact with Russell than with any other of his contemporaries. However, there does not seem to have been a great deal of exchange about art between them. They had no contact at all in the 1890s, the years that were surely the most formative artistically for both men. The 1908 buffalo roundup at Ronan, Montana is the first documented occasion in which they got together to sketch and talk about art. It is unfortunate that there is no record of what was specifically said in their conversations. Shortly after the roundup, Edgar tried a technique often employed by Russell: he modeled a horse in clay and then used it as a model for painting. But he did not pursue the technique thereafter.[5]

In 1912, Edgar and Russell again got together to paint. The occasion was their being commissioned, along with Montana landscapist Ralph DeCamp, to do murals for the new state capitol. They worked apart on the murals, but they occasionally got together at DeCamp's studio. There are stories of a few easel paintings on which all three painted. The author has identified one such painting, largely DeCamp's work and signed by him. Edgar's work is clearly distinguishable in it, mostly in the lower left. Artist Shorty Shope, who as a youth was a frequent visitor to Edgar's studio and also was acquainted with Russell and DeCamp, viewed the painting and indicated that Russell probably painted some of the mountains and the sky. Russell is known to have been a party to similar joint efforts in the studios of Edward Borein and Olaf Seltzer.

The few personal contacts Edgar had with other painters of western subjects are notable because they are so brief and so few.

There is evidence that Edgar was acquainted with Frederic Remington in the 1880s. In a 1948 interview, a daughter of Granville Stuart remembered that both Edgar and Remington were frequent guests at the Stuart ranch. She was certain that in 1888, the two artists were there together while Remington was engaged in painting Granville, his brother James Stuart and his son-in-law.[6] When Remington died in 1909, Edgar noted in his journal that he would send condolences to the artist's widow, an indication that there had indeed been some personal contact between the artists.

The other nationally known artists with whom Edgar had personal contact were Joseph Henry Sharp and landscapists Edgar Payne and James Stewart. These contacts occurred when the artists visited Edgar's studio. The only records of these visits are brief mention in Edgar's journals and the signatures of the artists, sometimes accompanying a drawing, in Edgar's guest register.

An overview of Edgar's painting reveals no great similarities between his work and that of the artists who have been mentioned here. Although his favorite artists were largely landscapists, he painted few pure

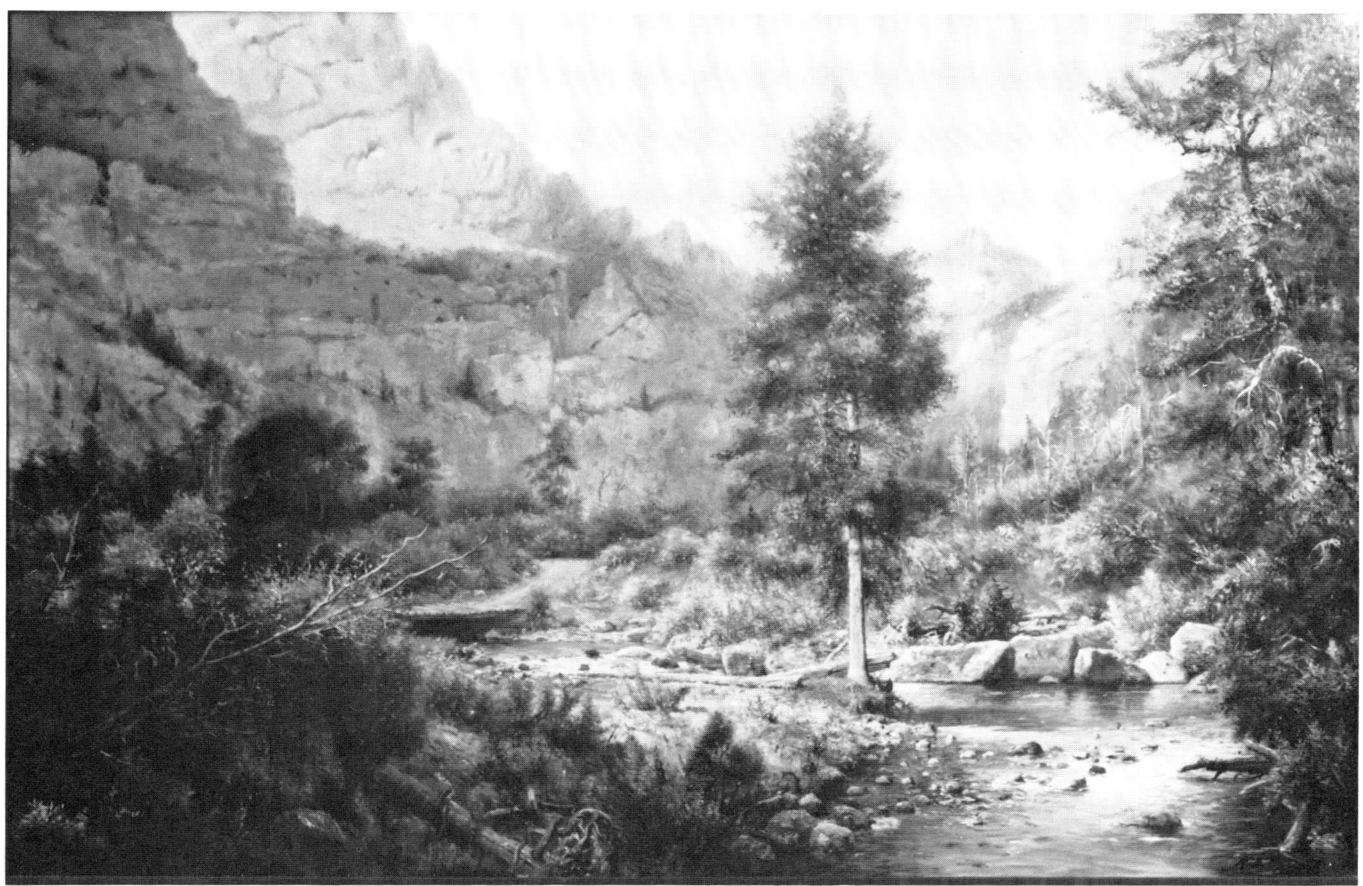

"Wolf Creek Canyon between Great Falls and Helena." Signed by Ralph DeCamp and mostly his owrk, this oil painting also contains work of Paxson and Russell. Paxson's contribution is especially discernable in the lower left. The painting is dated 1917. *Private Collection.*

landscapes. Landscape was an important part of his large paintings and it can be argued that the influence of Bierstadt is evident in some of them; but Edgar did not exaggerate mass and height of mountains and trees as did Bierstadt. And Edgar's human and animal figures are usually more prominent and central in his compositions, whereas Bierstadt often made his figures small and subordinate.

In a general way, Edgar's work may be seen as most similar to Russell's. This is not surprising since the two were nearly exact contemporaries (Edgar was twelve years older), both were self-taught and both matured as artists in Montana after experiencing the demise of the frontier there. The similarities in their work are most probably due to these parallels rather than the influence of either man on the other. And upon examination, the similarities are superficial, being limited to little more than the fact that the two painted Montana frontier subjects realistically, with an eye for authentic detail. The differences, however, are substantial. Edgar was more interested in portraying mountain men and pioneers than was Russell, but concerned himself very little with Russell's favorite subjects: cowboys and range life (to Edgar, Russell was always "the cowboy artist"). Russell limited himself largely to subjects with which he had first-hand knowledge. Edgar, having an intense interest in the history of the frontier, produced many paintings of historical events, which he researched before painting. Both artists, of course, were greatly interested in painting Indians and Indian life, but Edgar devoted more effort to portraiture. Russell, ever the storyteller, gave his paintings an anecdotal quality, often humorous and action-packed. Edgar, too, portrayed dramatic action, but in a more serious vein. Often his Indian scenes have little action; they project instead a sense of harmonious tranquility and quiet dignity. They reflect Edgar's own perspective of the Montana frontier, a perspective transferred to canvas by a naturally developed talent influenced only minimally by other artists.

Although Edgar began painting full-time rather late in life, he was a prolific artist. Evidence suggests that he painted approximately two thousand works. But because he sold his paintings widely during his lifetime and then his work lingered in obscurity for several decades after his death, the whereabouts of many Paxson paintings is not known, and it is difficult to determine the exact extent of Edgar's output. The author has compiled a record of approximately six hundred oils and watercolors based on examination of extant paintings, Edgar's journals, records of exhibitions, early photographs and the correspondence of William Paxson, Sr. with owners of Paxson works during the last twenty-five years. Edgar also produced several hundred—possibly close to one thousand—Indian heads in watercolor.

With few exceptions, Edgar signed and dated his

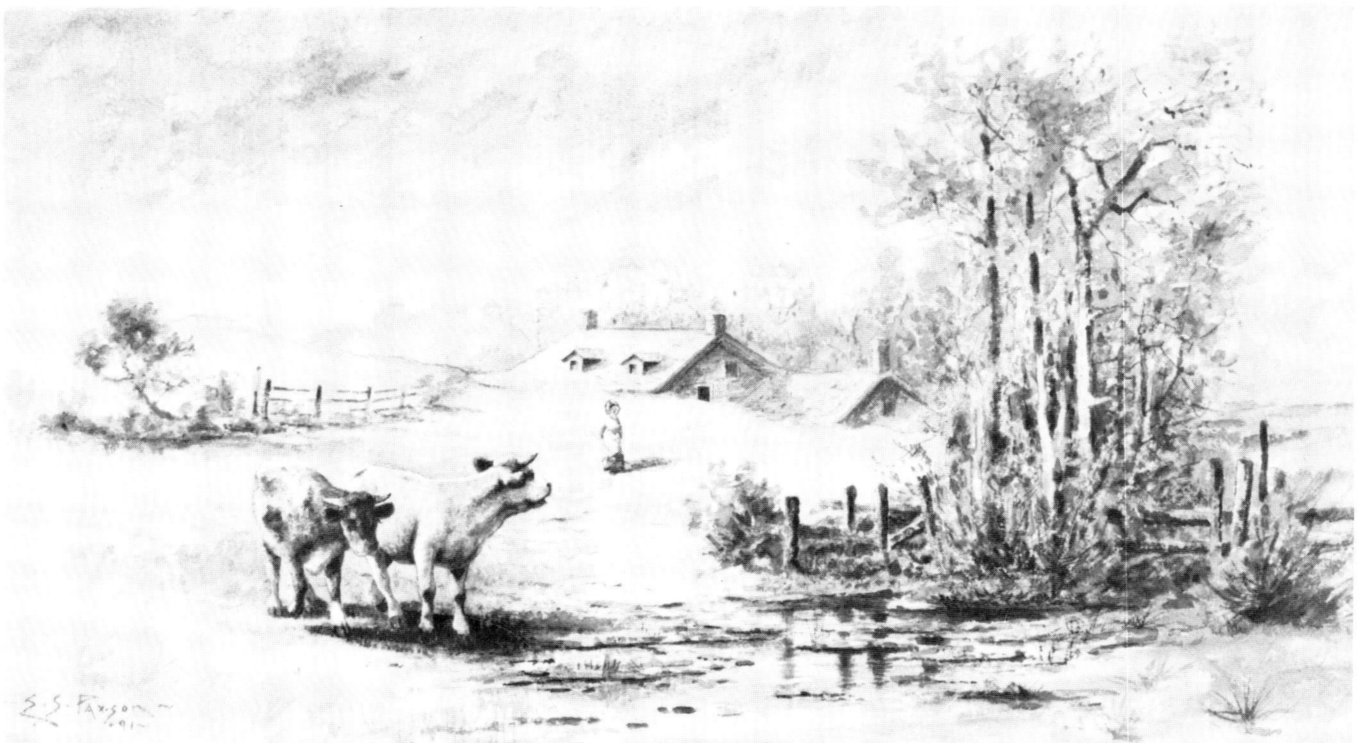

Title unknown. Watercolor, 1891, 14 x 25. This is an example of the artist's early genre painting before he devoted himself almost entirely to painting frontier subjects. *Private Collection.*

paintings, which helped the author greatly in sifting through references.

There is only a very incomplete record of Edgar's work before 1900. The author has evidence of only sixty-seven paintings before then. Certainly the artist painted considerably more. From 1900 to 1917, when Edgar painted on a nearly full-time basis, the records are better, but still incomplete. Very little of Edgar's work during the 1880s exists, and there is no record of how many easel paintings he did during these years. There is no evidence that he destroyed his early works. In later years he seemed more inclined to give away than throw away paintings with which he was not happy. It has been said that he traded paintings for basic necessities during his early years in Butte when money was scarce in his growing family. It is likely that the recipients of Paxson works through these trades were not enthusiastic art collectors, but, rather, friendly shopkeepers. Consequently, many of the paintings were probably forgotten, lost and destroyed over the years.

The earliest Paxson painting now known to exist is a remarkably skillful oil portrait of an early seventeenth century European. It is signed and dated on its back "Ed. S. Paxson, 1880, Deer Lodge." He undoubtedly copied it from a reproduction, but the actual source and subject remain a mystery.

Most of the few paintings Edgar is known to have done in the 1880s and early 1890s are typical of American genre painting. Genre art was popular in nineteenth century America. It satisfied the practical Yankee taste for pleasant, reassuring, realistic everyday scenes of farm life, village life and ordinary pastimes. Several of Edgar's genre scenes have settings outside the Old West. There are eastern rural scenes, a pilgrim scene and even a few seascapes. Two of his most ambitious are hunting scenes showing sportsmen and their dogs. They happen to be Montana scenes but could be easily taken for any eastern woods. There are also four known still lifes of ducks and grouse hanging to age after the hunt. These and the hunting scenes exude the spirit of the outdoorsman. Another sporting scene, *The Last Match*, depicts four marksmen in an autumn landscape. According to a newspaper clipping in Edgar's scrapbook, the four are likenesses of prominent members of the Butte Rod and Gun Club.

But these early efforts were an exercise, an exploration of his talent, for at the time his goal was to record the rapidly fading frontier in paint. After about 1895 Edgar's painting was, with few exceptions, of the Montana frontier.

Most numerous of Edgar's frontier subjects are his Indian portraits. He did several meticulous oils, but most of his portraits are small watercolors from four to twenty inches in height. Although he did several hundred of these watercolors, each is unique. The handling in each study is not highly stylized, but subdued, drawing attention to the character of the subject, not the artistry of the painter. Yet each is so distinctive that it can hardly be mistaken for the work of another artist. In the author's opinion, Edgar's watercolor Indian heads are, with possibly the exception of his *Custer's Last Stand*, his most important contribution to western art. But perhaps their greatest praise came from Charles Russell when he said, "I can't paint an Indian head with Ed Paxson."[7]

Edgar began painting his small watercolor Indian heads about 1900, in response to the shortage of adequate natural light for painting in oil during winter in smoky Butte. He found that by working in watercolor he could dash off complete images during brief periods of favorable light. He quickly became intrigued with these small studies and found that they were readily purchased by local buyers who could afford the five to fifteen dollars per head. He soon found his Indian heads to be his bread and butter work (he called them his "head trade"). His larger, more detailed efforts brought fifty to seventy-five dollars.

For most of Edgar's watercolor heads, it is difficult to determine exactly what the artist used for a model. Certainly many were painted from life. He never lacked live Indian subjects. Those portraits which have an obscure Indian name written on them in the artist's hand are very likely done from life or from sketches made from life. Many portraits were undoubtedly synthesized by the artist's imagination, drawn from the hundreds of Indians he had known and sketched. The many portraits titled with a tribe's name are most likely in this category. For example a portrait entitled *Nez Perce* is probably a study of the Nez Perce type. There are also several full-length studies in this category. In these Edgar captured the fine detail of beaded buckskins, decorated shields, weapons and the like. Sometimes the subjects are mounted on Indian ponies decorated for battle. As in the head studies, there is rarely any background.

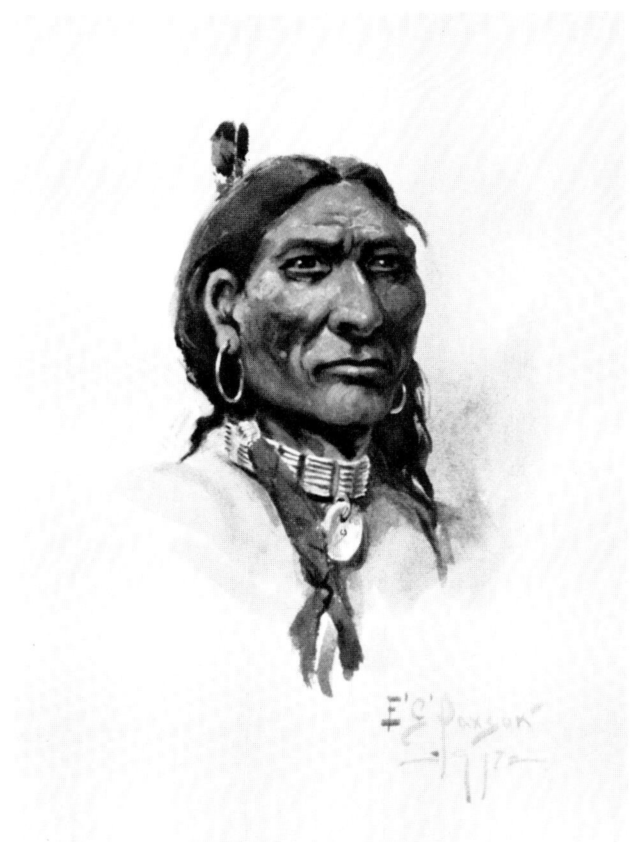

"Young Charlo," Watercolor, 1917, 13 x 10. *Private Collection.*

There are very few sketches extant that Edgar did before 1890, but he had opportunities during that time to sketch famous Indians whom he painted many years later. He wrote that he interviewed Chiefs Two Moon and Gall and Custer's scout, Curley on the Custer Battlefield. It has always been said in the Paxson family that he sketched them at the same time. He wrote that he met Chief Joseph in 1877-8. He sketched Joseph then, too, according to an 1897 Butte newspaper article.[8] A *Fine Arts Journal* article in 1905 stated that Edgar painted a portrait of Joseph in an elaborately beaded buckskin shirt, which was a gift of the artist. The gift is nowhere else documented. In the same article, Edgar was said to have made sketches of both Joseph and Sitting Bull "at a time before the disturbances with the settlers and the hostilities with U.S. troops had embittered them."[9] This is unlikely, because Edgar did not reach Montana until 1877. Joseph was disenchanted with white men at least a year before that time. Sitting Bull had from early on hated the white man.

It is possible that Edgar sketched Sitting Bull in the 1880s. Paxson family legend holds that he did. It is known that the old medicine man made himself available for photographers and artists on the Sioux reservation and when he toured with Buffalo Bill's Wild West Show. A recent article in a small New England newspaper relates a story (not originating from the Paxson family) that Sitting Bull did indeed sit for Edgar, but only on the condition that the painting would show Custer's ring prominently.[10] There is a painting by Edgar showing the ring very prominently on the third finger of the left hand, but there is also a published photograph in Edgar's scrapbook of Sitting Bull in a pose identical to the painting. This certainly discounts the story. Edgar did other likenesses of Sitting Bull, but there is nothing more known about the artist's sources for these portraits.

How much Edgar worked from photographs is not known. He did portraits of several famous chiefs who were deceased or geographically removed from him. Most likely he worked from photographs for these. Portraits of Geronimo, American Horse and Black Hawk are examples. It is known that he used photographs for likenesses of some of the Indians in his *Custer's Last Stand.*

There is no evidence that Edgar duplicated portraits except when he occasionally did a watercolor directly from one of his large oils, usually on request. Although he depicted a number of his subjects more than once, in each portrait he changed the pose, headress, attire or a combination of these. He sometimes received serveral requests for portraits of a chief who had recently died. This was true for Joseph who died in 1904, Charlo who died in 1910 and Geronimo who died in 1909. The author has a record of seven portraits of Joseph and ten of Charlo, these done in either oil or watercolor. Each study that has been inspected by the author was approached differently by the artist.

Although Edgar did far fewer portraits in oil, they were generally more ambitious, larger works. Some of these have been documented to have been done from life. Edgar recorded in his journal that Lemhi Chief Ten Doy, his half-brother Nag-a-shaw and Flathead Chief Louison sat for their portraits. Chief of the Northern Cree, Little Bear, visited the artist's studio in 1904, according to an entry in the artist's journal. but Edgar's only known oil portrait of Little Bear was completed several years later. Edgar painted an oil of Flathead Chief Charlo immediately after the chief's death. He had had, however, many opportunities to see the Flathead leader and perhaps sketch him, for the Flathead reservation was not far from Missoula. Edgar may also have used some rare photographs of Charlo given him by the chief's widow.

Next in number to Edgar's Indian portraits are his oil and watercolor compositions of frontier scenes. These range up to about twenty by forty inches, although a few are larger, and depict Indians, buffalo, pioneers and frontiersmen engaged in wilderness activities. There are quiet scenes of a few figures in a Montana landscape and there are depictions of dramatic action such as buffalo hunts and Indian-white conflict.

Edgar found his buffalo hunts to be some of his most well received works. A 1911 entry in his journal reads: "I plan to do a series of small buffalo hunts. It's what the people want." The author has documented roughly fifty buffalo scenes. Most of them are hunts, but a large portion are quiet scenes depicting one or more buffalo grazing or watering, usually with a powerful bull prominently featured, as if he were lord of the landscape.

The author has a record of twenty Paxson paintings depicting Indian-white warfare. At least three of these illustrate Edgar's personal experiences. Although he often insisted he was never an Indian fighter, he was certainly a witness to hostilities, found himself confronted with renegade Indians, and undoubtedly had to defend himself on occasion. The preliminary sketch for one painting depicting an Indian being shot bears this cryptic note in Edgar's handwriting, "A personal experience of the artist." Whether Edgar fired the shot or was only a witness will remain the artist's secret; the facts about the incident are lost.

There have been western art critics who have insisted Edgar was not very sympathetic to Indians and painted them from the perspective of an "Indian-scout and Indian-fighter...who accepted extermination of the Red-man as essential."[11]

They point to Edgar's *Good Injun* which depicts an Indian being shot as he flees with with a comrade on horseback. But in the light of the evidence to the contrary presented in this biography, a more logical interpretation is that the artist was motivated to paint the subject as an historian. The painting does not reflect a personal prejudice, but rather it is a record of the time. The title reflects the popular prejudice during the Indian wars manifested in the notorious quote by General Sheridan and widely circulated by the press, "The only good Indian is a dead Indian." Similarly Edgar painted *The White Peril* portraying the Indians' fears of white civilization threatening their way of life. Edgar had a penchant for titling his paintings after faddish phrases. He did so when President Wilson coined the phrase "Watchful Waiting" to describe U.S. policy toward the Germans at the beginning of World War I. Edgar painted his *Watchful Waiting*, depicting an Indian brave, prepared for war, intently searching the distance from a rocky outcrop.

In truth Edgar painted to ennoble both the whites and Indians who struggled along the frontier. He portrayed Custer and his men as valiantly fighting a losing battle and he portrayed Chief Joseph with sympathy and honor in his famous surrender. There can be no doubt that Edgar was sentimental in this. His desire was to record the lofty aspects of frontier times. He avoided portraying detestable perpetrations by both Indian and white. In his portrayal of violence, he emphasized the drama of confrontation, not ghoulish brutality and butchery. Nowhere in Edgar's work can there be found an act of scalping or mutilation, or dismembered bodies with dozens of arrows protruding, although such depictions were popular in the illustrated periodicals of the day.

Although Edgar wrote little about his own painting, there are a few brief references in his writings to his lofty view of Indians and pioneers. Edgar's paintings of Indians are aptly summarized by the following paragraph in a book from Edgar's library describing Indians before subjugation by the white man. Edgar marked the paragraph with a brief note—"as I knew them": "They wore an air of sturdy independence. They were equipped according to their natural requirements. Their minds were generally attuned to magnificent ideas of time and distance. They abhorred the limitations that the white man accepts as affecting his dwelling place. They were foes to be reckoned with, or they might be converted into friends worth having."[12] Edgar never painted Indians in the poverty and degradation they suffered after the white civilization overwhelmed them.

Of the pioneer, Edgar wrote this lofty vision: "Stern, hardy people who faced courageously each and every condition as it presented itself, not as in days of old, when warrior bold with lance and steel clad armor fought, but as knights robed in buckskin and 'linsey woolsy' with rifle on shoulder and ax in hand, fighting and hewing a broad trail, which was soon to carry from river to ocean prosperity and civilization."[12] These are certainly the pioneers depicted in Edgar's paintings.

For Edgar, tranquil wilderness scenes were well suited for depicting Indians as he knew them. One of his favorite subjects for large oil paintings was an Indian party winding its way single file down a wilderness trail. He did several variations on this theme. It is obvious from them that Edgar felt the Indian had achieved an admirable equilibrium with nature before encroachment of white civilization. The largest of these paintings is *The Last Gleam* (also called *Up Miner's Creek*), measuring four feet by seven feet. If Bierstadt had an influence on Edgar, it is manifest in this painting.

Although landscape was a key element in most of his paintings except portraits, Edgar painted few more than twenty pure landscapes. He once wrote, "A painting should always tell a story." Pure landscape rarely provided a story for Edgar to record on canvas.

Some of Edgar's landscapes were done on commission. Occasionally landowners paid him to paint a view of their property. In one instance Edgar was commissioned to paint Hamilton, Montana, with copper magnate Marcus Daly's ranch in the foreground.

Several of Edgar's pure landscapes were of subjects outside Montana, done from sketches or in the field while on his visits to California, Oregon and Washington in 1910 and 1915. They include watercolors of Crater Lake in Oregon, Sky-no-mish Falls in Washington, and oils of Mount Shasta and the head of the Sacramento River in California. Apparently the novelty of the new country inspired him to paint it. One of the few pure landscapes Edgar did of Montana country manages to tell a story of sorts: *The First Snow, 1917*, shows Mount Lolo and its foothills with a white mantle on their upper reaches. Another pure landscape is of Yellowstone Falls. Dated 1895, it is done in a thick oil impasto, very rare handling for Edgar. Although it is an effective painting, apparently the artist abandoned this style for unknown reasons and without any further exploration.

The author has uncovered evidence of eighteen books for which Edgar did illustrations. Several of these, however, may not have reached publication. Ten are known with certainty to have been published with Edgar's illustrations:

By Order of the Prophet A Tale of Utah, Alfred H. Henry. Published by Fleming H. Revell, Chicago, 1902.

Glengarry School Days, Ralph Connor (Charles Gordan). Published by Fleming H. Revell, Chicago, 1902.

The Trail of Lewis and Clark, Olin D. Wheeler. Published by Putnam and Sons, New York, 1904.

(The Man) On the Edge of Things, Ella W. Peattie. Published by Fleming H. Revell, Chicago, circa 1903.

Ramrod Jones, Clinton G. Brown. Published by Saalfield Press, 1905.

Life of Reverend L. B. Stateler A Story of Life on the Old Frontier, Rev. E. J. Stanley. Published by the Methodist Church, Nashville, 1907.

Following Old Trails, Arthur L. Stone. Published by Morton J. Elrod, Missoula, Montana, 1913.

Story of Montana, Kate Hammond Fogarty. Published by A. S. Barnes Co., New York and Chicago, 1916.

The Lure of the Frontier—A Story of Race Confllict, Ralph Henry Gabriel. Published by Yale University Press, New Haven, Conn., 1929.

Your National Parks, Enos A. Mills. Published by Houghton-Mifflin Co., Boston, 1917.

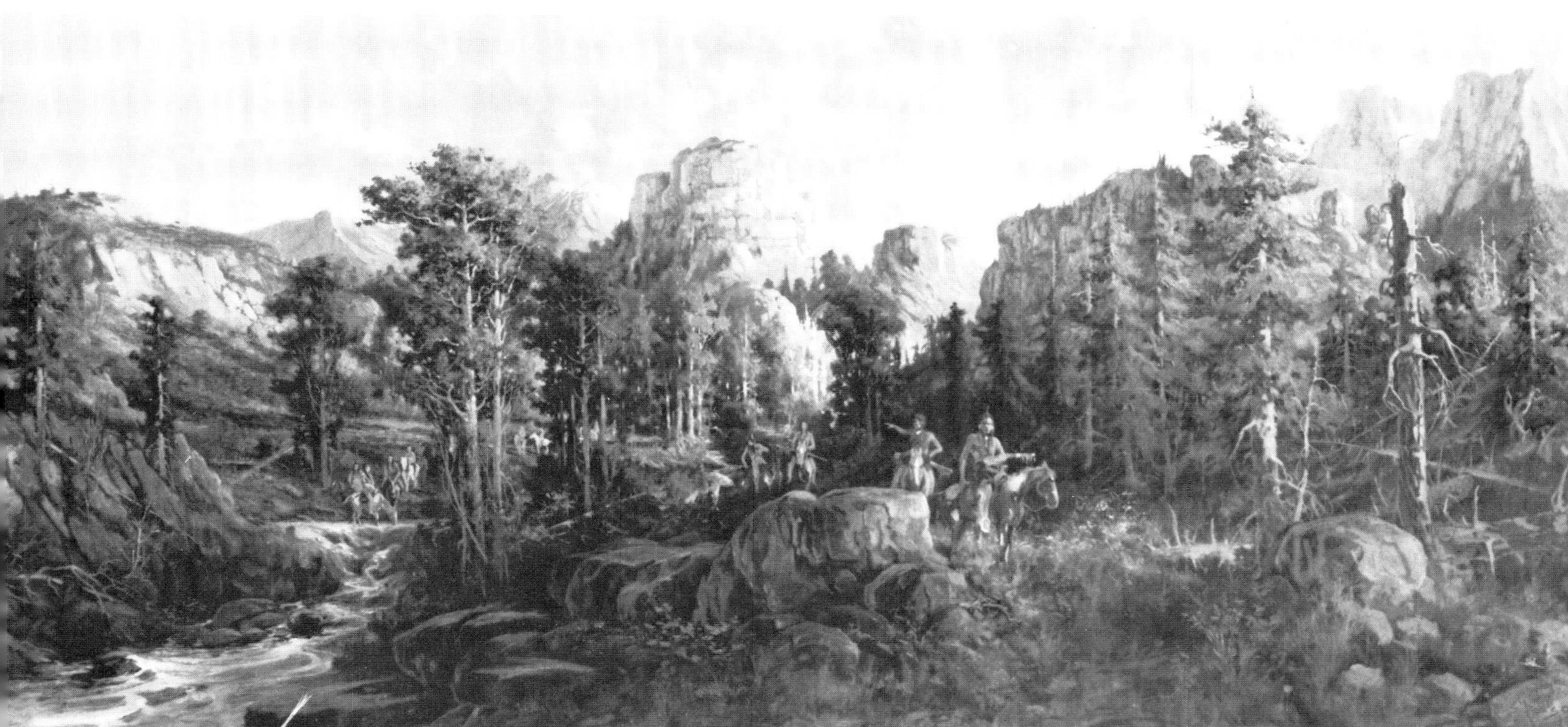

"The Last Gleam" (Up Miner's Creek). Oil, 1915, 48 x 84. *Private Collection.*

Three illustrations for *Ramrod Jones* by Clinton G. Brown, published in 1905. Oil. *Brown Heirs.*

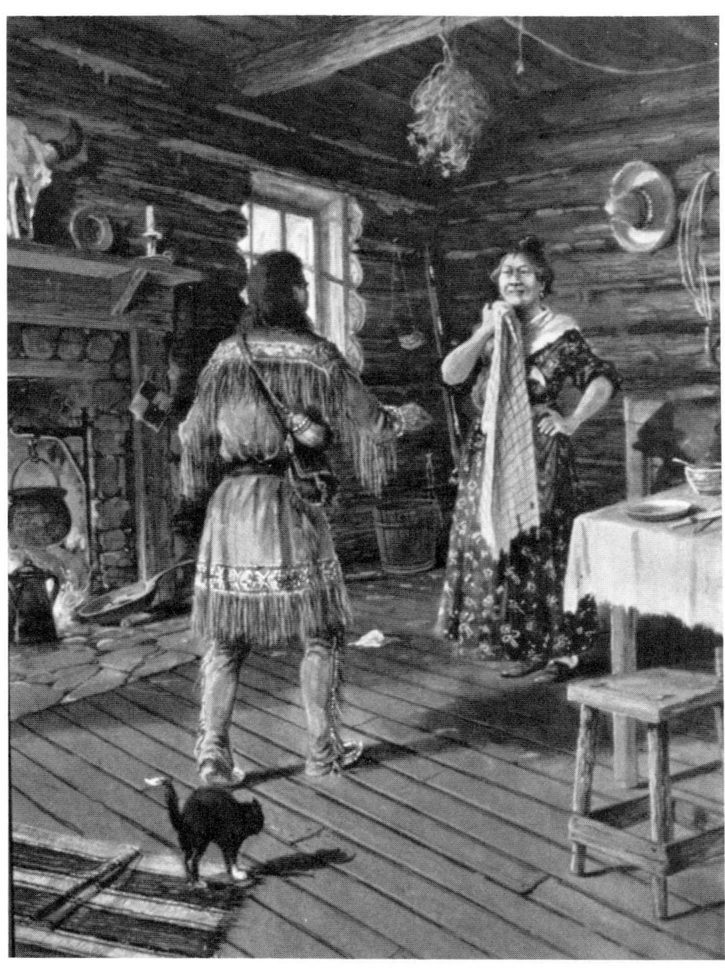

"Landsakes! It's Mr. Blalock. Excuse my greasy mouth."

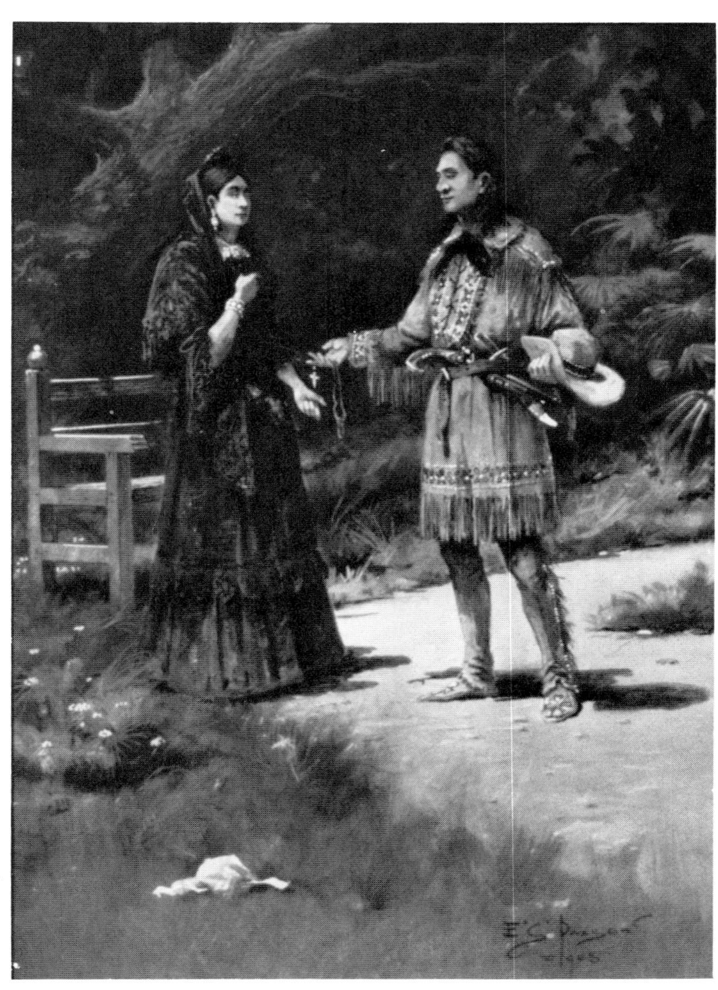

"So I took it from around my neck and put it in her hand."

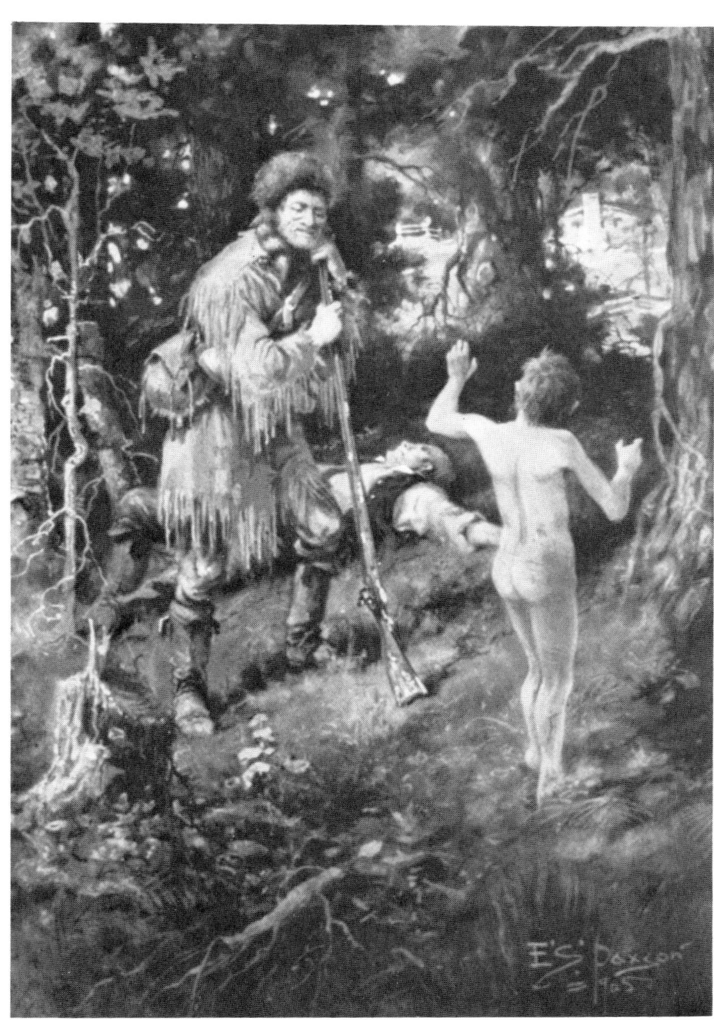

"There, there, sonny, don't be afraid. I ain't goin' to hurt you."

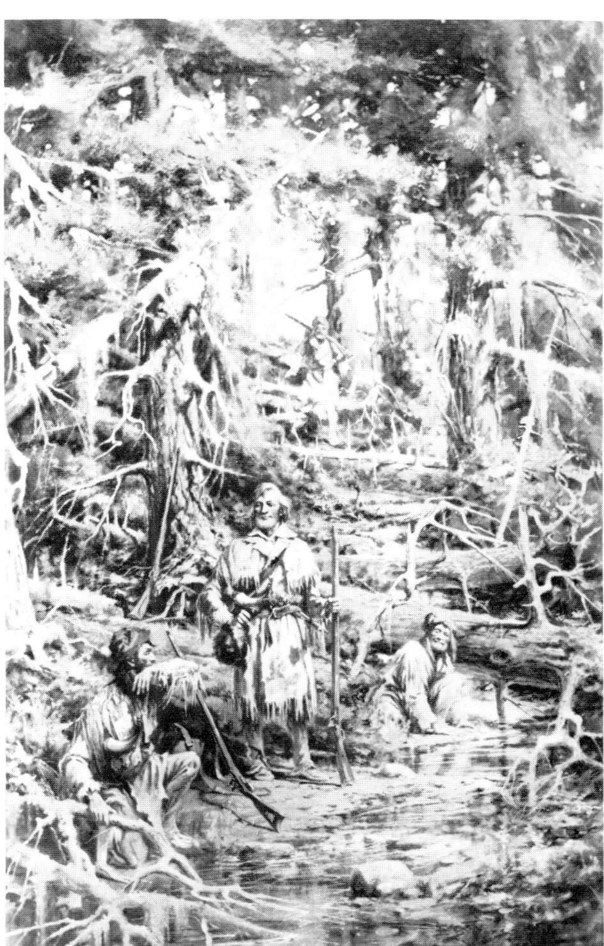

"1804" (Contemplation), oil, 1903. Reproduced from a photograph in the artist's album.

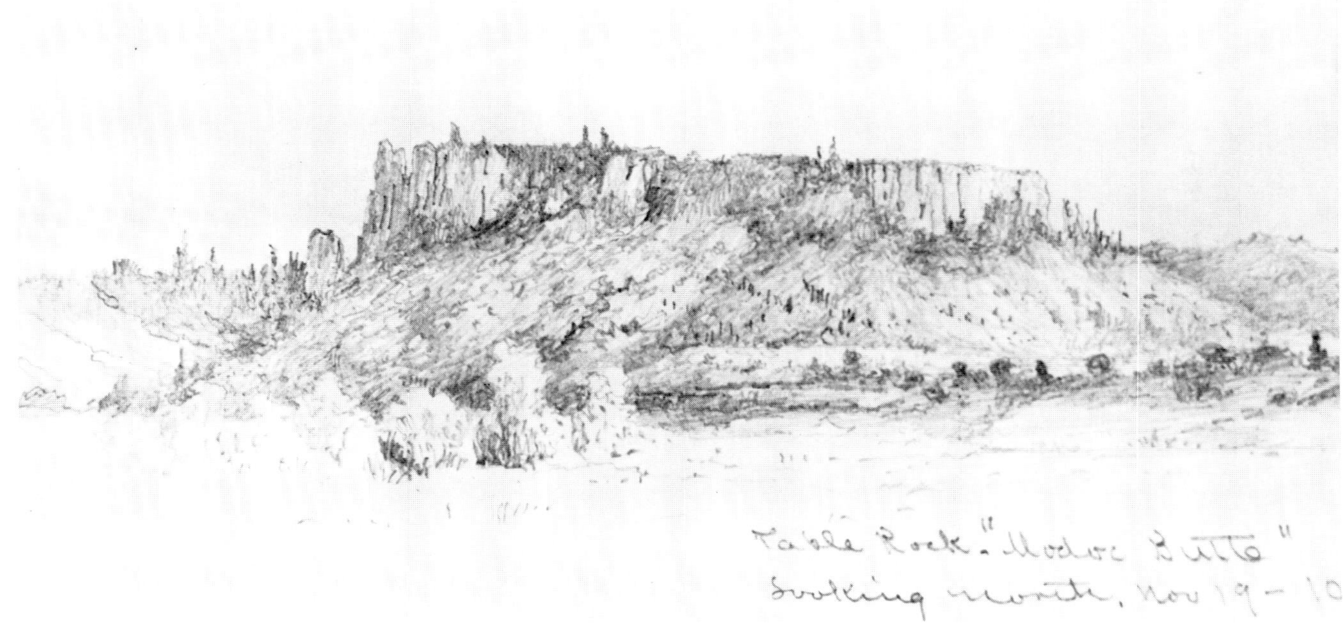

"Table Rock, 'Modoc Butte,' looking north, Nov. 19-10." Pencil sketch done in Oregon during a trip to visit relatives. *Private Collection.*

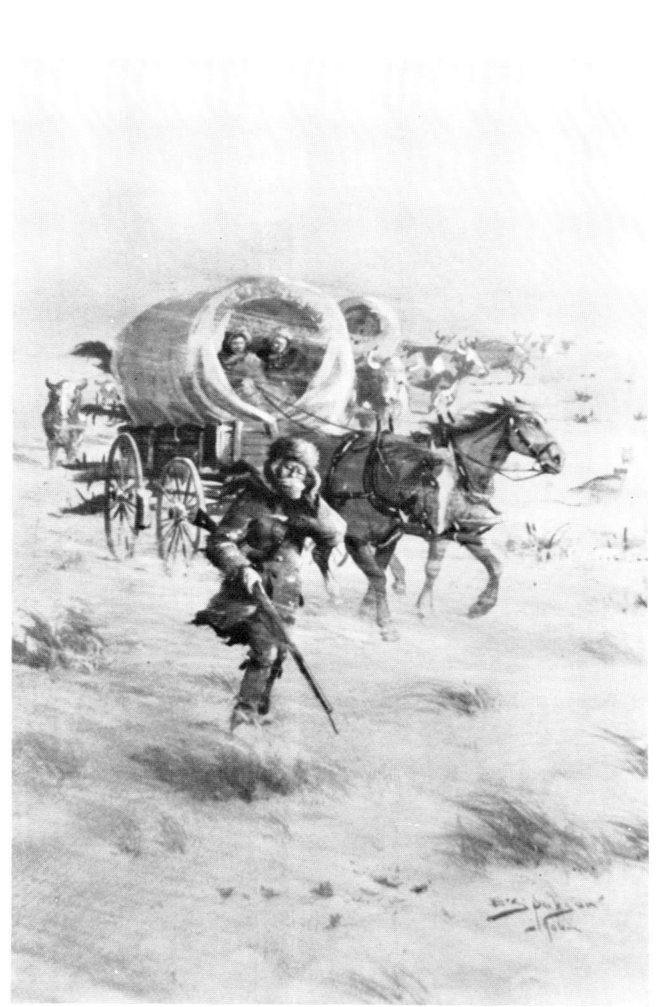

"Wearing the Winter Out," oil, en grisaille, 1906, 18 x 12. One of seven illustrations Paxson did for *The Life of Rev. L.B. Statler* by E.J. Stanley. *Private Collection.*

In at least one case, Eva Emery Dye's *The Conquest*, about the Lewis and Clark Expedition, the publisher rejected Edgar's completed illustrations in favor of less costly ones by another artist. Edgar also did illustrations for Frances Queen Victor; Texas historian, James De Shields; American author, Winston Churchill, and for other manuscripts by Eva Emery Dye. But it is unclear whether any of these books reached publication, or if so, whether they ultimately contained Edgar's work. Edgar normally did washes or oils on board *en grisaille* for use as illustrations. There are several such works in existence today which the author has not found represented in the books known to have been published. Some may have been used, however, in rare editions which are difficult to trace. In total the author has a record of forty-five paintings done by Edgar *en grisaille*, apparently for illustration.

In addition to his *Custer's Last Stand*, Edgar did many ambitious paintings depicting historic events and figures. The Lewis and Clark Expedition of 1803-6 was one of his favorite subjects. He is known to have painted thirteen works relating to the expedition. Two are murals in the state capitol and one is a mural in the Missoula County courthouse. He also painted four depictions of Sacajawea. One was used in *The Trail of Lewis and Clark*. Another, a large one now hanging in the University of Montana in Missoula, ranks with his very best work. In 1903, Edgar painted *1804* (also called *Contemplation*) for the 1904 Louisiana Purchase Exposition in St. Louis. It depcits Captain Lewis and three of his men, Shannon, Drouilliard and McNeil, resting at Lemhi Creek's headwaters. The party had just crossed the Continental Divide. Thus the creek's headwaters were the first they reached which flowed into the Pacific Ocean. Edgar also painted two more oils for use in *The Trail of Lewis and Clark*, one of the

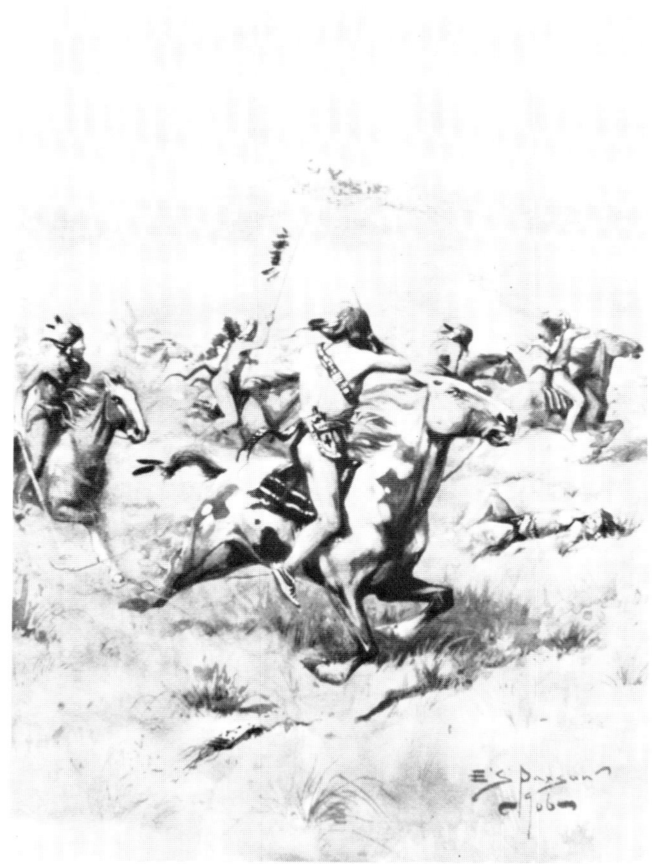

"Custer's Last Battle," oil, en grisaille, 1906, 18 x 12. Another of the illustrations done for The Life of L.B. Statler by Stanley. *Private Collection.*

expedition in camp at Lolo Creek and another of the expedition in the Bitterroot Mountains. For Enos Mills' *Your National Parks*, Edgar painted *John Coulter* for a frontispiece. Coulter had been a member of the expedition and is credited as the discoverer of what is now Yellowstone National Park. In 1912, Edgar painted a view of Mount Lolo during the time of the Lewis and Clark Expedition. He gave the sky a peculiar yellowish cast that was reported in the party's journals, the result of volcanic ash in the air from a tremendous volcanic eruption in Alaska at the time.

Edgar researched extensively for his depictions of the Lewis and Clark Expedition. He especially liked to supply historic detail, which he extracted from many works on the subject, including *The Complete Journals of the Lewis and Clark Party* with all the original maps, a massive set of seventeen volumes. Enos Mills wrote in his biographical sketch of Edgar:

> "He has so thoroughly absorbed books on the West that if the records of Western exploration were accidentally destroyed he could rewrite them from memory without the loss of an important fact or interesting incident.... The Journals of Lewis and Clark he has almost by heart, and discusses their contents with so much enjoyment, intelligence and enthusiasm that the actors in their pages live again before the listener, and act again their spirited parts. With his love for these books, with his experience and his artistic talent, how superbly he could illustrate their rare pages."[13]

Interestingly, this article was published in 1903, several years before Edgar's historical murals were done.

Sometimes Edgar delighted in adding obscure and minor historical details to his paintings. In one instance, he noted in his research that Captain Lewis gained a pet when a dog was left behind by an Indian band whose day-old trail they crossed. Edgar wrote in the margin next to the reference, "I will put this dog in one of my panels." It appears in *Lewis and Clark at Lolo Creek* in the Missoula County courthouse. In another courthouse mural, *Lewis Crossing the Clark's Fork*, Edgar put a spyglass in the hand of Lewis. He painted it from a photograph of the very one Lewis used, which was found in his effects after the explorer's death.

That the locales of events that Edgar portrayed were properly shown in his paintings was also most important to him, and he delved deep into his library to ascertain the exact locations. The time he reached, on his third attempt, Lewis' crossing place of the Clark's Fork River near Missoula, his companion on the sketching and photographing adventure exclaimed: "Colonel! We no doubt are the only ones on earth who can say absolutely that this is the identical place, as no one but you and I are so seriously

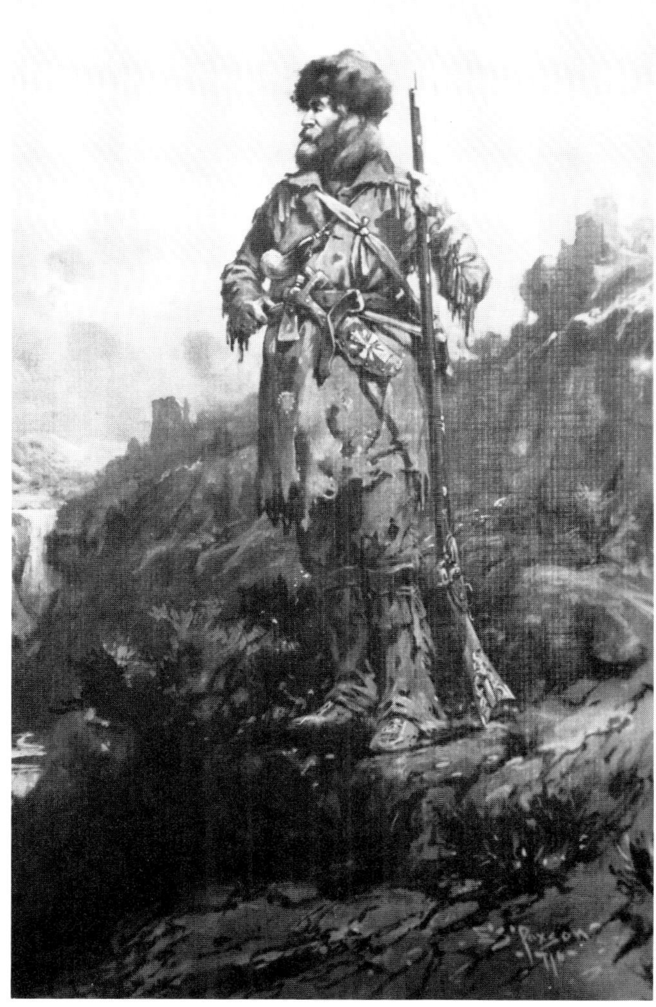

"John Coulter," oil, 1916. Reproduced from a photograph in the artist's album.

interested!" Edgar not only knew where Lewis crossed the river, he could trace Lewis' trail through Missoula from where Lewis and his nine men separated from Clark at the mouth of Lolo Creek. He knew that Lewis and his men camped with five Indians on the site of the University of Montana and then followed a trail, which was to be Stephens Avenue, past the site of Fort Missoula along a route which would later be the C&M railroad line to Bonner.

Edgar researched for his other murals as well. For his state capitol mural *Surrender of Chief Joseph*, Edgar had correspondence with Gen. Nelson Miles (who accepted the surrender) as well as firsthand accounts of old friends who had been there. And presumably Edgar used his sketches and interviews with Joseph himself and others of the Nez Percé who had surrendered at Bear Paw.

For another state capitol mural, *Seeking the White Man's Book*, Edgar consulted his old Flathead friend Chief Louison, whose uncle had been one of the four young braves to make the long overland trip on foot to St. Louis. Edgar was so moved by the story that he painted three more oil paintings depicting the four Indians' quest. The first shows four fine Indian figures striding along a mountain trail. The next shows the four, thin and trail-worn, meeting William Clark in St. Louis. The final painting shows a single exhausted brave, Bible in hand, being greeted by his tribesmen upon his return. The three other braves are conspicuously absent, for they had died of cholera in St. Louis. Edgar must have seen that the story symbolized what white civilization had done to the Flathead tribe, who had welcomed white settlers into their Bitterroot Valley home and had never raised their weapons against the newcomers, only to be ultimately forced from their ancestral valley onto a reservation.

Undoubtedly because of Edgar's sympathy for the Flatheads, he took some liberties with history in one of his Missoula courthouse murals. This mural depicts Chief Charlo leading the Flatheads from their beloved Bitterroot Valley to the Jocko Reservation in 1891. Edgar painted a proud and noble breed, with many horses, each brave with a rifle across his lap, the young braves shooting in the air, shouting and racing their ponies across the valley beneath Mount Lolo. Edgar also included the travois. In reality, Charlo's people moved in a ragtag procession. They wore castoff white man's clothing and hauled their belongings in wagons pulled by a few horses, as shown in photographs taken at the time. Furthermore, the braves had been advised by their chief to keep their rifles out of sight when near Missoula to avoid causing trouble with the townspeople. There were no shooting and whooping or fanning out across the prairie until the Indians were greeted by the rest of their tribe at the Jocko Reservation, far from Mount Lolo. Edgar must have known these facts, for he had interviewed some of those who had witnessed the event. Edgar mentioned in his journal that he had interviewed one witness just in time, for two days later the oldtimer "crossed the divide." Edgar had also acquired photographs of the Indians and scenes of that time from the widow of Major Peter Ronan, the Flathead Indian agent then. Mrs. Ronan, herself, had seen the event and described it to Edgar. But Edgar clearly refused to paint the Indian in a degraded state. He chose instead to infuse his mural with the respect he held for his Flathead friends by painting them in their former nobility.

Another historical painting of Edgar's about which there has been some controversy is *The Death of John Bozeman*. Bozeman's death at the hands of Blackfoot Indians near the Yellowstone River in 1867 is one of those intriguing incidents which are charged with the drama of the Old West and about which accounts differ on many points. In a monograph on Bozeman's life, Merrill G. Burlingame notes that the numerous accounts he used in preparing his paper were written many years after the incidents had occurred and were so distorted as to make it difficult to know the man they attempt to represent.[14] There are even versions of Bozeman's death which point to John Cover, the trailblazer's partner, as the murderer.

Edgar's conception of Bozeman's death was criticized by W. S. Mackenzie in a 1919 interview, fifty-three years after the event. Mackenzie had been a longtime friend of Bozeman. He said: "I have seen a number of pictures intended to represent the death of Bozeman, but all are inaccurate. One [Edgar's], a very pretty picture too, is in a store here today. The figure intended to represent Bozeman is heavily bearded and is a good likeness of Liver-Eating Johnson. It is attired in a gawdy buckskin suit. Bozeman never wore such a suit and did not wear a beard." Mackenzie went on to note additional details in the painting he said were inaccurate.[15]

There is no record of what Edgar did in the way of research for the painting. But a visit to the site of the incident will indicate that Edgar was familiar with the terrain. And Edgar was acquainted with George Irvine who knew Bozeman, having been with him when he selected the site of Bozeman, Montana, in 1862. There is also evidence that Bozeman sometimes wore buckskins. A published journal of a member of a wagon train led by Bozeman on the Bozeman Trail described the trailblazer as wearing "a fine suit of fringed buckskin."[16] Historians have pointed out that Bozeman, in order to be convincing, wore a buckskin suit while promoting himself as a guide to the Montana gold fields. But whatever Bozeman wore the day he died, it is not surprising that Edgar portrayed him as the essential trailblazer. It is very much in keeping with Edgar's intention to record, as he perceived them, the noblest and the most courageous aspects of the notable figures of the early West.

Although Edgar may have used artistic license on rare occasions, accuracy of representation was very important to him. His historical paintings and Indian portraits; his compositions of pioneers, Indians and buffalo in the western wilderness; his studies of trappers, warriors, half-breeds and scouts all share one important distinction: they are documentary. But not only do they present largely factual historical information, perhaps more significantly, they also express the perceptions and sentiments of one who experienced the frontier era and its rapid demise. They parallel in the literary world, not the history book written by a modern scholar, but the diary of a history maker himself. When Edgar used his imagination in creating his paintings, he was using the imagination of an authentic frontiersman.

Many acknowledged critics as well as self-appointed ones have and will classify E. S. Paxson, as they have Remington, Russell and many other western painters, as a western genre painter or simply as an illustrator, which dismisses him from fine art altogether. Commonly, the several "comprehensive" volumes on the history of American art devote only a few paragraphs to the late nineteenth and early twentieth century painters of the West. These painters, of whom only Remington and Russell are typically mentioned, are grouped in these volumes with the genre painters of the period and judged, as exemplified in this quote from *American Art to 1900*: "In retrospect the popular genre painters and illustrators said little that was profoundly revealing about American life in the late nineteenth century. At best their work was minor and nostalgic, at worst falsely sentimental."[17]

But a pictorial record of the fading frontier by one who was part of it can hardly be considered minor.

It is true that Edgar was sentimental. He of course had strong feelings of admiration for all that was heroic about the pioneer and the Indian. Intense feelings have always been primary inspiration for artists. But Edgar was not motivated to paint by nostalgia. He did not want to return to an earlier day. He wanted to record it as he saw it, in detail and in spirit for the benefit of future generations. He was not much concerned with providing the pleasant and familiar as genre painters were, nor was he painting primarily to entertain or satisfy the curious, as the illustrators were. His paintings were meant to be documentary by their creator and this documentary nature transcends both illustration and genre art. As the twenty-first century approaches, we and the generations to come surely benefit from these irreplaceable pictorial records. We are fortunate that the man toward whom Beaver Dick spurred his horse at a full run, fleeing from hostile Indians that late summer day in 1877, possessed a rare combination of foresight, artistic genius, and the single-minded determination to apply them to immortalizing the Old West he knew so intimately.

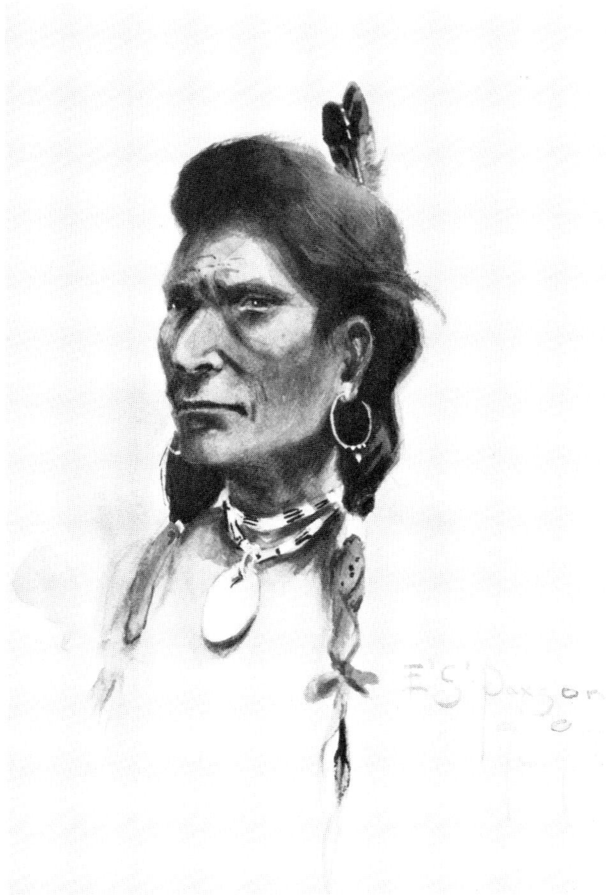

Title unknown. Watercolor, 1909. *Private Collection.*

Color Plates
A Selected Portfolio of E.S. Paxson Art

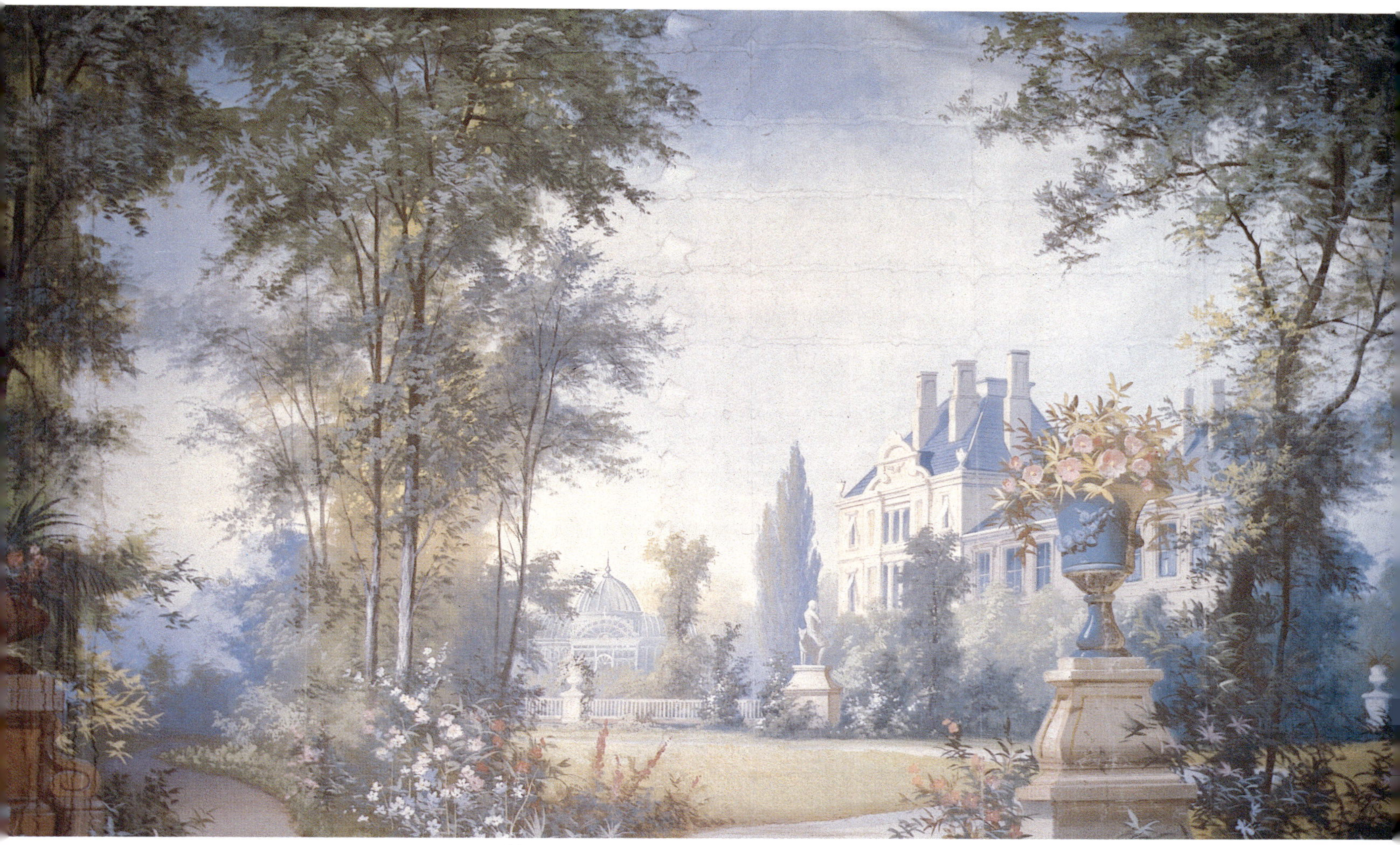

Theater set backdrop, McDonald Opera House in Philipsburg, Montana about 1891. *David Bird Burnham.*

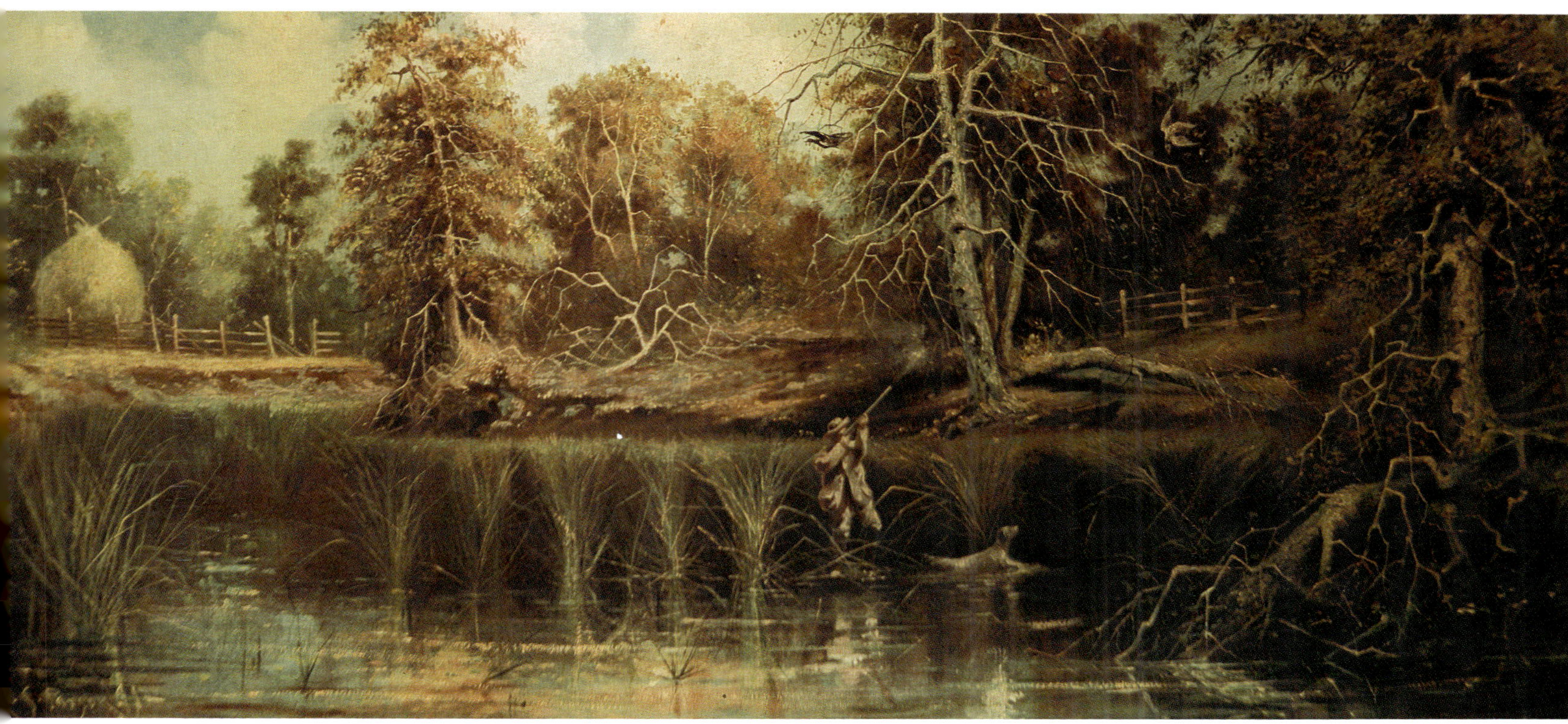

"Head of Horseshoe Lake, Cascade County. Oil, 1891, 18 x 40. *Private Collection, on loan to the Missoula City-County Library, Missoula, Montana.*

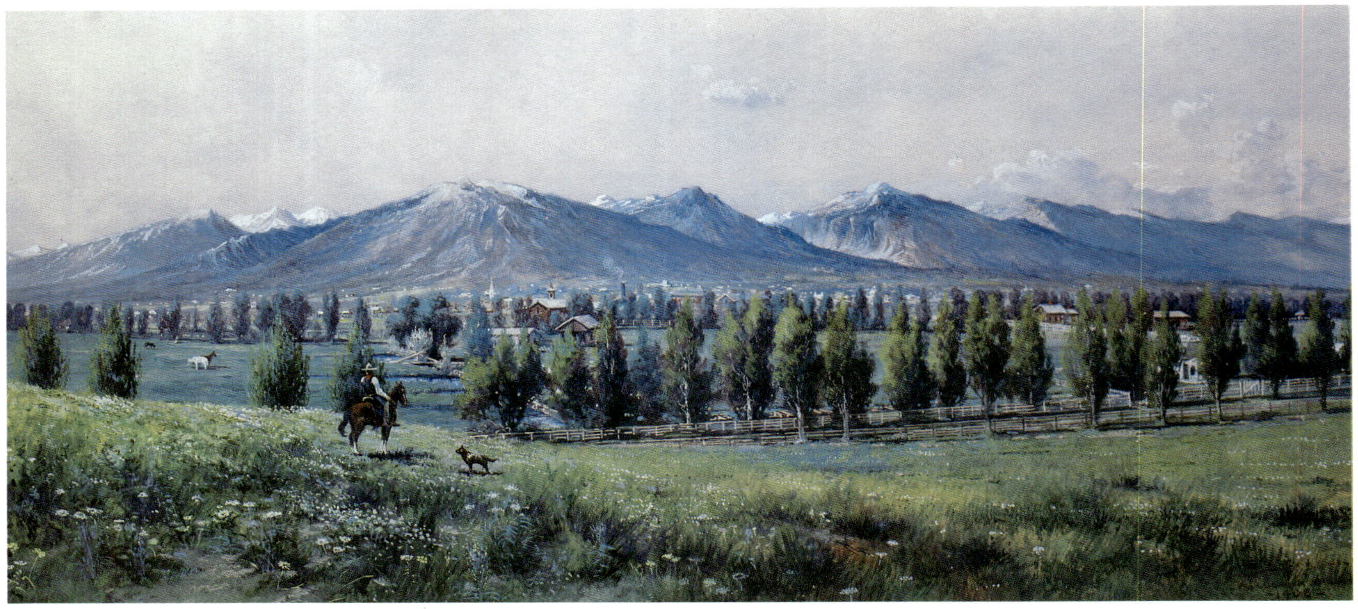

"Hamilton, Montana." Gouache, 1908, 22 x 48. *James Connelly.*

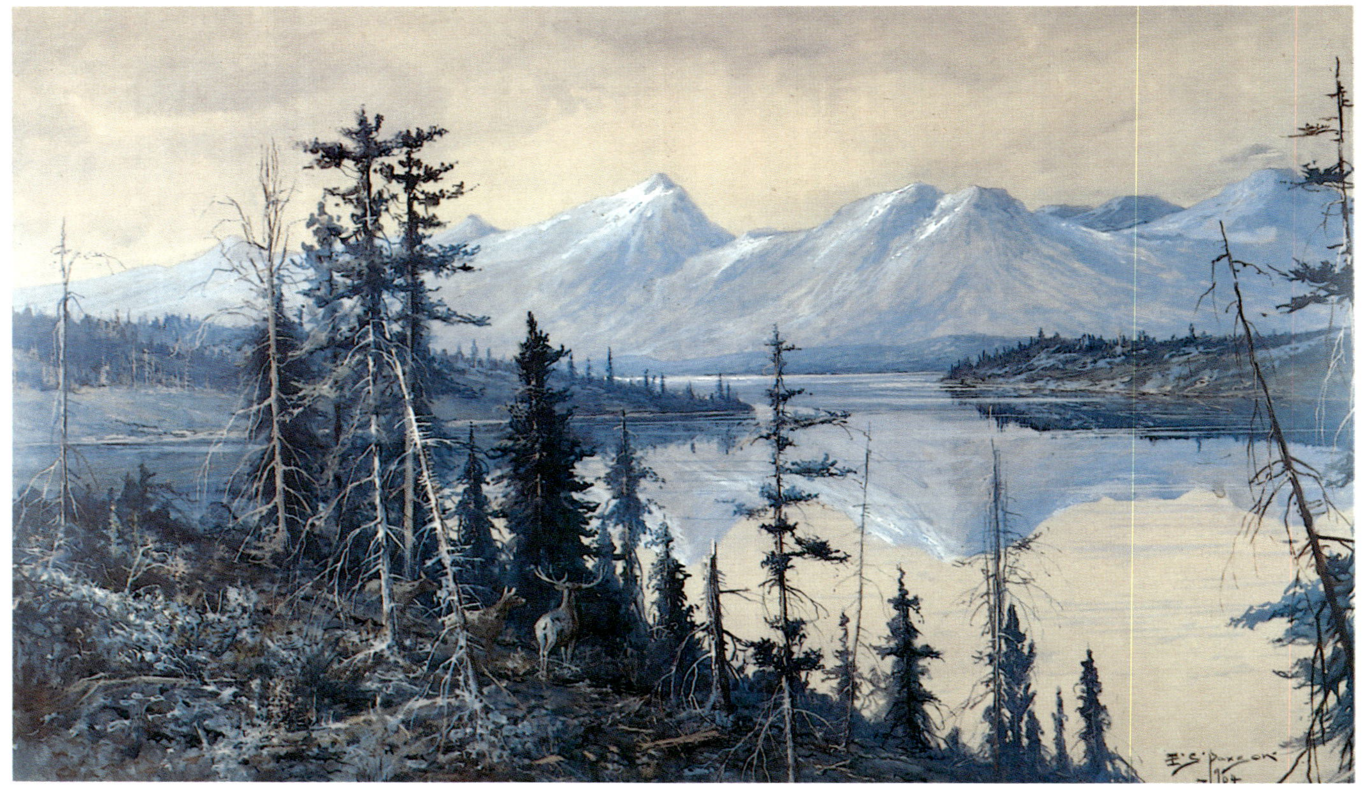

"Jackson Lake." Gouache, 1904, 16½ x 26½. *Dillon, Montana School District.*

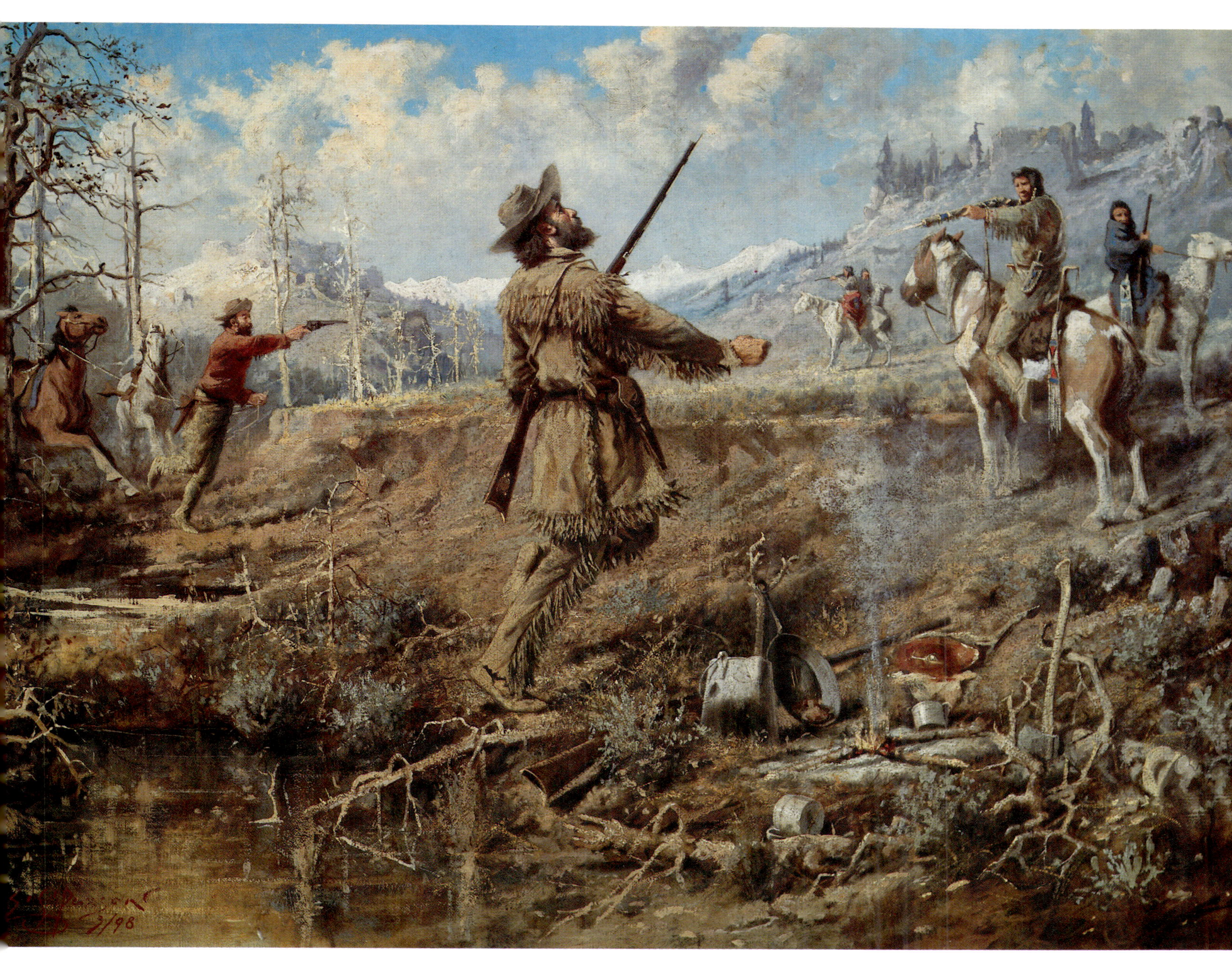

"The Death of John Bozeman." Oil, 1898, 21 x 48. *Robin MacNab, Bozeman, Montana.*

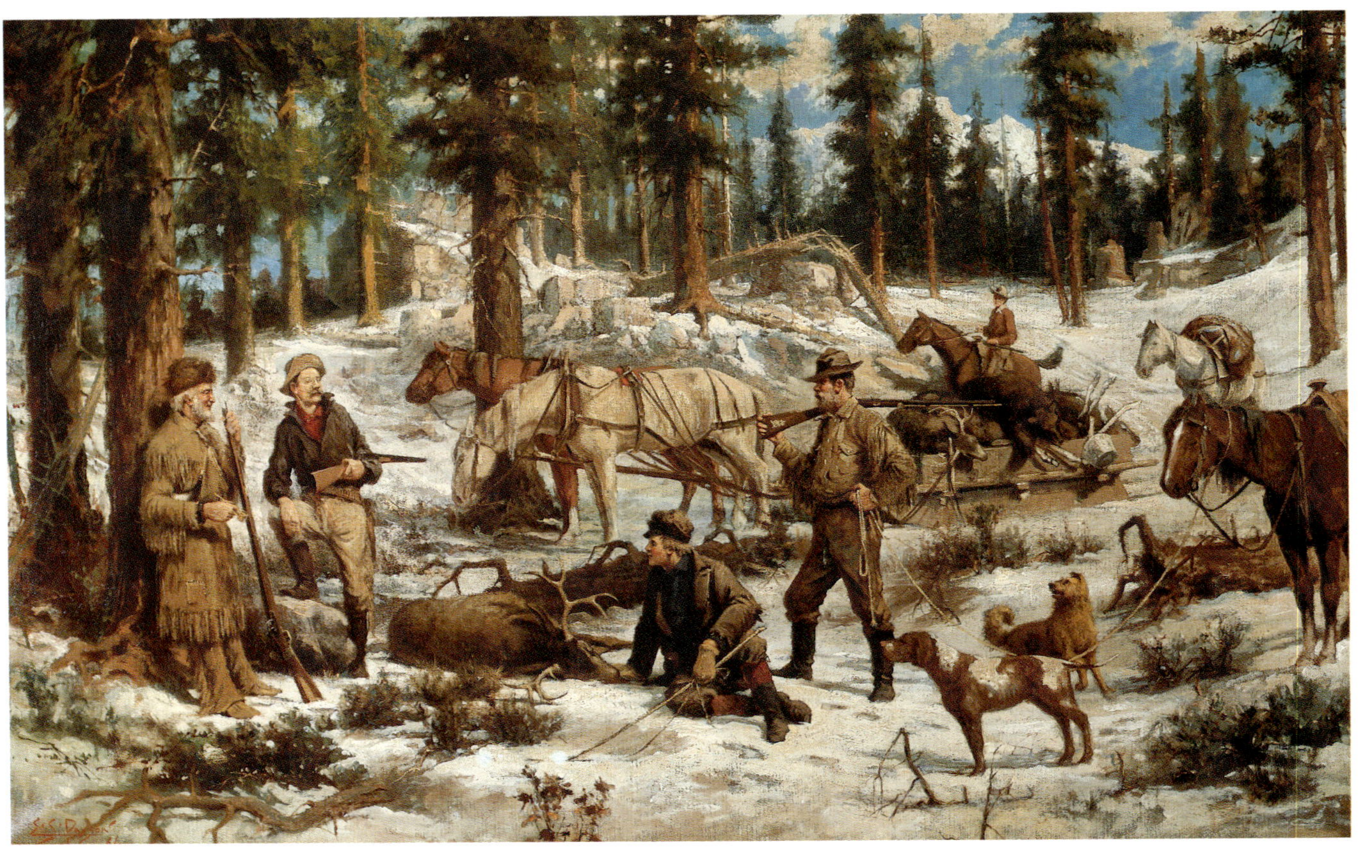

"Grandpa's Luck." Oil, 1899, 24 x 36. *James Fowler, Period Gallery West, Scottsdale, Arizona.*

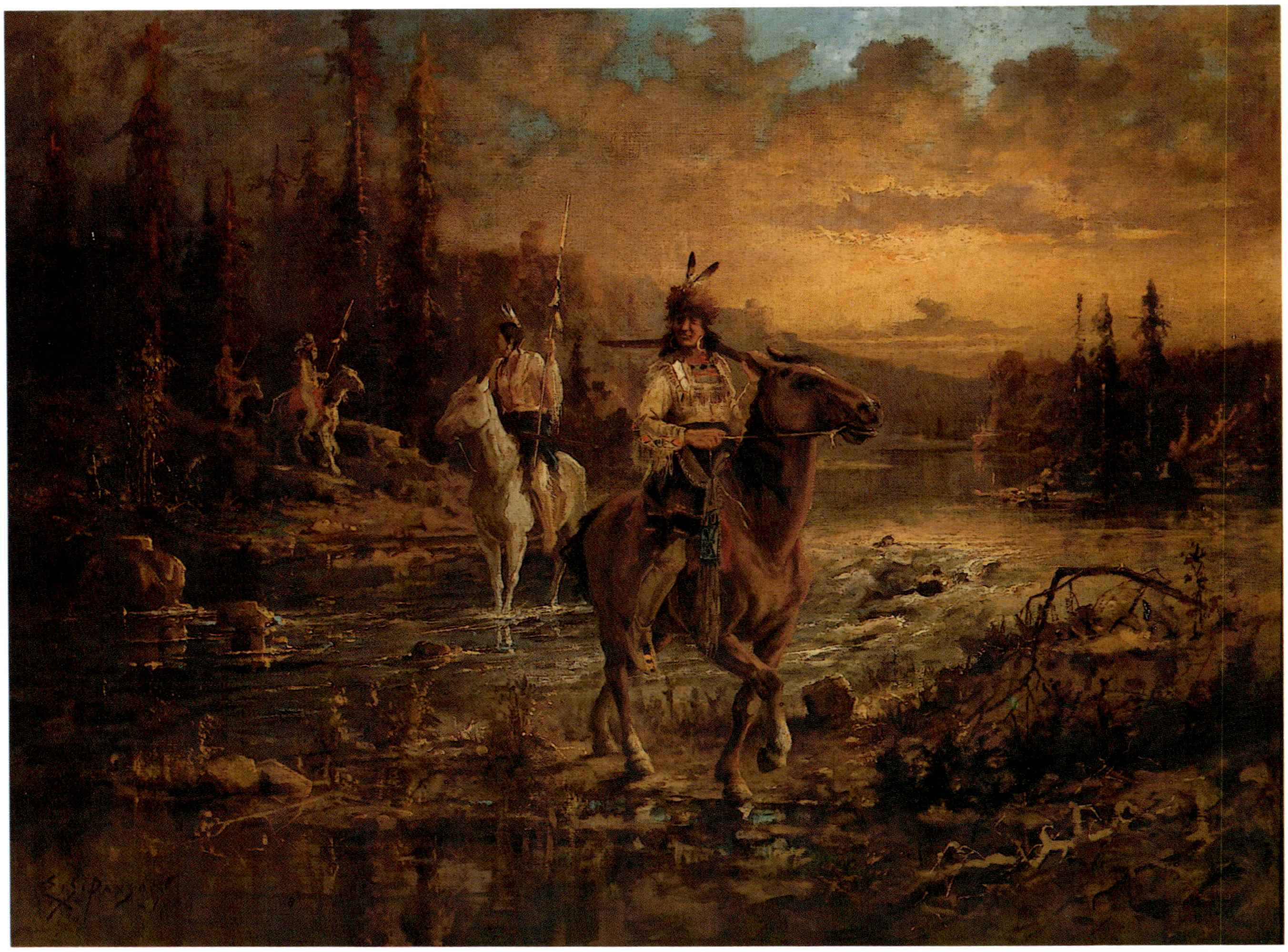

"Bound for Buffalo Country." Oil, 1899, 20 x 28. *Maxwell Galleries, San Francisco.*

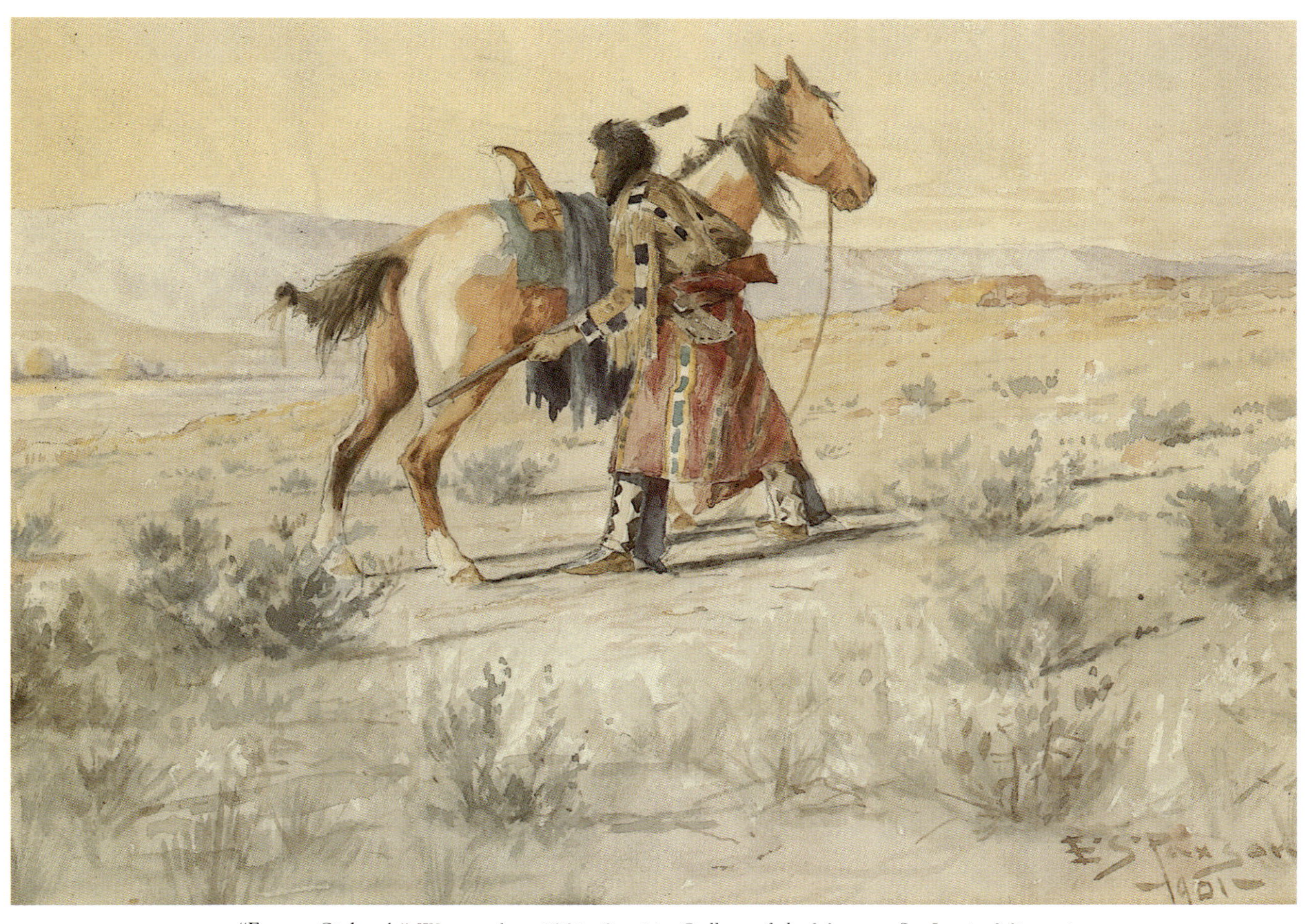

"Enemy Sighted." Watercolor, 1901, 8 x 11. *Gallery of the Masters, St. Louis, Missouri.*

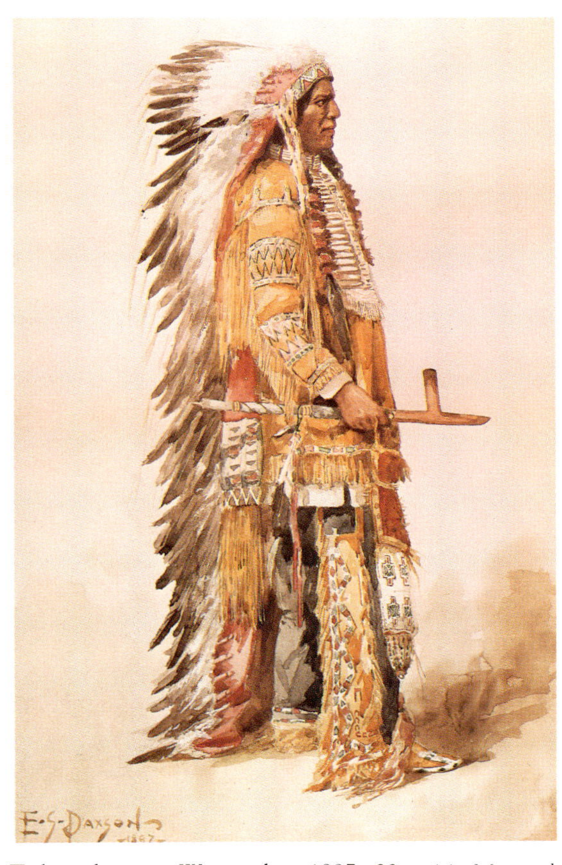

Title unknown. Watercolor, 1897, 22 x 14. *Mr. and Mrs. S.H. Rosenthal, Jr.*

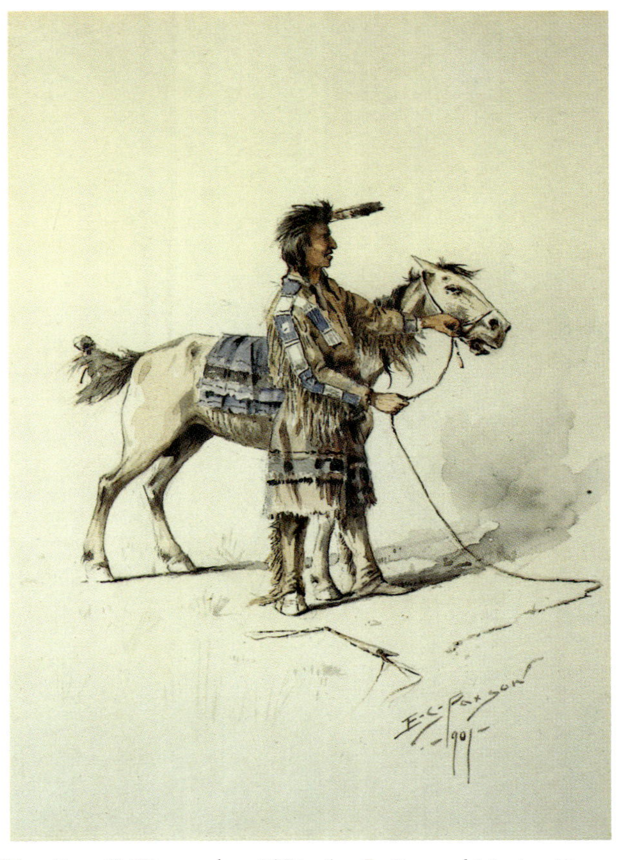

"You Swap?" Watercolor, 1901, 6 x 7. *Ray and Maxine Howser.*

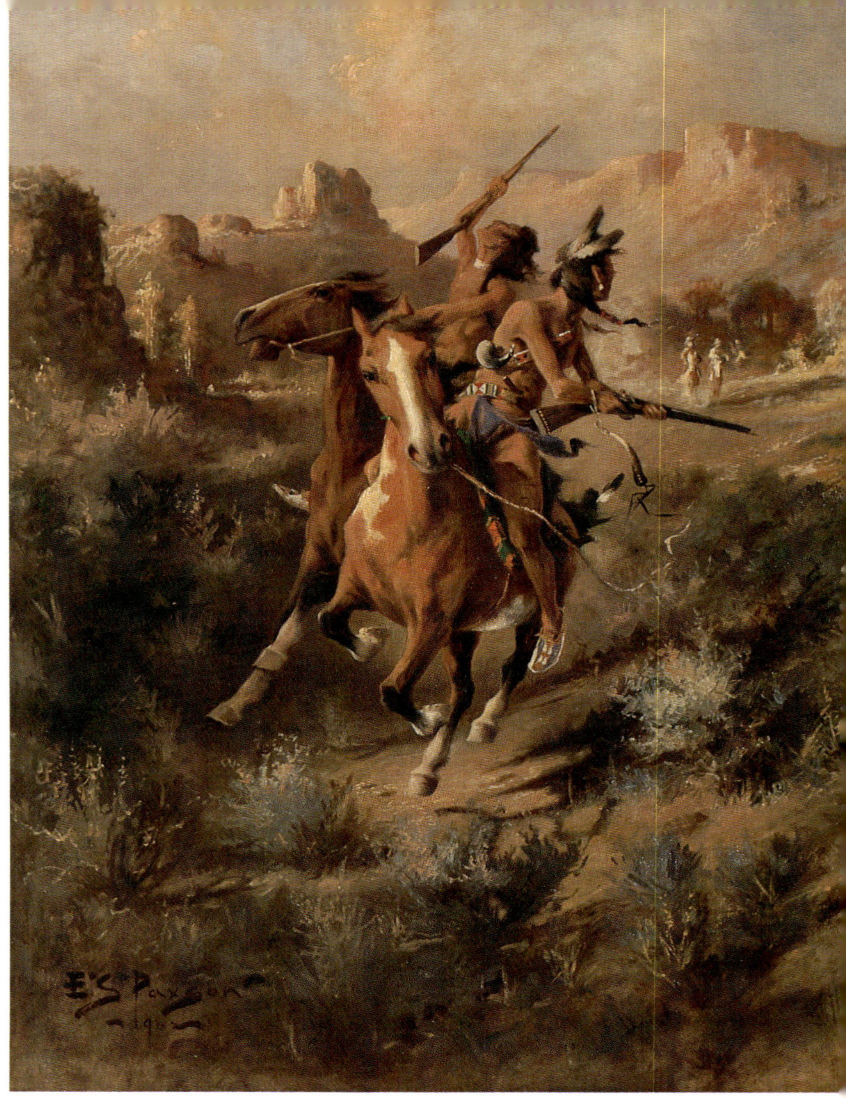

"The Last Shot." Oil, 1902, 20 x 26. *Jimmie and Sydney M. Shoenberg, Jr., St. Louis, Missouri.*

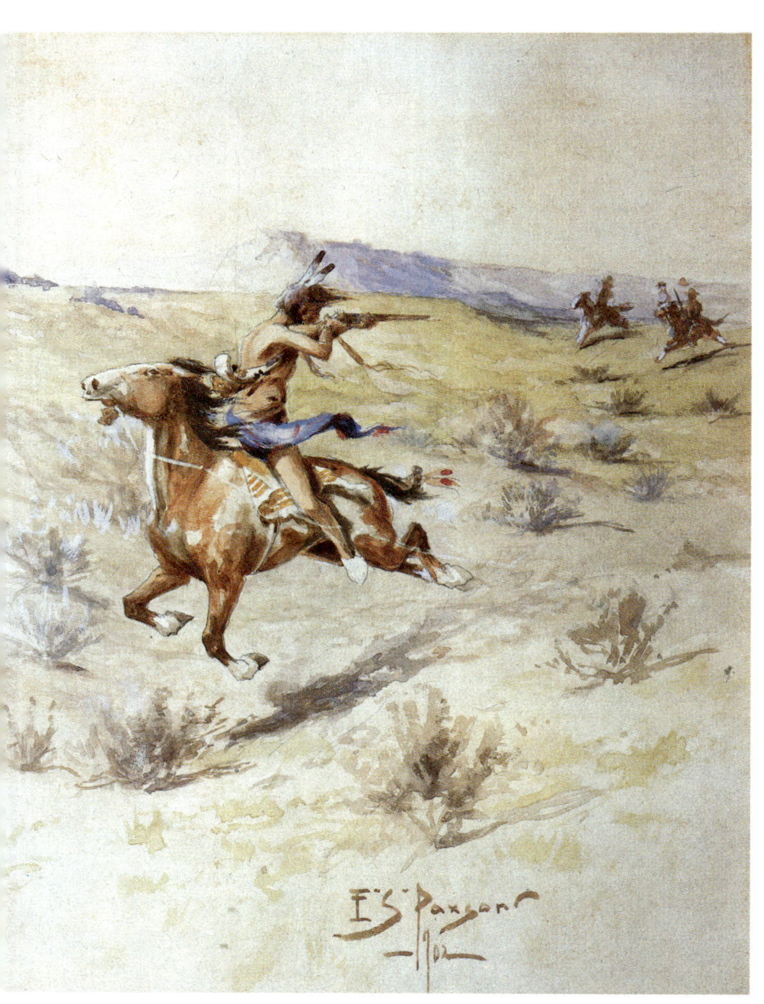

"The Last Shot." Watercolor. *Jimmie and Sydney M. Shoenberg, Jr., St. Louis, Missouri.*

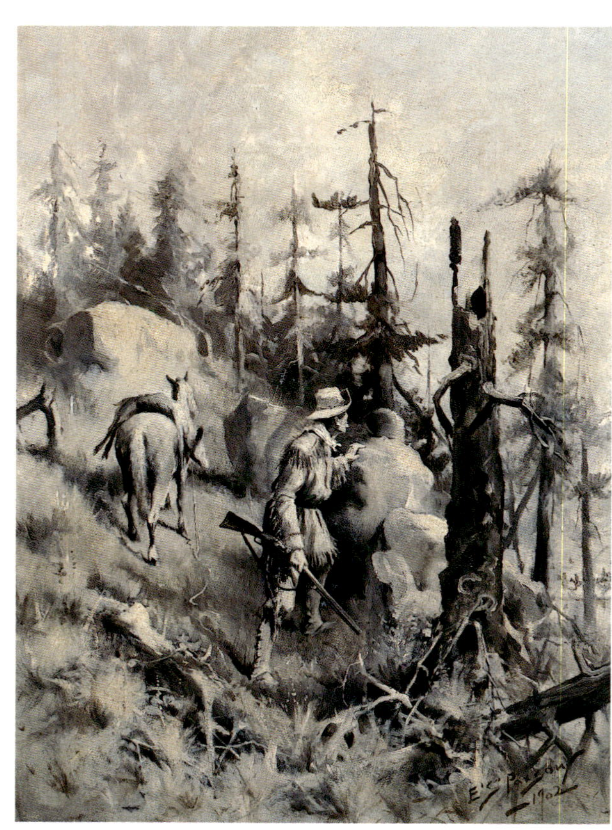

"Old Sol" (Spotting an Indian Party). Oil, en grisaille, 1902. *C.W. Edwards.*

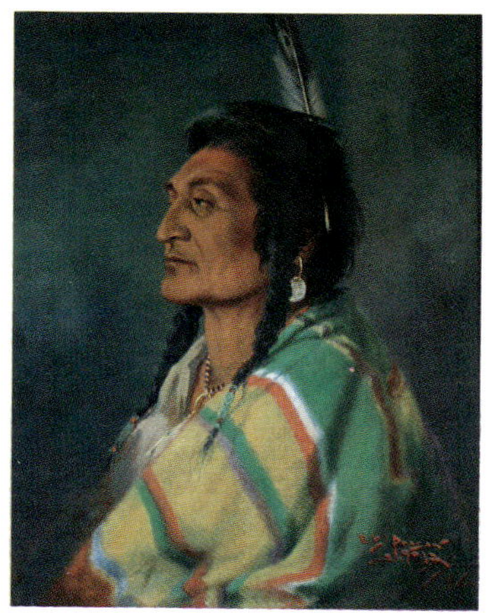

"Nag-a-Shaw, Shoshoni Scout." Oil, 1901, 25½ x 19½. *Judy and Al Goldman.*

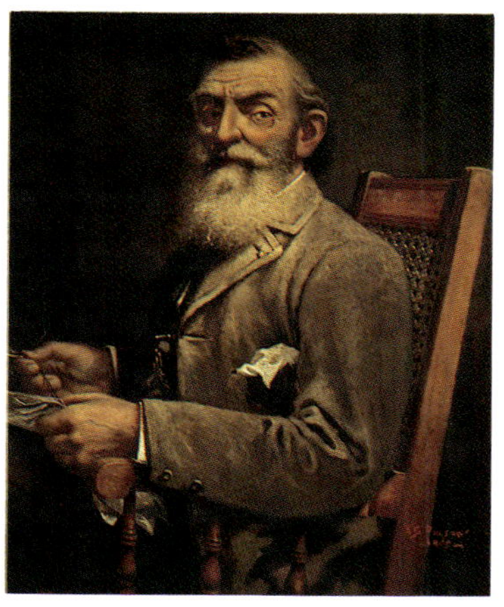

"William Hambleton Paxson." The artist's father. Oil, 1895, 29½ x 13½.

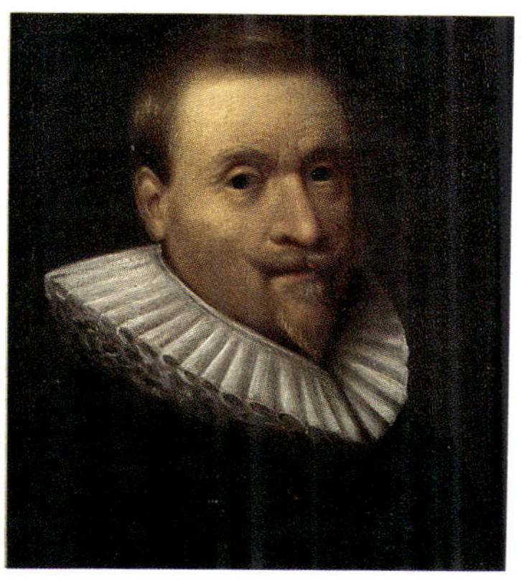

Title Unknown. Oil, 1880, 20 x 16. This is Paxson's earliest painting known to be extant by the author.

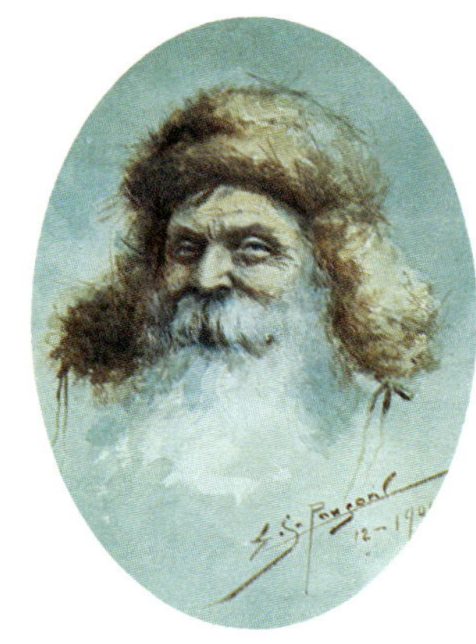

"The Happy Trapper." Watercolor, 1900. *Private Collection.*

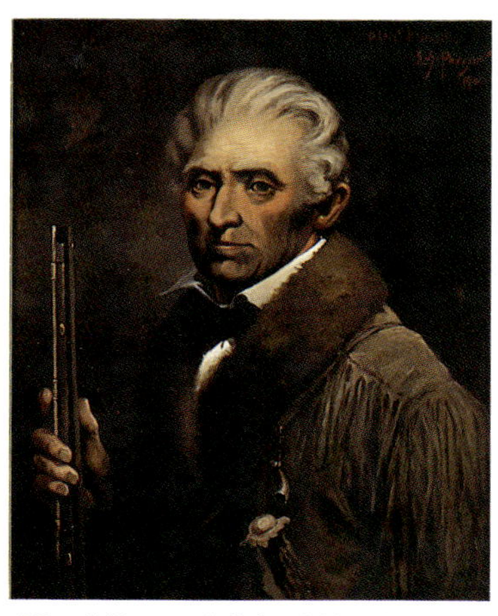

"Dan'l Boone." Oil, 1900. 18 x 13½. *Private Collection.*

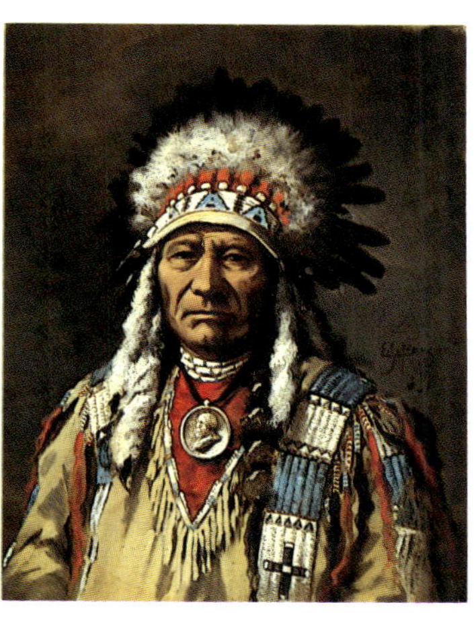

"American Horse." Oil, 1900. 14 x 10. *Private Collection.*

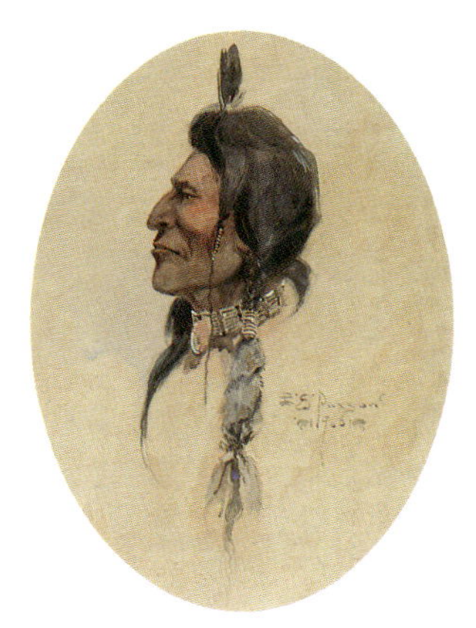

"Crow Brave." Watercolor, 1908, 10½ x 5. *Julliette and Pat Donlan.*

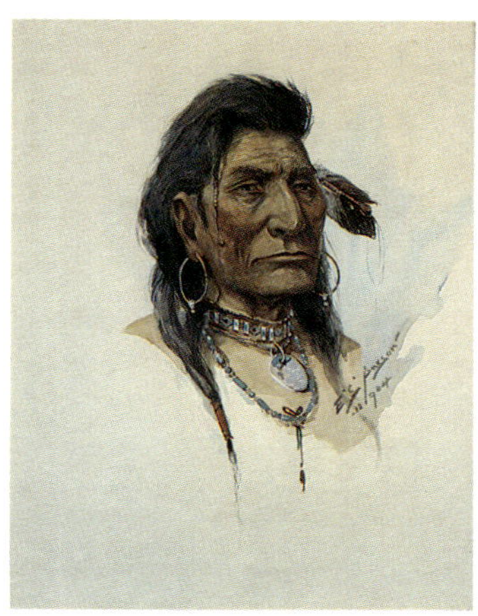

Title Unknown. Watercolor, 1904, 7½ x 6. *Private Collection.*

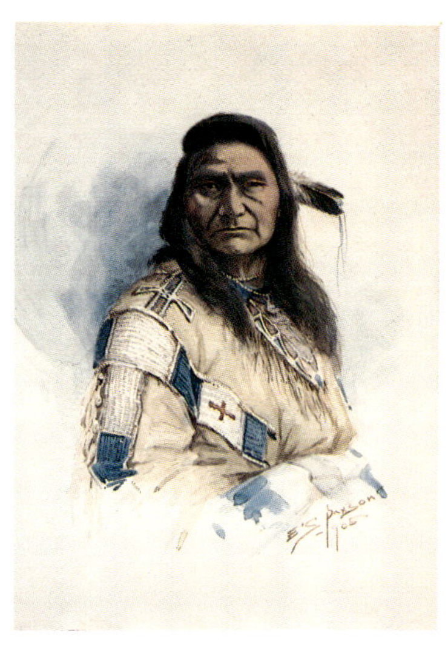

"Chief Joseph." Watercolor, 1905, 12 x 10. Private Collection.

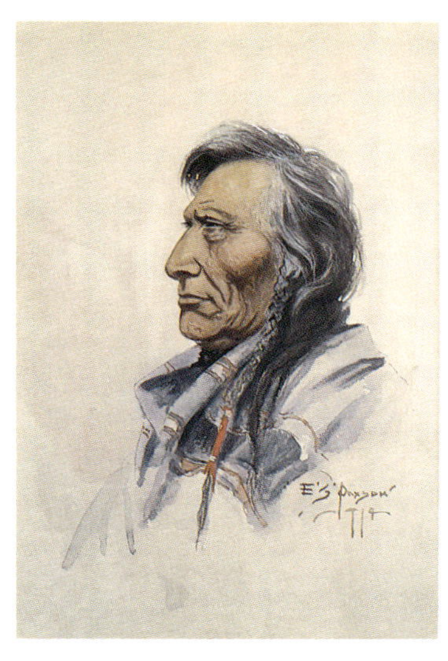

"Chief Charlo." Watercolor, 1904, 14 x 9. *Private Collection.*

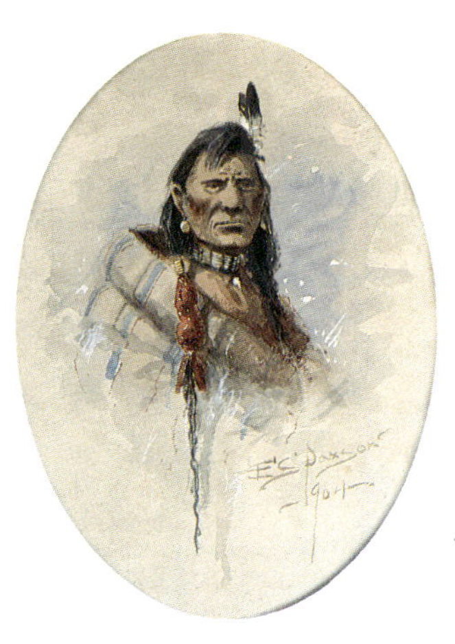

Title unknown. Watercolor, 1904, 7½ x 6. *Private Collection.*

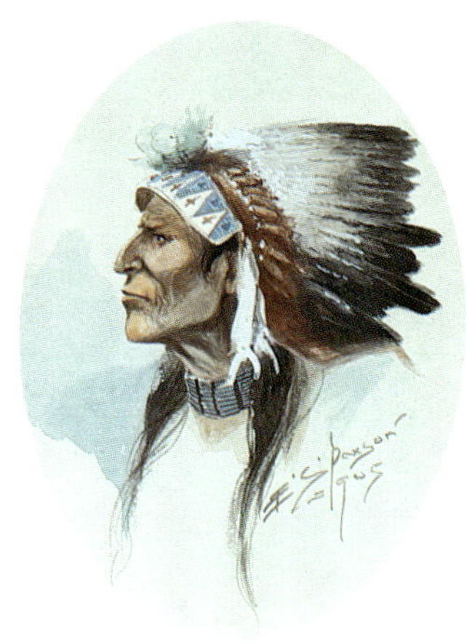

Title Unknown. Watercolor, 1904, 14 x 10. *Private Collection.*

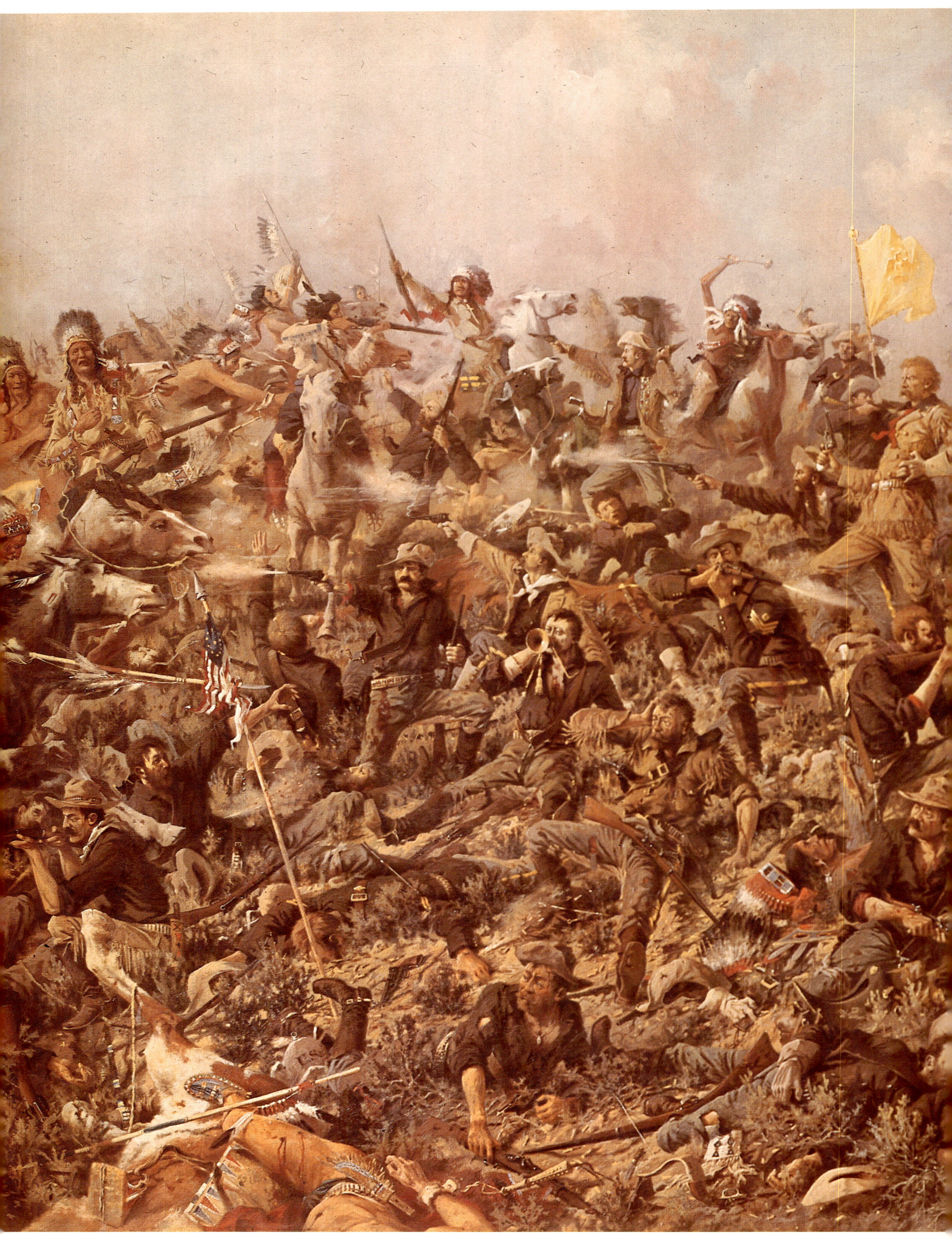

"Custer's Last Stand." Oil, 1899. *Buffalo Bill Historical Center, Cody, Wyoming.*

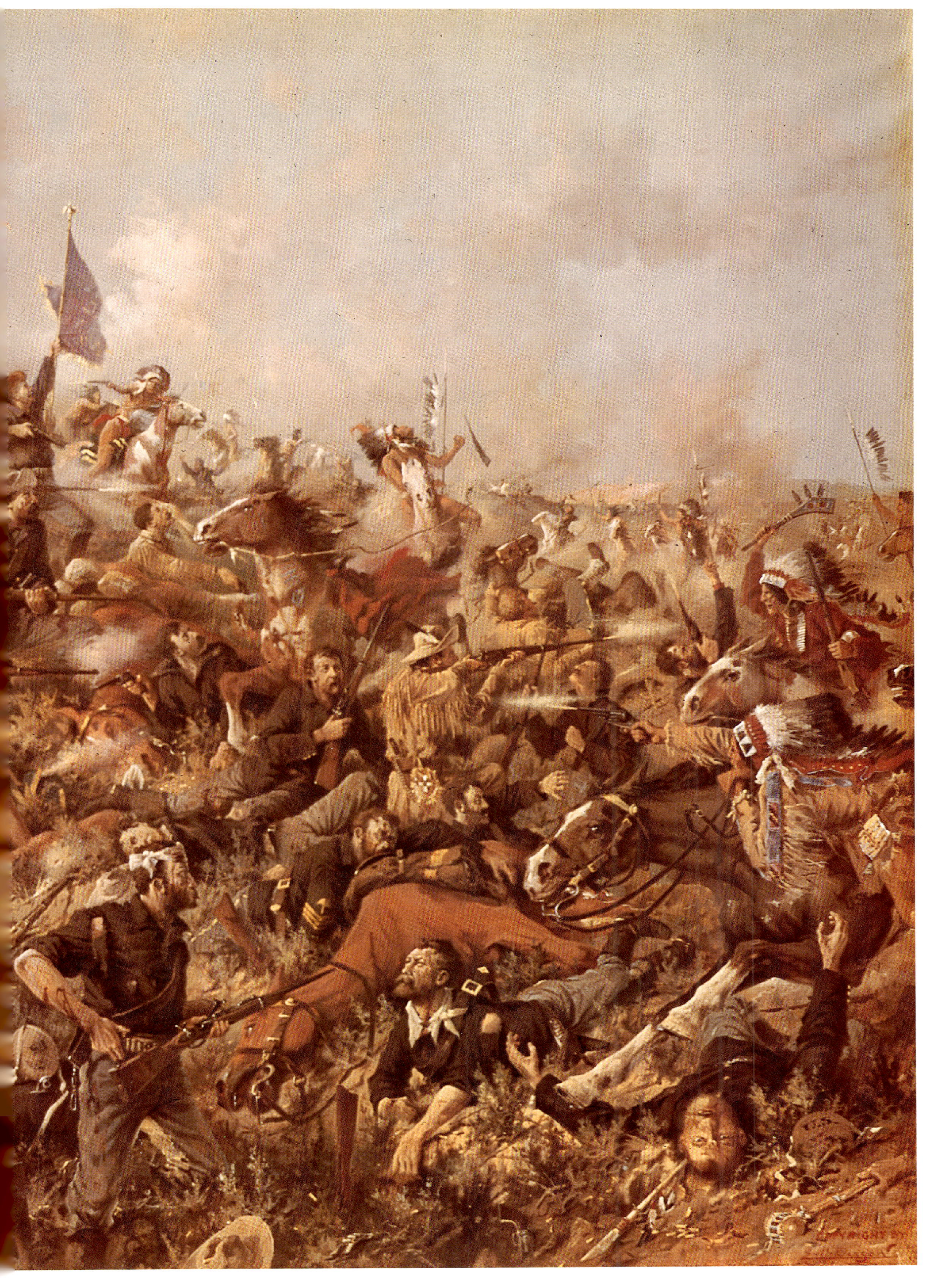
U.S.
COPYRIGHT BY

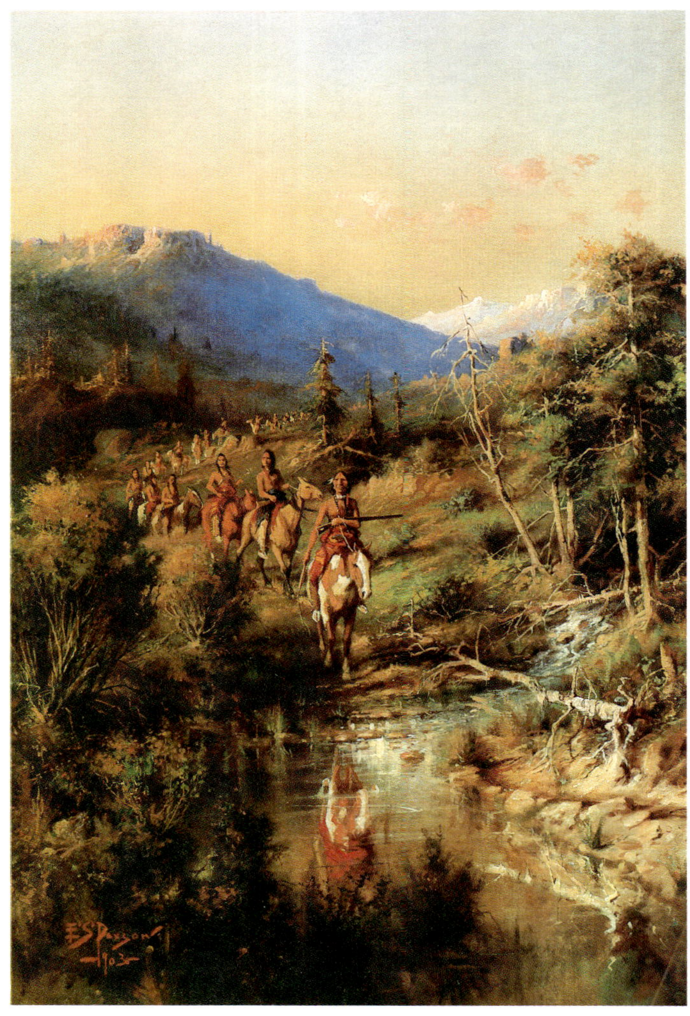

"Return from the Mountains of Chief Joseph and Tribe." Oil, 1903, 36 x 24. *Penny and Martin Kodner, St. Louis, Missouri.*

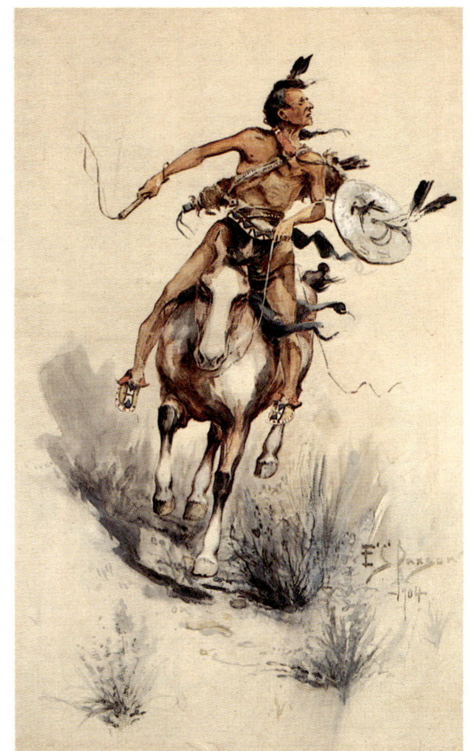

Title Unknown. Watercolor, 1904, 14 x 9. Private Collection.

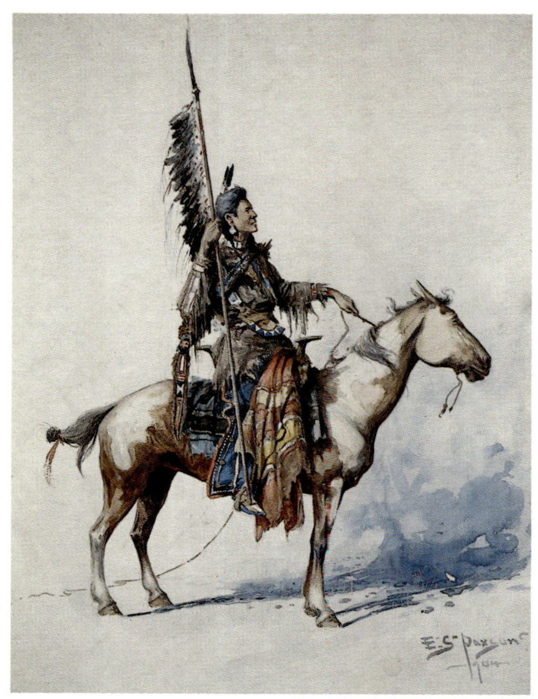

"Ready for a Coup." Watercolor, 1904, 17 x 12½. *Private Collection.*

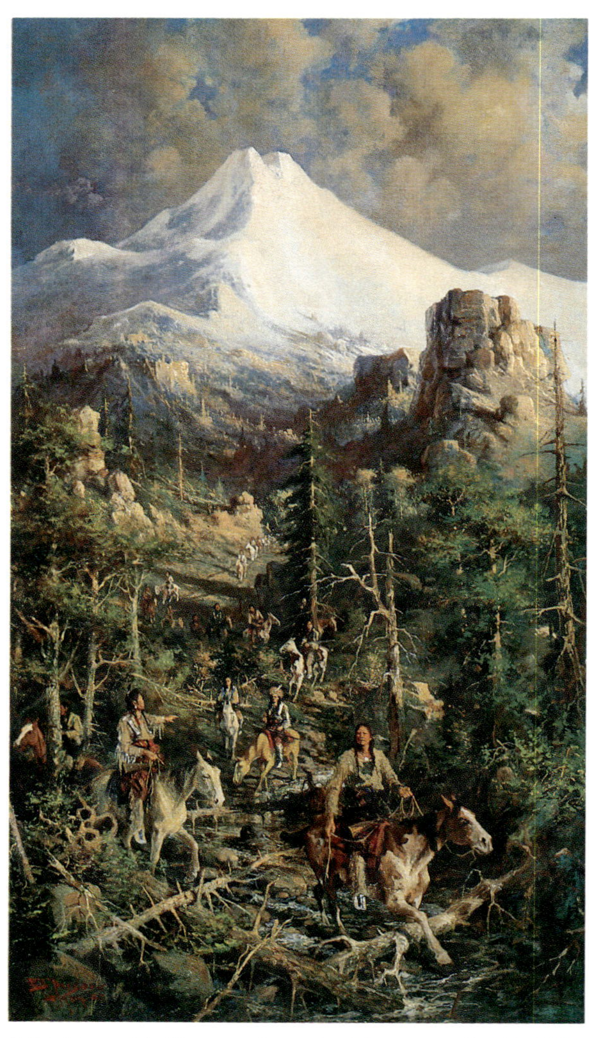

"Chief Joseph's Descent from the Mountains." Oil, 1904 52 x 34. *Felice and Robert Rubin, St. Louis, Missouri.*

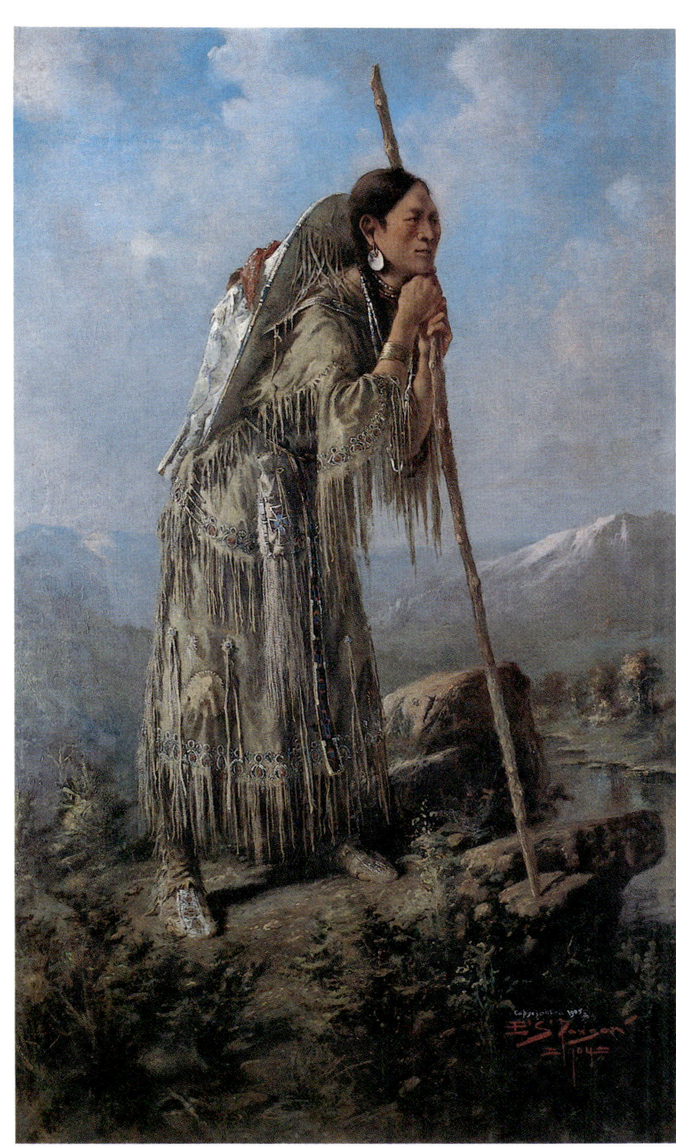

"Sacajawea." Oil, 1904, 50 x 29. *University of Montana, Missoula, Montana.*

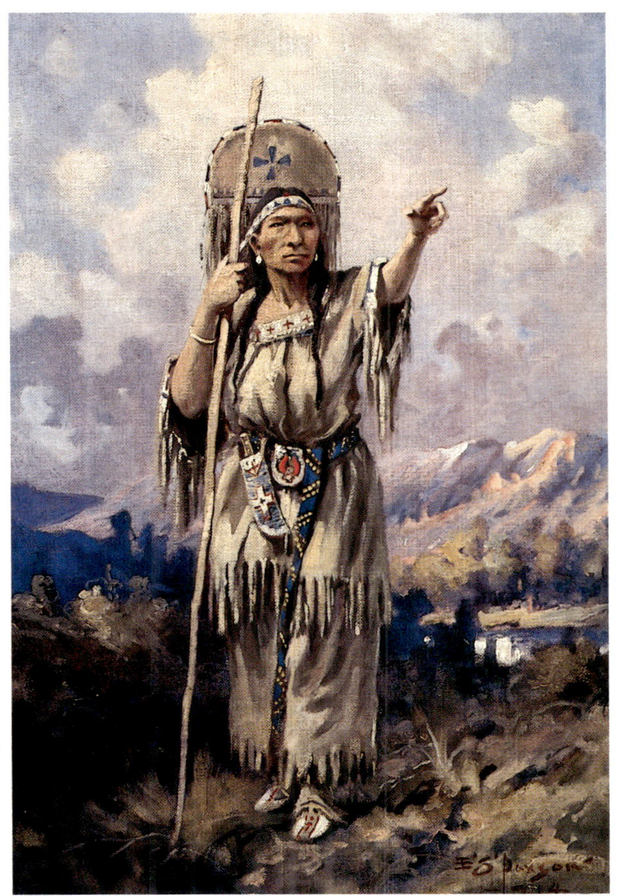

"Sacajawea." Oil, 1914, 17½ x 11½. *Private Collection.*

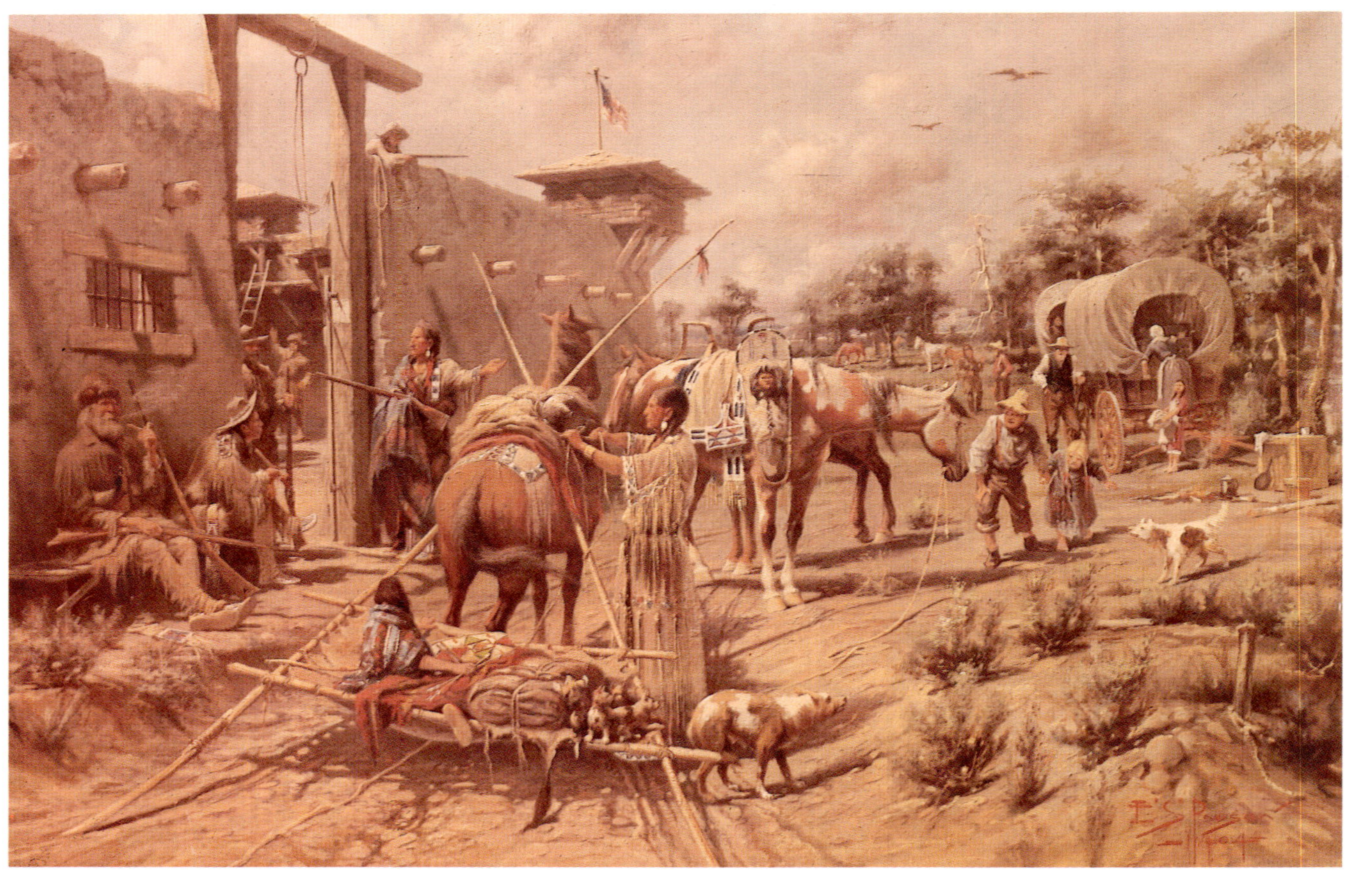

"*The Latest Arrivals.*" *Oil, 1904, 28½ x 42½. Montana Historical Society, Helena, Montana.*

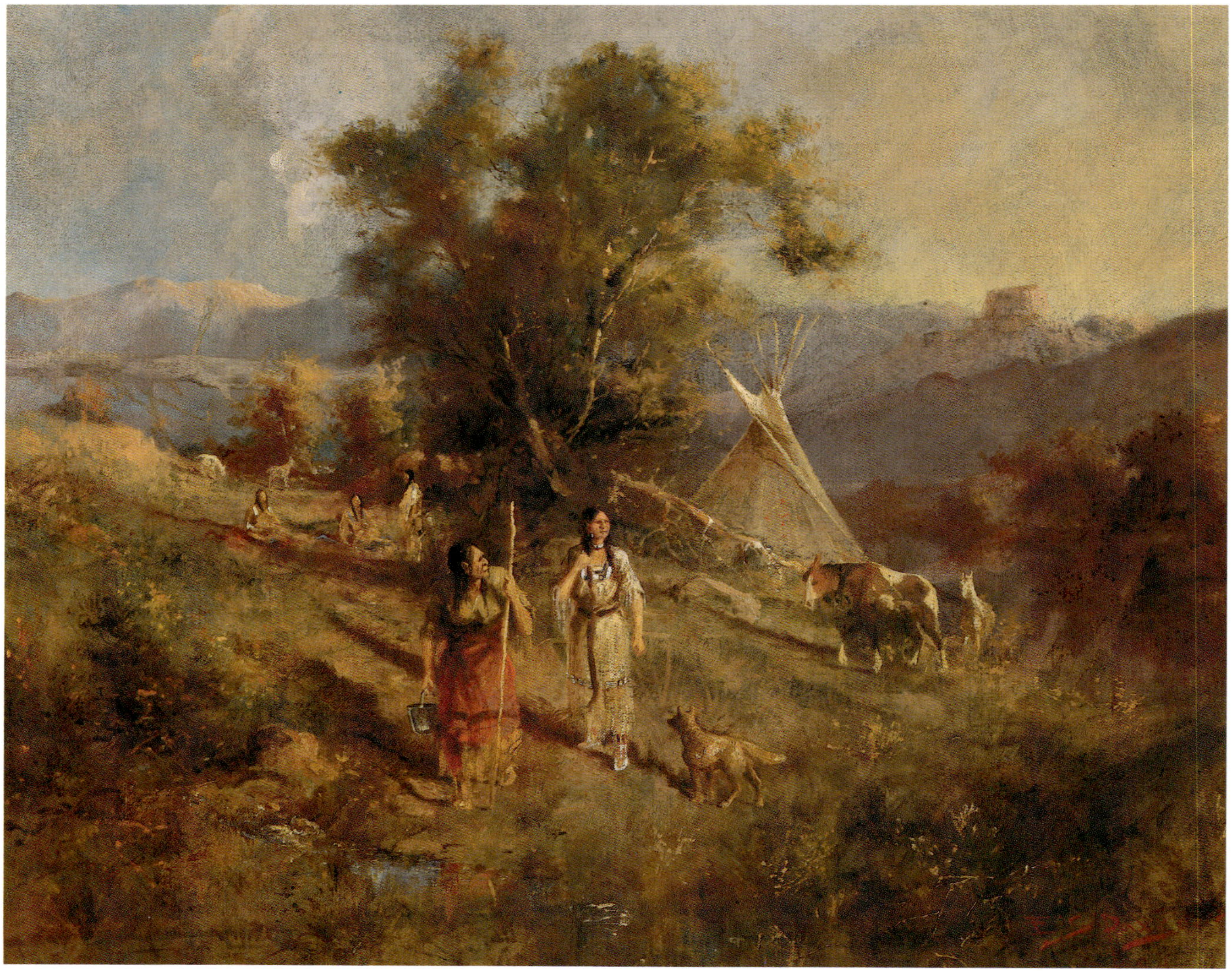

"Indian Encampment-Crow Village." Oil, 1904, 22 x 28. *Gallery of the Masters, St. Louis, Missouri.*

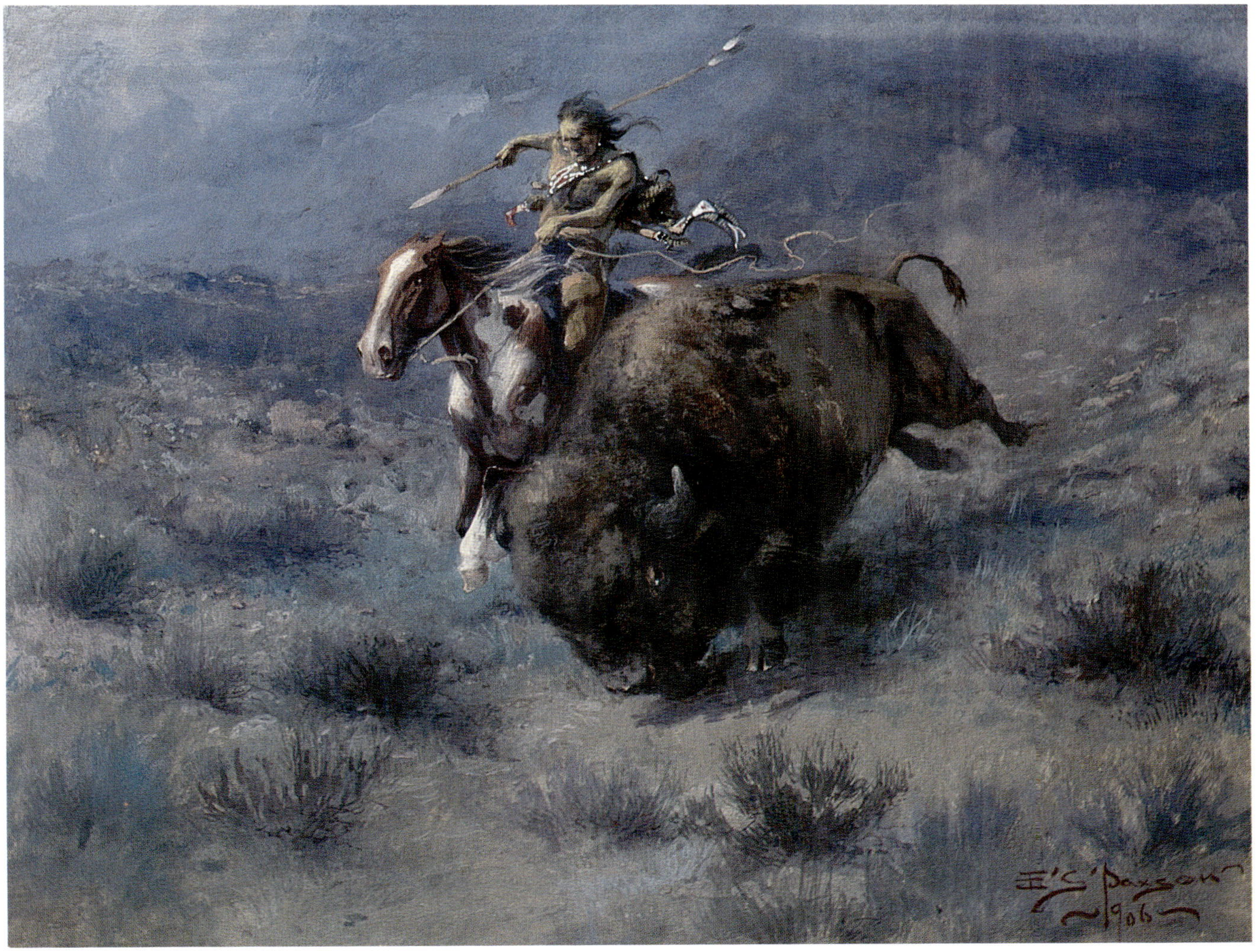

"Buffalo Hunt." Gouache, 1906, 17½ x 21. *Private Collection.*

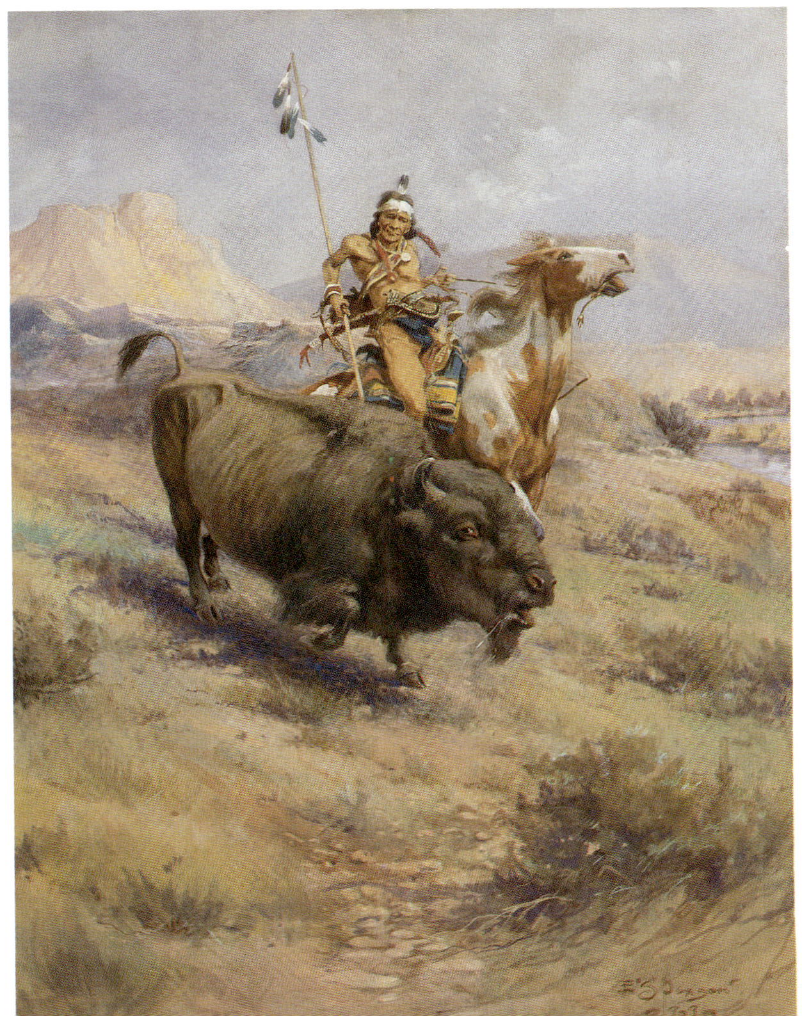

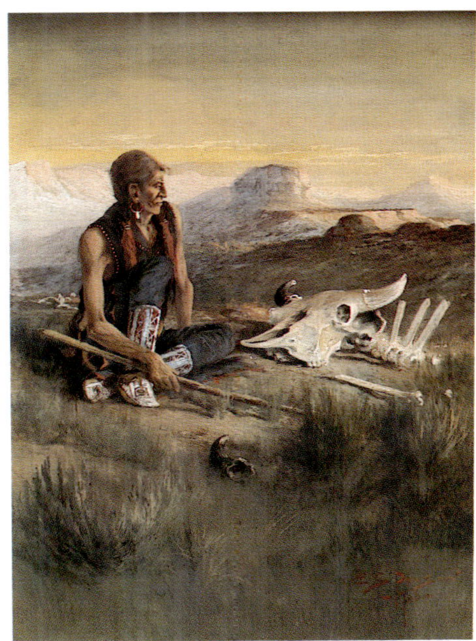

"Once We Were Great." Watercolor, 1906, 20½ x 16. *S.L.M., Inc., Corning, Arkansas.*

"Buffalo Hunt." Watercolor and Gouache, 1909, 28 x 22. *Penny and Martin Kodner, St. Louis, Missouri.*

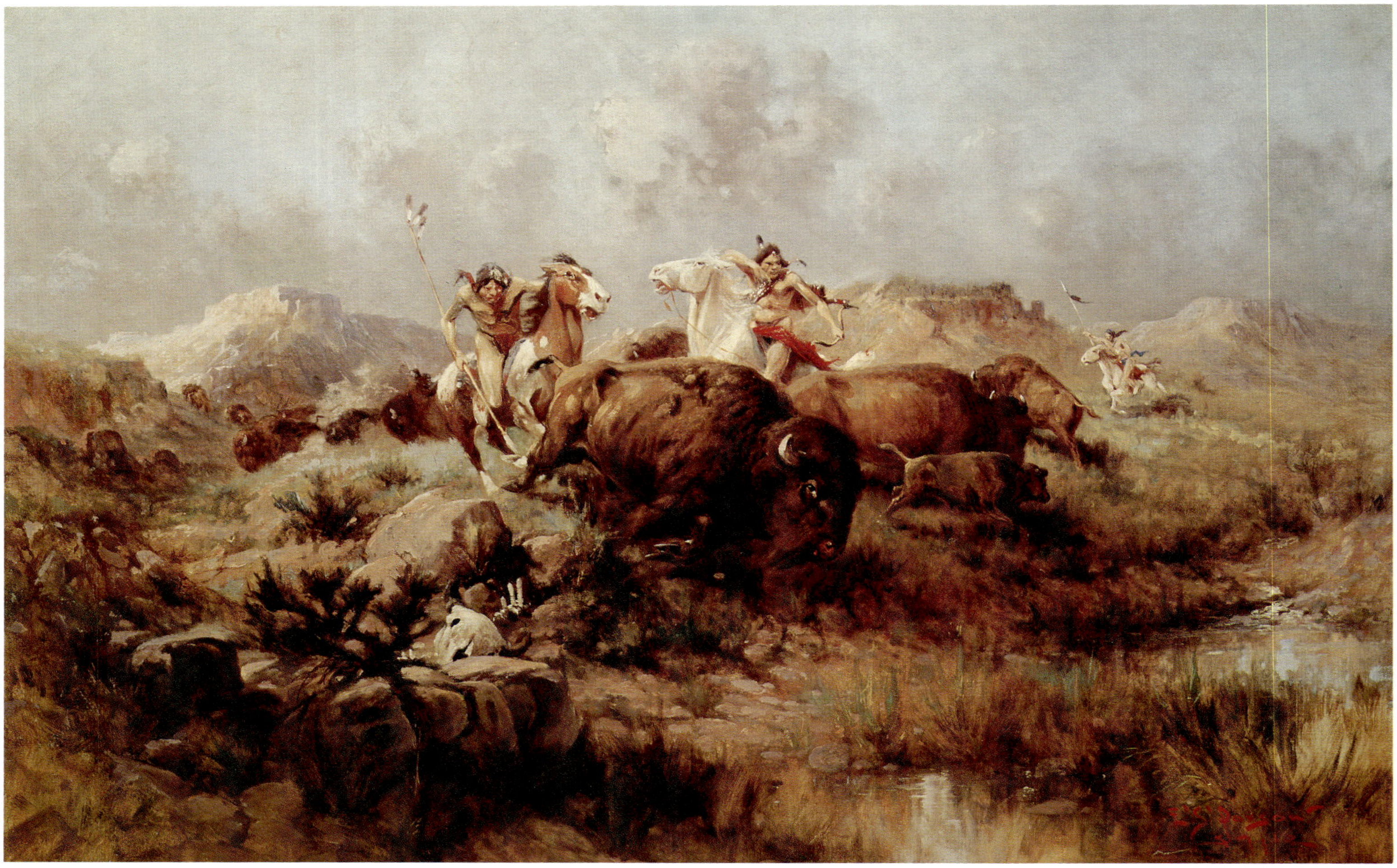

"Buffalo Hunt." Oil, 1911. *Private Collection.*

Title Unknown. Guasche, 1914. *Private Collection.*

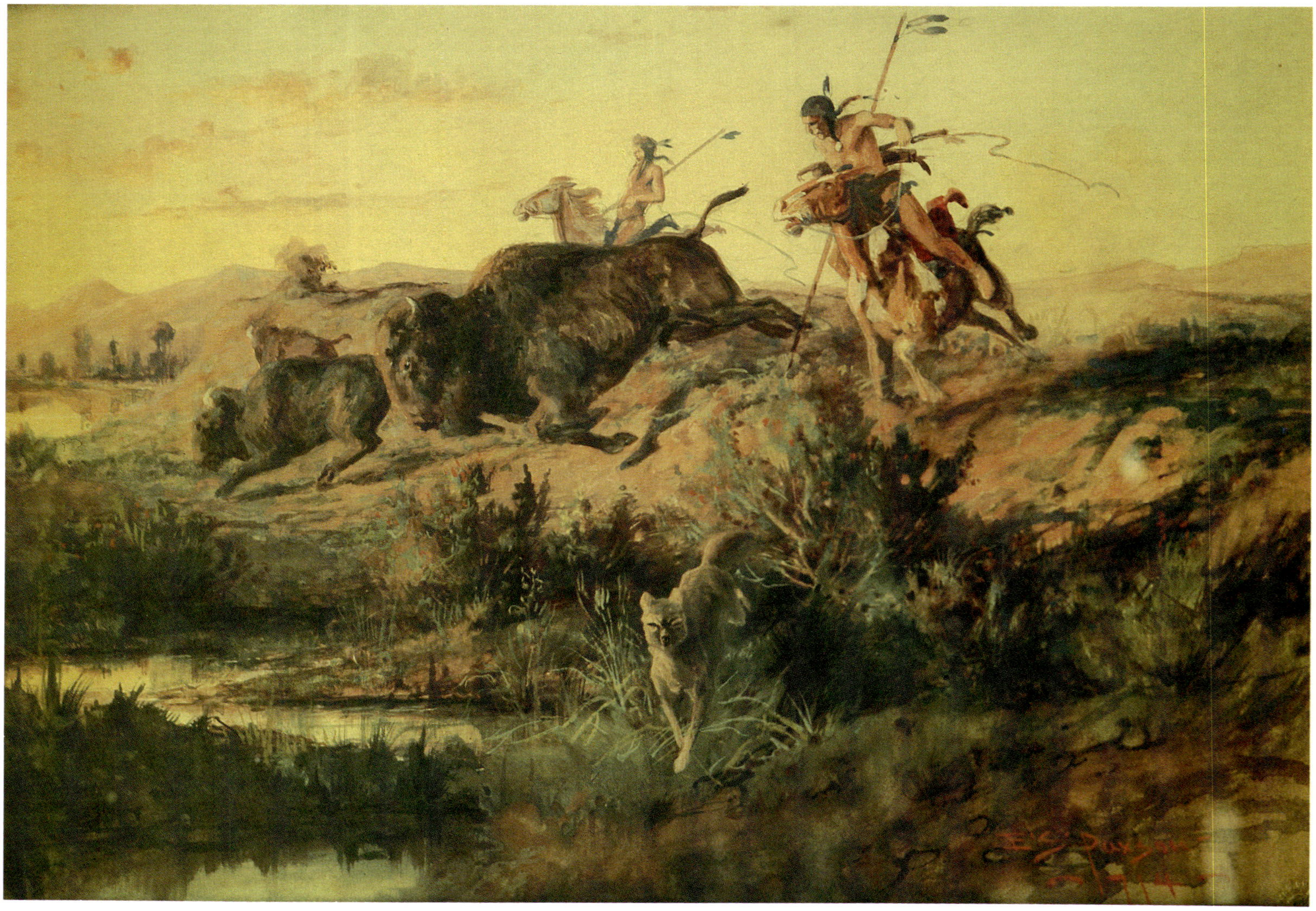

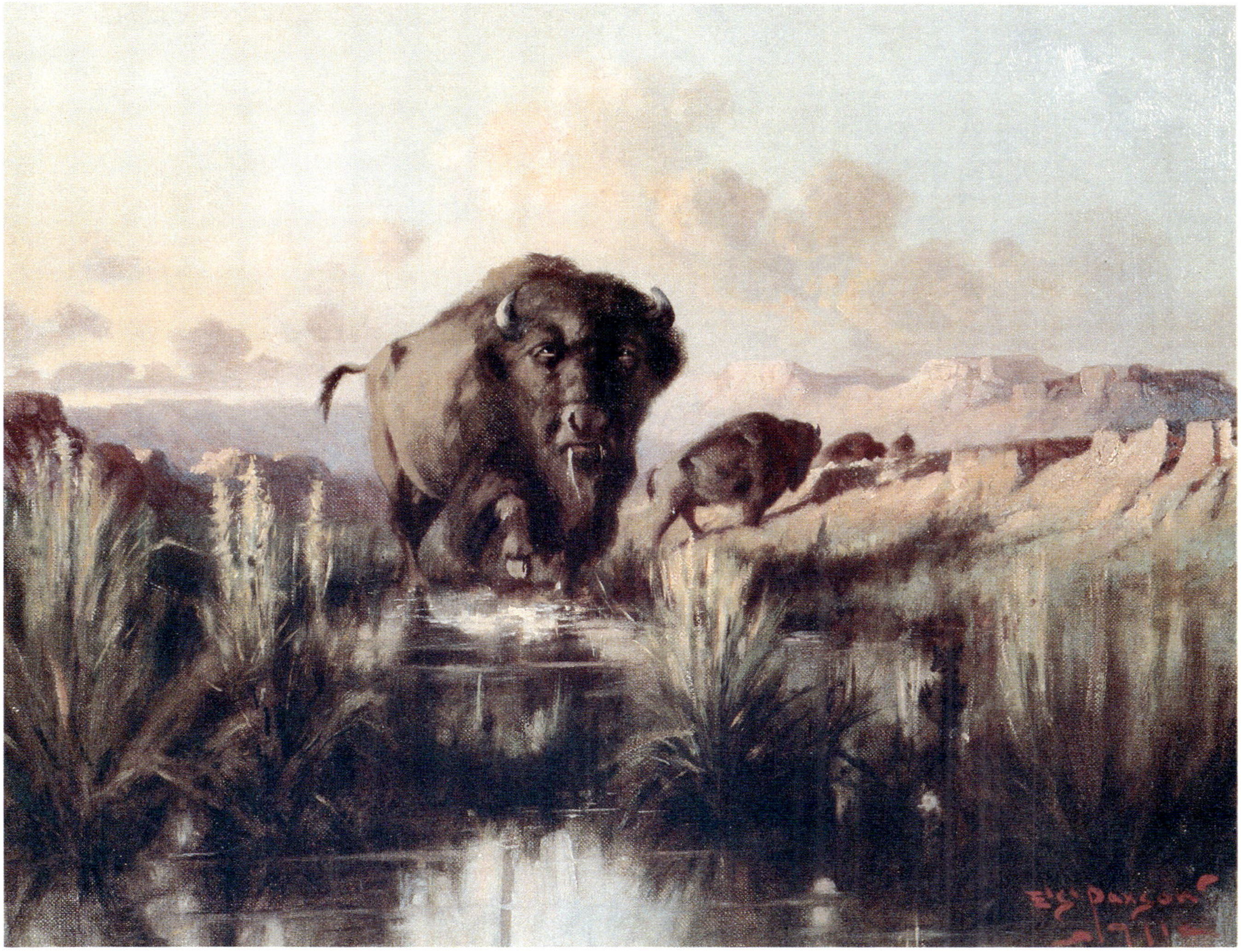

"Buffalos at Drink." Oil. *Mr. and Mrs. Gordon Fraser.*

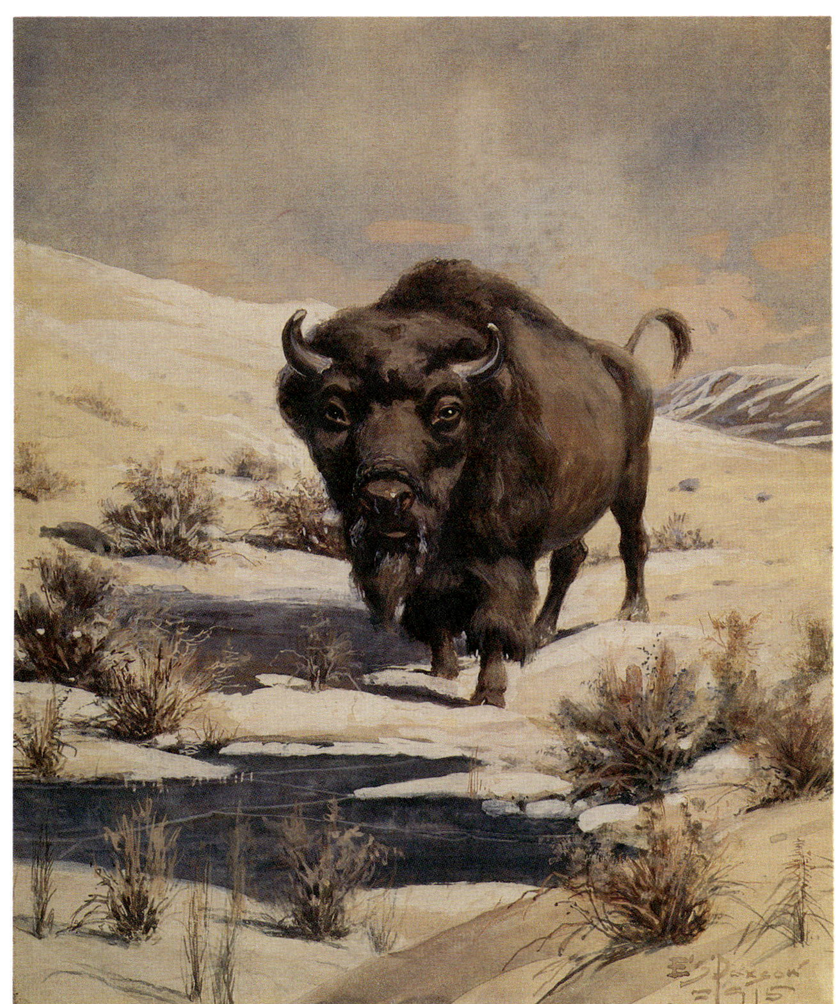

"Froze Up, by Thunder!" Guasche, 1915, 14 x 11. *Private Collection.*

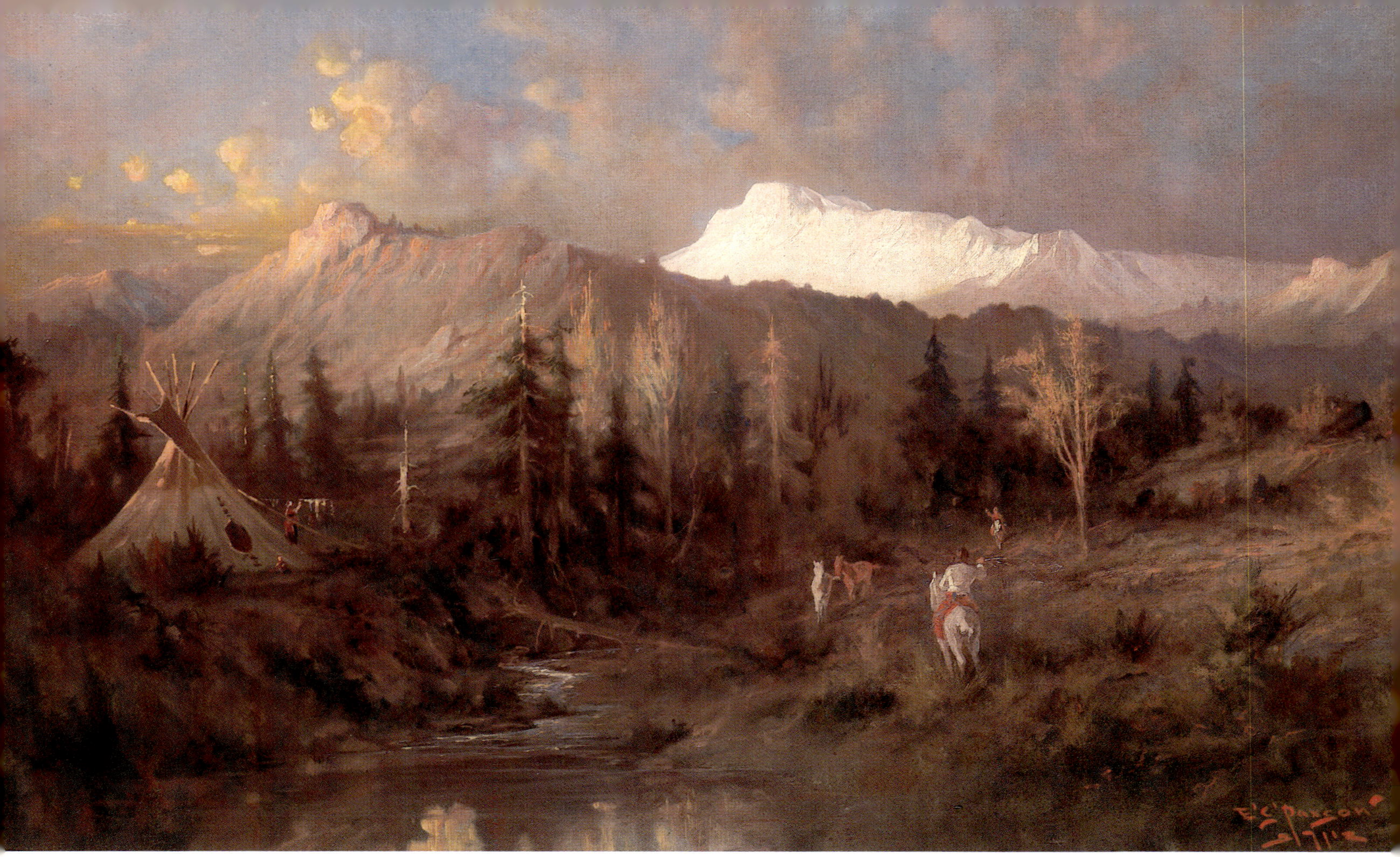

"Sunrise at Agency Creek." Oil, 1911, 22 x 36. *Petersen Galleries, Beverly Hills, California.*

"Selecting the Camping Place." Oil, 1911, 30 x 50. *Maxwell Galleries, San Francisco, California.*

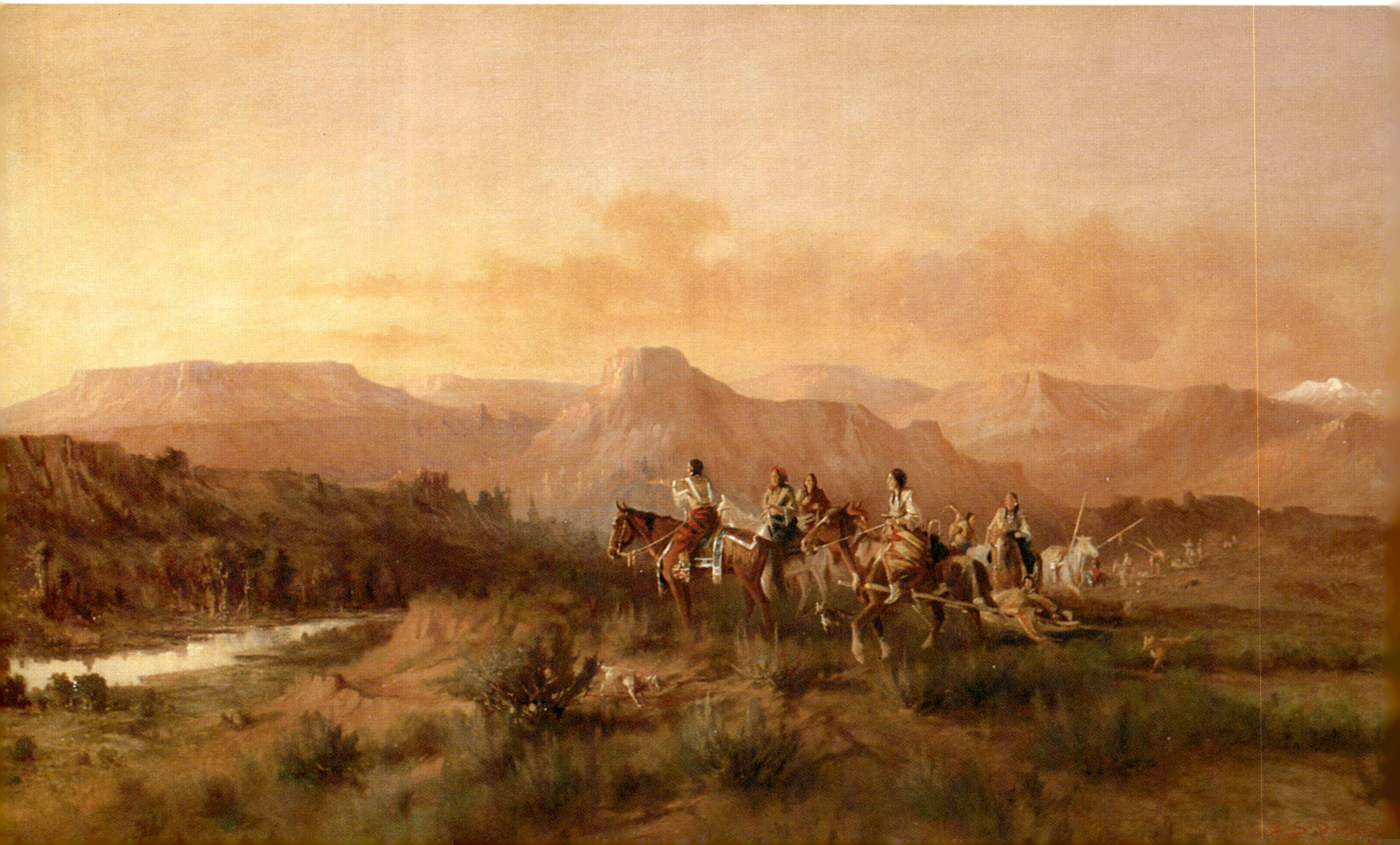

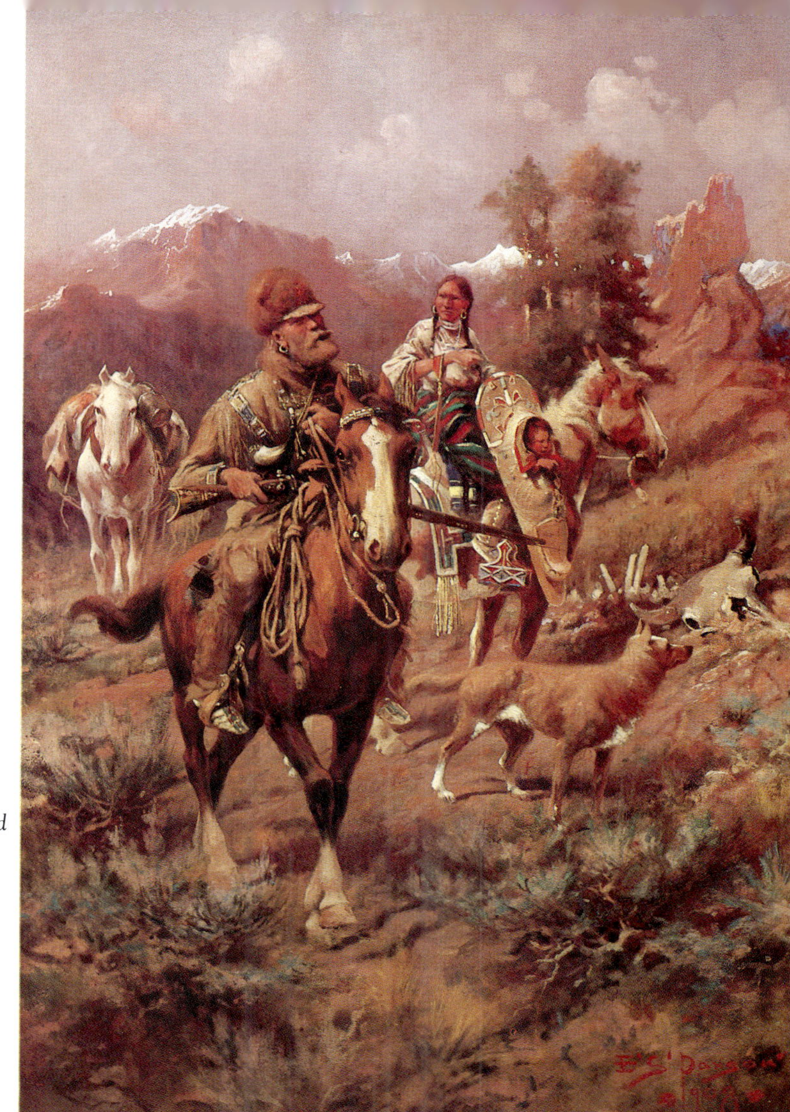

"The Squaw Man and His Outfit." Oil, 1908, 36 x 24. *Trail's End Collection, Dr. and Mrs. Van Kirke Nelson, Kalispell, Montana.*

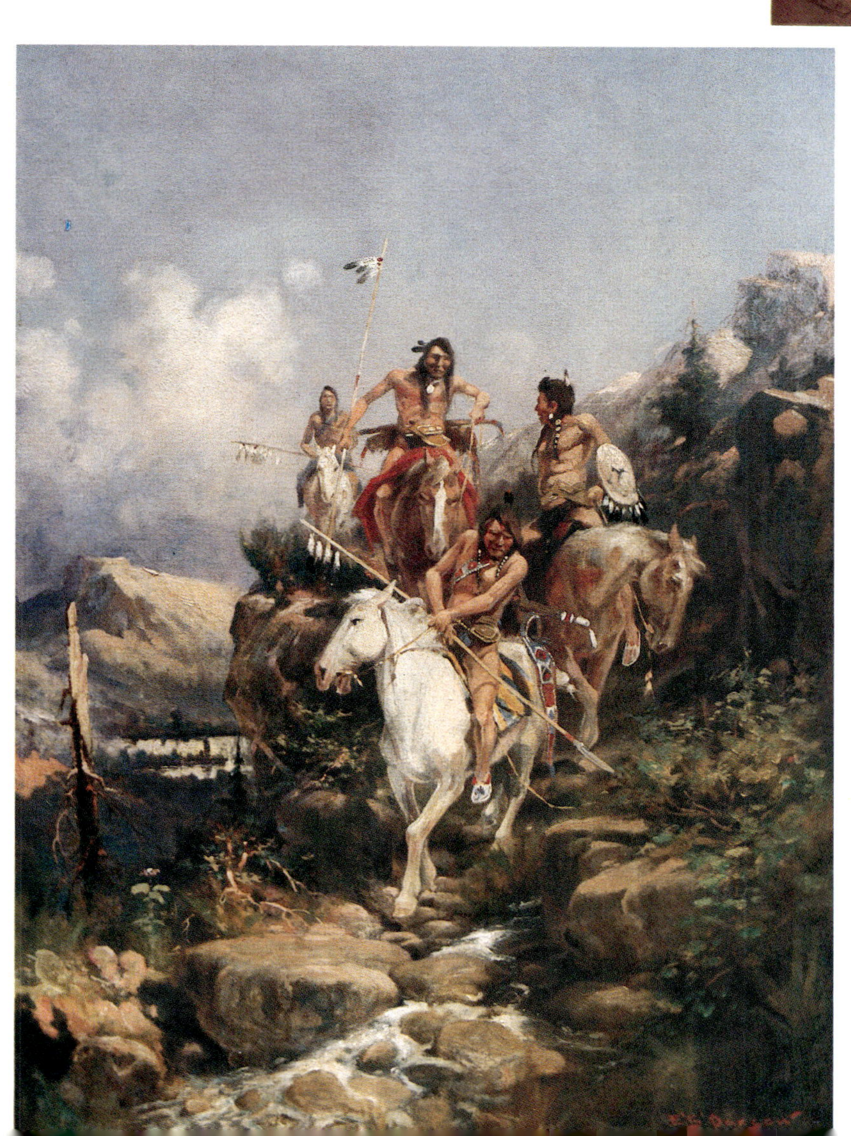

"Tracking." Oil, 1911, 30 x 20.

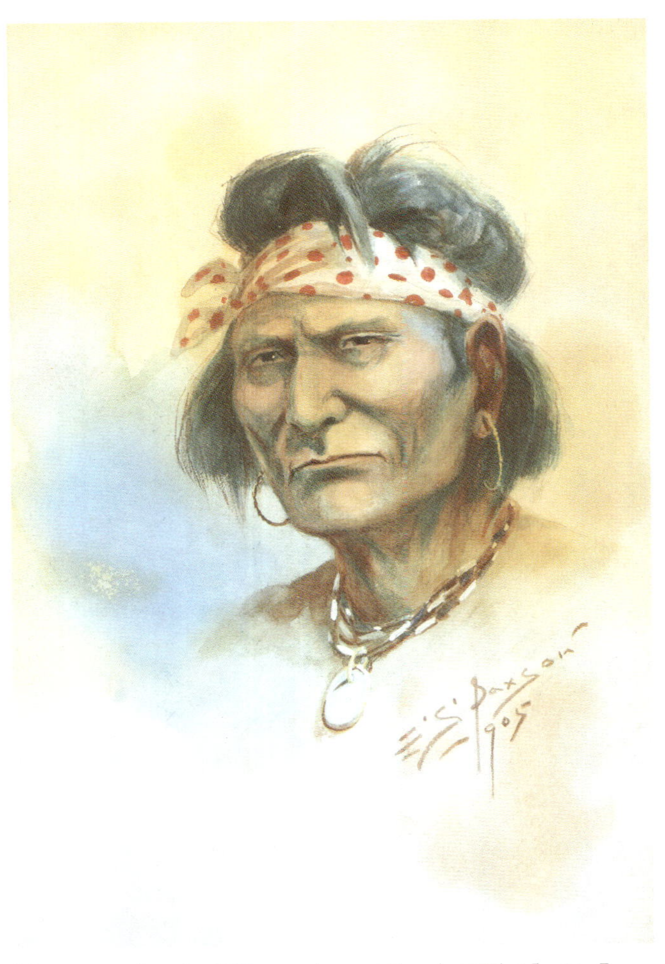

"Geronimo-Apache." Watercolor and Pastel, 1905, 15 x 11. *Penny and Martin Kodner, St. Louis, Missouri.*

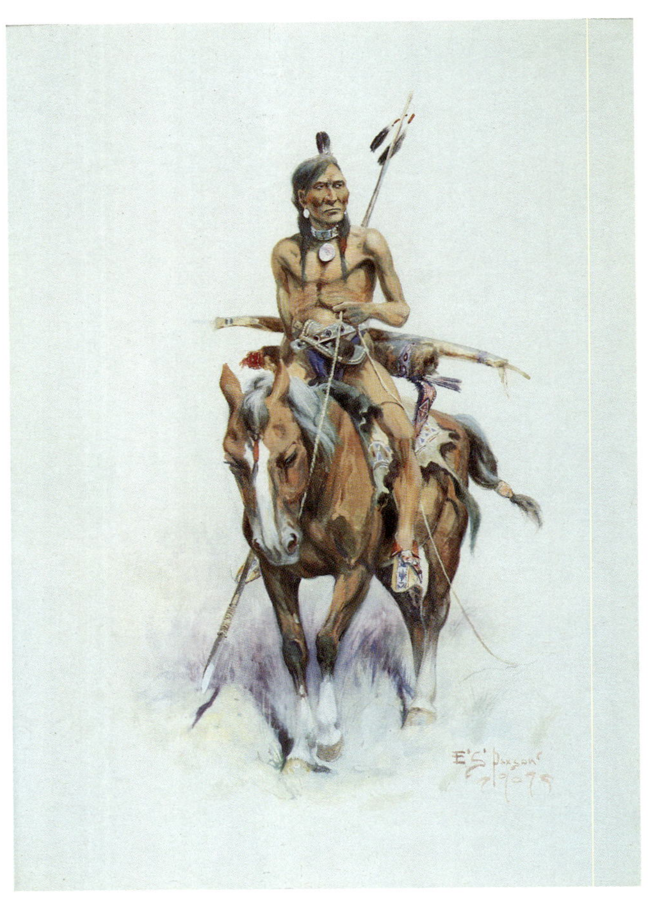

"The Old Warrior." Watercolor, 1909, 15 x 22. *S.L.M., Inc., Corning, Arkansas.*

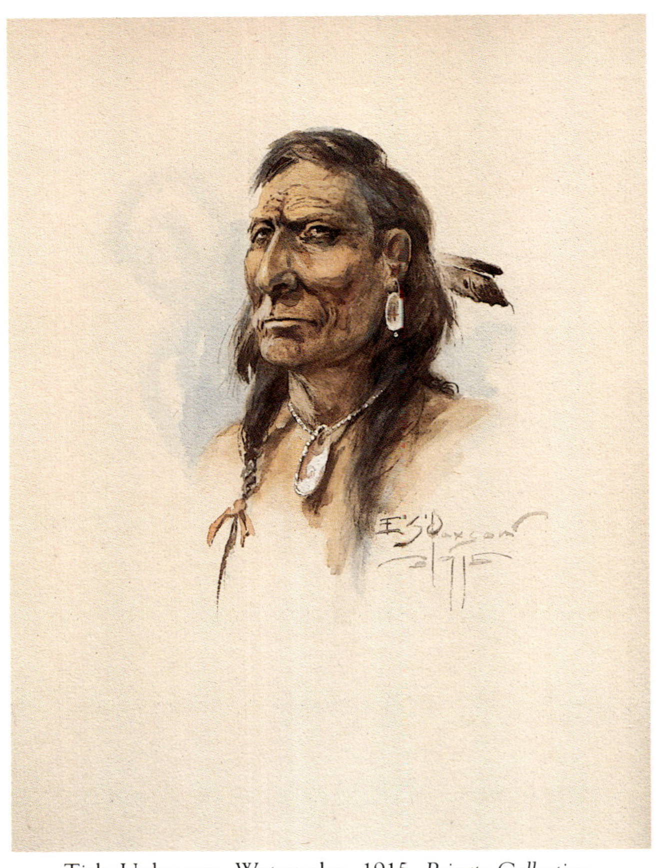

Title Unknown. Watercolor, 1915. *Private Collection.*

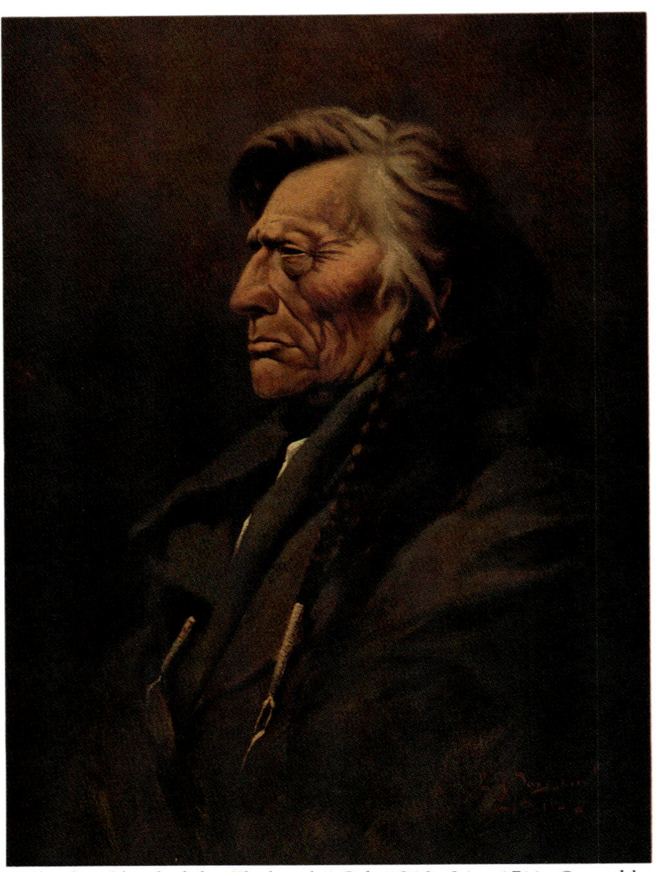

"Charlo, Chief of the Flathead." Oil, 1910, 24 x 17½. *Owned by the Women's Club of Missoula, Montana, and on loan to the Missoula City-County Library, Missoula, Montana.*

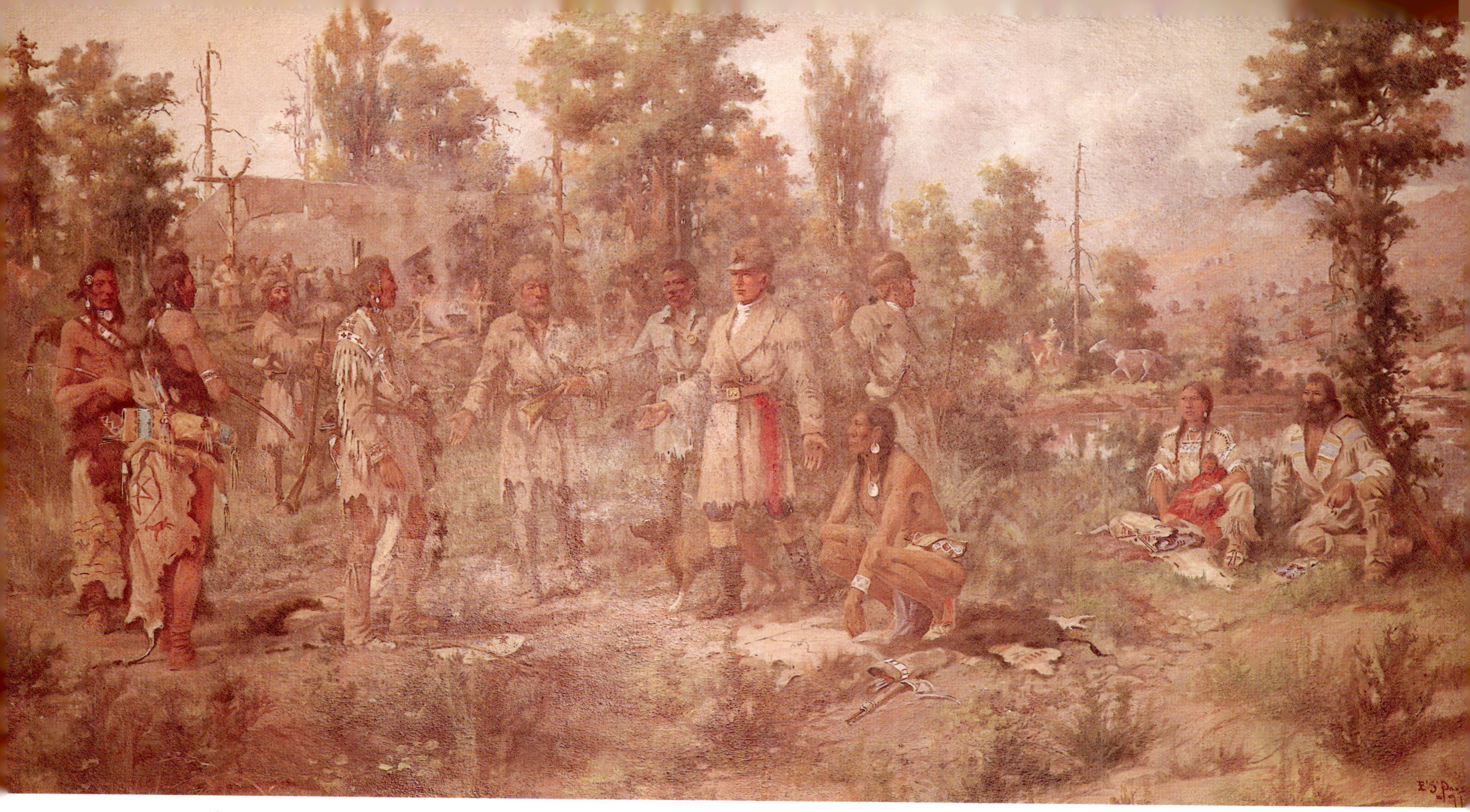

"Lewis and Clark's Camp at Travelers Rest, Lolo Creek, 1804." A hunter named Drewyer is presenting three Flathead Indians to Capt. Clark. The guide Sacajawea and her husband, the French trapper Charbonneau are seated to the right. Sacajawea holds her baby born at Fort Mandan on the Missouri River. Other members of the expedition pictured are John Coulter, leading a horse in the background; the Black, York; and Shannon, leaning on his rifle. *Missoula County Courthouse Mural.*

"Lewis' Party Crossing the Clark's Fork, July 3, 1806." The site of the crossing, just west of what is now Missoula, was located and sketched by the artist in his preparation for the mural. Depicted are the artist's conceptions of Captain Lewis, Sergeant Patrick Glass, the hunter Drewyer, Ruben Fields, Joseph Fields, William Werner, Robert Frazier, Hugh McNeal, John Thompson and Silas Goodrich. *Missoula County Courthouse Mural.*

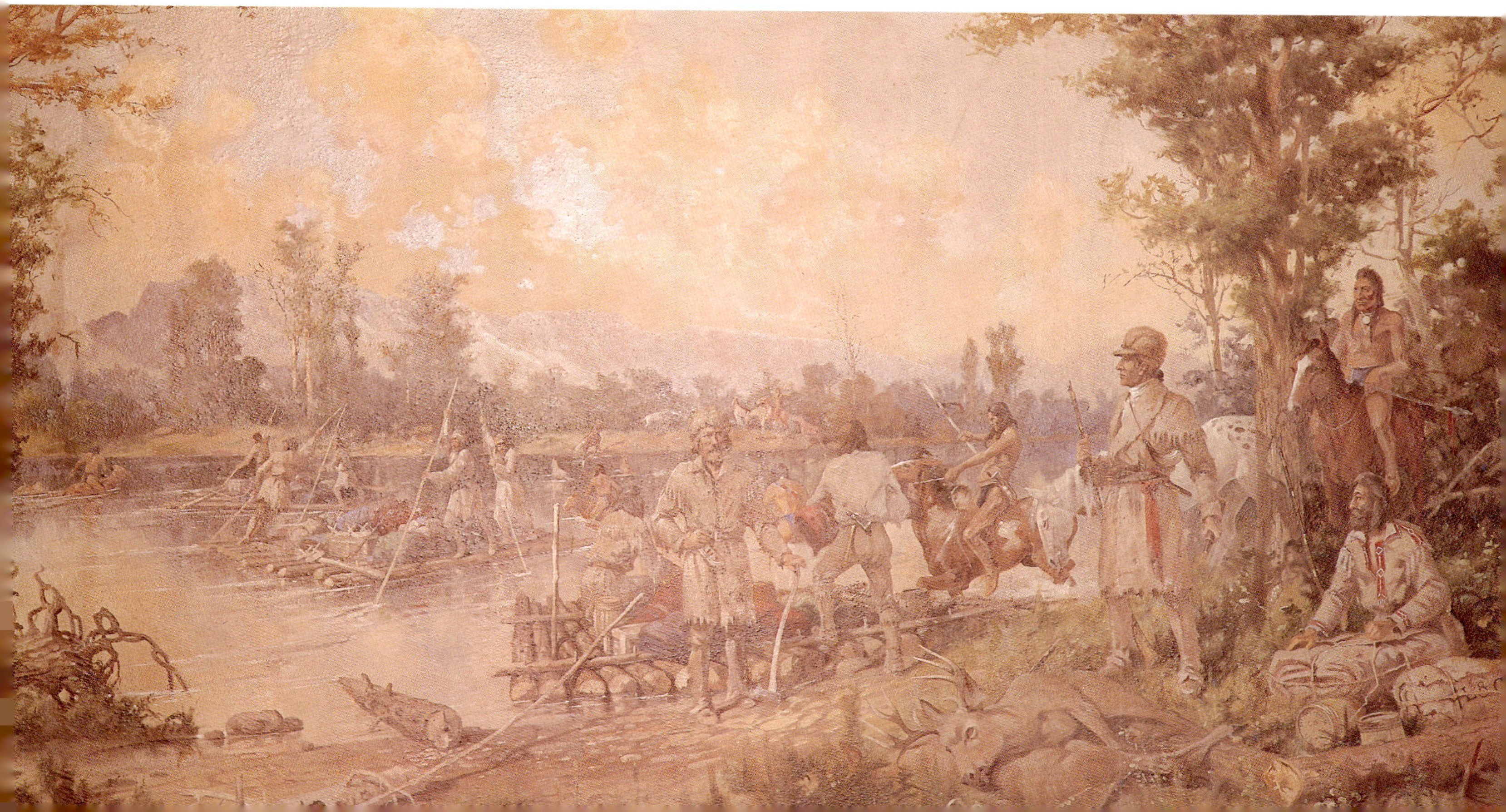

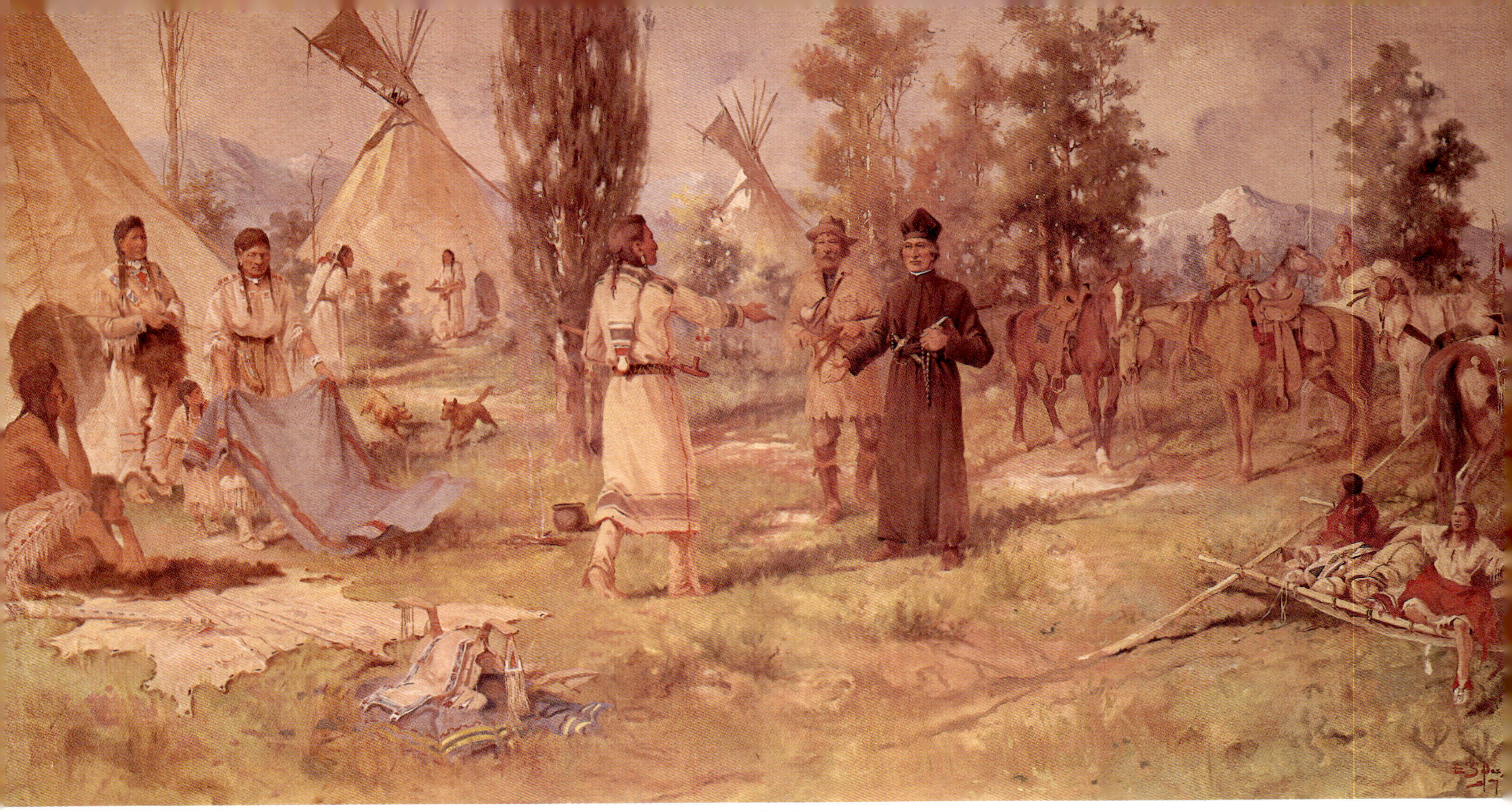

"Arrival of Father Ravalli at Fort Owen in September, 1845." 5½' x 10'. Having been escorted by a party of frontiersmen to Fort Owen, the priest is presented by Angus McDonald of the Hudson's Bay Company to Victor, chief of the Flathead (Selish) Indians. Moiese, a sub-chief is also pictured. The setting is near what is now Stevensville, Montana, in the Bitterroot Valley south of Missoula. Ravalli built St. Mary's Mission on the site. *Missoula County Courthouse Mural.*

Missoula County Courthouse Mural: *Governor Stevens' Treaty with the Pend d' Oreilles, Flatheads and Kootenais at Council Grove, July 9, 1855* (5½' x 5½'). Left to right are W.H. Pearson, guide and express rider; Christopher P. Higgins, packmaster and a founder of Missoula; Chief Alexander of the Pend d'Oreilles; James Doty, secretary; hunter and guide Delaware Jim; Governor Isaac Stevens; Chief Victor of the Flatheads; and Chief Michel of the Kootenais.

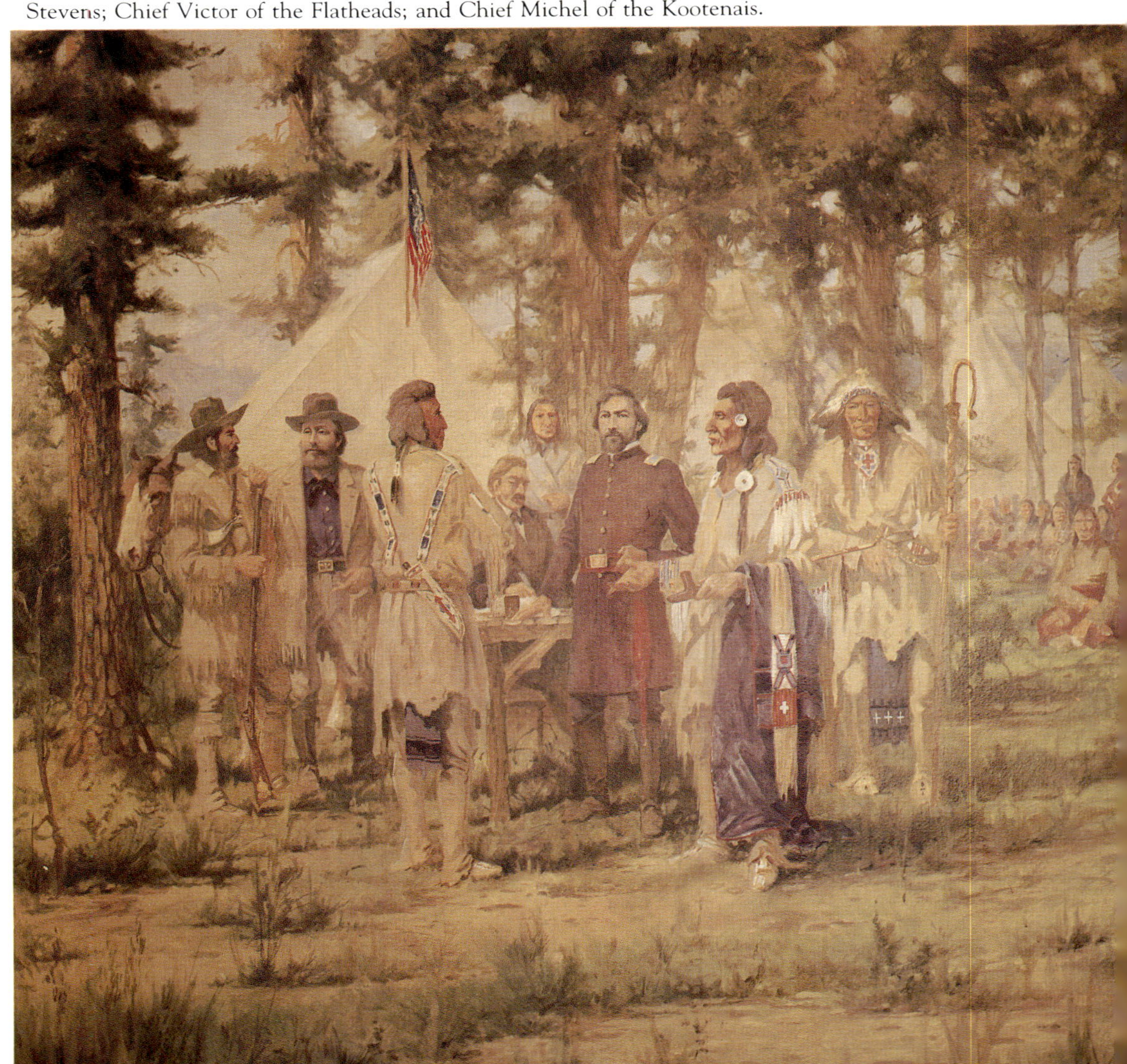

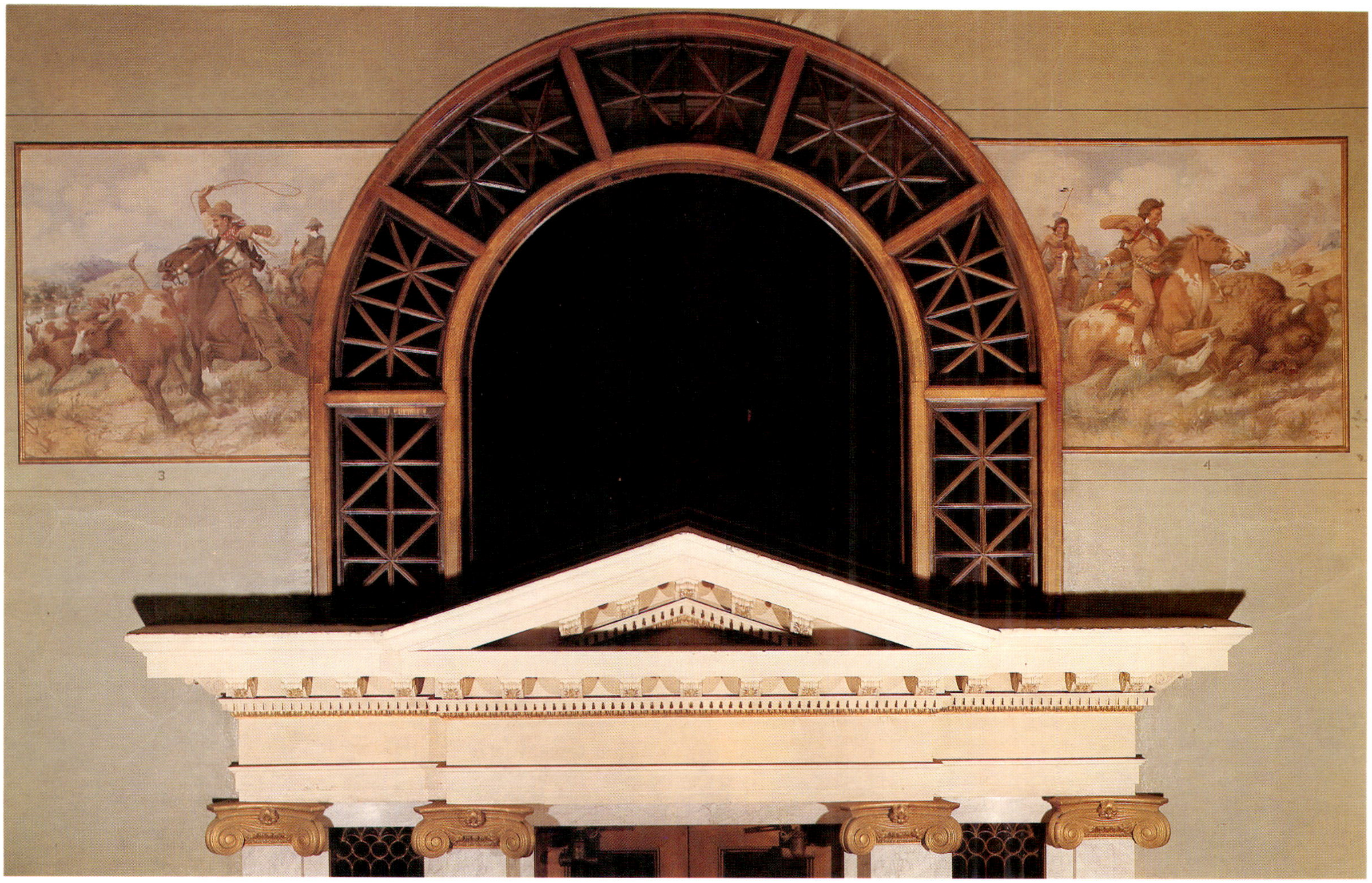

Left, "A Montana Roundup." 5½' x 6½'. Right, "The Flatheads in Buffalo Country." 5½' x 6½'. *Missoula County Courthouse Murals.*

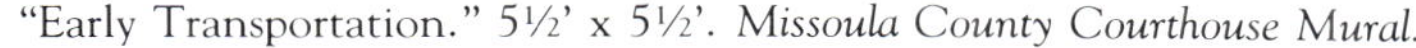

"Early Transportation." 5½' x 5½'. *Missoula County Courthouse Mural.*

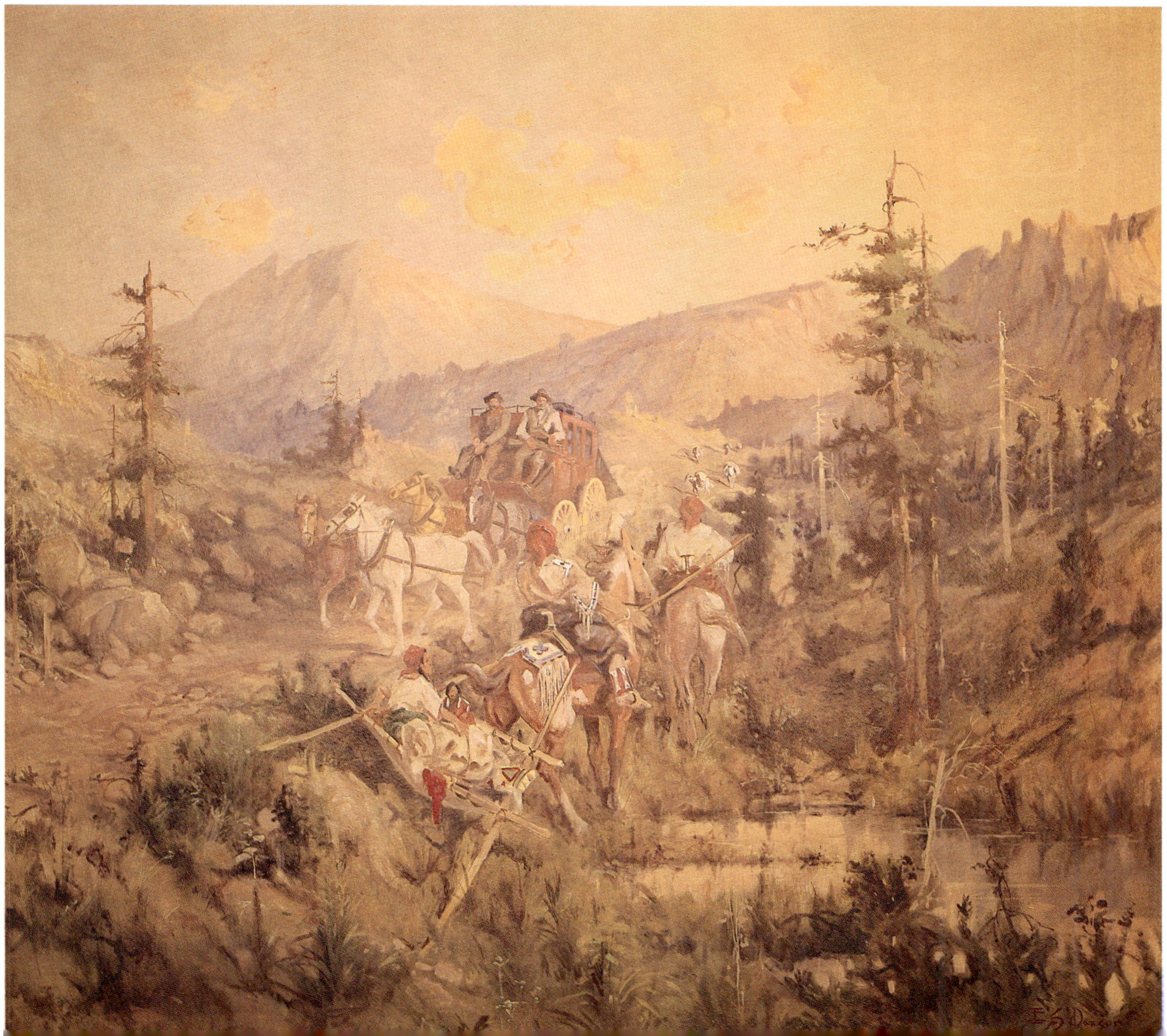

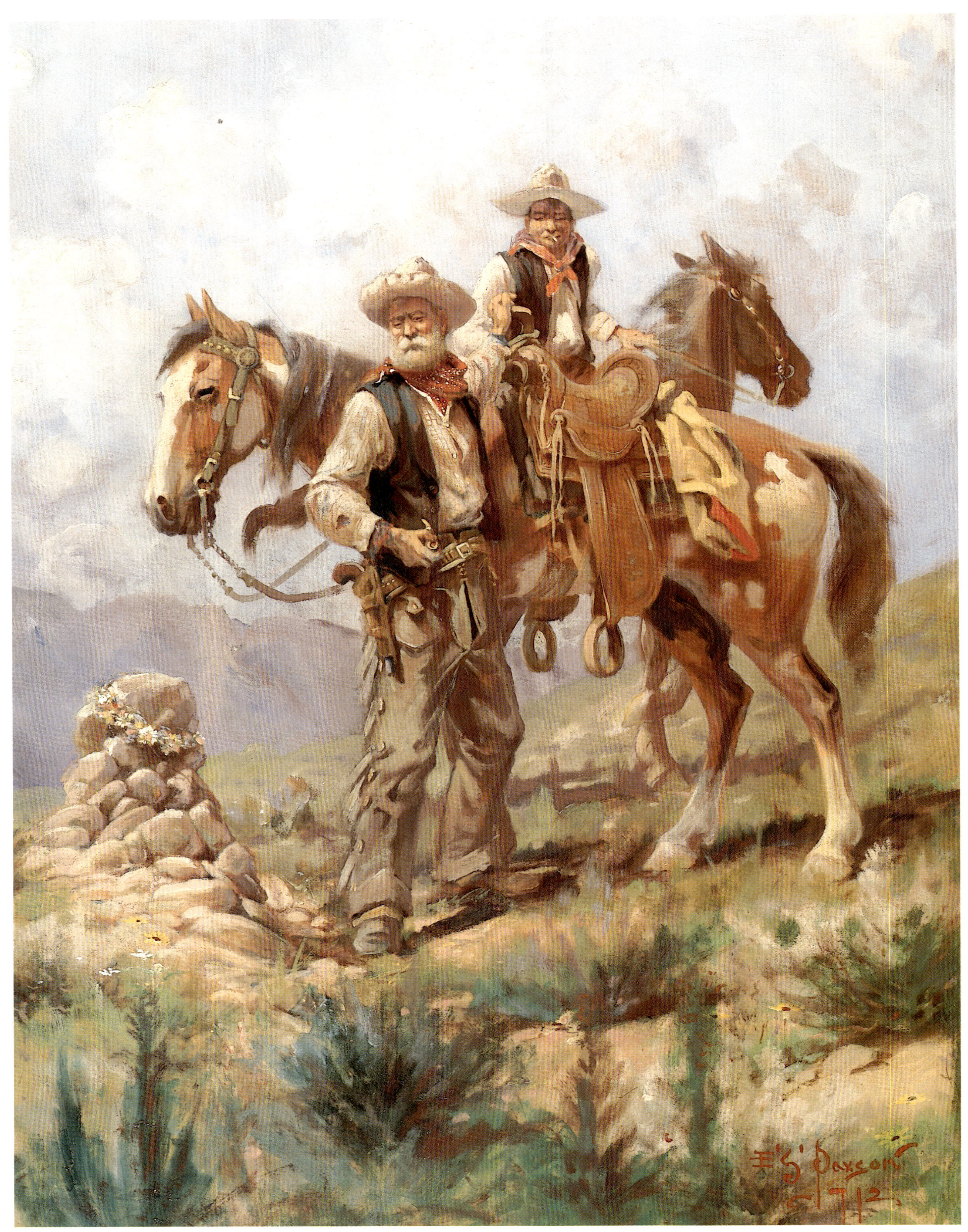

"The Cowbcy Memorial." Oil, 1912. *Stremmel Galleries, Ltd., Reno, Nevada.*

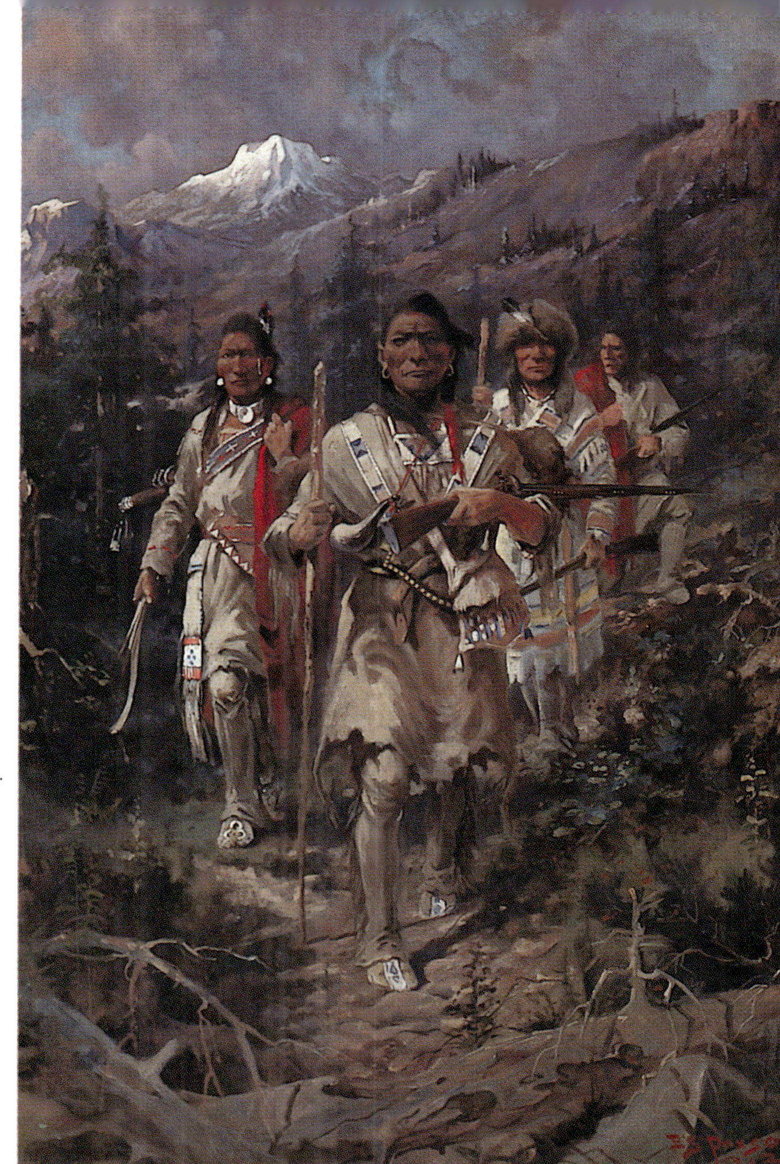

"Seeking the Whiteman's Book." Oil, 1912, 36 x 24. *Private Collection.*

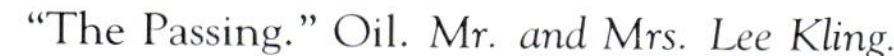

"The Passing." Oil. *Mr. and Mrs. Lee Kling.*

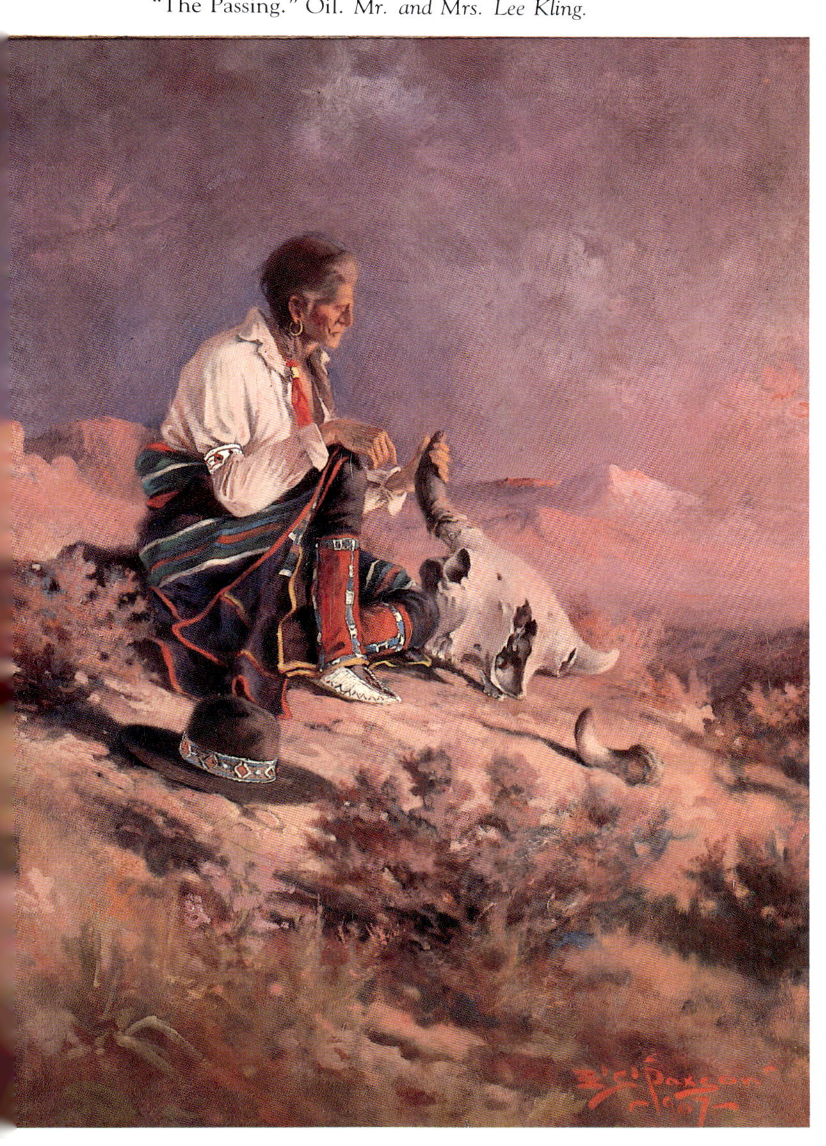

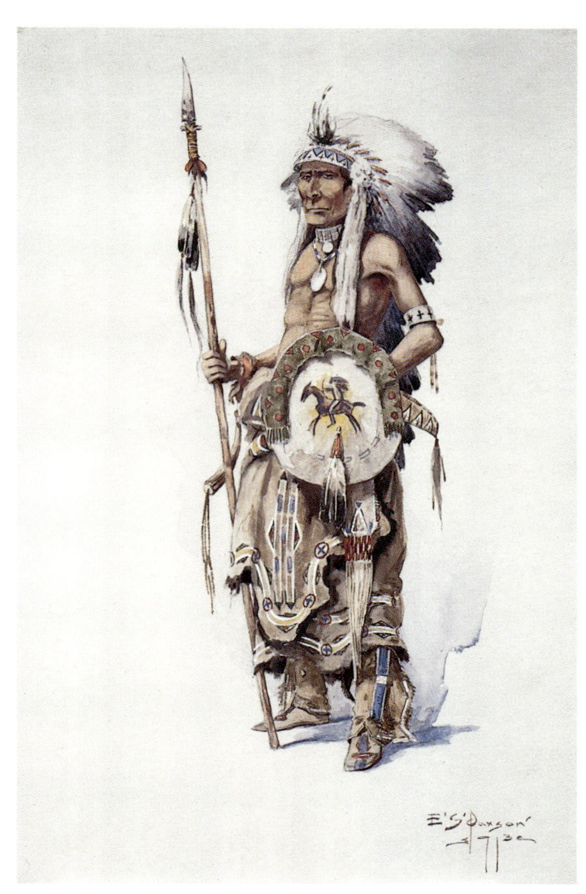

Title Unknown. Watercolor, 1913, 15 x 17 *Private Collection.*

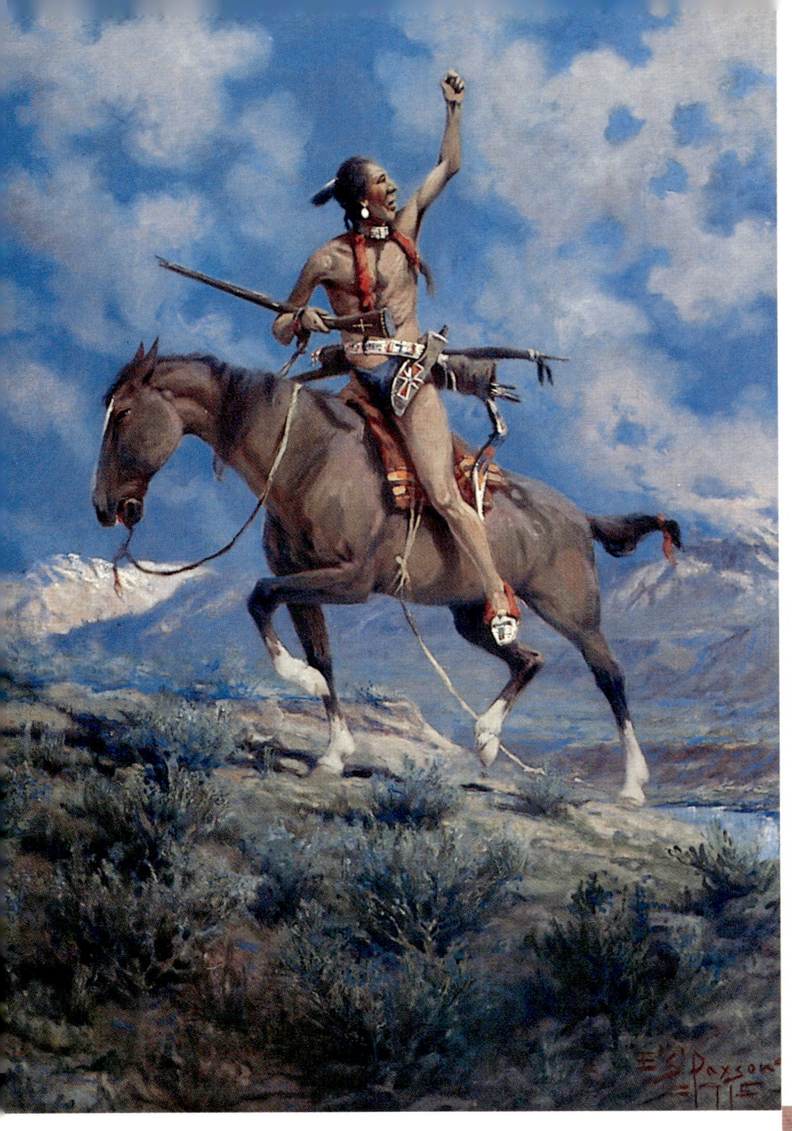

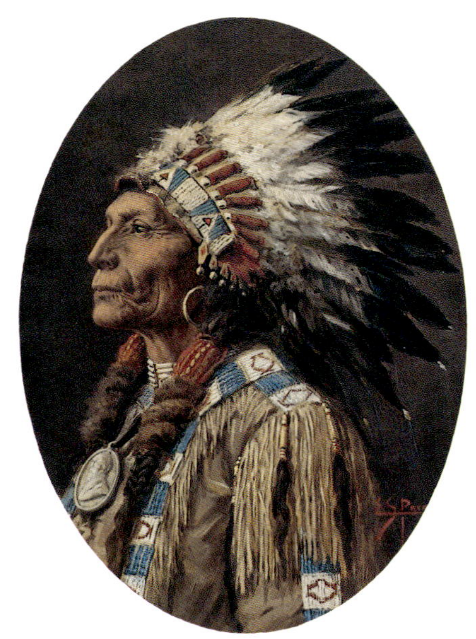

"Wolf Robe." Oil, 1899, 15 x 12. *Susan Sorelle.*

"His Defiance." Oil, 1915, 19½ x 27. Private Collection.

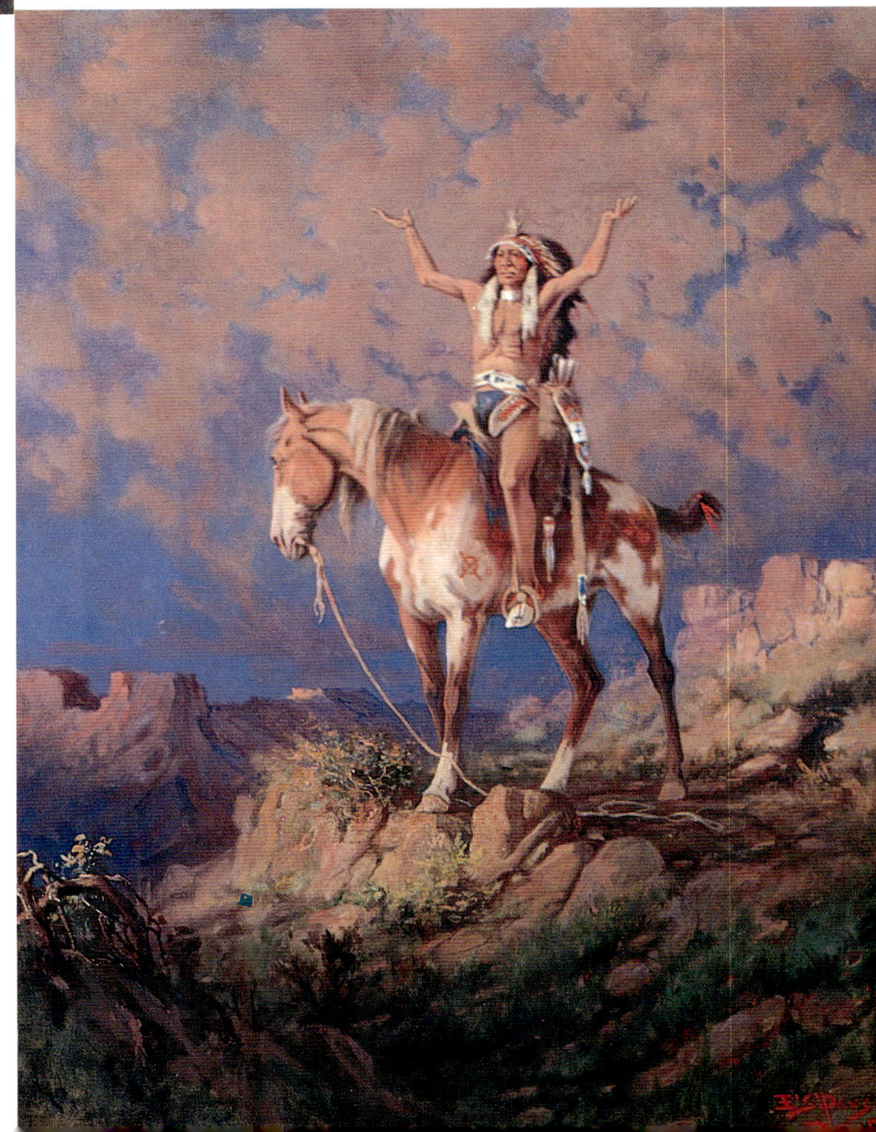

"His Manatou" (His God). Oil, 1915, 36 x 28. *Private Collection.*

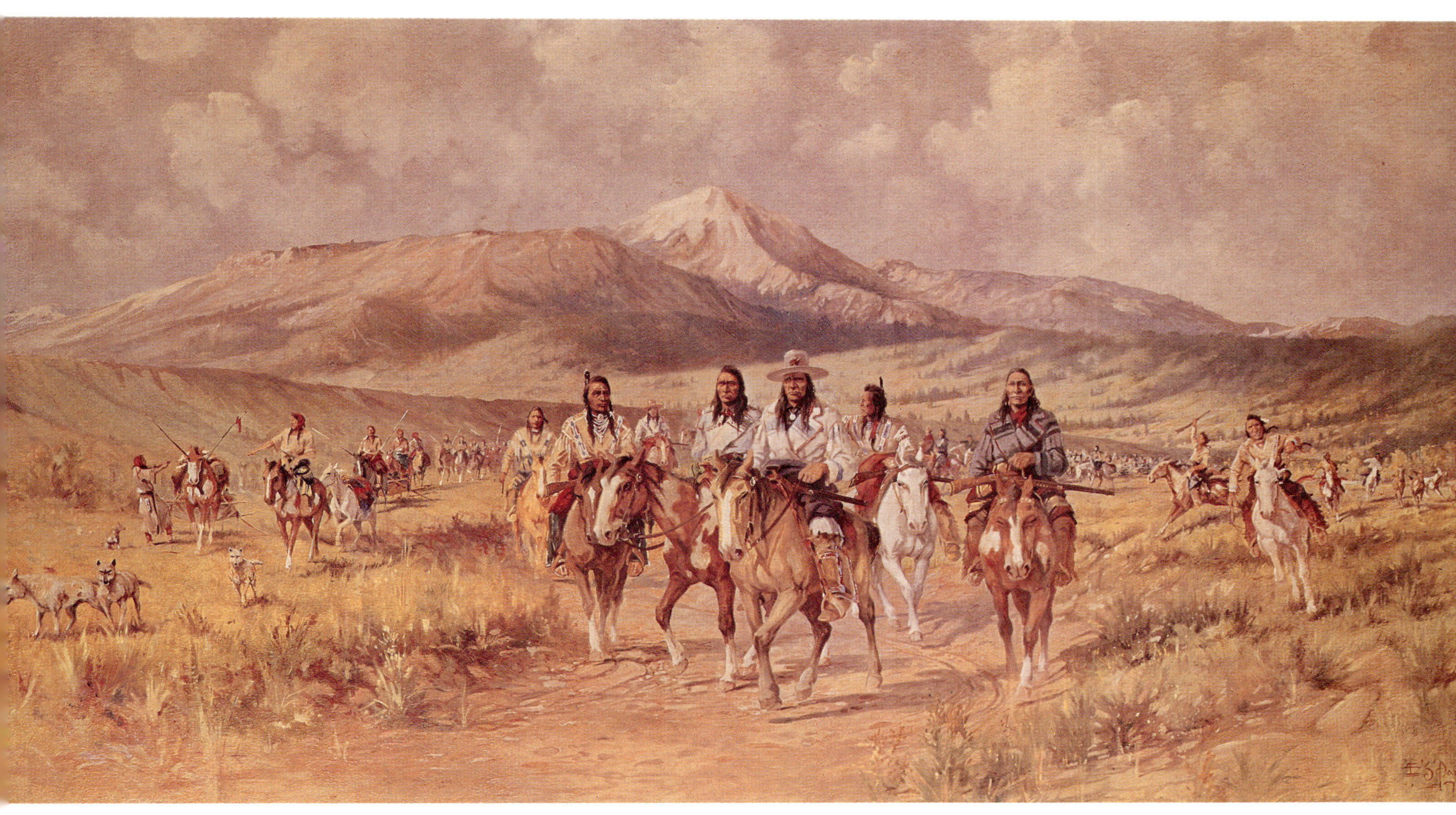

"Flatheads Leaving Their Bitterroot Home, October, 1892." 5½' x 10'. Chief Charlo is shown leading his people from their ancestral home in the Bitterroot Valley to their appointed reservation north of Missoula. Mount Lolo is seen in the background as they move along what is now Stephens Avenue in Missoula. Depicted in the foreground are tribal leaders. Left to right are Antoine Moise, Louis LaCoot, Charlo, John Hill and interpreter Pierre Francois. *Missoula County Courthouse Mural.*

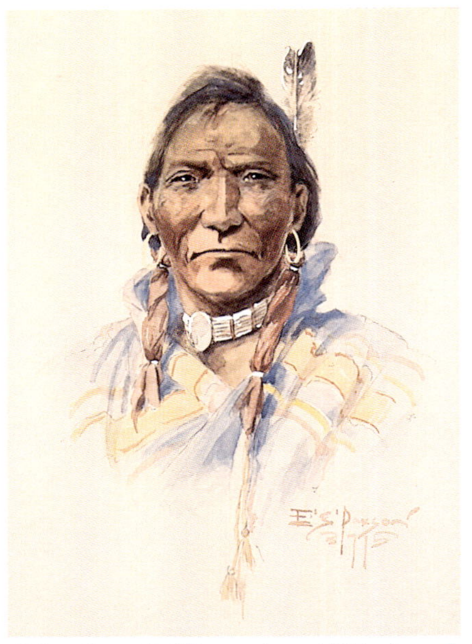

"Nez Percé." Watercolor, 1915, 9 x 7. *Private Collection.* This painting was originally sold by the artist for twelve dollars.

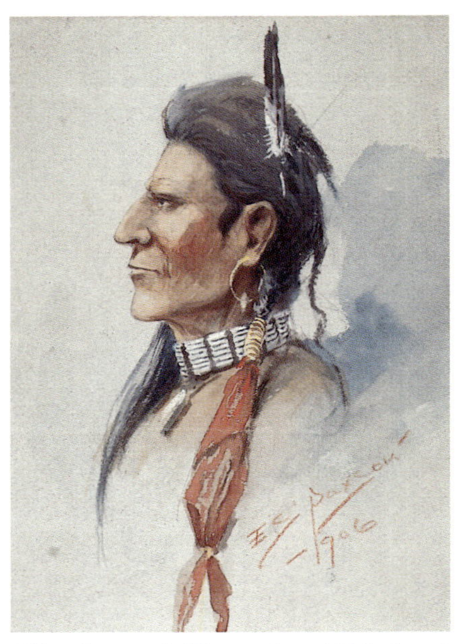

"Sho-sho-nee." Watercolor, 1906, 9 x 6. *Julliette and Pat Donlan.*

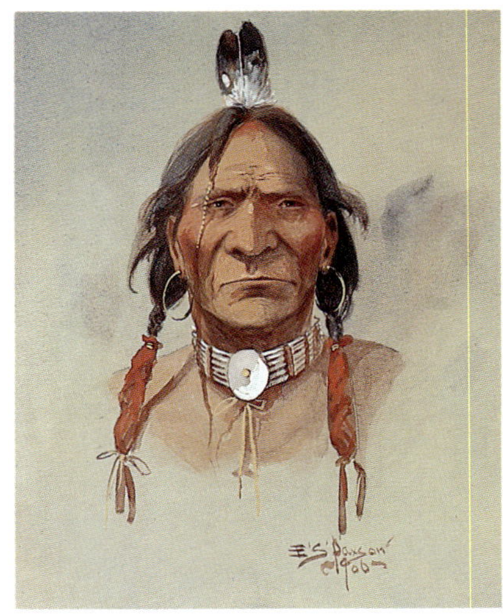

"Sioux." Watercolor, 1906, 13 x 10. *Robert and Juanita Ellithorpe.*

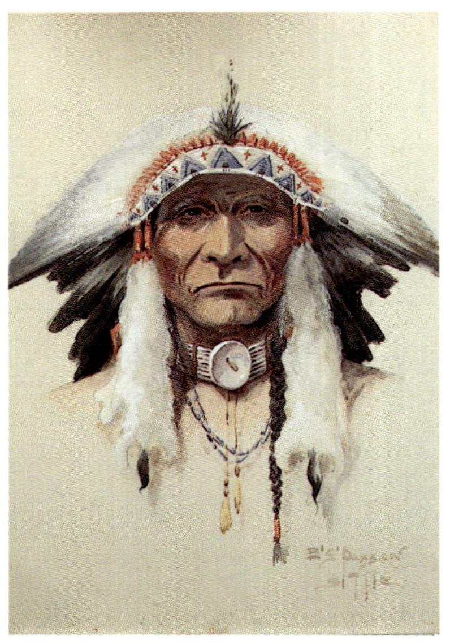

Title Unknown. Watercolor, 1911, 16 x 12. *Private Collection.*

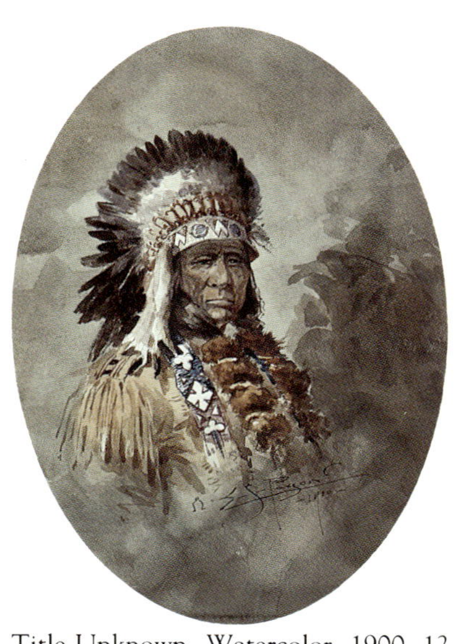

Title Unknown. Watercolor, 1900. 12 x 9. *Ray and Maxine Howser.*

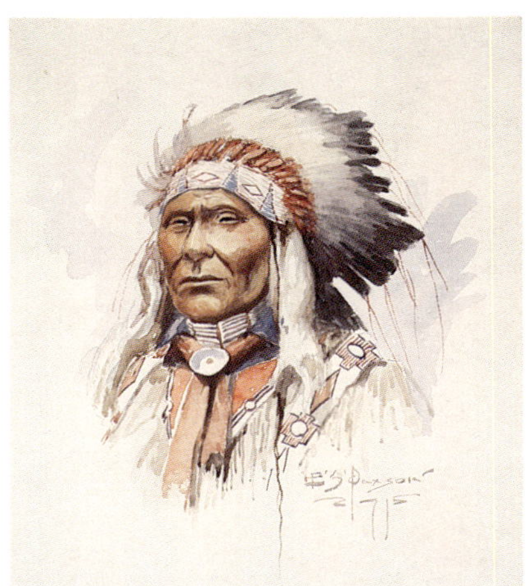

"Black Hawk." Watercolor, 1914, 8 x 7½. *Jean Walker.*

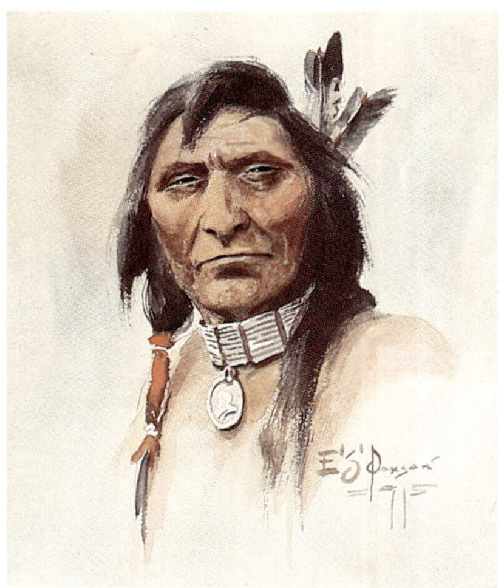

"Sho-sho-nee." Watercolor, 1915, 8 x 6½. *Private Collection.*

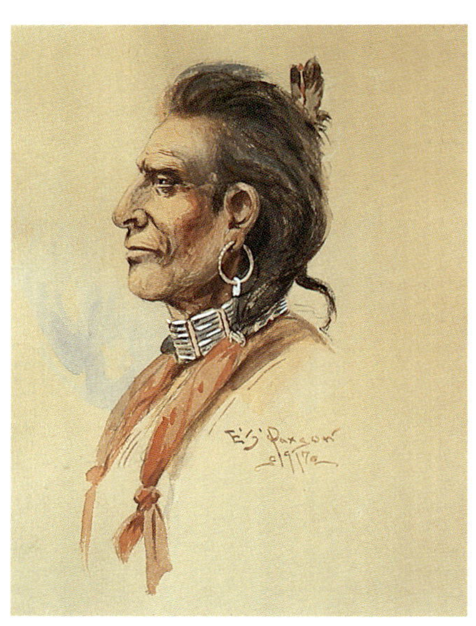

Title Unknown. Watercolor, 1917, 7 x 4. *Ray and Maxine Howser.*

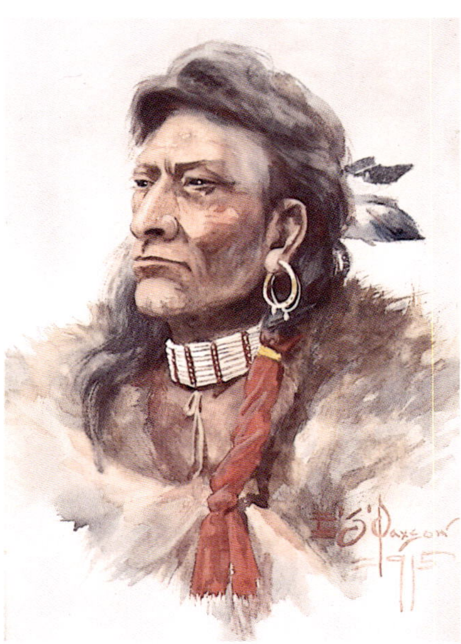

"Pon da Rey." Watercolor, 1915, 10½ x 7½. *Private Collection.* This painting was originally sold by the artist for twenty dollars.

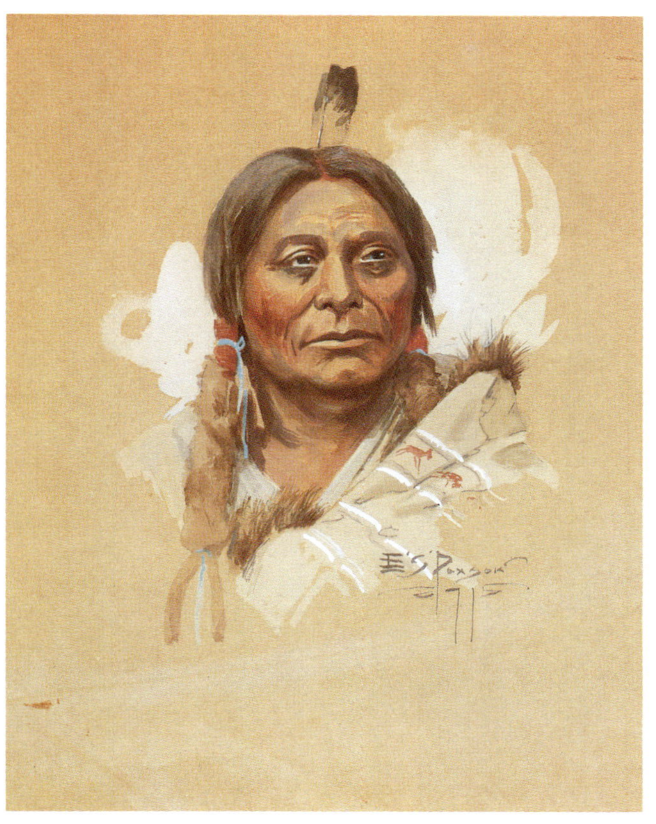

"Young Sitting Bull." Watercolor and Guasche, 1915, 12 x 10. *Gallery of the Masters, St. Louis, Missouri.*

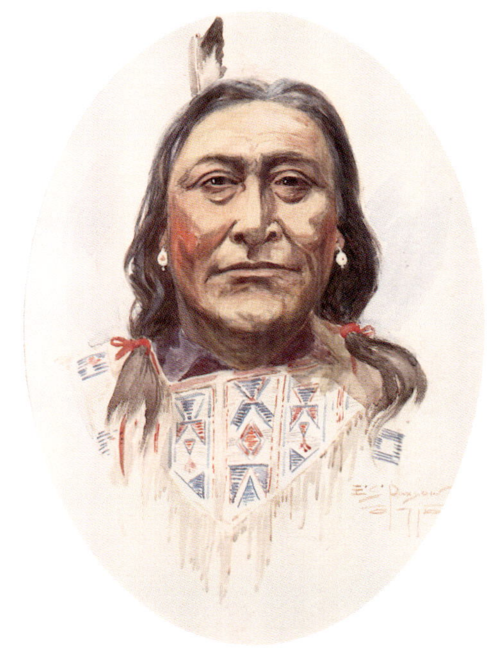

"Hollow Bear Horn." Watercolor, 1915, 14 x 9½. *Private Collection.*

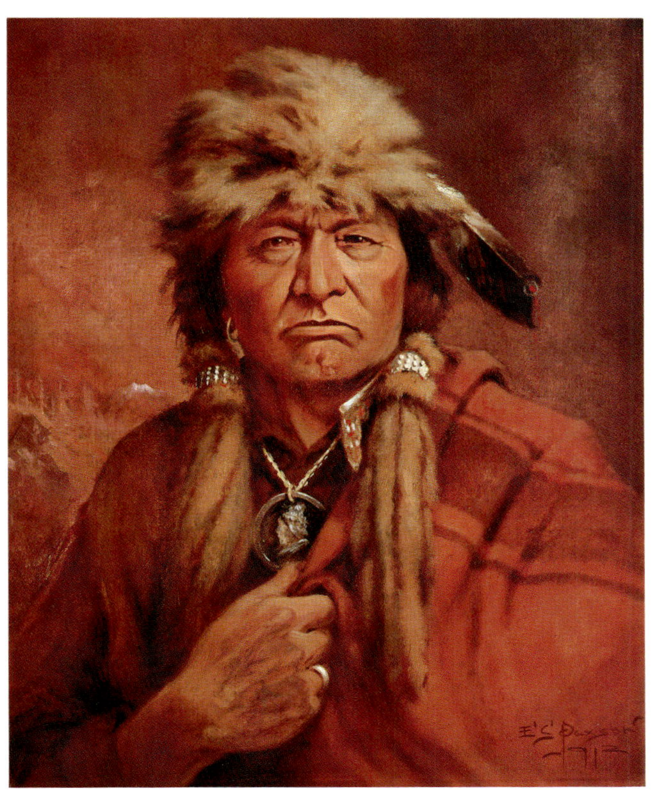

"Little Bear, Cree Chief." Oil, 1912. 22⅛ x 18¼. *The Los Angeles Athletic Club Collection.*

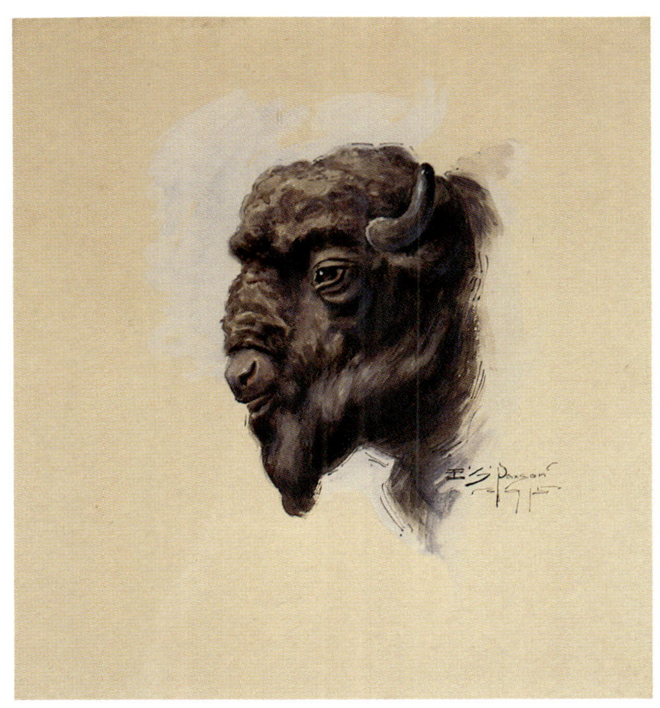

"Buffalo Head." Watercolor, 1915, 8 x 6. *Private Collection.*

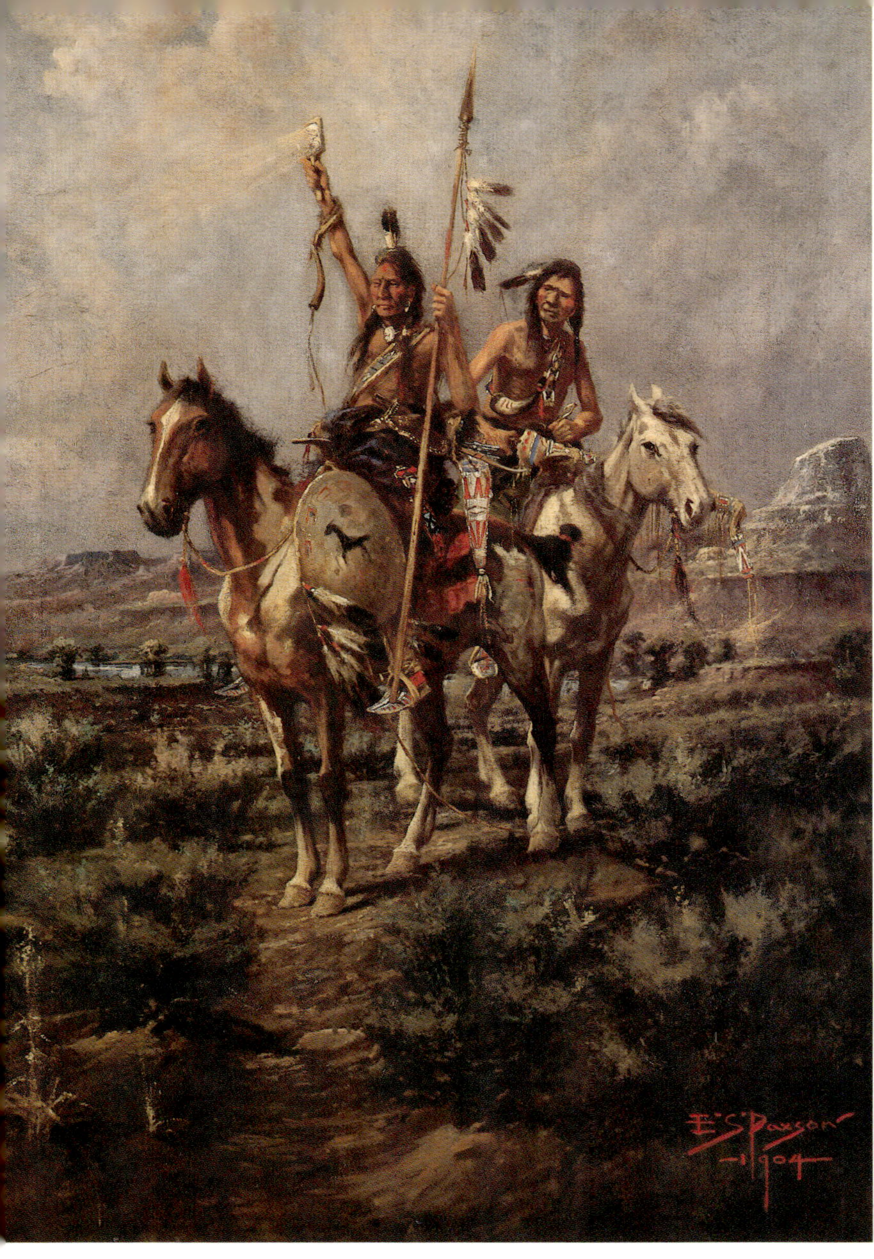

"La Heliographa" (The Signal Mirror). Oil, 1904, 36 x 24. *Trail's End Collection, Dr. and Mrs. Van Kirke Nelson, Kalispell, Montana.*

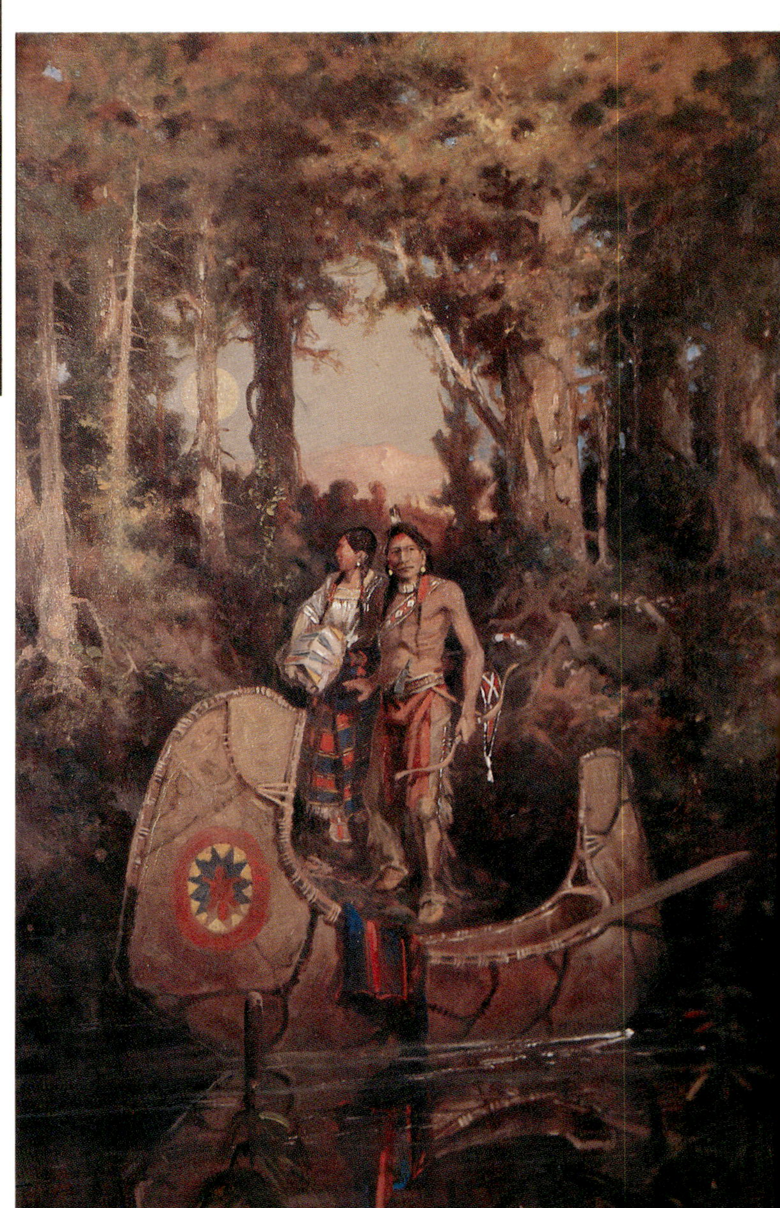

"Elopment of the Sioux." Oil, 1913, 22 x 36. *Museum of Native American Cultures, Spokane, Washington.*

Plate 28

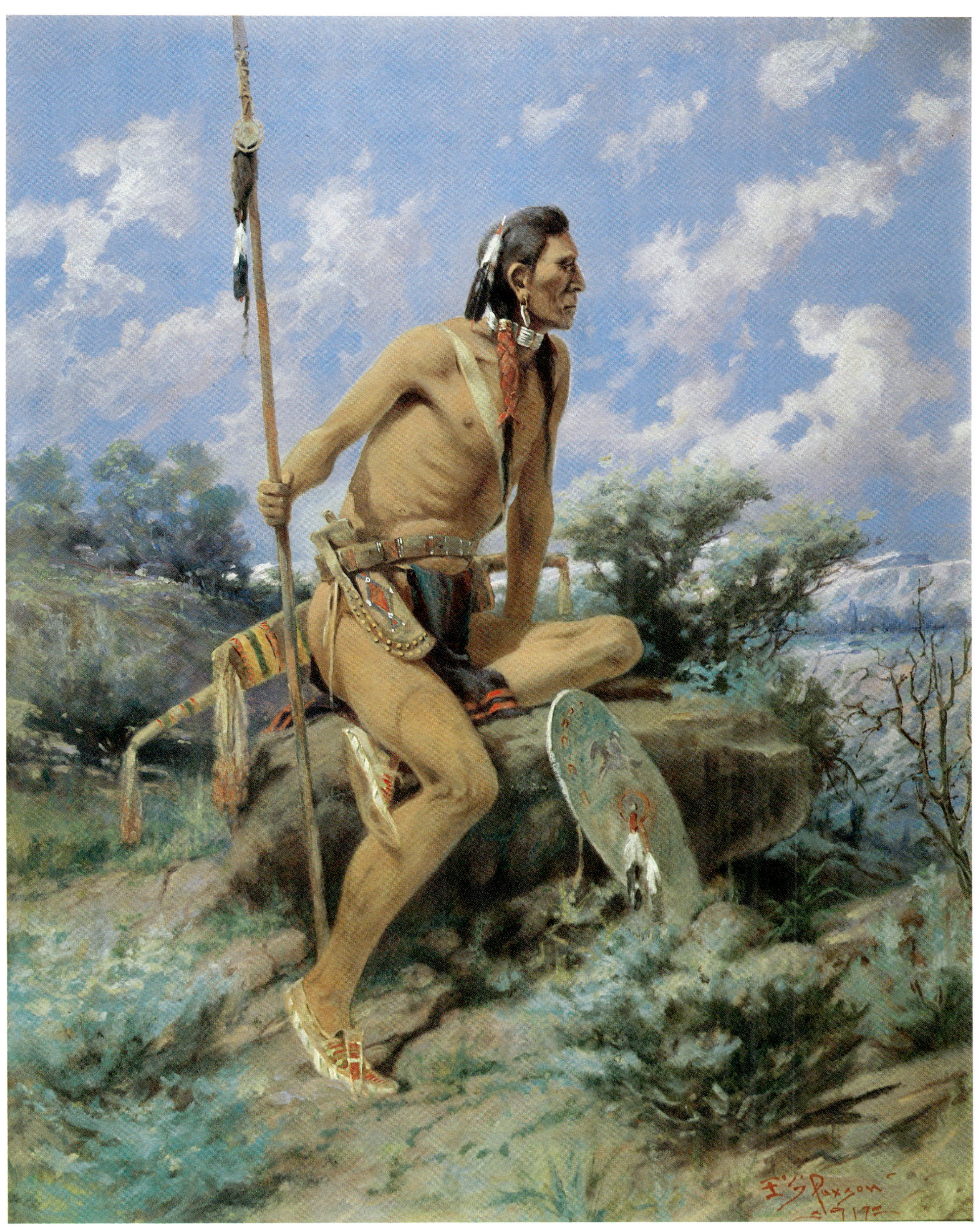

"Watchful Waiting." Oil, 1917, 40 x 30. *Jimmie and Sydney M. Shoenberg, Jr., St. Louis, Missouri.*

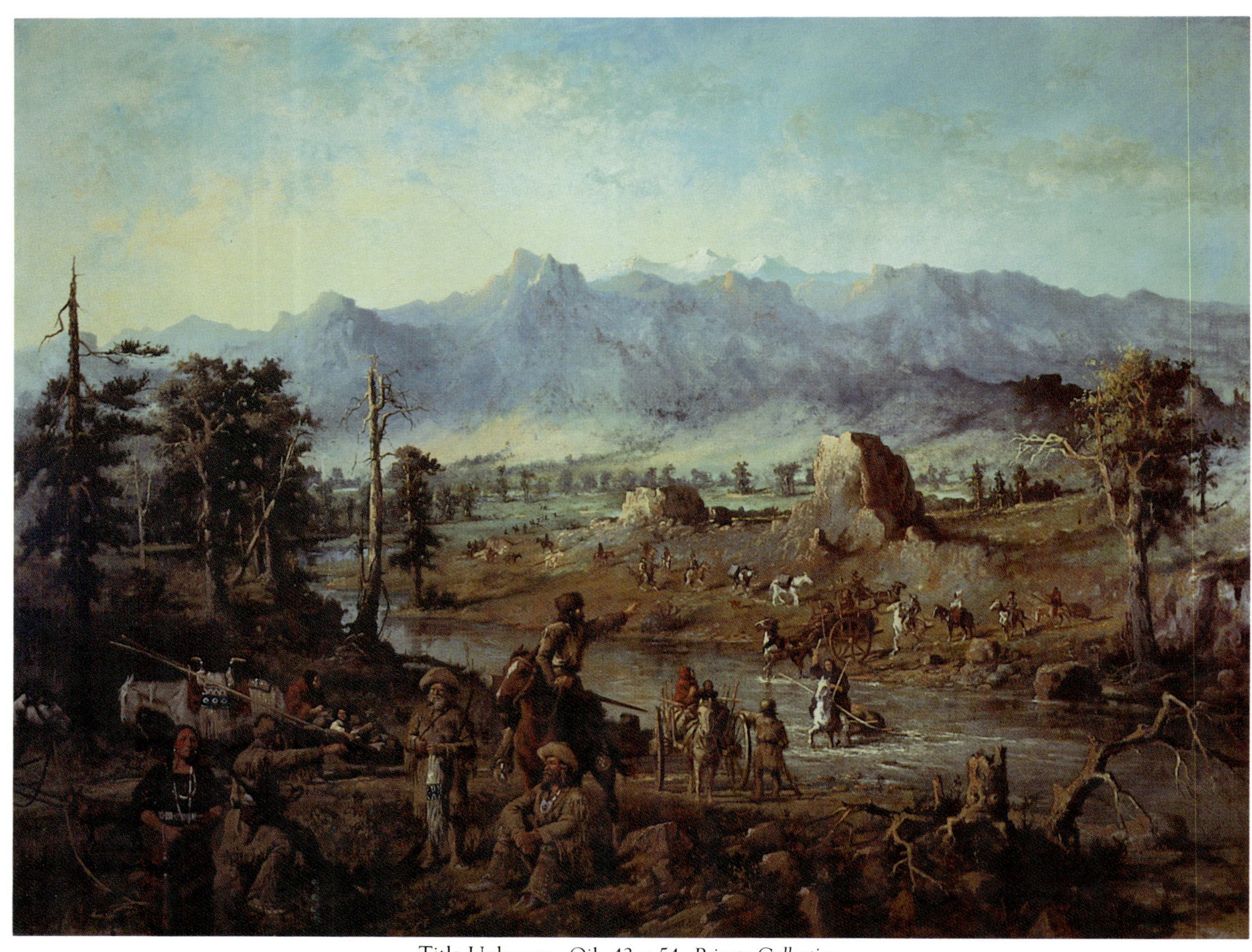

Title Unknown. Oil, 42 x 54. *Private Collection.*

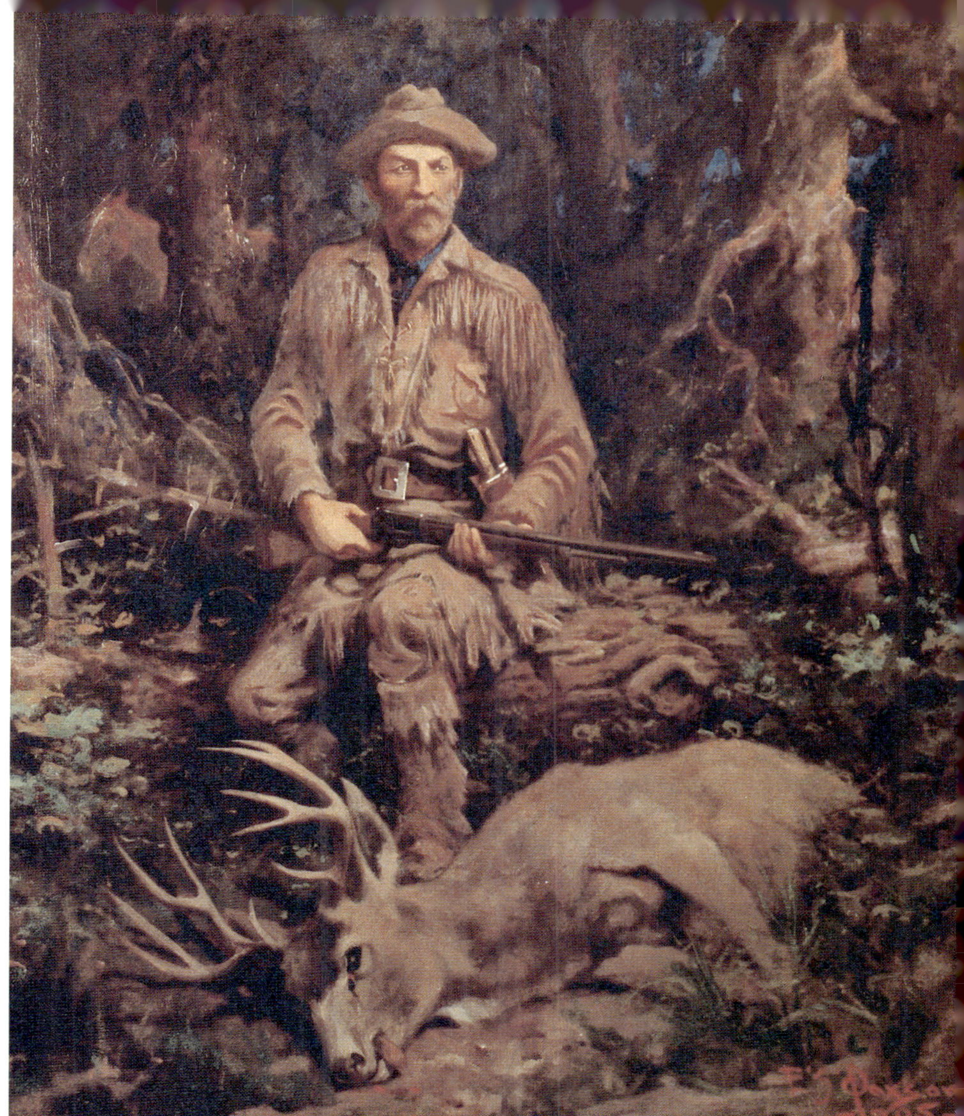

"Kit Carson." Oil. *Mr. and Mrs. Gordon Fraser.*

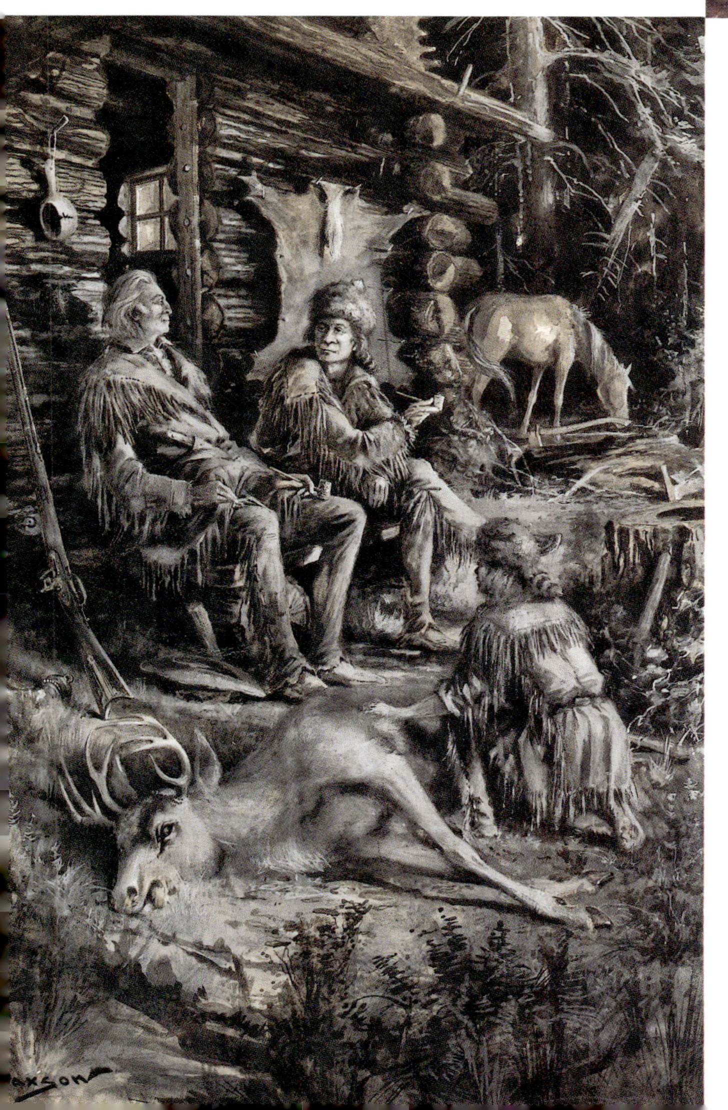

"Kit Carson's Cabin." Black and White,, gouache, 1903, 25 x 7. *Gallery of the Masters, St. Louis, Missouri.*

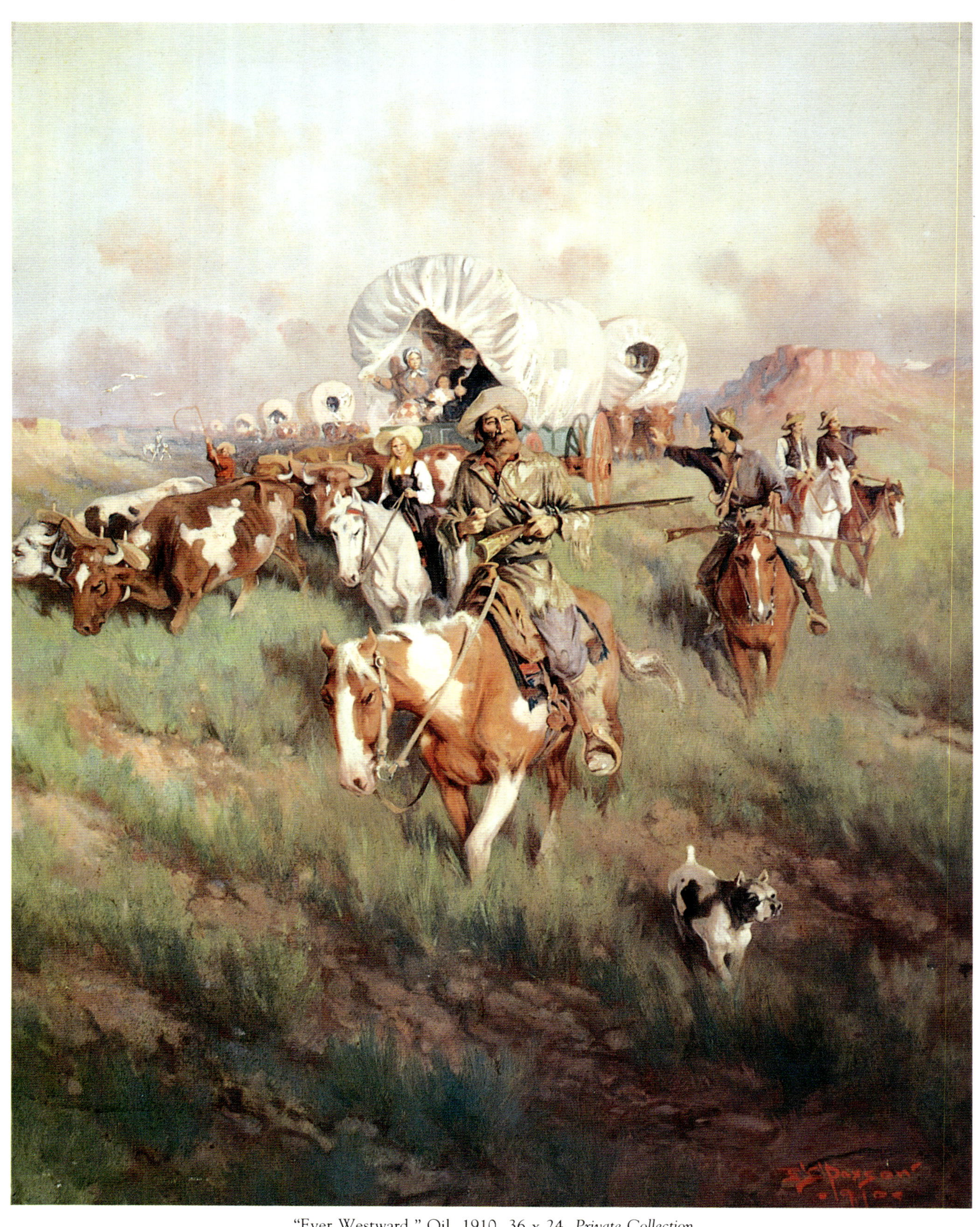

"Ever Westward." Oil, 1910, 36 x 24. *Private Collection.*

Checklist of Paintings by E.S. Paxson (by year)

Though obviously incomplete, this is, to the author's knowledge, the most extensive list of Paxson paintings to date. Watercolor Indian heads, of which there are hundreds, were omitted unless they were portraits of specific individuals and so titled. An asterisk indicates that a painting's date is approximate. A listing in bold type indicates that the work may be found in this volume. If the work is reproduced in color, the location reference will be a plate number; if black and white, a page number. Effort has been made to avoid using titles not the artist's own.

Title/Description	Medium	Size	Location/Reference
1880			
Portrait of a 16th Century European (after?) (Plate 7)	Oil	20" x 16"	Collection of William E. Paxson, Sr.
1885			
grouse	Oil	10" x 8"	Private collection
1890			
*grouse, ducks (set of two)	Oil	19" x 13" 19" x 13"	University of Montana
"Highland Chief," portrait of the artist's hunting dog	Oil	12" x 10"	Collection of Elizabeth Dartnell
1891			
Boy and girl at a stream	Watercolor	28½" x 21"	Private collection; formerly owned by the Butte YMCA
Farm Scene	Watercolor	14" x 25"	Collection of William E. Paxson, Sr.
"The Forest Sentinel"	Oil	11" x 15½"	Private collection
"Head of Horseshoe Lake, Cascade County" (Plate 1)	Oil	18" x 40"	Private collection; exhibited at the Missoula City-County Library
1893			
***"The Lolo Trail"** (Page 10)	Oil		Exhibited at Columbian Exposition, Chicago, 1893.
***"Me",** an Indian looking at a photograph of himself.			Exhibited at the Columbian Exposition, Chicago, 1893.
1895			
"Over the Trail of Lewis and Clark"	Oil	22½" x 18"	Montana Historical Society
"Yellowstone Falls"	Oil		Private collection
1897			
"Custer's Last Buffalo Hunt, Little Missouri River, Dakota Badlands"	Oil	69½" x 54"	Montana Historical Society
Full-figure Indian headress with pipe (Plate 5)	Watercolor	22" x 14"	Collection of Mr. and Mrs. S.H. Rosenthal, Jr.
*"The Last Match", four Butte sportsmen in an autumn scene			Newspaper clipping in the artist's scrapbook.
"Sitting Bull," **"Ta-ton-ka-i-yo-ton-k,"** ¾ portrait, seated, displaying Custer's ring	Oil	36" x 24" (approximate)	Private collection; illustrated in the *Daily Hampshire Gazette* (Northhampton, Mass.), c. 1962.
"Snuffed Out," Indian receiving a fatal bullet	Oil		Photograph in the artist's album
Standing Indian	Oil	12" x 18"	"E.S. Paxson-Montana Artist," by Franz Stenzel p. 32 (see bibliography)
"The Trapper," shooting a rifle (Page x)	Oil	12" x 18"	Collection of SLM, Inc., Corning, Arkansas; illus. in *Southwest Art,* Aug., 1978, p. 32
U.S. infantry soldier	Oil	12" x 18"	"E.S. Paxson-Montana Artist" by Franz Stenzel p. 32 (see bibliography)

Title/Description	Medium	Size	Location/Reference
1898			
Confessional and tent, Cavite, Philippines (Page 37)	Watercolor	9½" x 11"	Private collection
"The Death of John Bozeman" (Plate 3)	Oil	21" x 48"	Collection of Robin Mac Nab; exhibited at the Museum of the Rockies Montana State University
Filipino woman, full figure (Page 38)	Watercolor		Private collection

Title/Description	Medium	Size	Location/Reference
1899			
"Bound for the Buffalo Country" (Plate 4)	Oil	20" x 28"	Maxwell Galleries, San Francisco, Ca.
"Chief Gall", portrait			The artist's journal
"Chief Joseph", portrait			The artist's journal
"Custer's Last Stand" (Plates 8 & 9)	Oil	6' x 9'	Whitney Gallery of Western Art, Buffalo Bill Historical Center, Cody, Wyoming
"Cyclone"			The artist's journal
*"The Favorite Squaw"			Newsclipping in the artist's scrapbook
*"Geronimo", portrait			The artist's journal
"Grandpa's Luck" (Plate 4)	Oil	24" x 36"	Period Gallery West, Scottsdale, Arizona
"Of a past Generation"			The artist's journal
"A Parting Shot" ("The Last Shot")	Oil		Reproduced as a supplement to the October, 1901 *Fine Arts Journal;* illus. as *The Last Shot* in the January-February, 1901 and February, 1905 issues
"Sitting Bull", portrait	Oil	24" x 18"	Thomas Gilcrease Institute of American History and Art, Tulsa, Oklahoma
"Three Bears", ¾ figure			The artist's journal
"The Trapper's Reverie", ¾ figure, seated	Oil	22" x 18"	Illus. in "E.S. Paxson-Montana Artist" by Franz Stenzel, p. 10 see bibliography)
"Turning Eagle", portrait			The artist's journal
"The War Woop"			The artist's journal
"Wolf Robe", portrait (Plate 24)	Oil	15" x 12"	Collection of Susan Sorelle

Title/Description	Medium	Size	Location/Reference
1900			
"American Horse," portrait (Plate 7)	Oil	14" x 10"	Private collection
"Beaver Dick," full figure (Jacket)	Oil	17" x 11½"	Collection of Laurence Rockefeller
"Breaking the Pony," buffalo hunt (Page 29)	Oil		Illus. in *Outdoor Life,* vol. X, No. 2 (August, 1902), p. 2
"Dan'l Boone," portrait (Plate 7) (after?)	Oil	18" x 13½"	Private collection
"Happy Trapper," portrait (Plate 7)	Watercolor		Private collection
*"Lone Wolf," portrait	Oil		Illus. in *Fine Arts Journal* January-February, 1901, p. 7
"Painting the Robe"	Oil	14" x 9"	"E.S. Paxson-Montana Artist" by Franz Stenzel, p. 31 (see bibliography)
*Self-portrait with deer	Oil		Private collection
"Sitting Bull in the Little Bighorn Mountains"	Oil		Illus. in *Fine Arts Journal,* October, 1901, p. 363 and February, 1905, p. 75
"White Magpie, the Teton Orator," portrait	Oil		Illus. in *Fine Arts Journal,* January-February, 1901, p. 7 and February, 1905, p. 76
Young mountain sheep head	Oil	15½ x 11½	Private collection

Title/Description	Medium	Size	Location/Reference
1901			
"Beaver Dick," mounted, chased by Indians (Page ix)	Watercolor		Illus. for *The Trail of Lewis and Clark* by Olin D. Wheeler, published by Putnam and Sons, New York 1904; also illus. in *Outdoor Life,* October, 1901
"Black Eagle Falls"	Watercolor		The artist's journal
"The Chase," buffalo hunt	Oil		Reproduced as a supplement to the *Boston Sunday Journal,* November 17, 1901
"Cummin' Home from Meetin'" ("Goin to Church")	Gouache	18" x 14½"	Collection of SLM, Inc., Corning, Arkansas; illus. in *Southwest Art,* August, 1978, p. 37
"Enemy Sighted" (Plate 5)	Watercolor	9" x 12"	Collection of SLM, Inc., Corning, Arkansas
"Fording in Buffalo Skins"	Watercolor		Illus. for *Following Old Trails* by Arthur L. Stone, published by Morton J. Elrod, Missoula, 1913
"A Frontier Trading Post"			The artist's journal
"A Hunt of ye Olden Times, buffalo hunt			Illus. in *Outdoor Life,* vol. X, No. 2 (August, 1902), p. 7
Indian on a pony making a peace sign			The artist's journal
***"Injuns, By Gosh!"**			Reproduced as a supplement to the January (?), 1902 issue of *Fine Arts Journal*
"Kay Saba", full figure Indian	Watercolor		The artist's journal
"Nag-a-shaw", portrait (Plate 7)	Oil	25½" x 19½"	Collection of Penny and Martin Kodner, St. Louis, Missouri
"An Old-Time Frontier Scout"	Watercolor		Illus. for *The Trail of Lewis and Clark* by Olin D. Wheeler, published by Putnam and Sons, New York, 1904
*"The Parley"			The artist's journal
"Retreat"			The artist's journal
"Saving Thar Hair"			The artist's journal
"A Shot from the Cabin"	Oil en grisaille	22" x 16"	Illus. in "E.S. Paxson-Montana Artist" by Franz Stenzel, p. 5 (see bibliography)
"Soo-wite" ("That Way"), full figure Indian	Watercolor	14" x 10½"	In the Dr. and Mrs. Franz Stenzel collection sold at auction, Sotheby Parke Bernet, Los Angeles, June 24, 1980
"Soo-yop-pee"			The artist's journal
"You Swap?" (Plate 5)	Watercolor	6" x 7"	Collection of Ray and Maxine Howser

Title/Description	Medium	Size	Location/Reference
1902			
"After the Rain"			The artist's journal
"All for Gold" ('62)			The artist's journal
"Before any man lays a finger on Thomas here, he will need to begin with myself."	Gouache en Grisaille	24" x 18"	Illus. for *Glengarry School Days* by Ralf Connor, published by Fleming H. Revell, Chicago, 1902
"Burial on the Plain"	Oil en Grisaille	18" x 24"	"E.S. Paxson-Montana Artist" by Franz Stenzel, p. 31 (see bibliography)
"A Floral Offering"			The artist's journal
"The Forest Trail"			The artist's journal
"Heap Plenty Wind", portrait	Watercolor	12" x 8"	Collection of SLM, Inc., Corning, Arkansas
"He raised himself to see the bear."	Gouache en Grisaille	18½" x 12"	Illus. for *Glengarry School Days* by Ralf Connor, published by Fleming H. Revell, Chicago, 1902
"He studied the easy attitude of the sleeper."			Illus. for *By Order of the Prophet, a Tale of Utah* by Alfred H. Henry, published by Fleming H. Revell, Chicago, 1902

Title/Description	Medium	Size	Location/Reference
1902 cont.			
"He went to her and put his hand upon her shoulder."			Illus. for *By Order of the Prophet, a Tale of Utah* by Alfred H. Henry, published by Fleming H. Revell, Chicago, 1902
"Indian Chase" ("The Chase") (Page 18)	Watercolor	14" x 11"	Exhibited at Missoula Museum of the Arts, 1976
"The Injun and His Pony"			The artist's journal
"The Last Shot (Plate 6)	Oil	26" x 20"	Collection of Jimmie and Sydney M. Shoenberg, St. Louis, Missouri
"Laughing Horse, Sioux", portrait	Watercolor	5" x 3"	Montana Historical Society
"An Old French-Canadian Trapper"	Watercolor		Illus. for *The Trail of Lewis and Clark* by Olin D. Wheeler, published by Putnam and Sons, New York, 1904
"Old Sol" ("Spotting an Indian Party") (Plate 6)	Oil		C.W. Edwards, Ltd, Seattle, Washington
"The routine of travel soon became a matter of course." a wagon train			Frontispiece for *By Order of the Prophet, a Tale of Utah* by Alfred H. Henry, published by Fleming H. Revell, Chicago, 1902
"Slowly Thomas extracted the Manuscript from his trousers pocket."	Gouache en Grisaille	24" x 10"	Illus. for *Glengarry School Days* by Ralf Connor, published by Fleming H. Revell, Chicago, 1902
"She seemed the very personification of this entire movement."			Illus. for *By Order of the Prophet, a Tale of Utah* by Alfred H. Henry, published by Fleming H. Revell, Chicago, 1902
"Stop that young man! That's a coward's blow."	Gouache en Grisaille	24" x 18"	Illus for *Glengarry School Days* by Ralf Connr, published by Fleming H. Revell, Chicago, 1902

Title/Description	Medium	Size	Location/Reference
1903			
*"The Arrowmaker"			The artist's journal
"At the Crossing" (Plate 10)	Oil	35½" x 24½"	Collection of Debbie and John Capps, St. Louis, Missouri
"Chief Gall", portrait			The artist's journal
"The Crow Scout", mounted	Watercolor		Photograph in the artist's album
"Days Gone By", buffalo hunt	Watercolor		The artist's journal
*"The Death Shot", buffalo hunt			Reproduced as a supplement to the *Chicago Tribune*, January, 1904
*"Evening Shadows", Indians on a mountain trail			The artist's journal
"Geronimo", portrait			The artist's journal
"Goin' West"			The artist's journal
"Good Injun"	Watercolor		Illus. in *Montana Magazine of History*, spring, 1954, p. 24
Indian warrior, full figure	Watercolor	11" x 6½"	Museum of the Rockies, Montana State University
Kit Carson and cabin (Plate 31)	Oil	28" x 20"	Gallery of the Masters, St. Louis, Missouri
"Lewis and Clark in Camp on Traveler's Rest (Lolo) Creek, Montana"			Frontispiece for *The Trail of Lewis and Clark* by Olin D. Wheeler, published by Putnam and Sons, New York, 1904
"Lewis and Clark in the Heart of the Bitterroot Mountains"			Illus. for *The Trail of Lewis and Clark* by Olin D. Wheeler, published by Putnam and Sons, New York, 1904
"An Old Sioux Scout", full figure	Watercolor	16" x 9"	Illus in "E.S. Paxson-Montana Artist" by Franz Stenzel, p. 8 (see bibliography)
"Running from a Bear on the Missouri River, Montana	Watercolor	21" x 13"	In the Dr. and Mrs. Franz Stenzel collection sold at auction, Sotheby Parke Bernet, Los Angeles, June 24, 1980

Title/Description	Medium	Size	Location/Reference
1903			
"Sacajawea, the Bird Woman"	Watercolor		Illus. for *The Trail of Lewis and Clark* by Olin D. Wheeler, published by Putnam and Sons, New York, 1904
"Watching the Signal"	Watercolor		The artist's journal
"When Winter Comes on"	Oil		The artist's journal

Title/Description	Medium	Size	Location/Reference
1904			
"Chief Charlo", portrait (Plate 7)	Watercolor	14" x 9"	Private collection
"Chief Joseph", three separate portraits	Watercolor		The artist's journal
"Chief Joseph's Descent from the Mountains" ("Below the Timberline") (Plate 10)	Oil	52" x 34"	Collection of Felice and Robert Rubin, St. Lewis, Missouri
"Contemplation" (1804), Meriwether Lewis at Lemhi Creek's headwaters	Oil	50" x 30"	Exhibited in the Montana building, 1904 Louisiana Purchase Exposition, St. Louis
"Crowfoot", portrait			The artist's journal
"Curley", portrait (Page 64)	Watercolor		Reproduced by McKee Printing Co., Butte, about 1909
"Dan'l Boone Returning"	Watercolor en Grisaille	22" x 16"	Montana Historical Society
"El Telegrapho"	Oil		"E.S. Paxson-Montana Artist" by Franz Stenzel, p. 31 (see bibliography)
"Four of a Kind" (Page 17)	Watercolor	14" x 20"	Thomas Gilcrease Institute of American History and Art, Tulsa, Oklahoma
"Geronimo," portrait			The artist's journal
"Indian Encampment" (Plate 12)	Oil	22" x 28"	
"Jackson Lake" (Plate 2)	Gouache	16½" x 26½"	Dillon, Montana Schools
"Jim Bridger"	Watercolor		The artist's journal
"Jumping the Wagon Train, Scene at Coffin Butte on Yellowstone, Montana	Oil	28" x 40"	Thomas Gilcrease Institute of American History and Art, Tulsa, Oklahoma
"La Heliographa" ("The Signal") (Plate 28)	Oil	36" x 24"	Trail's End Collection-Dr. and Mrs. Van Kirke Nelson, Kalispell, Montana
"The Latest Arrivals" (Plate 12)	Oil	28" x 42"	Montana Historical Society
"Making the Sign"			The artist's journal
Mounted Indian	Watercolor	14" x 9"	Private collection
"Pack Train Crossing the Mountains"	Watercolor en Grisaille	18" x 12"	Illus. for *Life of Rev. L.B. Stateler* by Rev. E.J. Stanley, published by the Methodist Church, Nashville 1907
*"The Prospector"			The artist's journal
"Ready for a Coup", mounted Indian (Plate 10)	Watercolor	17" x 12½"	Private collection
"Sacajawea at Three Forks, Montana" (Plate 11)	Oil	50" x 29"	University of Montana
"Sumpthin' fer the Kittle"	Oil	17" x 23"	The artist's journal; dated 1911 in "E.S. Paxson-Montana Artist" by Franz Stenzel, p. 32 (see bibliography)
"A Supper in Sight"			The artist's journal
"When White Man Came"			The artist's journal

Title/Description	Medium	Size	Location/Reference
1905			
"The Backwoods Swain"			The artist's journal
"Canada Cree Trapper", full figure	Watercolor	18" x 13"	Montana Historical Society
"Chief Charlo", portrait	Oil		The artist's journal
"Chief Joseph", portrait	Oil		The artist's journal
"Chief Joseph", portrait (Plate 7)	Watercolor	12" x 18"	Private collection

1905			
"A Friendly Sign"			The artist's journal
Indians at a creek	Watercolor	17" x 24"	Western Montana College, Dillon, Montana
"In the Enemy's Country"	Watercolor	17½" x 21½"	Missoula Museum of the Arts
"Landsakes! It's Mr. Blalock. Excuse my greasy mouth." (Page 96)	Oil en Grisaille	18" x 14"	Illus. for *Ramrod Jones* by Clinton G. Brown, published by Saalfield Press, 1905
"Moving the Pack String" (Page 8)	Watercolor en Grisaille	20" x 12"	The Rockwell Museum, Corning, New York
*"Out in the Sunshine"	Watercolor		The artist's journal
"Saving His Scalp"	Gouache		The artist's journal
"The Scout's Warning"			The artist's journal
"So I took it from around my neck and put it in her hand." (Page 96)	Oil en Grisaille	18" x 14"	Illus. for *Ramrod Jones* by Clinton G. Brown, published by Saalfield Press, 1905
"There, there sonny, don't be afraid, I ain't goin' to hurt you." (Page 97)	Oil en Grisaille	18" x 14"	Illus. for *Ramrod Jones* by Clinton G. Brown published by Saalfield Press, 1905
"The Turning of the Worm" ("A Montana Buffalo Hunt")	Oil	26" x 38"	Whitney Gallery of Western Art, Buffalo Bill Historical Center, Cody, Wyoming
"A Visit to the other Tribe"			Photograph in the artist's album
"White Beaver", portrait			The artist's journal
"Who's Boss"			The artist's journal
"Winning His Coup"			The artist's journal

Title/Description	Medium	Size	Location/Reference
1906			
"Bernardo Pass Fight"	Watercolor		The artist's journal
Buffalo hunt (Plate 13)	Gouache	17½" x 21"	Private collection
"Colonel Sanders prosecuting George Ives, the Road Agent	Watercolor en Grisaille	18" x 12"	Illus. for *Life of Rev. L.B. Stateler* by Rev. E.J. Stanley, published by the Methodist Church, Nashville, 1907
"Custer's Last Battle" (Page 97)	Watercolor en Grisaille	18" x 12"	Illus. for *Life of Rev. L.B. Stateler* by Rev. E.J. Stanley, published by the Methodist Church, Nashville, 1907
"From High Places They Watched the Tide of Immigration" (Page 7)	Oil		Photograph in the artist's album
"Getting a Supply of Meat"	Watercolor en Grisaille	18" x 12"	Illus. for *Life of Rev. L.B. Stateler* by Rev. E.J. Stanley, published by the Methodist Church, Nashville, 1907
"In the Sunshine", (buffalo hunt)	Oil		The artist's journal
"The Itinerant Leaving Home"	Watercolor en Grisaille	18" x 12"	Illus. for *Life of Rev. L.B. Stateler* by Rev. E.J. Stanley, published by the Methodist Church, Nashville, 1907
"Just for Fun"			The artist's journal
"Once We Were Great" (Plate 13)	Watercolor	21½" x 16"	Collection of SLM, Inc., Corning, Arkansas
"Once We Were Great"	Oil		The artist's journal
"On the War Path"	Watercolor	20" x 14"	"E.S. Paxson-Montana Artist" by Franz Stenzel, p. 31 (see bibliography)
"Peep o' Day"	Watercolor		The artist's journal
"'Perhaps you are one-horse preachers,' rejoined one of the 'parsons' promptly and good naturedly,'"	Watercolor en Grisaille	18" x 12"	Illus. for *Life of Rev. L.B. Stateler* by Rev. E.J. Stanley, published by the Methodist Church, Nashville, 1907
"A Story of Other Days"			Photograph in the artist's album
"Sunday Morning Worship"	Oil en Grisaille	16" x 14"	Collection of SLM, Inc., Corning, Arkansas
"Stateler Preaching in Camp"	Watercolor en Grisaille	18" x 12"	Illus. for *Life of Rev. L.B. Stateler* by Rev. E.J. Stanley, published by the Methodist Church, Nashville, 1907

Title/Description	Medium	Size	Location/Reference
1906			
"Wearing the Winter Out" (Page 98)	Watercolor en Grisaille	18" x 12"	Illus. for *Life of Rev. L.B. Stateler* by Rev. E.J. Stanley, published by the Methodist Church, Nashville, 1907
"A Wilderness Toilet"	Watercolor		The artist's journal
"Wounded Buffalo", attacked	Oil		The artist's journal
"Wounded Buffalo" II, attacked by wolves	Oil		The artist's journal

Title/Description	Medium	Size	Location/Reference
1907			
"The Cowboy's Roundup," mounted cowboy and a pretty girl			The artist's journal
"Edna the Runner"	Watercolor en Grisaille	18" x 12½"	Private collection
"An Ishmaelite of the Plains"			The artist's journal
"Old Montana", buffalo herd			Newspaper clipping in the artist's scrapbook from the *Butte Evening News,* December 12, 1907
"Our Turn Next", wolves watching Indians cooking buffalo meat			Newspaper clipping in the artist's scrapbook from the *Butte Evening News,* December 12, 1907
"The War Bonnet"			The artist's journal
"The Women Did Their Part"	Watercolor	19" x 13½"	E.S. Paxson-Montana Artist" by Franz Stenzel, p. 31 (see bibliography)

Title/Description	Medium	Size	Location/Reference
1908			
"American Horse", portrait	Watercolor	10" x 6½"	Private collection
"General Custer", portrait	Watercolor	13" x 17"	"E.S. Paxson-Montana Artist" by Franz Stenzel, p. 32 (see bibliography)
"Goatland"			The artist's journal
"Hamilton, Montana" (Plate 2)	Watercolor	22" x 48"	Private collection
"He War a Pard o' Mine"			The artist's journal
"Kicking Bear, Sioux", portrait	Watercolor	9"x 7"	Montana Historical Society
Indian in headdress, portrait	Oil	22" x 17"	University of Montana
"A Mutual Surprise"	Watercolor		The artist's journal
"Nag-a-shaw in War Bonnet"			The artist's journal
"Signs of Winter", buffalo scene	Oil	19½" x 23½"	Private collection
"The Squaw-Man and His Outfit (Plate 17)	Oil	36" x 24"	Trail's End Collection—Dr. and Mrs. Van Kirke Nelson, Kalispell, Montana
"West Bound", wagon train	Oil		Photograph in the artist's album
"Wounded Buffalo"	Oil	27½" x 23"	"E.S. Paxson-Montana Artist" by Franz Stenzel, p. 31 (see bibliography)
Young Indian boy	Watercolor	8" x 11"	"E.S. Paxson-Montana Artist" by Franz Stenzel, p. 32 (see bibliography)

Title/Description	Medium	Size	Location/Reference
1909			
"Apprehensions of Trouble", mounted frontiersman	Watercolor		The artist's journal
"A Bit of Sunshine"	Watercolor		The artist's journal
"Blackfoot Scouts"	Watercolor		

Title/Description	Medium	Size	Location/Reference
1909			
Buffalo hunt	Watercolor	16" x 20"	Illus. in "E.S. Paxson—Montana Artist" by Franz Stenzel, inside front cover (see bibliography)
"Gathering the Bitterroot"	Watercolor		Private collection
"Greeting the Early Morn"	Watercolor		The artist's journal
"His Fate", buffalo hunt	Gouache	20½" x 13½"	Private collection
"The Old Warrior", mounted (Plate 18)	Watercolor	22" x 15"	Collection of SLM, Inc., Corning, Arkansas
"On the Alert"	Watercolor		The artist's journal
"The Referee", a coyote watching two buffalo fight	Watercolor		The artist's journal
"A Rocky Mountain Priscilla"	Watercolor		The artist's journal
"Taking a Chance"	Watercolor		The artist's journal
"Watching Custer's Advance on the Rosebud"	Oil	21½" x 17½"	Private Collection
"Watching for Sign"			The artist's journal
"When the Indian Worked", buffalo hunt			The artist's journal

Title/Description	Medium	Size	Location/Reference
1910			
"After the Shower"			The artist's journal
Buffalo at a water hole	Watercolor	14" x 22"	"E.S. Paxson-Montana Artist" by Franz Stenzel, p. 32 (see bibliography)
"Chief Charlo", portrait (Plate 18)	Oil	24" x 17½"	Owned by Missoula Women's Club; exhibited at Missoula City-County Library
"Ever Westward", wagon train	Oil	36" x 24"	Private collection
"A Family Affair	Watercolor	15" x 20"	"E.S. Paxson-Montana Artist" by Franz Stenzel, p. 31 (see bibliography)
"The Inspection", Indian scouting	Oil	26" x 19½"	Private collection; exhibited at Pacific Northwest Indian Center, Spokane, Washington
"Only a Dog"			The artist's journal

Title/Description	Medium	Size	Location/Reference
1911			
"After the Fight", buffalo scene	Oil	14" x 20½"	In the Dr. and Mrs. Franz Stenzel collection sold at auction, Sotheby Parke Bernet, Los Angeles, June 24, 1980
*"Apache Children")			The artist's journal
Buffalo hunt (Plate 14)	Oil		Private collection
"Clark Fork of the Columbia"	Oil	21" x27"	Private collection
"The Emigrant"			The artist's journal
"In Arizona"			The artist's journal
Indian portrait	Oil	20" x 14"	Montana Historical Society
"Louison", portrait	Watercolor		The artist's journal
"Old Fort Owen"	Drawing		Illus. for *Following Old Trails* by Arthur L. Stone, published by Morton J. Elrod, Missoula, 1913
"Selecting a Camping Place" (Plate 16)	Oil	30" x 50"	Maxwell Galleries, San Francisco
"Sumpin' Doin', buffalo	Oil	14" x 18"	Private collection
"Sunrise at Agency Creek" (Plate 16)	Oil	22" x 36"	Peterson Galleries, Los Angeles
"Tracking" (Plate 17)	Oil	30" x 20"	Private collection
"Ugly Cuss", buffalo	Oil	14" x 18"	Private collection

Title/Description	Medium	Size	Location/Reference
1912			
"The Borderland", mural (Page 70)	Oil	7' x 13'	Montana state capitol, Helena
"The Cowboy Memorial" (Plate 22)	Oil		Stremmel Galleries, Reno, Nevada
"Elopement of the Sioux" (Plate 28)	Oil	36" x 22"	Pacific Northwest Indian Center
"Lewis and Clark at Three Forks," mural (Page 66)	Oil	7' x 13'	Montana State Capitol, Helena
"Lewis at Black Eagle Falls", mural (Page 67)	Oil	7' x 31'	Montana State Capitol, Helena
"Lost Trail", a scouting party	Oil	23½" x 39½"	Private collection
"Mount Lolo"	Oil	17½" x 29½"	Private collection
"Pierre de Le Verendrye", mural (Page 66)	Oil	7' x 3'	Montana state capitol, Helena
"Seeking the White Man's Book" (Plate 23)	Oil	36" x 24"	Private collection
"Seeking the White Man's Book, mural (Page 68)	Oil	7' x 4'	Montana state capitol, Helena
"The Surrender of Chief Joseph", mural (Page 69)	Oil	7' x 4'	Montana state capitol, Helena
"What's Doing", buffalo herd	Oil	20" x 40"	Private collection

Title/Description	**Medium**	**Size**	**Location/Reference**
1913			
Indian chief, full figure	Watercolor	15" x 7"	Private collection
"Little Bear, Cree Chief," portrait (Plate 27)	Oil	22" x 18"	Los Angeles Athletic Club
"The Lost Pilgrim" (Page 16)	Gouache	16" x 14"	Collection of SLM, Inc., Corning, Arkansas; illus. for *Following Old Trails* by Arthur L. Stone, published by Morton J. Elrod, Missoula
"The Race"	Watercolor		The artist's journal
"The Spy", mounted Indian	Watercolor	9½" x 13½"	Private collection

Title/Description	**Medium**	**Size**	**Location/Reference**
1914			
"Ah-kene ah", Flathead	Oil	20" x 24"	"E.S. Paxson-Montana Artist" by Franz Stenzel, p. 32 (see bibliography)
"Arrival of Father Ravalli at Fort Owen, September 1845", mural (Plate 20)	Oil	5½' x 10'	Missoula county courthouse
"Black Hawk", portrait (Plate 26)	Watercolor	8" x 7½"	Collection of Jean Walker
"Chief Charlo" portrait	Watercolor	9½" x 8"	Private collection
"Early Transportation", mural (Plate 21)	Oil	5½' x 5½'	Missoula county courthouse
"The Flatheads in the Buffalo Country" mural (Plate 21)	Oil	5½' x 6½	Missoula county courthouse
"The Flatheads Leaving Their Bitterroot Home, October, 1892", mural (Plate 25)	Oil	5½' x 10'	Missoula county courthouse
"Gov. Stevens' Treaty with the Pend D'Oreilles, Flatheads and Kootenais at Council Grove, July 9, 1855, mural (Plate 20)	Oil	5½' x 5½'	Missoula county courthouse
"Lewis and Clark's Camp at Traveler's Rest, Lolo Creek 1804," mural (Plate 19)	Oil	5½' x 10'	Missoula county courthouse
"Lewis Party Crossing the Clark's Fork, July 3, 1806, mural (Plate 19)	Oil	5½' x 10'	Missoula county courthouse
"Louison, Subchief and Judge of the Flatheads", portrait (Page 83)	Oil	27" x 20"	Los Angeles Athletic Club
***"Mission Falls"**	Oil		The artist's journal
"A Montana Roundup", mural (Plate 21)	Oil	5½' x 6½'	Missoula county courthouse
"Sacajawea", full figure (Plate 11)	Oil	17½" x 11½"	Private collection
"Sunset Falls on the Sky-ko-mish, Washington	Watercolor	14½" x 10"	Montana Historical Society
"The White Peril"			The artist's journal

Title/Description	Medium	Size	Location/Reference
1915			
"Aeneas, Chief of the Flatheads", portrait	Watercolor	12" x 9"	Trail's End Collection—Dr. and Mrs. Van Kirke Nelson, Kalispell, Montana
Buffalo head (Plate 27)	Watercolor	8" x 6"	Private collection
"The Crossing" ("The Ford")	Oil		The artist's journal
"The First Snow, 1915"	Oil	21" x 34"	Private collection
"Froze Up, by Thunder!" (Plate 15)	Gouache	14" x 11"	Private collection
"His Defiance" (Plate 24)	Oil	19½" x 27"	Private collection
"His Manatou" ("His God") (Plate 24)	Oil	36" x 28"	Private collection
"His Solitude", buffalo			The artist's journal
"Hollow Horn Bear", portrait (Plate 27)	Watercolor	14" x 9½"	Private collection
"Interrupted", buffalo	Oil	23" x 17"	Private collection
"The Last Gleam" ("Up Miner's Creek") (Page 93)	Oil	4' x 7'	Private collection
"On the Head of the Sacramento River"	Oil	20" x 15"	Private collection
"On the Missoura"			The artist's journal
"Shasta Twins–Head of the Sacramento River"	Oil	20" x 16"	Private collection
"Summer Noon", Indian scene	Watercolor		Maxwell Galleries, San Francisco
"When Wilderness Was King"			The artist's journal
"Young Sitting Bull", portrait (Plate 27)	Watercolor	14" x 10½"	Collection of SLM, Inc., Corning, Arkansas

Title/Description	Medium	Size	Location/Reference
1916			
"Evening Hunt", buffalo hunt	Oil	17" x 28"	Private collection
"For the Home", buffalo hunt			The artist's journal
Indian scouts	Oil	36" x 28"	"E.S. Paxson-Montana Artist" by Franz Stenzel, p. 31 (see bibliography)
"John Coulter, the Discoverer of Yellowstone Park"	Gouche		Frontispiece for *Your National Parks* by Enos A. Mills, published by Houghton-Mifflin Co., Boston, 1917
"Northwester"	Watercolor		The artist's journal
"Off for a Treaty with the Other Tribe" (Jacket)	Oil	30" x 49"	Trail's End Collection—Dr. and Mrs. Van Kirke Nelson, Kalispell, Montana

Title/Description	Medium	Size	Location/Reference
1917			
"Charlo II", portrait	Oil	16" x 14"	Montana Historical Society
"Chief Charlo", portrait	Oil	19½" x 16"	Montana Historical Society
"Chief Charlo", portrait	Watercolor	14" x 10"	Montana Historical Society
"Chief Victor", portrait	Oil	16" x 13½"	Montana Historical Society
"The Dying Day"			The artist's journal
"A Mixup			The artist's journal
"Sacajawea and Her Dog, Scammon"	Oil	24" x 16"	In the Dr. and Mrs. Franz Stenzel collection, sold at auction, Sotheby Parke Bernet, Los Angeles, June 24, 1980
"Scouting for Custer"	Oil	20" x 31"	State of Montana
"Signalling Arrival of the Buffalo"	Oil	24" x 20"	"E.S. Paxson-Montana Artist" by Franz Stenzel, p. 31 (see bibliography)
"Watchful Waiting" (Plate 29)	Oil	40" x 30"	Collection of Jimmie and Sydney M. Shoenberg, Jr., St. Louis, Missouri
*"Watching Custer's Advance"	Oil	28" x 36"	Montana Historical Society
"Young Charlo", portrait	Watercolor	13" x 10"	Private collection
1919			
"The Signal"	Oil	20" x 24"	Collection of SLM, Inc., Corning, Arkansas

End Notes

Although Paxson's unpublished journals, notes and letters provided a substantial source of material for this biography, for simplicity they are not generally cited in the end notes except where they corroborate or supplement the cited sources.

Introduction

1. From "Beaver Dick," an article by E. S. Paxson in *Outdoor Life*, October, 1901. The article was accompanied by a reproduction of Paxson's watercolor painting illustrating the episode.

Childhood

1. Information on the Paxson family history has been garnered from a Hambleton family history, published privately in 1887, by Chalkley J. Hambleton and an unpublished family history began by Edward Heston Paxson and completed by Joseph P. Paxson in 1918.
2. This and other childhood anecdotes in this chapter are from Paxson's remembrances in his journals and in margins of books from his library.
3. This is a remembrance of Paxson's father, written in the form of a poem in the artist's guest register in 1903.
4. From an unpublished paper, "Edgar S. Paxson, Artist and Friend of the Red-Man" by Emma Corbin, February, 1910.

Going West

1. "Buffalo Bill Is Known to Missoula Old-Timers from Days of Long Ago," *Missoula Sentinel*, 1916.
2. Paxson's travels in the early 1870s are drawn from *A History of Montana*, vol. II, by Helen Fitzgerald Saunders. This material is partly corroborated and is supplemented by Paxson's remembrances in his journals and other writings.
3. "Buffalo Bill Is Known to Missoula Old-Timers...."
4. From a short talk by the artist to the Butte Women's Club, February 5, 1902. The text was published in the *Anaconda Standard* February 9, 1902.

Frontier Days

1. Saunders, *A History of Montana*, vol. II, generally corroborated by Paxson's notes and journals.
2. *Description of the Lolo Trail* by E. S. Paxson, 1893. The artist published this pamphlet himself.
3. Albert J. Partoll, "Mrs. Edgar Paxson, Widow of Famous Painter, Reminisces," *Great Falls Tribune*, April 10, 1932.
4. Paxson, "Beaver Dick."
5. Dr. Franz R. Stenzel, "E. S. Paxson, Montana Artist," *Montana Magazine of History*, Autumn, 1963. The author has not found clear corroboration for this story. Saunders relates in *A History of Montana* that once Paxson was captured by "a party of thirty Indians who had escaped from United States soldiers." He was held for forty-eight hours but escaped by "a piece of cunning." Perhaps this is the same incident related by Stenzel.
6. "E. S. Paxson, Artist," *Old-Timer's Handbook, the story of Butte* (a special number of the *Butte Bystander*), April 15, 1897. This is partly corroborated in the artist's notes.
7. From a brief newspaper clipping in Paxson's scrapbook from the *Butte Miner*, September 2, 1909, and from Paxson's notes in the margin of the clipping. This material is also supplemented by his journals.
8. Paxson's droving experiences are from Saunders, *A History of Montana*, supplemented considerably by Paxson's notes and journals.
9. Paxson's stagecoach experience is drawn from Albert J. Partoll, "Experiences of Noted Painter Recalled," *Great Falls Tribune*, November 3, 1940. The incident is also mentioned in Paxson's journals.
10. Paxson, "Beaver Dick."
11. Partoll, "Mrs. Edgar Paxson...Reminisces."
12. Frank D. Brown, "Nez Perces Massacre of M'Kay Gulch; Artist Paxton (*sic*) Warned Other Settlers," *Mineral County Independent* (Montana News Association insert), September 23, 1918. This is partly corroborated in Paxson's journals.
13. Information on Old Sol is drawn from Albert J. Partoll, "Paxson and Russell Close Friends; Led Parade at Missoula," *Great Falls Tribune*, January 15, 1933. This is supplemented by Paxson's journals and notes.
14. The account here is drawn from Paxson's notes in addition to the published version, as told to Merle Kettlewell, in the *Missoulian*, April 7, 1912, and in *Following Old Trails* by A. L. Stone.

Beginning Artist

1. From the artist's talk before the Butte Women's Club, published in the *Anaconda Standard*, February 9, 1902.
2. Stenzel, "E. S. Paxson, Montana Artist". Stenzel's source for Paxson's artistic efforts at Ryan's Canyon is not known to the author.
3. The "Indians are coming!" incident is drawn from Partoll, "Experiences of Noted Painter Recalled."
4. Published in the *Anaconda Standard*, February 9, 1902.
5. Information on John Maguire and Butte in this chapter is drawn from Neil J. Lynch, *Butte Centennial Recollections*. Paxson's remembrances in his journals provided material on his relationship with Maguire.
6. Saunders, *A History of Montana*, vol. II.
7. Information about Paxson's Cottonwood Theater curtain is drawn from an article in the Missoulian, date unknown.
8. From a newspaper clipping in the artist's scrapbook, about 1887.
9. From a newspaper clipping in the artist's scrapbook, source and complete date unknown.
10. The *Butte Evening News* article is recalled in Alan Goddard, "Y Closet Yields Paxson Find for Copper Camp Auction," Montana Standard, April 30, 1978.

11. Letter quoted from Ramon E. Adams and Homer B. Britzman, *Charles M. Russell, the Cowboy Artist, a Biography*. Trail's End Publishing, Pasadena, 1948, p. 187.
12. Partoll, "Mrs. Edgar Paxson...Reminisces."
13. The paper was presented at a Missoula high school.

Soldier

1. The riot account is drawn from Lynch, *Butte Centennial Recollections*, Paxson's part in quelling the riot is a remembrance from his journal.
2. The account in this chapter of Paxson's Spanish-American War experiences is taken from his detailed daily journal which he kept during the entire adventure.

The Artist's Masterpiece: Custer's Last Stand

1. The painting's title on the 1900 copyright is *Custer's Last Fight*. A descriptive pamphlet published about 1901 by the painting's leasee uses *Custer's Last Battle on the Little Bighorn*. In his journals, Paxson referred to his masterpiece as "my Custer painting" or simply "Custer." But the artist's heirs insist that late in life he referred to the painting most commonly as *Custer's Last Stand*, as did his wife after his death. Since that time the Paxson family has used *Custer's Last Stand* and this title has generally been accepted.
2. The original letter is on display in the Whitney Gallery of Western Art at the Buffalo Bill Historical Center, Cody, Wyoming.
3. Details of the agreement are taken from Stenzel, "E. S. Paxson, Montana Artist."
4. Peyton Moncure, "Custer's Last Stand—Is This the Way It Was?" *Minneapolis Tribune*, February 21, 1954.
5. Ruckstull, F. W., *Great Works of Art and What Makes Them Great*. New York: Garden City Publishing Co., 1925.

Successful Artist of the Old West

1. An 1897 newspaper clipping in Paxson's scrapbook states that the artist "will send a large number of his pictures to New York at the request of Kleckner, the biggest picture dealer in the country."
2. *Chicago Herald-Record* advertisement, April 29, 1901, quoted in the artist's journal.
3. Stenzel, "E. S. Paxson, Montana Artist."
4. Goddard, "Y Closet Yields Paxson Find...."
5. *St. Louis Globe-Democrat*, December, 1901, quoted in the artist's journal. Paxson recorded this quote with mixed feelings because it was part of an announcement that the newspaper would supplement its Sunday edition with a color reproduction of a Paxson painting—yet another that the artist had not copyrighted.
6. Marian A. White, "A Group of Clever and Original Painters in Montana," *Fine Arts Journal*, February, 1905.
7. "Missoula Has Paxson Art Treasure," *Missoulian*, March 25, 1928.

One of A Dying Breed

1. Partoll, "Paxson and Russell Close Friends...."
2. "Friendly Brushes between Artists," Missoulian, April 12, 1964.
3. Charles M. Russell, "An Appreciation of Edgar S. Paxson," published in Montana newspapers at the time of Paxson's death.

The Art of Edgar S. Paxson

1. Stenzel, "E. S. Paxson, Montana Artist."
2. Published in the *Anaconda Standard*, February 9, 1902.
3. Enos A. Mills, "A Western Artist," *Outdoor Life*, August 1902.
4. Mills, "A Western Artist."
5. In 1910 Paxson noted in his journal that he spent the day modeling in clay. In 1917 he noted that he modeled an Indian head in clay. These, along with the medallion and statue done in 1899 (see Chapter 4, p.000) are his only other efforts at modeling or sculpture known to the author.
6. Granville Stuart's daughter, Mrs. Edwin Abbot, was interviewed by John L. Temple.
7. Al J. Noyes, *In the Land of the Chinook or the Story of Blaine County*, p. 26. Russell added, "Nor can I mix his paints."
8. "E. S. Paxson, Artist," *Old Timer's Handbook, the Story of Butte* (a special number of the *Butte Bystander*), April 15, 1897.
9. White, "A Group...in Montana."
10. Eve Allen, "Oil Portrait of Custer's Foe in Amherst."
11. K. Ross Toole and Michael Kennedy, "A Portfolio of the Art of E. S. Paxson," *Montana Magazine of History*, Spring, 1954, p. 24.
12. James McLaughlin, *My Friend the Indian*, Boston: Houghton-Mifflin, 1910, p. 6.
13. Mills, "A Western Artist."
14. Merrill G. Burlingame, "John M. Bozeman, Montana Trailmaker," *Mississippi Valley Historical Review*, March, 1941, p. 27.
15. Boulder, Montana *Monitor*, October 25, 1919, quoted in Burlingame, "John M. Bozeman...," p. 27.
16. James Kirkpatrick, "A Reminiscence of John Bozeman," *Frontier*, May 1929, quoted in Burlingame, "John M. Bozeman...," p. 5.
17. Milton W. Brown, *American Art to 1900—Painting, Sculpture and Architecture*. New York: Abrams, 1977, p. 536.

Bibliographical Note

Much of the published material about E. S. Paxson is, understandably, cursory and sometimes inaccurate. The artist's dislike of interviews, the brief and modest national recognition he received during his career and his work's relative obscurity from the time of his death until recently are largely to blame.

The first significant magazine articles on Paxson's life and work, appearing January and October of 1901 in the Chicago-based *Fine Arts Journal*, were brief and, although based on biographical material provided by the artist, wander occasionally from fact. A third and similar article appeared in the same magazine in February 1905. Another brief profile, this by author Enos Mills, appeared in the August 1902 issue of *Outdoor Life*. It was based on an interview with the artist and edited for accuracy by him before publication.

The most complete of the first efforts at recording Paxson's life was done by Helen Fitzgerald Saunders. Based on interviews with the artist, it appeared in part in the *Overland Monthly* in September 1906 and in its entirety in Saunders' exhaustive *A History of Montana*, published in 1913. Running about 3,500 words and generally accurate, it has been a main source for most of the material written about Paxson since his death.

Some of the most interesting anecdotes about Paxson's frontier days appeared in Montana newspapers whenever the artist could be induced by an enterprising reporter to tell of his experiences in the '70s and '80s. Paxson's story about "A Lost Pilgrim" came to be published in this way. In 1902, he gave a short, but revealing, talk before the Butte Women's Club, the text of which was published in the local newspaper.

In 1901, Paxson wrote of some of his frontier experiences in a brief article for *Outdoor Life* entitled "Beaver Dick." He wrote the article in the third person, referring to himself cryptically as "Sam," thus leaving the reader unaware that the author was writing of his own experience.

After Paxson's death in 1919, little was published about him for thirty-five years, with the exception of occasional articles commemorating him in Montana newspapers. Most notable of these are a series done in the 1930s by Montana historian Albert Partoll, who retrieved some interesting material from oblivion through interviewing those yet living who had known the artist, most importantly the artist's wife, Laura.

In 1954, the Montana Historical Society published material on Paxson for the first time. Two essays appeared in the spring issue of the society's periodical, *Montana Magazine of History*: "E. S. Paxson: Neglected Artist of the West" and "Frontier Vermeer." Both essays consist largely of their author's opinions and presented no new biographical material on the artist.

In 1963, the Montana Historical Society published the most ambitious effort up to that time at chronicling Paxson's life and work. Authored by Franz R. Stenzel, M.D. and containing about thirty pages, it appeared in the autumn issue of the society's magazine and was published separately as a booklet entitled *E. S. Paxson—Montana Artist* (#14 in the Montana Heritage Series). Although it brings together most of what had been written about Paxson over the previous sixty years, it contains inaccuracies of minor and not so minor import. One curious example is Stenzel's statement that in her last years, Paxson's wife "was constantly more dependent on her husband for companionship and, in her illness, for his help" and that "her death was a severe loss to Paxson." In fact she outlived her husband by nineteen years!

Since 1963 William Paxson, Sr. has written articles on the artist and his Custer masterpiece. These have appeared in magazines devoted to the history of the American West.

There have also been several other biographical sketches in recent books and magazines dealing with the history and art of the West. These have all been drawn from previously published material.

Paxson's unpublished writings and his scrapbooks

are certainly the most valuable sources for this biography. Much of this material, rediscovered in a trunk by William Paxson, Sr. in 1962, has been heretofore kept under wraps by the Paxson heirs. Paxson's journals form the bulk of this material. They cover most of 1898 and 1899 when Paxson was a soldier in the Spanish-American War. They begin again January 1, 1901, and continue, rarely missing a day, until his death in 1919. Toward the end when he was unable to write, the journal entries are in his wife's hand, either dictated by her husband or entered on her own. The rest of Paxson's writings consist of letters; notebooks of visits to Chicago in 1893 and to the Custer battlefield in 1896; and his extensive notes in the margins of books he owned. His studio guest registers have also been important sources in revealing his relationships with other artists and notable Westerners.

In the bibliography that follows, the author has attempted to present a reasonably complete list of written material, both published and unpublished, on the life and work of E. S. Paxson. References not included are those of an entirely summary nature. Least complete in the list are the newspaper references. Several newspaper articles have not been listed because, although they appear in the artist's scrapbooks, the dates and sources are missing. Some newspaper articles have not been included because they repeat material published concurrently in those newspaper sources listed.

Bibliography

Books and Booklets

Hambleton, Chalkley J., *A Geneological Record of the Hambleton Family*. Published by its author, 1887.

Hunt, David C., *The Missoula County Courthouse Murals: A Brief History of Their Creation and Restoration*. Missoula Museum of the Arts Foundation, 1980.

Lynch, Neil J., *Butte Centennial Recollections*. Butte: Pioneer Printing, 1979.

Montana House of Representatives, "House Resolution to the Memory of Edgar Samuel Paxson, Artist, Painter and Writer." *Journal of the Montana House of Representatives*, February, 1949.

Noyes, Al J., *In the Land of the Chinook or The Story of Blaine County*. Helena: State Publishing Co., 1917.

Saunders, Helen Fitzgerald, *A History of Montana*, vol. II. Chicago and New York: The Lewis Publishing Co., 1913.

Stone, Arthur L., *Following Old Trails*. Missoula: Morton John Elrod, 1913.

Periodicals

Anon. "Edgar S. Paxson, Our Cover Artist." *Golden West*, January, 1966.

Burlingame, Merrill G. "John M. Bozeman, Montana Trailmaker." *Mississippi Valley Historical Review*, vol. XXVII, No. 4, March, 1941. Revised and reprinted by Museum of the Rockies, Montana State University, Bozeman, Montana, 1983.

Godfrey, General Edward S. Letter to Edgar S. Paxson, January 16, 1896. Published as "After the Custer Battle," Albert J. Partoll, ed. in *Frontier and Midland Magazine*, vol. XIX, no. 4 (1939) by Montana State University. Reprinted as Number Twenty-nine in Sources of Northwest History Series by Montana State University. Also appeared in "Paxson's Picture of Custer's Last Stand Called Remarkable," Albert J. Partoll, *Great Falls Tribune*, January 28, 1934. Original letter on display at Whitney Gallery of Western Art, Buffalo Bill Historical Center, Cody, Wyoming.

Manatt, Sam L., Jr. "Edgar Samuel Paxson (1852–1919)." *Southwest Art*, August, 1973.

Mills, Enos A. "A Western Artist." *Outdoor Life*, vol. X, No. 2 (August, 1902).

Paxson, Edgar S. "Beaver Dick." *Outdoor Life*, 1901.

Paxson, William E., Sr. "'Custer's Last Stand': The Painting and the Artist." *True West*, October, 1963.

________. "Paxson." *Westerner*, December, 1971.

Saunders, Helen Fitzgerald. "Edgar Samuel Paxson—Pioneer, Scout and Artist." *Overland Monthly*, September, 1906.

Simons, Antoinette E. "Worked Twenty Years on One Picture." *American Magazine*, July, 1915.

Stenzel, Franz R., M.D. "E. S. Paxson, Montana Artist." *Montana Magazine of History*, Autumn, 1963. Reprinted as Number Fourteen in the Montana Historical Society's Montana Heritage Series, 1963.

Toole, K. Ross and Michael Kennedy. "A Portfolio of the Art of E. S. Paxson." Includes two essays: Toole, "Neglected Artist of the West" and Kennedy, "Frontier Vermeer." *Montana Magazine of History*, Spring, 1954.

White, Marian A. "E. S. Paxson, American Painter of Western Life." *Fine Arts Journal*, January-February, 1901.

________. "A Group of Clever and Original Painters in Montana." *Fine Arts Journal*, February, 1905.

________. "Our Matted Supplement" and "Gems from Private Galleries." *Fine Arts Journal*, October, 1901.

Newspapers

Allen, Eve. "Oil Portrait of Custer's Foe in Amherst." *Daily Hampshire Gazette* (Northhampton, Massachusetts), date missing (about 1962).

"Associated Artists Open Their First Exhibition." *Chicago Tribune*, March 17, 1903.

Brown, Frank D. "Nez Perces Massacre of M'Kay Gulch; Artist Paxton (*sic*) Warned Other Settlers." A Montana News Association insert in the *Mineral County Independent*, September 23, 1918.

"Buffalo Bill Is Known to Missoula Old-Timers from Days of Long Ago." *Missoula Sentinel*, 1916 (complete date missing).

"Butte Artist Who Has Won Pinnacle." *Butte Intermountain*, 1902 (complete date missing).

"Edgar S. Paxson, Famous Artist, Dies in Missoula." *Missoulian*, November 10, 1919.

"E. S. Paxson, Artist." *Old Timer's Handbook: The Story of Butte* (a special edition of the *Butte Bystander*), April 15, 1897.

"E. S. Paxson Is Honored in Display of Works at Historical Museum." *Missoulian*, February 28, 1954.

"Federation of Women's Clubs Starts Campaign to Hang Famous Paxson Painting 'Custer's Last Stand' in Capitol at Helena." *Anaconda Standard*, April 4, 1920.

"Four of Artist Paxson's Paintings in State Capitol." *Missoulian*, June 17, 1912.

"Friendly brushes between Artists." *Missoulian*, April 12, 1964.

Goddard, Alan. "Y Closet Yields Paxson Find for Copper Camp Auction." *Montana Standard* (Butte), April 30, 1978.

"Illustrations by Paxson." *Butte Intermountain*, July, 1904 (complete date missing).

Mackenzie, W. S. (interviewed). *Monitor* (Boulder, Montana), October 25, 1919.

"A Masterpiece." *Butte Intermountain*, February 10, 1900.

"Military Men Commend It: Paxson's Picture of Custer's Last Battle Exhibited in Washington." *Butte Intermountain*, May 30, 1900.

"Missoula Has Paxson Art Treasure." *Missoulian*, March 25, 1928.

Missoulian. Articles about Paxson undertaking Missoula County courthouse murals in editions of March 17, 1912; December 15, 1912; December 25, 1912; July 4, 1913; July 16, 1913; August 19, 1913; June 26, 1914; August 7, 1914; November 8, 1914; November 10, 1914.

Moncure, Peyton. "Custer's Last Stand—Is This the Way It Was?" *Minneapolis Tribune*, February 21, 1954.

"Montana Pictures at the Worlds Fair." *Butte Intermountain*. December 24, 1903.

Partoll, Albert J. "Experiences of Noted Painter Recalled." *Great Falls Tribune*, November 3, 1940.

———. "Montana History Vividly Portrayed by E. S. Paxson." *Great Falls Tribune*, February 22, 1931.

———. "Mrs. Edgar Paxson, Widow of Famous Painter, Reminisces." *Great Falls Tribune*, April 10, 1932.

———. "Paxson and Russell Close Friends; Led Parade at Missoula." *Great Falls Tribune*, January 15, 1933.

———. "Paxson's Picture of Custer's Last Stand Called Remarkable." *Great Falls Tribune*, January 28, 1934.

Paxson, Edgar S. Autobiographical lecture to the Butte Women's Club. *Anaconda Standard*, February 9, 1902.

"Paxson Enters Arena of Eastern Art Work." *Butte Intermountain*, May, 1902 (complete date missing).

"Paxson's Painting Is Monument To Heroes." *Missoulian*, February 18, 1915.

"Paxson's Works Creating a Rage." *Butte Intermountain*, October 28, 1903.

"Plea For Purchase of Paxson's Masterpiece Made Here Last Friday." *Missoulian*, November 10, 1919.

Smith, Steve. "Profile: He Got Off the Train with Ten Cents in His Pocket." *Missoulian*, April 7, 1980.

Stone, Arthur L. and Merle Kettlewell. "A Lost Pilgrim." *Missoulian*, April 7, 1912. Reprinted in Arthur L. Stone, *Following Old Trails*. Missoula: Morton John Elrod, 1913.

Stone, Arthur L. "State's Debt to Paxson Unrealized, Says Stone." *Missoulian*, November 10, 1919.

"Viewed in Washinton." *Anaconda Standard*, June 20, 1900.

Unpublished Material

Corbin, Emma R. *Edgar S. Paxson; Artist and Friend of the Red-man.* MS, 1910, in the collection of William E. Paxson, Sr.

MacNab, Robin. *Incident at Cady Coulee.* MS in progress.

Paxson, Edgar Samuel. *Journals (1898–99, 1901–1919), notes and letters.* In the collection of William E. Paxson, Sr.

Paxson, Edward Heston and Joseph P. *The Paxson Family in America.* MS duplicated by multigraph, 1918. Copy in the collection of William E. Paxson, Sr.

Paxson, Lelia Everetta. *Custer's Last Stand.* MS, 1916, in the collection of William E. Paxson, Sr.

———(Mrs. R. H. Hale). *Edgar S. Paxson.* MS, 1946. Copy in the collection of William E. Paxson, Sr.

Temple, John L. Letter to William E. Paxson, Sr. August 8, 1962. In the collection of William E. Paxson, Sr.

Index

Illinois, 48
Indian Samiah, 11
Indian sign language, 29